Table of Contents

ASMP

Professional Business Practices in Photography

The American Society of Media Photographers

Allworth Press, New York

Published by Allworth Press
An imprint of Allworth Communications
10 East 23rd Street, New York, NY 10010

"Keys to Success in Production Stock Photography" ©1995 Jon Feingersh

"Image Protection Standards for the Digital Era" © 1994, 1997 Roger H. Ressmeyer

Cover design by Douglas Designs, New York, NY

Book design by Sharp Des!gns, Holt, MI

ISBN: 0-927629-14-3

Distributor to the trade in the United States and Canada:
Writer's Digest Books
An imprint of F&W Publications, Inc.
1507 Dana Avenue, Cincinnati, Ohio 45207

To order additional copies of this book, call toll-free 1-800-289-0963.

Acknowledgments

The American Society of Media Photographers, Inc., thanks the following people who contributed to this book and to the *ASMP Business Bible: A Guide for Professional Media Photographers,* which was the foundation for this, the Fifth Edition of the *ASMP Professional Business Practices in Photography.*

- Editor: Peter Skinner (ASMP Communications Director)
- Production Coordinator: Cilla Skinner (ASMP Production Editor)
- Editorial Review: Jay Asquini, James Cavanaugh, Terry Pagos, Victor S. Perlman, Esq., Robert Rathe, Richard Weisgrau
- ASMP Executive Director: Richard Weisgrau
- ASMP General Counsel: Victor S. Perlman, Esq.

Writers and Other Contributors

Craig Aurness, David Barnes, Bruce Blank, Thom Bunting, James Cook, Jon Feingersh, Ira Mark Gostin, Paul Henning, Scott Highton, Bill Hurter, Don Luce, Jean Miller, Annette Laabs Paajanen, Victor S. Perlman, Esq., Maria Piscopo, Allen Rabinowitz, Roger Ressmeyer, Barbara B. Roberts, Stephen Seeger, Peter Skinner, Amy Stone, Vince Streano, Mark Tucker, Susan Turnau, John Uppgren, Emily Vickers, Richard Weisgrau.

Information Providers and Other Assistance

Mikkel Aaland, Beverly Adler, Jay Asquini, Craig Aurness, Lee Balgemann, Annie Barrows, Janie Bennett, Lou Biscotti, Barbara Bordnick, Reagan Bradshaw, Matt Brown, Nancy Brown, J. W. Burkey, Janet Swan-Bush, Dick Busher, Alan Carey, James

Cavanaugh, Dwight Cendrowski, James Cook, Maura Damacion, Catherine DeMaria, Lisl Dennis, Beverly Don, Jim Drake, Dana Duke, Tom Egner, Enrico Ferorelli, Michael Furman, Gary Gladstone, David R. Godine, Paul Gottlieb, Daniel Grotta, Sally Wiener Grotta, Charles Hagen, Don Hall, David Heiser, Matt Herron, Scott Highton, David Hiser, Cliff Hollenbeck, Robert Holmes, Ryszard Horowitz, Bill Hurter, Walter Iooss, Lou Jacobs, Jr., Mike Jensen, Lou Jones, Mark Kaproff, Ed Kashi, Greg Kinney, Kathleen King, Douglas Kirkland, Don Klumpp, Bob Krist, Frans Lanting, George Lepp, Harry Liles, Andrei Lloyd, Harvey Lloyd, Don Luce, John M. Lund, David MacTavish, Alen MacWeeney, Jerome Magid, Jay Maisel, Tom Mason, Georgia McCabe, Forest McMullin, Sam Merrell, Robert Meyer, Jean Miller, Gordon Munro, Ken Newton, Charles D. Ossola, Esq., Terry Pagos, Gloriana Palancia, Victor S. Perlman, Esq., Jim Pickerell, Robert Rathe, Michael D. Remer, Esq., Roger Ressmeyer, Les Riess, Anne Rippy, Herb Ritts, Bill Ross, Neil Sapienza, Henry Scanlon, Bob Schmolze, Brian Seed, Stephen Seeger, Robin Simmen, Jeff Smith, Rick Smolan, Richard Steedman, Amy Stone, Bill Straus, Laura Straus, Vince Streano, Randy Taylor, Rebecca Taylor, Scott Taylor, Jerry Tovo, Steve Umland, Frank Van Riper, Emily Vickers, Garie Waltzer, Richard Weisgrau, Art Wolfe, Tom Zimberoff.

Introduction

As photographers we love to make photographs, but if you want to make this your profession, photography becomes more than an art and a science. It is also a business. And if you are to stay in business you must apply sound principles, develop and implement marketing strategies, be adept at estimating and pricing, and learn how to harness the new technologies to make your business more efficient.

The very nature of freelance photography tends to keep photographers in relative isolation and at times it can seem like you're trying to do it all yourself. Fortunately, there are professional trade organizations such as the American Society of Media Photographers (ASMP) to help you.

Founded in 1944, ASMP has been dedicated to educating photographers in the business of photography and in over more than half a century has produced numerous publications to achieve that goal. This, the Fifth Edition of the *ASMP Professional Business Practices in Photography,* represents the business knowledge of thousands of people and we trust that you will be able to apply some of that knowledge to your business.

This publication has its foundation in the long line of previous ASMP books and is based to a large extent on the *ASMP Business Bible: A Guide for Professional Media Photographers,* which is provided to all ASMP members as a member benefit. The *ASMP Business Bible* is being expanded constantly and it, along with numerous other benefits, is a tangible reason to be a member of ASMP. However, there are many other reasons why photographers should belong to professional associations such as ASMP. One of these is the camaraderie, the networking, and the access to experienced professional colleagues who can help you grow as a photographer and a businessperson. With almost forty chapters nationwide and members throughout the United States and in many other countries, ASMP does have an important international network of professional photographers.

ASMP was founded on the principle of photographers helping photographers, and while the industry has changed and evolved over the years since 1944—and seen tremendous technological advances—ASMP has never wavered from its initial mission.

As a trade organization, ASMP cannot tell its members or other photographers how to run their businesses, nor can the Society fix terms, conditions, or rates. However, ASMP can provide the information and the tools to help photographers in their business transactions. This book is one of those tools.

On behalf of the many people who have contributed to this publication, I wish you the best in your career and I hope that the information here helps you.

REAGAN BRADSHAW
ASMP President

Chapter 1

The Business of Assignment Photography

Annette Laabs Paajanen and Peter Skinner

Assignment photography covers a wide spectrum of fields and while each specialty has its own requirements, numerous business details are common to many fields. Vital to any business dealing is making sure you and the client understand and agree on what the job entails, what the final product will be, and the terms of usage. Knowing what your costs will be, and what you have to charge to stay in business while producing what the client wants, are essential to any successful operation. Refer to the chapters on "The Art of Pricing and Estimating" and "Formalizing Agreements," which provide a wealth of information and sample forms which can be tailored to virtually every assignment, regardless of the field. Assignment photography is highly competitive, and constantly evolving. To succeed in it, professional photographers must be talented and skilled in photography and in business.

In general, "assignment photography" implies projects specifically commissioned by clients, while "self-assigned photography" means work done in the photographer's own interests for stock, experimentation, and promotion.

To succeed in assignment photography, it simply is not enough to take wonderful pictures. You have to know how to find your niche, how to market your images and yourself, and how to manage your business. Successful marketing is the key to sales. Sales keep you in business.

The competition in assignment photography is fierce and the number of practition–ers has expanded. Also, the profession has no licensing or certification requirements; anyone can hang up a shingle. Photography has become a popular profession and many more institutions are offering courses.

Business education, unfortunately, is not a strength of most photography programs and this is where organizations like ASMP become so important to professional pho-tographers. Economic conditions in recent years have meant tight money. Budgets are being scrutinized. Photographers have to know their costs and be able to justify the value of their work to clients. They have to know how and what to negotiate. Because they lack the necessary skills and knowledge, many photographers unknowingly give away their work—which makes it difficult for everyone in the profession. It's hard to compete with someone who is losing money. As one sage noted, however, many photographers don't seem to mind losing money, but they do hate to see other people make money from their images. Thus the concern about electronic transfer of images. Certainly the technology to manipulate computerized images raises copyright issues, but the technology also facilitates the global expansion of markets. And, as photographers know well, things change and images will need updating. Just as photographers need not fear being replaced by machines, electronic imaging probably doesn't constitute a major threat either, if photographers take steps, just as they do in other media, to protect their rights.

The competitive nature of the business demands quick decisions and sound business judgments. You must be a shrewd financial manager, a savvy marketing and sales expert, an effective negotiator, an astute administrator, a skilled casting agent and an understanding employer—not just the person clients look to as the creative expert behind the camera.

Service

Competition is not all bad. Many photographers welcome it as an incentive to produce better images and to work more efficiently, providing better service to their clients. It is essential to remember that assignment photography is a service to business: the quality of that service will make a lasting impression, is as important as the quality of the images and the way you conduct your business.

Communication is critical—you and your clients must go into a shoot with the same expectations. Ensure all questions are addressed.

Professional Responsibility and Ethics

You need to be attuned to your clients' needs and objectives, both in the spirit and in the letter of your agreement with them.

For example, a photographer accepts an assignment to photograph a grandmother and grandchild for use in an advertising brochure by a pharmaceutical manufacturer. The client uses one photograph and returns the outtakes—one of which is similar to the image used in the brochure—to the photographer. Should the photographer offer the outtake photograph for advertising use by another pharmaceutical company? The answer is not simply a matter of legality and ownership of the outtake—the photographer owns the copyright—it is a question of propriety and ethics. The photographer has a responsibility to the client to make sure that the use of the image is protected to the fullest extent for the period of the license.

Ethical dilemmas like these have contributed to clients wanting to buy all rights. Some photographers, particularly those new to the business, may be reluctant to bring up the complex-sounding rights issues. Clients, too, would rather not bother with figuring out when they can or cannot use an image. This problem is best addressed through education of both photographers and clients. It behooves you, as a professional, to know the ins and outs of rights and usage which this publication will teach. You also have to make it easy for your clients to understand these issues and to explain why it might not be in their best interests to buy all rights. This is part of the service and value offered by your business.

It's in your best interests to make sure your clients get full exclusive usage of images, including similar outtakes, for the full duration of the rights period. This hinges on the concept of "fairness." Just as photographers want to be treated fairly by clients, clients also deserve to be treated fairly by photographers. This is simply good business.

When you earn your living by taking photographs, you become a professional. Your work and manner of operation are judged by professional standards and, therefore, you must understand both the ethical and the business aspects of your profession. The way you conduct business helps set the standard for the whole profession. You can help educate clients about the business of photography. One way might be to send new and potential clients the ASMP brochure *On Buying Photography.* Your actions speak loudest so treat your clients as you want to be treated.

What it really comes down to is this: If you want dignity, respect, and compensation for what you do as a photographer, you must act in a professional, ethical, and businesslike manner. This does not minimize the importance of an artistic approach to your work, but don't overlook the practicalities that relate to ethics in a business setting—insurance coverage, legal matters, and business forms. (See chapter 6, "Formalizing Agreements.")

Most photographers really love their work. Therein lies a dilemma. Photographers often give their work away just for the opportunity to ply their craft. Unfortunately, being in business entails certain costs, and photographers who don't have a good handle on those costs may find themselves out of business. Few photographers go out of business because of their photography. Poor business skills are usually their downfall.

The pressure on photographers to deliver more service at lower prices can be tremendous. There is a trend for clients to seek concessions from all suppliers, including photographers who, because of their love for their work and, often, their lack of business skills, are particularly vulnerable. You must know your production and business costs and set fees accordingly. Ask for compensation which reflects your costs of doing business. Reasonable fee increases won't necessarily scare off clients. Other vendors raise their prices periodically to cover cost increases; clients are used to it. Don't be afraid to seek fair compensation for your work.

Business Skills

If you think being an assignment photographer will keep you behind the camera all the time, think again. More than 50 percent of your time will be spent dealing with universal business matters—sales, collections, billing, bookkeeping, management, and other administrative operations. The reality is that only when those business skills bring in an assignment can the photographer practice the artistic and technical aspects of the profession.

Some skills can be obtained through paid consultants, others can be provided by reps and studio managers. But for the typical solo photographer, the skills have to be learned and developed to achieve success. Some required talents are obvious. You must coordinate, schedule, shoot, and deliver a job as promised. Other necessary skills include planning, estimating, marketing, promotion, sales, negotiation, administration, secretarial, and financial. These skills can be learned and ASMP, through its network of members and chapters, and this publication, can help you.

A most important skill is marketing. You can't afford to wait for the phone to ring. Although some photographers rely to a certain extent on others to sell their work, clients ultimately want to meet the photographer since this is the person they are hiring. You're going to have to take a break from shooting to sell your work.

Decide what kind of projects you want to do and for which clients you want to do them. Maybe you know an art director at an ad agency or a creative designer you'd like to team up with. Use your portfolio as your primary marketing tool. Find out as much as you can about the clients you're approaching. Determine what their needs might be and tailor your portfolio to reflect those needs. Clients in manufacturing, for example, won't be interested in soft-focused images of home interiors.

Some photographers take an even more aggressive approach by anticipating a client's needs. They will put together a detailed proposal outlining a project, including information on how this project can benefit the client.

Equipment and Facilities

Trying to do assignments without the proper facilities or equipment invites failure, or results in photographs of unacceptable quality. While you do need some basic pieces of equipment, it may be more prudent to rent, especially during the first few years in business. Rental costs often can be billed to the client. Initially, it's more important for an assignment photographer to invest in marketing than in lots of equipment. You simply shouldn't overextend yourself when starting, particularly since a typical investment in equipment ranges from $50,000 to $100,000, a formidable amount of money.

A problem bigger than the lack of equipment—which can be remedied through ingenuity or equipment rental—is a lack of interest. Accepting work that doesn't thrill you is common, and most professionals usually can muster enough short-term enthusiasm to do a good job. However, taking assignments you enjoy and that are within your capabilities is a better path to success. The fact is, you will generally do the best work on the jobs you like best.

Assessing your capabilities can be a daunting proposition. Many photographers work with consultants, others rely on hired sales representatives or "reps" to give them guidance.

Markets and Specialties

Assignment photography is a broad field that can be broken down into sectors which define markets in the broadest sense. Most assignments fall into one of three broad sectors: advertising, corporate, and editorial. Each sector is defined primarily by the purpose for which the photographs are used, not by the subject matter.

In dense markets, the only way to compete effectively may be to specialize in some way. However, to describe their work as strictly advertising, corporate, or editorial photography, might not be the best course of action for many photographers. In reality, the same level of skill is compensated differently in different sectors. Limiting yourself to one sector is going to limit your client base and your ability to operate in diverse markets.

For example, making a photograph for the editorial pages of a magazine often requires all the expertise needed to do the same shot for an advertisement. The demand for an excellent image may be identical. But, generally, you will get paid less for it when it's for editorial use.

In addition, pictures made for one purpose, such as an advertisement, may have many other uses. An advertising photograph might also appear in a magazine article or in the advertiser's annual report. With a proper contract in place, you should be paid for these multiple uses.

Regardless of a photographer's specialty, assignments are usually derived from five major sources: advertising agencies, design firms, public relations firms, client direct (including in-house marketing departments), and in the case of photojournalists, magazines.

The actual photographs may be the same from one market to the next, however, the practices of each business are a little different (as explained below). Each business services different needs for the end-user. In all but in-house marketing departments, the end-user is a client on contract for a specific period of time and budget. In some cases, companies may contract with all three types of marketing companies (ad agency, design firm, public relations firm) as well as have its own in-house marketing department. When soliciting assignments, it's best to investigate all sources of photo buyers that a company might have.

The following are the primary photographic markets with special considerations when doing business with each.

Advertising Agencies

Advertising agencies plan strategy, produce materials, and buy media for their clients. Media purchases that involve photography may include print ads (magazine and newspaper), outdoor (billboards and transit), and television.

In some cases, an agency will also be involved in the creation and distribution of collateral materials for the client, especially when it ties in directly with the total marketing concept. Such materials may include brochures, packaging, point-of-purchase, and direct mail. (Because of the multiple uses that a photograph might have, you should be clear about what rights you are licensing to the agency.)

Larger agencies often have public relations sections who handle responsibilities associated with PR campaigns and often their efforts will dovetail with paid advertising in an overall marketing strategy.

Your contact for working with an advertising agency will be an art director who is responsible for details of the layout and art direction of the final ad. Some firms also have creative directors, which is a senior art director position, and art buyers, who negotiate contracts and estimates with photographers. When details of a shoot involve client coordination, you may have to deal with an account executive.

When working with advertising agencies be clear about to whom your bill should be sent and how soon it will be paid. It is often not the art director, although sending him/her a copy of the invoice would be a courtesy.

Design Firms

Graphic design firms are an ever increasing client base for photographers. These companies produce a wide range of collateral (non-advertising) material for their clients who have needs from almost all of the photographic specialties. Collateral material may include annual reports, brochures, direct-mail pieces, and even trade show displays. Design firms seldom involve themselves in media placement.

While large design firms are well-established in the communications industry, the advent of desktop publishing and sophisticated computerized design technology has resulted in an increase in the number of independent graphic designers. These smaller firms, or sole operators, constitute an important and growing source of business for photographers, especially in smaller markets.

Even though it's common for a client to attend shoots, the designer will be the photographer's principal contact and director. In such cases, an independent graphic designer would perform a variety of roles—as the art director, art buyer, and production coordinator for example—and will work very closely with the photographer on both creative and business aspects.

Billing could be either direct to the client, or to the designer, depending on what arrangements are made prior to the assignment. In either event, make sure you know to whom the bill is sent.

Public Relations Firms

The role of public relations firms is varied, and essentially is to enhance communications between their clients and the people those clients want to reach. These firms use a wide range of methods to get their client's message across, from products (brochures, press kits and releases, newsletters) to events (trade shows, product "roll outs," press conferences, and audiovisual presentations). And photography is used extensively.

Because public relations companies focus on publicity and promotional activities, it is unlikely that your photography will be used in advertising. But be sure that fact is established ahead of time. Editorial uses of photographs for press releases are most often published without credit or use fee to the photographer. Therefore, be sure to include a blanket editorial usage in the fee and do not expect further compensation.

Your contact in a public relations firm typically would be an account executive whose job is to arrange the details of the shoot. It is not uncommon for the account executive to be absent from the shoot.

In-House Agency/Client Direct

Large corporations will often have in-house marketing departments who hire photographers directly. They may function similarly to design and public relations firms creating annual reports, newsletters, company magazines, brochures, and even advertising. These corporations might also have in-house creative departments who hire photographers. With large companies, the buyer of photography could be a marketing director, director of public relations or corporate communications, or a graphic designer. Again, be clear which person or department should be sent the bill.

Start-up companies, particularly in smaller markets, will often produce their own publications and advertisements at first. Often these clients will place great responsibility on the photographer to turn concepts into reality, with the barest of thumbnail sketches to work from. In some cases you could do your client, and yourself, a great service by suggesting a graphic designer be hired. Entrepreneurs might know their business well, but they might not know how to get their message across visually.

If there is any concern about the solvency of a company, it would be wise to check its credit background, and to get a substantial advance.

Professional photographers usually find that they are drawn to certain types of photography more than others. These types of photography, called specialties, describe the nature of the subject matter and include areas such as still life, fashion, people, architectural, industrial, sports, and medical photography. Although each specialty requires a unique approach using specific equipment, they can all exist in any market of assignment photography. For example, a portrait could be used as an advertising image, a corporation's annual report cover, or as an editorial illustration.

In order to become a successful assignment photographer, you must be honest about your capabilities. Determining what you are able to do best and what you like to do is very important. Working on jobs that you literally detest or are ill-equipped to handle will almost surely ruin the job and your reputation as an honest presenter of your capabilities. Do that too often and your business may also be in ruins.

Markets

Advertising photography

Advertising photographs are used to sell a product or service. The photographs appear in many different types of media including magazines, newspapers, direct-mail pieces, point-of-purchase displays, package design, billboards, posters, catalogs, television, and World Wide Web pages. Electronic media, including CD-ROM and multimedia, is an ever expanding market.

The costs for media space are paid for by the company which sells the product or service. The photographer's contact, however, is usually the company's advertising agency or in-house advertising department.

Normally, photography for advertising purposes is assigned to a photographer by an art director, who also produces a layout (varying from rough sketches to comprehensive four-color illustrations). The art director gives the layout to the photographer as a guide for the illustration.

For a "rough" layout, a photographer may be asked to determine the spatial relationships and style within the image. A "tight" layout, on the other hand, may require the photographer to reproduce the illustration with precise rendering of the elements within the image. In either case, a photographer may be asked to shoot variations of the layout to provide the art director with a choice of images.

If you are ever asked to copy, either totally or substantially, a layout that includes an actual photograph taken from, for example, an ad in a source book, don't! It's illegal. Photographer, agency, and client are all liable in the case of copyright infringement. Explain the facts of copyright, and the penalties for infringement to the art director. (See chapter 7, "Copyright.")

Advertising photographers must have the creative ability to translate the idea of the layout, whether rough or tight, into photographs of real people, scenes, and objects. Sensitivity to nuances in the look of models, clothes, props, and backgrounds is essential, as is the technical expertise to position and light all the elements needed to achieve the final image. The photographer's taste and ingenuity will be apparent in most assigned photographs, which explains why many art directors are very particular about selecting the photographer.

The business of advertising photography has become increasingly complex, attributable to higher production costs, higher model fees, and drastically increased media costs. Because more money is at stake, there is greater concern about liability and awareness about legal rights. Usually, photography for an ad or ad campaign is assigned only after the advertising agency and client have agreed on a total strategy for direction, design, and media placement.

Budgets are carefully developed, approved, and controlled, usually under the watchful eye of the art buyer, the person hired within an agency to relieve art directors of negotiations, estimates, forms, releases, and paperwork.

All assignments should have a written estimate or assignment confirmation. Based on the art director's layout, the estimate is provided by the photographer. The written estimate includes the creative fee and all the production expenses required to produce the assignment. It is designed to protect both the photographer and the client from misunderstandings about the scope of the assignment. (For more information, see chapter 3, "The Art of Pricing and Estimating.")

Use/reproduction rights: Photography fees were once loosely based on a percentage of the media buy for the ad being produced. Now that media costs have escalated far beyond what is considered acceptable photography costs, fees are most often based on the primary use of the work, with additional compensation for additional uses thereafter. Production charges are calculated separately.

To reduce the possibility of misunderstanding, the use of the work being prepared should be spelled out in writing, for example: "Photographs of product X intended solely for magazine test market for six months." The specific usage should be included on the estimate, on the assignment confirmation or purchase order, on the assignment delivery memo, and again on the final invoice.

Copyright protection is not granted for the "idea," but rather for the "expression" of the idea. Thus, it is the photographer—not the client—who owns the copyright in the resulting image. Users of photography are increasingly asking for ownership of photography on the line of reasoning that, "We're paying for the pictures and therefore we're entitled to own them," or, "We need to ensure exclusivity; you can't use them anywhere."

Often, such users seek ownership by way of "work made for hire" agreements, or "all rights" (sometimes called "buyout") agreements. These all result in the photographer's surrendering of rights, ownership, and control in the creation and, ultimately, of the opportunity to realize additional income from future uses of the work.

ASMP has long sought to educate both users and photographers that the user, more often than not, simply does not need to own all rights. Instead, both sides should look realistically at what rights are really needed by the user, and what fees should be paid to the photographer for those rights.

Corporate/Industrial

This area of photography covers an extraordinary amount of ground because it requires the use of many forms of photography for a wide variety of purposes.

A corporate/industrial photographer's work can encompass every conceivable kind of photography—illustration, photojournalism, still life, portraiture, studio and location—anything from photographing a company's product for a catalog to shooting portraits of the chief executive for an annual report. Corporate/industrial photographers also shoot for brochures, promotional literature, audiovisual programs, annual reports, and in-house publications, typically called collateral material.

Photographers in this field generally enjoy a great deal of freedom in image design and they get much satisfaction in forming close working relationships with corporate employees. They should be capable of interacting and directing a wide range of people, and be able to make them feel comfortable in front of the camera. Corporate/industrial photographers also need to be experts at making mundane subjects—for example, manufacturing plant interiors—into an exciting image.

Assignments in the corporate/industrial field are made either by the corporation or, increasingly, by a design firm or public relations agency engaged by the corporation to manage a particular publishing project. On a major item such as an annual report, a designer or art director will usually consult closely with its corporate client before making the final selection of a photographer.

This field may involve shooting dramatic illustrations of consumers using a company's products or services. It also often includes photographic coverage of the client's corporate activities and its facilities. For major corporate clients with nationwide or worldwide operations, the result often is a heavy travel burden for the photographer. To a lesser extent, the field also embraces the studio photographer whose assignment may be to illustrate the client's products and/or services for an annual report or for other publications.

Corporate/industrial assignments are executed normally on a day rate or on a creative fee basis plus all expenses. In a few situations, particularly those involving studio still lifes, the photographer's rate may be determined on a per shot basis. The field is idiosyncratic in that one or two big jobs can make a tremendous difference in total billings for a year.

Because highly detailed layouts from an art director or other administrator are not common, broad coverage of the site in the form of a shot list is usually desired and should be based on carefully considered general visual concepts. Considerable preparation and coordination with the client's line employees, plant managers, and executives are frequently involved and often result in long hours. Reimbursement for expenses reflects these operating factors.

Multiple locations, often requiring complex lighting capabilities and heavy equipment, plus extensive technical demands and coordination, often make it necessary to hire an assistant. Most clients recognize this and accept the assistant's fee and expenses as reimbursable items. It is advisable also to set down estimates for food and hotel expenses. (See chapter 3, "The Art of Pricing and Estimating," for examples of expenses involved.)

Photographers in this field customarily get all travel expenses paid in advance. It's also common to get one-third of estimated expenses for any assignment in advance, with another third paid halfway through and the final third paid upon completion.

In addition, given the nature of these assignments, the photographer is normally compensated for travel and scouting expenses, other prep and editing demands, and layover and standby days. For example, two shooting days sandwiched between three travel days (one day going out, one day between the two locations and one day to return) is an unprofitable assignment unless a reasonable fee is paid for travel time. ASMP surveys show that compensation for travel appears to vary from a full day's fee to 50 percent of that fee, depending on the circumstances.

Additional compensation for unusually long hours is common. This is true particularly in those instances where a photographer's professional responsibility may involve a series of days that begin before dawn and end only after evening setup shots, or following long hours of planning for the succeeding day's shooting.

Usage: All uses beyond those for which the assignment was initially undertaken require additional compensation to the photographer. This is a clear, acceptable practice—but always get it in writing.

For example, photographers invariably negotiate additional payment when a client decides later that photographs taken for, and used in, a recruiting brochure would also be desirable for a paid advertisement or annual report. Similarly, photographs taken for one particular year's annual report should not be used in another year's report (or in a paid advertisement) without further compensation to the photographer.

It is crucial that the photographer and the client have a clear understanding, in writing, of ultimate use before an assignment is executed. Getting credit for published images is another issue. Photographers get credit for annual report work in the back of the book about half the time, and rarely get credit next to their work unless it is their only photograph in the book; other formats—even newsletters—may be more problematic. The client needs to be educated on industry practices, and the potential legal implications if they deviate from these well-accepted practices.

While many photographs taken in the corporate/industrial field might not be suitable for sales to stock agencies, photographers should always be prepared for this possibility for further earnings. This is why they should, as much as practical, get their own releases—which use the term "anybody photographed"—from employees. This should be agreed upon with the client and negotiated as a non-exclusive shoot before getting releases. This is an important liability issue: If employees don't like the photograph that was used, they can sue. Also, if a division gets sold (not an infrequent occurrence), releases held by the company can get misplaced or lost all too easily.

Photographers also should be cautious if asked to sign any documents when preparing to shoot, for example, in a manufacturing plant. While the stated purpose of the document may be to protect the company from having trade secrets revealed, the document's practical effect may be to negate the photographer's copyright by requiring that any images (mainly drawings or sketches) be turned over to the company.

Editorial Photography

Editorial photography is visual reporting of personalities or events to illustrate general interest and specialty stories and information in magazines, books, calendars, newspapers, television programming, posters, and, more recently, on the Internet. Photographers in this field enjoy fairly independent working situations with little control exercised over what they do on the job.

The field is divided basically into two categories. The first is photojournalism in which the photographer tries to tell a story in pictures. The goal is to produce a photo essay through a series of photographs taken over an assigned period of time, and assembled at a later date by the assigning publication. The photojournalist tries to be a "fly on the wall" so that events are not influenced by the camera's presence. Documentary photography, which is similar to photojournalism, portrays the events and aspects of daily life in photos taken for social purposes.

Part of the appeal of photojournalism is its immediacy. This is a field which appeals to photographers who thrive on working under demanding conditions and who possess the ability to solve problems often with few resources. It requires special talents and aptitude.

Because many aspects of doing business in this field are unique, ASMP has created the Photojournalism Specialty Group to address specific concerns. Photographers particularly interested in photojournalism should make contact with ASMP for more information on this specialty group.

The second category, photo illustration and portraiture, involves creating photographs that visually describe the ideas, concepts, or personalities in a story.

One trend in recent years has been the changing role of some editorial assignments from that of photojournalistic to one of photo illustrative. Photographers must often be able to capture the essence of a story with a single image rather than with a series of photos. Illustrative portraits make up a large chunk of the editorial business.

Editorial photography can necessitate extensive travel; it's not uncommon to be on the road half of the year. And as with general travel photography, this takes a lot of planning, particularly for international work. Good sources of information are consulates, visitors bureaus, film commissions, and photographers based in those countries.

Photographers who specialize in editorial work for magazines also advise maintaining close contact with editors and photo buyers who have given you assignments. These people develop their own source of suppliers and if they change jobs, as many do, invariably they refer to their resource list in their new job. By keeping in touch, you increase your chances of obtaining work from the publication they move to. And there is also the possibility of continuing to get work from the publication they left if you make contact with their replacement. In this field, as in many others, success can depend to a great extent on knowing the right people.

Releases, which are usually not necessary for editorial work can be difficult to obtain in some situations. However, if editorial photographers think the images might have resale potential in brochures or advertising, they should try to get releases.

It's also smart for photojournalists to get a script from clients outlining in writing the major points wanted in the story. This avoids costly miscommunications. It's essential to keep copies of photo captions sent to magazines, in case the subject sues because the published captions are inaccurate. Captions are important and should include the basic who, what, where, when, and why and other pertinent information which could boost sales potential.

Fees and expenses: When negotiating fees with a client, be specific about what that fee encompasses. As outlined in the following section on usage there are established guidelines in this market. But with the emergence of electronic magazines and other products, such as CD-ROM, and other on-line uses, photographers are urged to check agreements to ensure payment for additional usage will be made. Some magazines may try to avoid additional usage payment for their on-line editions—and other secondary uses—by not mentioning them in their agreements. It's okay to change an agreement, so don't sign anything you're not happy with until you're satisfied with the language. Also, the practice of charging a less-than-minimum fee, with the understanding that an additional fee will be charged if the project is published, is a form of speculation that experienced photographers avoid.

Photo illustration might require more time spent preparing for the shoot than shooting. Photographers should weigh this when they determine their illustration fees. They also need to project what else—stylists, hairdressers, wardrobe, special lighting, other equipment and props, studio space, and models—should be in a budget, besides prep time, film, and processing. A photo illustrator's expenses may be much like those of the advertising photographer, which is why all parties should have at least a rough estimate of expenses in order to avoid surprises and misunderstandings.

Customarily, all expenses necessary to complete the assignment are billable to the client. For the photojournalist, the principal items (in addition to film and processing) often are travel related: transportation, hotels and meals, and long-distance phone calls. The fees and expenses of an assistant might also be included for major assignments which involve complex scheduling and lighting setups.

Because of the increased costs of supplies and services today, it's a smart business practice for photographers to obtain an advance before beginning an assignment. A rule of thumb is that if an assignment will take longer than a week or involves special expenses such as airfare, hotels and rental cars, the client should provide an advance.

Usage: The long-established tradition in editorial photography is that the client's basic fee covers one-time use in the designated publication in its primary territory and language (for example, one-time English-language North American rights). All other rights, including copyright, belong to the photographer. Ensure that all usage rights are agreed on in writing. Experienced editorial photographers advise getting, at the very least, a confirmation of fees and usage from the client before an assignment. Simply ask the client to fax that information on his or her letterhead.

This limitation on use is critical for professional freelance editorial photographers, since rates for this field are considerably lower than for advertising or corporate clients. Resale income is vital to the photographer's financial well-being, given the relationship between overhead costs and the current editorial rates, whether by day or by page. This is consistent with the principle that artists are entitled to own the results of their creative efforts—a position solidly backed by the Copyright Act. (See chapter 7, "Copyright.")

Credit and credit lines: It is part of the historical contract between editorial clients and editorial photographers that pictures are given an adjacent credit line. Both photojournalists and photo illustrators have the right to legible credits next to each photograph (or on the contents page if their photo is the magazine's cover). Having the credit adjacent to the photograph is the most widely accepted practice. This helps photo researchers recognize photographers' work.

The form of credit line is also important. Many photographers use a proper copyright notice: "© (or 'Copyright' or 'Copr.') year photographer's name." The year indicates the year of first publication.

This notice indicates clearly that the copyright belongs to the photographer, and defeats the defense of "innocent infringement"—a defense which can significantly reduce the amount of damages that a photographer can recover. With today's proliferation of scanners and transmission of pictures by modem, the adjacent copyright notice is more important than ever before.

The issues of placement and form of credit line are regarded as important by the entire profession. Many photographers state their requirements on business forms or stamp the back of their prints with this line: "Adjacent credit to read: © (or 'Copyright' or 'Copr.') year photographer's name. Failure to provide such shall result in triple billing."

The purpose of this is to ensure proper credit and to protect against the real loss of income that can result from omission, rather than to provide additional income. Traditionally, the credit line has been deemed part of the value received by the photographer because it helps to ensure the image's residual value.

For the illustrator, additional and crucial credit may be needed for any suppliers. Clothes, manufacturers, stylists, resort locations, transportation companies, and others often provide goods or services—either for no charge or at reduced rates—in exchange for appropriate credit on the editorial pages of the publication in which the photographs appear. These arrangements can add up to great savings, but photographers shouldn't make guarantees to suppliers about credit arrangements. Photographers usually have no control over what ends up in print and should just have the supplier make arrangements directly with the publication. As a general rule, however, this practice might best be avoided by photographers.

Specialties

In the following section are examples of several specialties and the nuances of doing business in them. This is not intended as a comprehensive list of all specialties and how photographers ply their craft within them, but will give photographers an insight into specialties such as aerial, architectural, fashion and beauty, nature and wildlife, publicity/promotional, sports, still life/product/food, and travel photography. The principles of doing business in these fields can be applied to many others.

As an example of the number of fields open to photographers, ASMP members list almost sixty specialties. These are: advertising, aerial, agriculture, animals, animation, annual reports, architecture, automobiles/trucks, beauty, biomedical, catalogues, celebrities, children, computer generated, corporate/industrial, documentary, editorial, entertainment, executive portraiture, fashion, features, film, fine art, food, forensic, glamour, graphics, historical, horses, human interest, illustration, interiors, landscape, marine, multi-image, multimedia, medical, nature, nudes, panoramics, people, performing arts, personalities, photojournalism, portraiture, products, public relations, scenics, scientific, special effects, sports, still life, stock, television, travel, underwater, video, and wildlife.

Aerial Photography

This is a demanding specialty which, because of the expense and potential danger involved, allows no room for errors, and no tolerance for inexperience.

Aerial photographers must make rapid decisions, and must learn to solve problems under unusual circumstances—and deal calmly with any potential hazards. The physical risks are significant, but the reward is seeing the earth as few others do. Clients can include real estate developers, construction companies, cruise lines, airplane manufacturers, museums, hotels and airlines, and recreation and sports complexes, who expect distinctive photography for advertising, brochures, magazines, and books.

While aerial photographers who work with organizations such as cruise lines and international hotel chains can spend up to half of each year traveling, the majority of practitioners usually work closer to home. Often they piggyback assignments, photographing for two or more clients at the same time, and also shoot stock.

If working internationally, planning and confirming all of a trip's myriad details—hotels, flights, translators, and people who will work on the shoot—are essential facets. Time spent on these details in advance, however, means that location time can be spent taking pictures, rather than solving logistical or personnel problems. Similarly, a shoot in one's backyard should also be well scripted so no important subject matter is overlooked.

Technical and practical concerns: Photographic equipment must be in top working condition at all times; it might be impossible to fix or replace in remote areas. Have all equipment cleaned and lenses checked for alignment every six months or so.

Aerial photography requires some specialized equipment. Zoom lenses are useful because they allow for a quick switch of focal lengths, and a gyro-stabilizer is a great help in keeping cameras stable at all speeds, and compensating for aircraft motion.

Safety is paramount and aerial photographers need to be able to determine which aircraft is most suitable in a particular situation. On location, they must evaluate the flying capability of the available light plane or helicopter and determine if weather poses any problems. They also need to know what safety gear they'll need while aloft, particularly if, for example, they plan to hang out of the aircraft, or for extended overwater flights.

Because of the expense, clients need confidence in the photographer's ability to do the job. Also, the photographer and the client and the creative director must agree on what the assignment entails and its goals. On location the photographer will need to coordinate logistics with people, such as cruise ship captains, hotel managers, and especially the pilots.

Fees and budgets: Aerial photographers command a creative fee reflecting several elements: the scope, complexity and risk involved, which will impact the time needed to complete the assignment; purchase rights and usage required by the client; and the photographer's experience and reputation.

Advances are necessary because of the time required for assignments. For some expenses, clients are billed directly, after the photographer approves the invoice.

Because of the extraordinary expenses in this field, the photographer and client should go over a proposed budget very carefully and make sure they agree on all details. Budgets should reflect all expenses but should also allow for unforeseen expenses. Here are some points to consider:

Production time: To cover, for example, logistical details and editing slides later. If the client isn't billed directly for this time, it should be a part of the fee.

Weather days: It's best to agree on a fair estimate of extra days with the client.

Special equipment: The photographer and the client need to decide who will pay for special items that might be needed, such as a gyro-stabilizer, land or marine radio use, special lenses or camera bodies or camera maintenance charges.

Aircraft estimates: Be aware that fees for helicopters and light aircraft rented in countries outside of the U.S. will probably be higher. Estimate accordingly. Include travel time to and from the aircraft base.

Film: Allow for plenty of film and processing, because of the need to bracket a lot.

Insurance and liability: The client should pay for liability and insurance coverage costs, which will vary from assignment to assignment. Aerial photography can be dangerous and it is important to make sure you have full insurance coverage for medical or death. Before undertaking an aerial assignment ensure that your policies cover you or your employees and be aware that some policies have clauses stating that injury or death resulting from unscheduled flights are not covered. This could include flights chartered for aerial photography. Also, photographers are advised to check with both the client and the flight operator to determine what insurance coverage is in place for injury, death or liability. Some photographers injured in aircraft crashes have found, after the fact, that the flight operator has had minimal coverage. Inquire before you fly—from your insurer and from the client and flight operator. Also, many experienced photographers make a point of informing their clients that they (the photographer) have liability coverage and carry proof of that coverage. This is a professional approach, for all assignments, not just aerial.

Assistant's wages/fees: Up-to-date information of overtime, which will be inevitable, should be kept so the client can be billed accordingly.

Air time is expensive, but the client might be willing to pay for scouting time, particularly for a large advertising campaign. If possible, the photographer should, at the very least, have time budgeted to scout the area on foot to get familiar with the landmarks. If specific colors or images are required for the photograph, the budget may need to include having a car and driver on call. Photographers should always have a backup plan in mind as conditions in the sky can change quickly; they also should be ready to take advantage of those conditions to get the unexpected image.

Aerial photography terms for assignment contract: Aerial photography can be affected by a number of factors including, but not limited to, climatic conditions, Federal Aviation Regulations, pilot safety requirements, aircraft performance, and certain local laws. The photographer's judgment as to the safe and effective execution of all aerial photography must be followed. If for any reason the original layout or design cannot be followed, client may request that photographs not be made. In any event, the client is responsible for all costs incurred on the flight. For a number of reasons, under some circumstances, a person's expectation from aerial photography may differ from the actual photograph that is taken. Although the photographer will use every effort to insure that the aerial photograph will correspond to client's expectations, such aerial photography must be purchased as shot, even if there is a deviation from the original layout or design.

Architectural Photography

Because many aspects of doing business in this field are unique, ASMP has created the Architectural Photographers Specialty Group to address specific concerns. Photographers particularly interested in architecture should make contact with ASMP for more information on this specialty group. The information in this section provides an overview of doing business in the field.

This area of specialization involves photographing man-made structures for illustrative purposes. Typical clients include architects, interior designers, contractors, engineers, developers, the hospitality industry, plus numerous manufacturers of products such as furniture, lighting, carpeting, and building materials. Client usage varies: portfolio, display, brochures, editorial, and advertising in trade or consumer media.

Architectural photographers need a sense of composition and sound technical skills because of the wide variations in lighting and spaces, and extreme patience (waiting for the right weather and lighting conditions) and must be particular about details (they might have to pick off every dead leaf from a tree). The physical demands of location work and heaving lighting equipment require good health and strength (or at least a strong assistant).

Usage and fees: Many clients for this type of work commission photography only occasionally, and some degree of client education regarding rights and usage often is required. It is also not unusual for first-time clients to be naive about the time required to photograph interiors, especially in mixed lighting conditions, and in large complex spaces. Also clients should be clear about copyright ownership belonging to the photographer.

Just as in other specialties, fees are based on a combination of a creative fee and usage. For example, photographs taken for hotel brochures should command a higher fee than the same photographs taken for an architect's portfolio; this reflects the type of usage and the value of the image to the client.

As with other specialties, most architectural photographers have a minimum creative fee which is based on experience, talent, capital investment and overhead, plus a desired profit margin.

For architects and interior designers it is customary to grant a non-exclusive license to use the photographs for portfolios, display, slide presentations, self-promotional brochures, awards competitions, and editorial usage. Photo credit should accompany photographs used in this way.

Fees charged for advertising usage of architectural photographs are based on the same criteria used for any other type of photography, namely: placement, number of insertions, length of use, and exclusive versus non-exclusive use, etc. (See chapter 3, "The Art of Pricing and Estimating.")

It is extremely important to obtain a property release and a model release, when appropriate, for any image with resale potential. While many images at first glance do not appear to have resale value, they may, in fact, have tremendous resale potential. Without adequate releases and permissions, however, many sales are impossible and you may be needlessly cutting yourself off from future income.

It is not uncommon for two or more clients (say, the architect and a supplier) to share usage of a shoot and to split the total cost. Since the usage is increased and the time required to service these clients is increased, it is customary to charge a higher-than-normal fee for this situation. With similar usage for all parties, a typical surcharge might be 30 percent of the day rate for two clients, 50 percent for three clients, etc.

Typically, the photographer retains the exclusive right to license usage of photographs for commercial use to any third party. This right should be made explicit in the contract in order to avoid any possible confusion. Such third party sales represent a significant source of income for most architectural photographers and should never create a conflict of interest with usage by the commissioning client. A good working relationship with the client will help ensure that any third party requests for usage will be referred to the photographer.

Fees for usage by third party clients are comparable to fees paid by the commissioning client, or higher if warranted by usage. These fees also may reflect the cost to recreate the photographs, and the photographer's experience and reputation.

Catalog Photography

There are two main areas of catalog photography: fashion and product. Potentially lucrative, extremely hard work, and laden with pitfalls, is how some practitioners describe this specialty. The number of photographs used in catalogs is enormous but before taking the leap into this specialty there are some considerations.

If all your work comes from one or two large clients, you will be expected to be available at all times, at short notice, otherwise clients will call other photographers. This will leave little time for marketing yourself to other clients, or servicing smaller clients you might already have. Also, large companies going out of business often take their suppliers—including photographers—down with them. And a store might suddenly decide to install an in-house photography department. If you lose a major client, for whatever reason, you suffer a double blow: loss of immediate business, and time lost trying to find new clients.

Of course there are advantages to having large clients, including, regular work, big projects, and potentially good income.

Catalog photography is used primarily in a company's direct-mail marketing campaigns but there can be overlap with some of the same photographs used in advertising. It is important to know exactly how the photographs will be used before submitting an estimate. (See chapter 3, "The Art of Pricing and Estimating.")

Because of the variety of photography, with speed being essential, the catalog shooter must be proficient with all formats of equipment, have strong lighting skills on location and in the studio, be able to follow a layout, and be comfortable working with people and products. Being able to perform under the intense pressure of tight deadlines—and usually for long hours each day—is a must. Catalog photography at its most hectic is incredibly demanding.

The work can be in the studio or on location (nearby or distant) and each involves its own pricing structure. Once the job moves away from the photographer's studio, travel, accommodations for the photographic crew and models, per diem, and other costs associated with location work, figure into the total fee.

The models used in catalog fashion photography are usually hired through an agency by the client and usually bill directly. At times the models' fee will be billed through the photographer's studio who will pay the agency.

Practitioners in fashion work stress the importance of having excellent relationships with model agencies. In addition to performing their obvious role, agencies can also help in business areas such as knowing clients' paying habits, and keeping an eye out for unauthorized use of photographs.

Catalog fashion photography fees are usually based on the number of shots taken during a day. Typically, the store or client's art director will project how many days a shoot will take and the photographer will negotiate a fee based on completing the job within that projection. Some clients will expect a certain number of shots to be completed each day, say, in the range of eight to ten. This figure will vary depending on the complexity of each photograph.

Because fashion photographs have a limited life span, in the vicinity of three months, their re-usage value, as stock for instance, is limited. Also, models' fees are high and are paid by the client. To use fashion photographs for other reasons, you would have to pay a model fee. These factors must be weighed into the photographer's fee and many catalog fashion shooters, while admitting it's preferable to retain rights to the pictures, will negotiate the sale of all rights and will charge accordingly.

Having determined the extent of the shoot the photographer will submit an estimate with a full description of the job. On its acceptance an advance, usually a third, is expected. Another payment of a third is expected at some point during the project—this depends on the total projected length—and the balance is due within thirty days of completion.

If reshoots are necessary, for reasons other than equipment or other technical problems, the client is expected to pay an extra fee. This should be clarified, in writing, before the job starts.

Trends: An increasing amount of catalog photography, especially of products, is being photographed digitally and while conventional photography, particularly of people, still plays a significant role in this specialty, vastly improved digital equipment is changing how catalog photographers work.

The advantages of digital photography for product work include not only the speed with which images can be made but the elimination of several steps from original image to printed page which are involved with conventional photography.

To remain competitive in catalog work, and because many clients are now requesting images in digital form, more studios are becoming electronic and this transition will increase as manufacturers continue to improve image capturing equipment. Obviously, this requires considerable investment by studio owners, a factor which will be have to be weighed when considering the viability of becoming an electronic studio.

Fashion and Beauty

To succeed in this highly competitive field, several mandated skills are vital: an intense interest in fashion and beauty, and the ability to create a distinct style—a look. Breaking into this field is not easy, but once in, photographers often have freedom to use their own interpretation to convey style.

The field is segmented according to how business is conducted. The three major areas—defined basically by usage—are advertising, retail, and editorial. They share some common areas, but each has its own compensation and peculiarities.

Advertising: As in other specializations, this pays the most because of the value of the image to the client. One image, which may take several days to make, is often the goal.

Retail: When shooting for stores, photographers often use day rates and space rates, which generally fall between advertising and editorial rates. The photographs are usually for flyers and catalogs and newspaper advertising.

Editorial: Some photographers have seven-figure contracts with magazines. Usually based on the size of the photograph, however, editorial rates pay the least amount of money—both to photographers and to models. The images can offer great advertising for photographers because of the photo credit. Advertising and retail clients often use magazines to seek photographers—and models—who can produce the "look" they want, which then leads to assignment work.

Much contemporary fashion/beauty photography entails shooting for catalogs, something many photographers used to denigrate. They felt the work was too stultifying, because the items had to be shown exactly as they looked. Photographers now have more freedom, with the result that many of the photos are image pieces. A few upscale catalogs even give credit lines. Wholesale or manufacturers' catalogs also provide work for photographers in this field.

Fees and usage: Usually creative fees in fashion/beauty photography are similar to those in other fields: they're determined primarily by usage. Advertising work commands the highest fees, editorial jobs pay the least, and retail rates fall somewhere in between. However, within this framework there is much deviation. Fees are fluid; advertising photographers who are in demand can get paid a tremendous amount of money, while others get paid significantly less. Fees for catalog work vary substantially, depending upon the client and the type of catalog.

As in other areas, fashion/beauty photographers—whether editorial, retail, or advertising—bill certain expenses and production charges to clients. Some of these items include assistants, stylists, hairdressers, location scouting, props, sets, transportation, hotel, meals, and film and processing. Photographers do not normally bill for models, however. Clients—ad agencies, companies, or magazines—take care of selecting (although photographers may make recommendations) and booking models. The clients also negotiate fees and pay the model agency directly.

Magazines, when travel is necessary, typically make all the arrangements, book hotels and transportation, and give the airline tickets to the photographer and crew.

While fashion/beauty photographers retain the copyright of all images (unless there is an agreement stating otherwise), releases from the models must be obtained for resale of images. Also to be considered is whether a release is required from the fashion designer. And the licensing agreement between the models and the client should be checked to ensure there is no conflict. Generally, resale of fashion is usually limited by time—fashions become outdated—while beauty photographs tend to have greater longevity. It should be noted that models sometimes demand residuals from resales so this aspect should be clarified from the outset.

Trends: This field is undergoing changes including the fact that photographers are moving away from studio ownership, which entails tremendous overhead costs, especially in the fashion and cosmetic areas. Many photographers are finding it expeditious to rent a studio as needed. This gives the flexibility of having access to different studio space and facilities to meet different needs.

Not being tied to studio space also allows fashion/beauty photographers more flexibility to take advantage of growing opportunities internationally. The field is becoming more global, particularly in fashion and cosmetics, and fashion photographers may spend up to half of the year out of the country. European editors tend to give more stylistic freedom to photographers, and the resulting images often lead to work in the U.S.

The global trend has spawned an international way of doing editorial business. The client takes care of all the myriad pre- and post-production details, and the photographer travels to the foreign country with cases of cameras, shoots in a rented studio, and gets paid a creative fee and goes home. While some clients will offer to handle film and processing, photographers should discourage this. Clients should pay for film and processing, but photographers should supply film and control processing to ensure quality.

A practice first common overseas but now gaining popularity in the U.S. is for clients to coordinate the logistics and pay models' and assistants' fees. Traditionally, most photographers prefer to use their own assistants and crew with the client paying their fees but now it is not unusual for clients to rent and pay for the studio, book the models, provide transportation, and provide everything else needed. This trend was introduced to the U.S. by the large department stores.

Nature and Wildlife Photography

The attractions of this specialty—being in the great outdoors photographing flora, fauna, and spectacular scenery—might lose their gloss after a few hard truths hit home: (1) there's fierce competition from established, dedicated practitioners; (2) working conditions can often be arduous and uncomfortable; and (3) the financial rewards might not meet your needs.

Nature photographers, who must have incredible patience and often mechanical aptitude in building special equipment or making repairs in the field, can lead the life of a vagabond. They might spend half the year in the field—anywhere from rain forests to Arctic tundra—and much of the rest of the time marketing their work, preparing for the next trip, and in general, taking care of business.

The most successful practitioners have a background in nature or biology, and know where to find what they want to photograph—often with the help of scientists, biologists, or environmentalists. The field grew from a hobby among a small group of photographers with a love for nature. It has exploded in the last ten years as growing concern about the environment and nature became an important and socially desirable issue. The field is dominated by a handful of professionals possessing business acumen and photographic skills. Their work is driven by a desire to bring nature to people; their intent is to help preserve it.

Business concerns: Major markets in this field include national magazines, nature books and, to a lesser extent, advertising. Nature photographs often have strong resale value, and stock sales can provide significant income, particularly after photographers get established. Typical stock sales would be for calendars, posters, cards, wall decor, and murals. Nature images generally don't get outdated and lend themselves to international publishing opportunities.

An office per se isn't really needed; photographers just need to be available to clients by fax or phone, have access to mail or courier service, and be able to get to an airport.

An all-terrain vehicle or one that enables the photographer to stay out in the field for extended periods of time, such as a camper, trailer, or van, often is useful. Film and processing costs are usually high because photographers in the field can't do snip tests and the nature of their work makes reshoots unlikely. Therefore, they tend to use a lot of film.

Travel, especially to foreign countries, brings its own difficulties. Photographers might need to figure out the logistics of moving equipment to a remote area on a small plane. They may also need to be able to work through customs and maneuver around bureaucracies that may be less than receptive to the photographer's presence. (See Travel Photography, below.)

If a nature photographer lands a specific assignment, expenses such as airfare, hotel, meals, and film and processing should be paid in advance by the client.

Depending on the area of nature photography, equipment and technical skills vary. Some nature and wildlife shooters simplify their approach, relying on available light and basic equipment, somewhat akin to photojournalism. But minimal equipment might not be good enough to compete. Others go to great pains in preparing for a shoot—such as building platforms high above the ground to photograph tree dwellers—and use sophisticated lighting and special lenses to achieve their goals.

Some specialties include landscape, usually the domain of large format equipment; macro, where special close-up equipment is essential; and general wildlife, for which long lenses are usually required. Investment in equipment—quality lenses, auto focus cameras, and electronic flash—can be extensive and expensive.

Hobbyists abound in this field because nature photography is a good excuse to get outdoors. It's an expensive hobby, however, so people look for ways to make money. The result is a depressed market for stock sales.

This explains why photographers in this area also tend to be involved in a multitude of diverse projects—giving lectures, teaching classes, leading photo tour groups, writing columns, and publishing books—with the goal of boosting their livelihoods.

Use and releases: Fees are generally based on usage. For editorial photographs, the going rates and practices in the editorial field apply. Although advertising assignments in this field are rare, sales of stock for advertising use are growing. Part of the reason for this is the desire for companies to portray themselves as nature friendly.

Because of the subject matter many practitioners don't bother with releases. Most photographs are taken outdoors; there's no one to sign in most situations. Photographs including people will have greater stock sales potential if released, and cannot be used for advertising unless released. If you rent animals and hire the services of a handler, ensure that you obtain releases.

National and state park services are also exerting greater restrictions on commercial photography in parks. Permits are usually required if the photographer has special needs such as crowd control, or does something different from other visitors. Rather than risk problems, you are advised to check restrictions on photography with the park authorities. Permits, if required can be obtained from either the National Park and Wildlife Service, or from a state park service, depending on who controls the park. Application for permits can take time to process, so inquire well before you intend making commercial photographs.

Publicity/Promotional Photography

This field is a hybrid of all the sectors of photography, incorporating elements of advertising, corporate, and editorial photography. It demands separate treatment, however, since it has some of its own peculiar practices.

Publicity/promotion pictures are used by producers, press agents, public relations firms, corporate directors of communications, and individual talents handling their own public relations. Clients often are associated with theater, television, sports, dance, film, tape, politics, book publishing, music, and, to some degree, general corporate activities.

Photographers need broad skills to succeed in this field, because they have to work in a wide range of settings, from on location in the workplace to a table top in a studio. Many practitioners can be found in smaller markets, where they need to do considerable educating of clients about rights and usage.

Financial considerations: Financially, this field incorporates elements of both photojournalism and the more commercial pursuits. Assignments may be seen by the client as satisfying purely commercial objectives. Nonetheless, to the photographer, these journalistic elements are present:

- The work is likely to appear in a wide variety of print and related media, frequently as illustrations used with reviews or similar editorial copy.
- The work is editorial in nature, often involving coverage "in performance" or in a portrait setting. Accordingly, the practices that have developed reflect a compromise between the wider use negotiated with clients in some of the more commercial specialties, and the limited one-time-use-only terms (and accompanying reuse income for the photographer) normally associated with editorial photography.

What this boils down to is this: in public relations assignments, fees may be more modest than in other commercial assignments, so reuse income is important for the photographer.

The photographer's ability to achieve publication in the right places can be a factor in determining who secures an assignment particularly with "special" still coverage on motion pictures. Avoid making guarantees about publication and press prospects, since final editorial judgment can be made only by the publication itself.

Usage: Photographers in this field often try to get clients to focus on usage when discussing fees, in an attempt to move away from the concept of day rates. Under current practice, a photographer's basic fee usually covers only these client uses: press kits; brochures; and certain editorial use in newspapers, trade publications, television, and local poster displays.

Publication is restricted to announcements, reviews, and other editorial situations where the subject of the photographs is mentioned specifically. The permitted duration of usage is normally for the life of the event, which for ballet or opera is the season or engagement, and for politics is the current campaign. Remember that in politics, especially during a campaign, business is traditionally done on a COD basis. A losing candidate might not pay bills after the election. For a book promotion or jacket, limitation pertains to the precise title and edition involved, and is limited to the specific photographs agreed upon for use.

Other uses normally result in additional or reuse income to the photographer from the publication, electronic medium, etc., that uses the material. Examples of media that typically may be charged for reuse of photography include:

- Publications: General-circulation magazines and major Sunday supplements.

(Note: Most major magazines and Sunday supplements expect to pay separately for all uses.)

- Television: Additional fees are usual for any editorial use, such as documentary-type features, not referred to as part of the photographer's basic fee.
- Commercial offshoots: These include program books, T-shirts, album covers, and book jackets that are not part of the initial assignment.
- Advertising: Paid national ads, nationally distributed posters and similar uses normally command additional fees. Local ads, however, are a gray area. Although sometimes permitted without extra charge (as part of the initial shooting fee), it is becoming more common to negotiate additional fees for such uses.
- Individual talents: Photos shot for the public relations client generally command additional use fees. Also, an author may pay more for publicity uses of shots taken initially for book jackets. Practically speaking, however, restrictions on usage in this area are difficult if not impossible to enforce. Local newspapers often use publicity photos without credit lines; in such situations, particularly in smaller markets, it might be detrimental from a business standpoint to take action against either the client or the publication. Photographers have to walk a fine line when negotiating these issues.

Credit lines: Adjacent credit line, preferably in proper copyright form (© year photographer's name), should accompany every use. Furthermore, many experienced photographers state on all forms that omission of, or incorrectness in, the credit is subject to triple billing. Protection of the copyright on a book jacket requires placement of the copyright notice on the jacket itself. A book jacket is considered a separate work which is not part of the book proper.

Negatives and transparencies: All negatives and transparencies should be returned to the photographer immediately after use.

Usage notice: It is customary (and advisable) to require a statement of use on the front of each photograph—on an overlay or on the border—in press kits, etc. This notice, together with the notice to the client of liability for any violation of usage restrictions, is important to prevent unauthorized use in publications.

Photographers in this area should get both property releases and model releases from corporate employees, or at least keep the company's releases in their own files for safekeeping. Even though this might be difficult to do from a diplomatic standpoint, getting a release at the time of the photo shoot can prevent problems with disgruntled former employees who, for example, might be unhappy about being included in a photograph used in a brochure which might be an offshoot from the original assignment. Signed releases also put the photographer in the position of being able to take advantage of any potential resale opportunities.

Sports Photography

Because many aspects of doing business in this field are unique, ASMP has created the Sports Photographers Specialty Group to address specific concerns. Photographers particularly interested in sports should contact ASMP for more information on this specialty group. The information in this section provides an overview of doing business in the field.

This primarily editorial field appeals, obviously enough, to photographers who love and understand sports. If you don't find sports exciting, or know little about them, this is probably not for you. But the stiff competition in breaking into sports photography indicates that many do thirst for the thrill of photographing the action and making a living from it.

If you have an intimate knowledge of sports—or a particular sport—and have a knack for knowing where the action is going to be, and have photographic skills and quick reflexes, you've probably got some of what it takes. But stepping right into the big time is unlikely and access to major events can be difficult unless you're willing to photograph from the stands. A better bet is to start photographing local sports where you can get better access. Your market could be the local paper, or high school or college magazines.

Once you've developed contacts and have tear sheets with credits, your chances of getting press credentials and opening doors to bigger events and athletes are better.

Developing your photographic skills takes practice. So does developing your business skills and in this field you are in essentially the same freelance market as any other editorial shooter. Stock sales for sports—especially released images, and those symbolic in nature (power, speed, etc.)—can be more lucrative than the original assignment. Some veteran sports photographers make considerably more income from sales of sports personality photographs used by sponsoring companies than for their editorial work.

Investment in equipment can also be expensive. Before taking the plunge seek advice from veteran sports photographers. Newspaper photographers usually have the experience to advise on ideal equipment combinations for different sports.

The working arrangement you have with clients will depend on how well you know them. A long established client with tight deadlines might require you to submit unprocessed film so it can be processed and edited immediately, and potential future selects kept on file. Some photographers see this system as an advantage as it means the client might use more material. However, it does reduce the control you have over your pictures.

Electronic transmission of sports, and other news photographs, might also demand quick processing by someone other than your own lab. Be aware of these possibilities before an assignment.

Sports assignments come under the same basic guidelines as editorial work. For example, releases for editorial purposes are not usually required but if an unreleased sports photograph is later used for an ad or promotional purposes, it could lead to legal problems. If such a use develops, or is anticipated, get a release.

Sports advertising photographs, especially of prominent athletes, are usually arranged—and set up—through an advertising agency. If photographs taken in competition of an athlete or team are to be used for advertising, releases from the individuals—and often from the league or competition organizer—must be obtained. Currently, a major concern is the move by sports leagues to limit access to events and to control licensing of images. ASMP is fighting for photographers' rights in this regard.

Still-Life, Product, and Food Photography

Still-life and food photography are usually studio assignments requiring special lighting and camera equipment and skills. The field incorporates some aspects of both advertising and editorial photography.

Clients can include corporations, advertising agencies, and design firms with photographs likely to be used in advertising, magazines, and cookbooks and on food packaging.

Still-life photography entails shooting inanimate objects, including food. A food photographer is assumed to be capable of shooting still life, but a still-life photographer is not assumed to be able to work with food.

While most of the work is table top within the controlled environment of a studio, it can require a larger set or be on location. As is true with many assignments, the successful still-life photographer must be able to visualize the final image and ensure that all the elements are on hand for the shoot. At times the client might provide only a vague idea for a layout leaving the photographer to control creativity.

Special requirements: The business of still-life photography is like the business of advertising or editorial photography in production planning requirements, shooting expenses, and usage and fees. Studio space and equipment are basic requirements and a food photographer has the added investment in kitchen appliances and utensils.

Photographing food often requires additional specialists or equipment whose costs are billed to the client. These could be:

- Food stylist/home economist—the most critical need is for a food stylist and perhaps an assistant stylist hired directly by the stylist. Some stylists shop for food, while others rely on shoppers. Food stylists charge day rates and get overtime.
- Food shopper—another critical crew member is a food shopper who knows butchers and produce people, and where to get food year round. Sometimes a shoot will have to be scheduled around the availability of the food which sometimes has to be shipped in.
- Prop stylists—buy or rent props. At times a prop maker might be called upon to design special items.
- Appliances and kitchen—special-purpose equipment such as deep fat fryers, additional refrigerators, freezers, and ovens are often needed and these can be rented.

The elements of food photography are difficult to control. Food moves and changes, unlike, for example, a piece of jewelry. Every food has a different life span so art directors, food stylists, and photographers have to rely on their ingenuity and problem-solving experience. Veterans in this field recommend that photographers not try to style food themselves.

Productions for shooting food can be complex and practitioners liken it to a controlled explosion: everything has to be ready at the climactic moment and the photographer has to catch that moment. Props, lighting and camera angle are all arranged, and then the food is placed in the set.

This might not be the end of the photo session, which can take hours longer than anticipated—accidents happen and food is unstable—and requires great patience. The cheese pull on a pizza doesn't last long, for example, and the photographer might use many pizzas before getting *the* shot.

Food stylists have many tricks of the trade to make the subject look good enough to eat, and this is standard and acceptable practice. However, if a photograph is of a particular product, say a hamburger with a stated amount of meat, ethically the photograph must be of that product with all the correct ingredients.

Usage and fees: Advertising work, the largest part of this specialty, commands a greater fee than editorial work. As with other assignment photography, usage is important. A shot for a national ad campaign will require a larger fee than one for trade publications. Copyright, unless negotiated otherwise, belongs to the photographer, who negotiates limited rights with the client for a specific duration.

Standard usage for packaging images is unlimited exclusivity, usually for one year and sometimes up to five years.

Cookbooks can provide photographers with a good publicity vehicle. Often photographers will team up with a writer and stylist on these projects and, while they may not always be a big money maker, the variety of work can comprise an excellent portfolio. Food photography for cookbooks and magazines is basically editorial work, with the photographer getting a credit line but commanding less pay than for other uses.

Travel Photography

Travel photography might also seem an ideal way to make a living: make photographs of exotic places, stay in plush resorts, and have all expenses paid. But it's not that simple. Successful travel photographers combine a love of travel (and the ability to cope with all the attendant stress) with the vision to see familiar places in fresh ways. They must have all-round photographic skills and business/marketing acumen to exploit every possible market from each trip.

And they must be capable of working solo—being the producer, stylist, and lighting expert. Being able to function independently comes with the territory—the client or photo editor might be thousands of miles away. Attention to detail both pre-trip and while on location is vital.

While it might sound paradoxical, within this specialty being a generalist is necessary. Landscapes, cityscapes, night scenes, people, food, interiors, architecture—all come within the domain of the travel photographer. What buyers usually look for is "freshness"; a new way of seeing old subjects.

There is demand for travel images, in fact it's huge. But so is the supply. And payment, for what is largely an editorial market, is not. This is why the travel shooter must glean every possible sales outlet from each assignment.

Veteran travel photographers will usually develop a network of clients and notify them whenever making a trip. Hotel chains, or airlines, with tourist facilities in different countries might need new pictures. Marketing imagination is vital.

Be familiar with cultural and political taboos when in foreign countries. Taking photographs is not a right, and crossing a cultural boundary could lead to abuse—or worse. The U.S. Government offers advice on international travel, including warnings about potential dangers, which can be obtained by calling the State Department's Citizens Advisory Center in Washington, D.C., at (202) 647-5225.

Experienced photographers who can work their way through bureaucracy, who are familiar with cultures of foreign countries, and who can be working soon after arriving at a destination, are valuable to clients, and can command higher payment. Gaining that experience might require initial self-financed assignments. Some travel shooters augment their income by leading workshops and tours, but this too is an undertaking for experienced travelers.

The commercial market, especially in tourism, pays better. Clients such as cruise ships, hotels, airlines, credit card companies, banks, and, to a certain extent, car rental agencies use photos for capability brochures or advertisements. Major tourist organizations occasionally need work done for travel brochure photographs.

Travel is expensive, which puts time at a premium—your own if it's a speculative trip, the client's if it's an assignment. Travel photographers don't relax much. Clients expect them to work fast and to be cost-effective, one reason why assistants are rarely hired for editorial assignments.

For photographers on assignment, travel expenses (airfare, hotel, meals, local transportation) generally are covered by the client. Other expenses that should be covered include film and processing, special equipment or props, models and shipping. Clarify and agree on these issues before the assignment begins and negotiate for advances on all assignments—commercial and editorial.

As in other fields, travel clients are seeking more rights. Check the wording on every contract, even those with established clients because travel photographs have potential for stock sales and you don't want to limit that potential.

Be careful of sending travel photographs to foreign clients. Violation of rights in some countries might be hard to combat and it might be better to channel those sales through a stock agency.

Generally, travel images for editorial use don't require releases and many magazines don't ask for them. Releases do increase the potential for advertising stock sales, and photographers are advised to obtain them. A supply of simplified releases in the language of the country you are visiting is a good insurance. However, many people, especially in foreign countries, might not understand the concept of releases, and language and other barriers might make it impractical to obtain releases. Also, in some cases, your subjects might be illiterate and unable to read a release, even in their own language. For these reasons, veteran travel photographers with an eye to stock sales will often hire models. Making people unidentifiable is another way to circumvent the need for a release.

Shooting on location: As the name suggests, this involves working away from the photographer's home environment and can be as simple as setting up an executive portrait in the office next door, or as complex as an advertising assignment in a foreign country.

Specializing in location work usually means that the photographer doesn't have a studio or the studio is a base to produce from rather than in.

Location photography and travel photography have much in common. They both require thorough planning of logistics, and practitioners are usually people who relish the challenges of problem solving, often without the convenience of on-the-spot suppliers and resources.

As one shooter said, survival in location photography is a great experience. And veterans in the field usually have extensive check lists, based on their experiences, to ensure that slip-ups and oversights occur only once. These check lists, or production guides, are used to walk the shooter through the job long before arriving on location. Every detail from film and equipment to personnel, transport, accommodations, and visa requirements must be checked.

Getting advances to cover all expenses for the trip is vital. Travel costs, especially for a group, are expensive and photographers should not have to subsidize them. Clarify with the client, before the shoot is completed, such things as costs that require pre-payment and bills to be paid on location.

Frequent communication is necessary for the smooth operation of all stages of the project. Some photographers recommend prior meetings with all the people who will be working on location. Everyone must know what to expect and what is expected of them. Brief meetings at the end of every day on location are useful for evaluating the day's work, and for making final preparations for the next day.

Clients also need to know what to expect. All details, financial and otherwise, should be in writing. How will weather problems be handled? What transport will be needed on location? What accommodations? Rent for storage space for equipment, access to phones, fax machines, or computers, and meals all need to be arranged and agreed on.

Confirm everything by fax the day before leaving for the shoot. This is a reminder and also makes sure everything is in order. Include information on whom to expect, the schedule, the number of pictures, number of rooms needed, and transportation requirements.

Personnel requirements vary with each assignment, but a typical assignment would include a production manager to set up the project and to make sure it runs smoothly, an assistant, a stylist, a location scout, models, and a hairdresser. These can be either full-time employees or freelancers, preferably experienced in location work. Depending upon the project and the client's relationship with the photographer, the art director might also be there.

Often location shooters will have experienced personnel as a nucleus of a crew and train new people on less demanding shoots.

Photographers need to be aware of security while on location. An assistant may be assigned to stay with the equipment at all times, even sleeping in the same room with it. Exposed film may be locked in a special case which stays with the photographer at all times. Hiring local guides or guards, particularly in unfamiliar territory, is another alternative.

Many photographers maintain that it is far preferable to pay excess baggage charges rather than to travel to a distant location and not have what is needed. They suggest taking twice as much as estimated in equipment, film, batteries, and walkie-talkies. Make arrangements to purchase extra film locally. Carry a medical kit, any necessary notes from doctors, and well-labeled prescription drugs. Some photographers have crew members trained in cardiopulmonary resuscitation and prefer good swimmers.

It is helpful to have a local company representative assigned to work with the entourage. This person can help solve problems and be a liaison with local vendors and others. Deal with well-known and established companies when renting cars or contracting for other services. Ask other photographers for recommendations on reliable suppliers. This is where ASMP colleagues can be great resources.

Because of the physical demands of travel, it's suggested that the location crew arrive the day before shooting begins. This allows them to be better rested and to scout the location ahead of time. Experienced photographers schedule a day off after three- or four-days' work. If the job entails more than one location, have an assistant travel to the next stop a day ahead of time to smooth the way and to make last-minute arrangements.

Location work can be in any of the major markets. Advertising clients, which traditionally pay higher fees, include credit card companies, banks, hotels, major tourist organizations, communications companies, software companies, recreational companies, and airlines.

Editorial clients include primarily magazines and some newspapers. Depending on the use, compensation is commensurate with either advertising or editorial rates.

Foreign travel: Any location work is demanding but traveling internationally requires special preparations. Some photographers even hire language tutors before going to a foreign location. They want the production staff, if not fluent in the local language, to at least be able to communicate. This helps them to get greater cooperation from local people and keep staff out of trouble. They also want staff to know something of the culture and to respect its customs, such as: who do you tip and how much, what behaviors to avoid, what is acceptable attire? Attention to these details can make the shoot go much smoother.

Paperwork to be done ahead of time includes passports, visas, insurance, and permits to bring equipment into the country. Location veterans suggest that because of its immediacy, fax is the best way to handle this paperwork. It also saves time and money making phone calls, and written communication can avoid misunderstandings.

Ensure that all paperwork—equipment lists with make and serial numbers, passports, visas, and driver's licenses—for all personnel is easily accessible, and that officials will be able to inspect your equipment against your lists. Check if a carnet, an official document covering equipment to be taken in and out of a country, is required. A carnet can also save you hassles when returning home, especially if you took new equipment. Before departing the U.S., let Customs officials know what equipment you are taking with you, otherwise you could have to pay duty when you come home.

If possible, have the client write, in the local language, a letter of introduction to the local company representative explaining who you are, that they should assist you, and to call the home office with any questions. Also carry a letter of introduction from your banker addressed to a local banker in case you need extra currency or other financial services.

The Photographer/Agent Relationship

The primary function of an agent or representative is to secure assignment work for the photographer or to arrange sales or licenses of the photographer's existing stock pictures. Some agents work solely on securing assignments. Others handle only stock pictures. And there are agents who do both.

Basically, there are two kinds of agents: individuals and stock houses. The individual representative (or "rep") may handle the everyday affairs of the photographer—like the personal manager of, say, an actor. But usually the rep's emphasis is on securing jobs for the photographer—the way the actor's agent does. There may also be some effort to sell existing stock material.

Once a photographer's gross income from fees amounts to somewhere in the neighborhood of $75,000 to $100,000, operating costs often begin to rise geometrically. This can be frightening. It can bankrupt the photographer. This situation obviously has to be watched with great care. An aware representative can help to control the situation generally and, in particular, make sure that all job-related expenses are included on estimates and invoices.

The extent of the rep's authority is a private contractual matter between him or her and the photographer. That authority should be clearly spelled out in the agreement between them.

A stock agency, on the other hand, is an organization that handles the work of numerous photographers. It can be an entity of as many as several hundred people, or as few as two or three. It maintains extensive subject-oriented files of existing stock photographs. The stock agency, of course, seeks to license the use of that file material as widely as possible.

It is essential to keep close contact with a representative. Photographer and representative should have regular discussions regarding the trend of assignments and financial progress.

Among the first things to be thoroughly understood in a photographer-representative relationship are the applicable fees and specific markets worth aiming for. A good representative should know these fields. Likewise, a photographer should be realistic about which markets are suitable and which are not. Any photographer worth a representative's selling effort is an individual with something positive to offer visually. A good representative sells the unique qualities of that person.

Doing Business

Representatives are the contacts with the art directors and other originators of photographic assignments. Most important, the representative's job includes ironing out all financial details in advance in the hope that those matters will not encumber the photographer/client relationship. Representatives must therefore be highly professional in their dealings, much as photographers are required to be, in matters such as meeting deadlines and having deliveries ready as promised. (In many cases, representatives make the deliveries themselves to protect the account and to get a quick reaction. It is to both the photographer's and the representative's advantage to deliver prints, transparencies, etc., personally.)

Freelance representatives who operate their own businesses normally finance themselves. They also usually gravitate to representing photographers of reasonable status within their area of business experience, and ones with whom they are compatible. At this time there probably are more photographers looking for good representatives than representatives looking for good photographers. Yet some of the highest-level representatives will also add that the appearance of exceptional new photographic talent is equally hard to find. Actually, representing may offer a swifter financial advance for an intelligent and creative and/or patient person than photography itself, and, where the representative works closely and creatively with the client, it is a satisfying profession.

It is normal for a good, busy representative to employ other people. But it is absolutely necessary that the representative personally devote enough time to each photographer to make the association worthwhile. In some cases, it may also be worthwhile for the photographer to provide the representative with office space, perhaps file space, and perhaps a telephone. In this case, the representative remains responsible for payment of all his or her expenses, including telephone calls.

Assignment Representative Contracts

The sample photographer/assignment representative contract at the end of this section does not establish a single uniform standard. That would be impossible given the varying circumstances under which photographers and their reps work together. Each time this sample contract form is used, it should be negotiated individually. Minor modifications can take care of any particular approach the photographer or representative has in his or her association. The contract entered into must be fair to both parties. As with other important documents, it may be useful for the photographer to seek expert guidance from an attorney or other advisor.

The following information refers to both the photographer's and the rep's primary areas of concern in the course of their working relationship and provides an essential background for understanding the technical contract details in the sample contract form that follows. The discussion indicates the variety of ways a particular topic may be handled in the contract itself, especially in the areas of commissions, house accounts, promotional expenses, and termination.

Commissions

Although 25 percent of the fee has become the generally accepted percentage a well-established representative receives, there are other rates and forms of agreement. Some very successful photographers have their representatives working for a salary, some for a salary and a percentage bonus. Some agreements are made at 20 percent and less; some grant a higher percentage on out-of-town accounts, perhaps another 2½ to 5 percent because of higher telephone and service costs.

As a yardstick, a representative's fee in the New York market on television commercials is usually 5 to 7 percent of gross billings.

Remember that an advance or "draw" against future commissions, unless clearly documented as a loan, might be legally considered a salary and may be nonreturnable. Taxes and social security may have to be paid on this. It is a situation worth avoiding by proper documentation.

House Accounts

House accounts are primarily those clients the photographer has been working with before any relationship with the new representative. They are often not commissioned, or they are commissioned at a lower rate than normal for a specific period of time.

In addition, lower paying accounts such as magazines would probably best be reserved by the photographer as house accounts, or commissioned at a lower rate. So should lower paying television editorial work, experimental film editorial work—and, in fact, experiments of most sorts. If, however, house accounts are not commissioned at all, they may be neglected and die for lack of attention. To make sure this does not happen, it might be a good idea to cut the representative in on house accounts from the start, although at a lower fee—some arrangements simply provide a continuing commission at half the usual rate (sometimes less) for house accounts. This often continues until it is clear that the photographer and representative are going to be together for a while. Thereafter, often within six to twelve months, the house accounts may become fully commissionable.

A representative with a long successful record may insist on full commissions from the beginning. This is a matter of negotiation. But retention of house accounts by the photographer is insurance against the representative in the early months of a relationship.

Other arrangements provide for an increase on house-account commissions in steps based on percentages of increases in the photographer's overall billings. (For example, starting the commission on house accounts at 10 percent—or on any level, for that matter—and increasing it by 5 percent increments with each 10 percent increase in the photographer's total billings, up to a 25 percent maximum commission). While the particular percentages must be negotiated individually, the principle can be applied to a variety of situations.

In any event, until photographer and representative have been together for a substantial period (perhaps a year or even longer), the photographer may wish to exclude house accounts from commissions following any termination. The reason for this is simple: the representative was not responsible for initiating work from those clients and may not yet have a major impact on the continuity of their work. Of course, if the facts are to the contrary, then the termination clause will have to reflect that.

Naturally, a representative receives no commission on those expenses which are normally billed to the client above the photographer's fee, such as props, models, travel, living on location, messengers, set construction, film and processing, stylist, and hairdressers.

There are occasional jobs—these are rarities—on which photographer and representative must come to an understanding on expenses that must "come off the top" of the fee (before calculating the commission) because, for example, unusual equipment is required or unusual setup or location searches may be involved that cannot be fitted into the client's budget. A representative who has bitten the bullet by bringing in an outsize job will be aware of the difficulties, and this problem should be thrashed out between photographer and representative before shooting. In special cases with unusual problems, the client should be informed in any event. Generally, such expenses are charged to the client, who should be aware of them before shooting or billing.

There must be a clear understanding between photographer and representative on jobs undertaken on a flat-fee basis. The occasional benefits in doing things this way should not be lost through misunderstanding about the expenses that must come off the top before the commission is calculated. A photographer who knows costs will be able to make a fair estimate of the expenses. Honesty and fairness must prevail, because blowing expenses up out of all proportion does not fit well in a relationship that can be terminated on a simple thirty-day notice.

Representative's Territory

If a photographer or studio engages more than one representative, the areas of work and territories should be spelled out carefully. Reps should rarely, if ever, approach the same agencies; it is certain that they should not be seeking the same accounts. Space is allowed in the sample contract Section 2(a) for such specifics as: New York market, Los Angeles market, San Francisco or Chicago markets; U.S.A., foreign, and even some agencies under certain conditions. Space is allowed in the contract's Section 2(b) to list such specialty specifics as: advertising, editorial, industrial, and television.

Invoicing

In general, the photographer is personally investing time and advancing expenses in producing the work, and therefore, should be the one to bill, to collect, and to handle the books. The photographer must also be scrupulous in paying the representative as soon as money is received. This is a contractual obligation. Where a photographer is too inexperienced to run a balanced set of books, the representative should handle the money and billing.

The representative should be consulted on bills, and wording should be carefully watched. The representative should acquaint the photographer with the idiosyncrasies of each client. For example, some clients do not like to see "messengers" on the bill; some insist it be called "shipping." In one instance, an item of $150 for "lumber" was entered as "lunch" by the photographer's accountant. It was caught by the account executive—luckily a friend—but if the item had reached the client it could have been the end of a fine account.

Promotional Expenses

In most cases, promotional expenses—such as mailers, directory advertising, etc.—are shared between photographer and representative. There are various ways to do this. Some split it 50-50, others make it 75-25 in accordance with the typical fee split.

At least one leading photographer ties in-house accounts and promotional expenses in this way: the photographer reasons that it is best to have the representative exert maximum efforts with all accounts, whether they are new ones or established house accounts. Accordingly, that representative receives 25 percent on all advertising accounts, including the house accounts. However, partly as a trade-off, the photographer also reasons that the representative has the parallel responsibility of bringing in all the assignments and paying whatever promotional costs are required in that regard. Accordingly, that representative does in fact pay 100 percent of all promotional expenses.

Termination

A photographer-representative contract based on a thirty-day period of notice of termination is obviously only going to exist for an extended period if each party to it is studiously correct in his or her dealings with the other. "There are problems in the whole relationship of photographer-representative," as one articulate representative put it. "The problem reps face is the unsuccessful photographer . . . the problem for photographers is the unsuccessful rep." There is nothing this discussion, or the sample contract, can do for those problems except perhaps lead to a graceful termination without litigation.

The termination clauses of the sample contract form contain the best advice obtainable from those who work actively in the field. Plan only to enter into an association that has a good chance of enduring. Either party can terminate on thirty-days' notice, but a short, scrappy association is simply a waste of valuable time and money to both. Make a fair contract and follow it carefully.

Termination involves some of the most sensitive issues in the photographer-representative relationship. In most situations, the representative is entitled to some compensation, usually reflecting substantial efforts to secure certain accounts that have at least a reasonable chance of remaining with the photographer for awhile after termination.

On the other hand, if that compensation is excessive it could harm the photographer's ability to secure another representative, while the representative may have no such problem in securing another photographer.

In addition, unless the relationship extends over a reasonable period of time (probably one to two years or possibly longer), the question arises whether the representative should be sharing in any of the original house accounts after termination unless special services were rendered respecting certain of those accounts. Another possible way to handle this is to provide for a reduced commission on house accounts on termination after the photographer and representative have been together for a reasonable period.

It is often stated that the representative is entitled to receive full commission for six months on accounts that are active at the time of termination after the photographer and representative have been together for a reasonable period. This is an oversimplification, if, when the relationship first began, the active accounts were the result of earlier efforts made by the photographer or by a past representative.

Accordingly, for approximately the first year it is often agreed that the commissions on termination shall be limited to approximately a three-month period, increasing by regular intervals to a maximum of six months after a period of around two years (with special rules, as appropriate, for house accounts). This type of situation obviously has to be individually negotiated in every instance. It is important because it protects the photographer against excessive demands after an early "breakup" while protecting the key long-term relationship for the representative.

Another possibility is to compensate the representative at full commission on all house accounts from the beginning of the contract and to provide, as a trade-off, for no compensation whatsoever after termination.

Whatever the final arrangement, it is the photographer's responsibility to stick to the agreed-to financial terms scrupulously. It is the representative's responsibility to return the portfolios and samples immediately upon termination.

Note: If there is no agreement, either written or oral, then the employment of the agent is deemed "at will" and no termination compensation may be called for. This may need the advice of a local attorney.

Sample Contract Between Photographer and Representative

AGREEMENT made this _____ day of _____ (year)_____, by and between [Photographer's name and address] (hereinafter referred to as "Photographer") and [Representative name and address] (hereinafter referred to as "Representative"). The parties agree as follows:

1. Definition of terms

As used for the purposes of this agreement:

(a) The term "Active Account" is defined as follows: An account is an active account when it generates assignments currently; it is either a product worked on, an art director worked with, or the original individual buyer for whom assignments have been initiated. An account may be a single order or a continuing campaign. An active account must consist of assignments initiated or assignments done within a period of (six) (twelve) months.

Upon the initiation of an assignment of any sort, oral or written, that constitutes an order for work, an account becomes active.

(b) The term "House Account" is defined as follows: A house account is an active account reserved to the Photographer or to the studio, from which the Representative is restricted in service of solicitation and on which the Representative does not receive commission, but with specified conditions may receive partial commission. When full commission is given the account is no longer a house account.

(c) The term "Library Account" refers to a general assignment which is undertaken on the basis of payment per picture use, where the pictures are to be paid for by the client for current use and are intended to be used and paid for by the client in the future, as well. A library account assignment represents an income source which extends in to the future and which, therefore, generates future commissions for the representative.

(d) The term "Stock" is defined as follows: Stock refers to photographs taken either independently or on assignment on which publication or use rights revert to or are retained by Photographer or the studio after use or rejection of the original stock. Stock rights belong solely to Photographer or the studio.

2. Representative shall use his or her best efforts to solicit assignments, contracts, and other work for the Photographer.

(a) Representative shall work in the following geographic territory: _____

_____

(b) Representative shall represent the Photographer in the following fields of work: _____

_____

3. During the term of this agreement, Representative agrees not to represent any other photographer [Option: any photographer other than those enumerated on an attachment to this Agreement] without the written consent of Photographer. Photographer shall not use one or more other representatives in the territory and the field(s) described above without first obtaining the written consent of the Representative.

4. The following are house accounts:

a. _____

b. _____

c. _____

d. _____

At any time hereafter, if Photographer is solely responsible for obtaining an account, said account shall become a house account.

5. Representative's commissions shall be as follows:

a. Advertising _____

b. Stock _____

c. House Accounts _____

d. Library Accounts _____

d. Editorial _____

6. Commission shall be calculated against the net photographic fee; i.e., the photographic fee exclusive of expenses chargeable to the client. In the event that a "flat fee" shall be set, the net photographic fee shall be that remaining after actual expenses directly relating to the specific job have been deducted.

7. Representative's claim to commissions shall arise when the Representative obtains a new assignment from an active account, subject, however, to Photographer's acceptance and completion of the assignment. Representative shall have no claim to commissions if for any reason Photographer refuses an assignment or if, after accepting it, Photographer does not complete the assignment.

8. Representative shall pay his or her own expenses, including telephone, entertainment, delivery, and general business expenses.

9. Billing shall be made in accordance with subparagraph [specify (a) or (b)] below. In the event an election is not made, subparagraph (a) shall be deemed to have been adopted.

(a) Photographer shall be responsible for all billing, shall be named in all purchase orders, and shall provide Representative with monthly statements, or copies of all bills rendered, for accounts Representative has serviced. Upon reasonable demand, Representative shall have the right to examine Photographer's bills and receipts for accounts Representative has serviced. Payment to Representative shall be made within 10 days of receipt of moneys.

(b) Representative shall be responsible for all billing and for all purchase orders on accounts for which he is responsible, and shall provide Photographer with monthly statements, or copies of all bills, for all accounts which Representative has serviced. Photographer shall be named in all billing. Payment to Photographer shall be made upon receipt of moneys. Upon reasonable demand, Photographer shall have the right to examine the Representative's purchase orders, bills, and receipts on all accounts Representative has or is servicing for the Photographer.

10. Both Photographer and Representative warrant that each has now in effect, and agrees to maintain during the term of this agreement, personal liability insurance with coverage in the amount of at least $100,000.

11. The relationship between Photographer and Representative shall be that of independent contractors, and nothing contained herein shall constitute this arrangement a joint venture or partnership.

12. Photographer retains the right to refuse any assignment obtained by the Representative.

13. Photographer shall not be bound by any representations or statements made by Representative unless Representative is specifically authorized by Photographer to make such statements or representations.

14. Photographer agrees to provide Representative with samples of work, to replace same as they deteriorate, and to provide a reasonable amount of fresh work from time to time.

15. Representative shall not acquire any rights in any of Photographer's work, and shall return any and all of said work on Photographer's demand.

16. This agreement shall terminate 30 days after receipt of written notice of termination given by either party, subject to the provisions of paragraph 17.

17. Termination

(a) Upon termination, Representative shall receive commissions from all active accounts as provided for under this agreement for a period of ____ months; however, on library accounts Representative shall receive commissions for a further period of ____ months. Representative shall be entitled to no other or further commissions, or remuneration of any kind.

[Alternative]: Upon termination, Representative shall receive commissions from all active accounts as provided for under this agreement for a period of ____ months. After this agreement has been in effect for ____ months, the period for such commissions shall be extended by an additional ____ months [optional: and commissions will also be paid on house accounts at the reduced rate of ____ percent for ____ months]. On library accounts, Representative shall receive commissions for ____ months. Representative shall be entitled to no other or further commissions or remuneration of any kind.

(b) If Representative is replaced with a new representative, notwithstanding paragraph 17(a) above, at any time after termination the parties shall have the option to mutually agree in writing as follows: Upon the effective date of an agreement between Photographer and a new representative. Representative shall receive half commission. Such Entitlement shall last for the period from the effective date of Photographer's agreement with the new representative until the final date for termination compensation as provided above in this agreement. Such mutual agreement between Photographer and Representative shall specify those accounts from which Representative shall be entitled to receive half commission. In the event of such mutual agreement, Photographer shall provide in the agreement with the new representative that all such specified accounts shall be serviced by the new representative for the duration of Representative's payment period. In the event of such mutual agreement, Representative shall not be entitled to any other or further commissions or remuneration of any kind.

(c) Notwithstanding paragraphs 17(a) and (b) above, at any time after termination the parties may mutually agree in writing to provide for a cash settlement which shall discharge all obligations and duties owed to each other under this agreement. Under this cash settlement procedure, Representative shall relinquish all rights to any future commissions payable under this agreement.

(d) In the event Representative shall have been responsible for billing under paragraph 9(b), upon termination Representative shall supply Photographer on demand with copies of all outstanding purchase orders and bills.

(e) Upon termination, either party shall have the right to notify third parties of the termination of this arrangement.

18. Any controversy or claim arising out of or related to this contract or the breach thereof shall be settled by arbitration before a single arbitrator in the City and Sate in which it has been executed in accordance with the rules of the American Arbitration Association or, at the election of both parties, in accordance with the rules then obtaining before the local Joint Ethics Committee, if any. In either instance, the award rendered may be entered in any court having jurisdiction thereof.

19. This agreement is personal to the parties and is not assignable by either party, unless the assignment is to a corporation in which the assignor is and remains the majority stockholder. This

agreement shall be binding upon and shall inure to the benefit of the respective heirs, legal representatives, successors, and assigns of Representative or Photographer.

20. This agreement constitutes the entire understanding between the parties and no modifications shall be of any force and effect unless made in writing and signed by the parties hereto.

21. Notice shall be given to Photographer at _____

_____

and notice shall be given to Representative at _____

_____

Notice shall be deemed received on the date of personal delivery thereof, or two days after the date of mailing such notice by U.S. Mail.

22. Both parties agree to execute and deliver such further documents as may be necessary or desirable to effectuate the purposes of this agreement.

23. This agreement shall be governed by the laws of the State of _____

Photographer: _____

Representative: _____

Date: _____

City and State: _____

Sample Notice of Termination

Under Paragraph 16

To: Chris Representative

Please be advised that I am giving you notice of termination of our agreement of _____ _____ (date), and that thirty days after your receipt of this notice our agreement is terminated.

Unless we enter a further agreement providing for termination payments to you under paragraph 17(b) or 17(c) you will be paid in accordance with paragraph 17(a).

At the end of thirty days, please return to my studio all my art work which you now have.

[Since you have been doing the billing, please turn over to me within 30 days copies of all outstanding purchase orders and bills.]

_____

(Pat Photographer)

Sample Agreement

Under Paragraph 17(b)

_____ (date),

To: Pat Photographer

I understand that our agreement of _____ (date), (was) (will be) terminated on _____ (date), which is thirty days after my receipt of notification of termination from you.

I further understand you have entered into an agreement with another representative, (Mr.)

(Ms.) _____ and that (he) (she) will start working as your representative on _____, (year)____.

In consideration of my release herewith of all claims which I may have against you on account of commissions or otherwise, you agree to pay me half commission from _____ (date), until _____ (date), on the following accounts:

1. _____

2. _____

3. _____

I also understand that you have arranged to have your new representative service these accounts during the above period.

If this letter sets forth your understanding, please sign below and return the signed carbon to me.

By your signature you will acknowledge receiving copies of the following bills and purchase orders which had been made by me on your behalf:

1. _____

2. _____

3. _____

Sincerely yours,

_____

(Chris Representative)

Accepted and Agreed to this _____ day of _____ (date)

_____

(Pat Photographer)

Sample Agreement
Under Paragraph 17(c)

To: Pat Photographer

I have your notice of termination of _____ (date)

In accordance with Paragraph 17(c) of our agreement of _____ (date) , I hereby release and discharge you from all claims which I now have under that agreement, in consideration of your payment to me of $_____, receipt of which I hereby acknowledge.

Sincerely yours,

_____

(Chris Representative)

Accepted and Agreed to this _____ (date)

_____

(Pat Photographer)

Chapter 2

The Business of Stock Photography

Craig Aurness, David Barnes, Thom Bunting, James Cook, Jon Feingersh, Paul Henning, Victor S. Perlman, Esq., Barbara B. Roberts, Peter Skinner, Richard Steedman, Vince Streano, Susan Turnau, John Uppgren, and Richard Weisgrau

Simply stated, stock photography is existing photography: that which is available for licensing from photographers or their agencies for specific uses. Buyers who see what they want in catalogs—print or electronic—or from submissions they have requested, have the advantage of knowing what they are getting. From that aspect it is risk-free photography for buyers, or licensors. For photographers, stock photography is not risk free. It involves investing time and money in planning, creating, editing, inventorying, and marketing images which might never sell. Elsewhere we will examine what it takes to get into and produce stock. At this juncture, photographers should be aware that while stock photography offers the attraction of freedom from shooting to the specific needs and deadlines, of assignments, it is fiercely competitive.

Stock photography is not a new business, nor are contemporary photographers the first to capitalize on their library of photographs. From a historical view, Matthew Brady, who sold images from the Civil War that he and other photographers made, could be credited with founding the first stock agency. However, even the entrepreneurial Brady could not have envisaged the staggering volume of stock photographs which are licensed today, nor the effect the growth of this segment of photography has had. Credit for the first twentieth-century agency, and for the first stock catalog, goes to H. Armstrong Roberts whose agency's main business was movie stills, and later cute shots of babies. Former *Collier's* editor Ewing Galloway founded his agency in New York in 1922, specializing in servicing the textbook market with the aid of worldwide files of travel photographers Burton Holmes and Dean Dickerson. The Galloway and Roberts agencies have stood the test of time and are still in business today.

Other groups, some photographers' cooperatives, followed the paths set by Roberts and Galloway and new agencies and syndications sprang up. And when, under the impact of television, many mass-market picture magazines lost readership in the late 1960s, photographers found new and burgeoning markets created by smaller circulation, special-interest publications. Other markets including textbook publishers, poster, greeting card, and other paper product companies and the growing audiovisual production business added to this demand.

Stock photography is widely accepted and respected, and the quality and quantity of material available will satisfy most buyers' needs. A 1996 *Graphic Design: USA* survey of readers to ascertain their opinions of stock found that:

- 82 percent of respondents used stock visuals for graphic design and related work and most are satisfied with the quality, content, and choice available.
- 37 percent said they used stock more than ten times during the year.
- 62 percent said they used stock more than six times during the year.
- Creatives are increasingly turning to stock images to cope with the pressures of time and budget.

The most common use of stock was for sales promotion/collateral/brochures, followed by advertising, direct mail, annual reports and corporate literature, point-of-purchase displays and exhibits, presentations, comps, packaging/covers, Internet/CD-ROM/multimedia, and editorial/publication design.

Nearly all of the survey respondents either already used CD-ROM and other digital methods for image selection or planned to begin doing so within the next year. These respondents indicated they were in tune with electronic technology and some 63 percent said they were currently using a digital method for search, selection, and/or delivery of stock visuals.

However, while digital selection and delivery are gaining wider and accelerating acceptance, many buyers still prefer the traditional print catalogs and other print material to find stock images. Regardless of how the photographs are found, the demand is high and many buyers like the versatility and convenience of stock.

Photographers involved in stock photography should be aware that while markets are there, creative talent and prolific production alone are no guarantees of success in this business. The successful stock photographer is invariably a good businessperson, one who understands what makes a salable stock photograph, how to create that image, and possesses the marketing acumen to get images into the most lucrative marketplace. And the business is not for the faint of heart. It is fraught with risk, demands hard work, and requires an acute perception of visual communications and trends.

While it is extremely competitive, there are practitioners who see great potential in the field and are excited at the future stock offers. These are the people who believe that smart photographers capable of fulfilling market demands and providing excellent service to clients and agents face limitless opportunity and rewards.

The growth of the industry, the proliferation of photographers eager to capitalize on new and seemingly insatiable markets, the emergence of hundreds of agencies and the establishment of international networks of agencies, and the streamlining of delivery systems have taken stock to new levels of sophistication. This success has both strengthened stock's position as an industry and threatened to dilute the individual photographer's revenues. There is an oversupply of photographers working in stock. But industry experts say that surprisingly few, perhaps only two hundred, photographers supply a large percentage of all stock worldwide. Their contention backs up what other bullish photographers are saying: the opportunities are increasing if you shoot the right subjects.

But there are bears out there too. These are people who contend changes are in store—and not necessarily good ones. They predict that the market has peaked, CD-ROM clip art has affected the generic subject market to such an extent that only model-released people are worth spending production funds on photographing. This in turn will, they say, create an oversupply of released people. Some stock specialists are turning to creating digital products to augment their stock, some are seeking assignments again.

Generally though, optimism reigns. A huge demand for images is forecast, the multimedia market will make up in volume for the drop in price per image, and photographers capable of creating powerful pictures with style and flair will command top prices.

Perhaps the biggest impact on stock—and communications generally—has been the advent of the Internet. Stock veterans see the Internet and World Wide Web pages as having enormous effect on, and potential for, the industry. (More on this, and how to develop a presence on the Internet, is discussed later in this chapter and in chapter 8, "Electronic Technology.")

Industry authorities also say that while the complexion of stock has changed, developments of several years ago continue and new ones have emerged. These include:

- Greatly increased quality. This was never more true. Buyers maintain that the quality of stock is very high, the variety is so wide and diversified that virtually every picture they need can be found in stock. This is not surprising considering the caliber of photographers whose work is available as stock.
- Increased market. In addition to the traditional markets, the new technologies have created many more markets and, according to industry pundits, their demand for images will be huge. Agencies have become more aggressive in reaching these markets and competition is driving their efforts. Additionally, there is a growing number of niche markets, special-interest publications, and short-run publishing ventures, all of which need images.
- New marketing techniques. These are more sophisticated and while most agents say that traditional methods of print catalogs, source books, and direct mail are essential, new channels of communication such as faxes, CD-ROM, on-line services, and the Internet are providing access to potential buyers on a large scale.
- Proliferation of new agencies and photographers selling their own work. Stock is big business and it has attracted many more agencies and photographers eager to take advantage. The advent of CD-ROM catalogs and print catalogs for individual photographers, as distinct from catalogs for agencies, have provided photographers with other avenues for selling their own work.
- Increased competition. Long gone are the days when stock comprised of assignment outtakes. Thousands of photographers are trying to cash in on stock, the field is overcrowded.

- Established agencies harder to get into. Many of the larger agencies or those which have set limits to the number of photographers they will represent are harder to get into. However, there are still openings for photographers who are willing to shoot high-quality, well-targeted images with a fresh and different look.
- More agencies requiring exclusive contracts. While this posed a problem for photographers in the late 1980s and early 1990s, many of the top stock producers now have no qualms about going exclusively with one agency. Agencies cite the need to provide buyers with rights to an exclusive usage and the wish to avoid conflicts and legal problems. Also, agencies invest heavily in market research which they share with their photographers and don't want this information to benefit other agencies.
- Production stock replacing assignment outtakes. Many of the top stock photographers create productions and with them all the detail and logistics which go into a major shoot. They hire models, set builders, designers, and stylists.
- The advent of CD-ROM clip art photography. There has been a proliferation of clip art discs and many photographers claim their emergence has eroded the market for generic stock, e.g., sunsets, clouds, travel, and similar. Others say that despite initial fears about clip art discs damaging the stock industry, they appear to have filled demands of low-end markets and in fact might have steered nonstock buyers toward traditional stock when the quality of clip art photography did not meet their needs. Additionally, one agency owner pointed to clip art discs as "giving us a wake up call; making us more aware that we have to produce better, more exciting images to stay ahead of what's available on clip discs." Many individual photographers are emphatic that the emergence of CD-ROM clip art has damaged their sales. As the quality of unrestricted material on CD-ROMs rises, there could be greater adverse effect on stock photography.

  Stock veterans maintain that while they don't like the advent of CD-ROM clip art discs, they are here; don't get involved with them but get used to them and make your work better than what's available as clip art. There is also the feeling that top-end buyers want their product to look different and clip art will all eventually all look the same. ASMP has advised photographers to avoid licensing all rights for clip art discs.

Over the past two decades, the growth and development of the stock picture business have provided photographers with significant and surprisingly consistent income from their pictures. Even during recent recession periods, stock usage grew and most photographers saw little drastic downturns in their stock income. But photographers' view of income from stock pictures has changed—no longer is it "gravy" or found money. As perceptions changed, so did business practices. Contracts have replaced handshakes and procedures between stock agencies and photographers that had become the norm have been reexamined. In a nutshell, stock is no longer an "on-the-side" business for photographers who want to make serious money. It is competitive, complex, and what was once traditional and acceptable stock might now be passé, and more in the domain of the CD-ROM clip art market.

There are still many photographers for whom stock is an adjunct to their assignments, but the number who are making stock shooting a significant and sometimes major part of their work is increasing. Also, there is a growing group who shoot stock exclusively, treating stock shoots as assignments with all the attendant logistics and budgets. More about stock production will be discussed later.

As during any period of major change, concerns are emerging. Some of these include photographers feeling the pressure from agencies to sign exclusive contracts; some photographers who have several agencies and also market their own stock say they could face contract termination if they don't accede to the demands of agencies who want exclusivity. Also, there is a trend toward larger agencies acquiring smaller ones resulting in photographers' being subjected to the contractual requirements of the parent agency. Acquisition and control of content have become major factors with millions of dollars being spent in those areas. Photographers should realize just how valuable their copyright is and retain control of their work and the rights that go with copyright ownership.

This is an industry in flux and elsewhere in this publication we have the views of several authorities who gaze into their crystal balls to predict the future of stock. There seems little doubt that stock photography as an industry will prosper. The main question is: how will individual photographers fare?

Several years ago an agent summed up what was needed to succeed in stock photography: brains, talent, hard work, and a business plan. That is still true. Also true is one other fact: to make big money you have to shoot great pictures.

The *International Report on Stock Photography* published by Westlight in Los Angeles, California, states: "The next image revolution could be shaped by a few individuals and their stock agencies, photographers who will take their cues from the demands of art directors, designers, and editors. There is a tremendous need to break out of the 'copy mode,' whereby even some of the best-known stock photographers and their agencies copy past successful stock images. Success will come to the few photographers and their agents who see and study creative problems, translate them into concepts and ideas, and turn them into great, new stock solutions."

This advice is echoed by other leading practitioners and agencies. The markets are growing, as is the competition. It's possible to make a good living from shooting stock, but not without a lot of hard, smart, and focused work backed up by sound business principles.

Getting Into Stock

So, you want to shoot stock. It sounds like the ultimate in photographic freedom. Travel, photograph what you want, when you want, deliver your images to your agent, and the money rolls in. No clients to satisfy, no art director dictating the parameters of the shoot. Sound easy? Perhaps. And there are some photographers (very few) to whom the above description might apply. Those who are successful stock specialists would probably be among the first to concur that stock does have innumerable advantages and benefits. But for the majority, the harsh realities of stock photography are vastly different and no photographer who ventures into this field should have illusions of just how competitive it is, or how expensive it can be to be competitive.

And it is expensive to get into stock. Photographers established in other fields but who want to expand into stock have an edge in this area; they have covered the initial investment in equipment and have the technical skills. Also, practitioners who market stock as an adjunct to assignments also have a decided advantage. But even veteran photographers who specialize in stock are quick to point out that it takes constant work to stay competitive. An analogy could be a steam locomotive: it takes a huge amount of energy to get started and you've got to keep stoking the boiler to keep it going. "The markets are changing all the time, trends come and go, and there are so many more photographers wanting to capitalize on stock. Even though there are new marketing opportunities and sales are up, there are so many people trying to get a slice of the pie. "It's harder now than before and to be successful you really have to be committed and shoot smart," said one photographer who shoots stock exclusively and is represented by one major agency.

The warning from another authority, the *International Report on Stock Photography,* is even more sobering. If an average image grosses $2 a year, the photographer will net $1 per year per filed frame. And how much did it cost to produce that image? Even on a tight budget, the serious stock professional cannot survive on less than $50,000 a year; $100,000 is a more practical figure to aim for. To generate $100,000 in stock annually could require an initial investment of well over $100,000, and probably closer to $200,000. Some of the investment can be recycled from sales, but it takes years to build up to a level that is substantial enough to support more stock.

It will cost even the best photographer thousands of dollars to buy into stock. Consider this: the best producers struggle for at least five years, sacrificing two or more days a week for stock, plus every extra dime their assignment work makes them.

Photographers should be very critical and analytical about what it costs them to produce stock. Because most are "part timers," they probably don't have a realistic financial picture of their stock photography. The occasional check is nice, but does their stock make a true profit?

The table on page 50 showing scale and supporting text, reprinted with permission of the *International Report on Stock Photography,* shows the estimated cost of film to produce 25,000 marketable frames, with film calculated at $15 per thirty-six–exposure 35mm roll. Additional costs would include travel, studio rentals, equipment, accommodations, assistants, models, and other production expenses.

Because of the competition, travel and scenics may offer a return of only $1 per image. Thus, a photographer will need 50,000 salable frames to make $50,000 a year income. The table shows the dollar figures for half this many frames, so you must double the figure that the table shows. For 50 percent salable frames, the table shows $20,835; therefore, you must invest $41,670 in film. Since film is half your total expense, this means you must spend twice $41,5670, or $83,340, to make an annual return of $50,000.

Model-released people or sports might be more profitable because of the higher price of sales and less competition. These subjects might offer a return of $3 or $4 per image per year. On the other hand, these subjects waste a greater amount of film, as each action sequence usually yields one peak moment that is the best of the series. Changes in clothing and hair styles also may shorten the life span of some shots.

There are inexpensive subjects, but they are rapidly being filled in all agencies. It is now common for a serious stock production photographer to spend $5,000 to $10,000 on a single shoot, or more than $100,000 a year to produce serious stock. This is competition.

Casual stock photographers rapidly fill the travel, scenic, and other generic files that age slowly. Dedicated stock producers work primarily in subjects that are more of the moment, such as released people, technology, and skylines. While the generic files are quietly being filled by the casual shooters, the serious producers have to keep reinvesting to stay ahead.

The rewards are there for the photographer who approaches stock as a business venture which needs a business plan, a good product, and a marketing strategy, whether that be through an agency exclusively, a combination of being with an agency or agencies and selling their own work, or by selling their own work.

Here are some general comments from people in the industry which provide insight into the potential and pitfalls. These comments might help photographers weigh their situation and make the decision on whether stock, in some form or other, is for them.

- Success is keyed on producing stock consistently. Set self-assignments, week in and week out. Assign yourself and keep doing it.
- My cost of a production can range from $1,000 to $5,000. If I get ten good images from a production which sell consistently for, say, three years, I can get three or four times the investment of the shoot. After producing like this, week after week, sales become significant.
- Agencies are always in need of new talent, people who can photograph in new and refreshing ways. But it is harder for photographers to get into established agencies unless they can bring in something new. Most agency files are full of the timeless, generic subjects.
- It just doesn't pay to shoot some subjects anymore—there are just too many of them—unless they are really spectacular examples of that subject (e.g., sunsets, clouds, general scenics). But something like lifestyles, with a documentary approach, are in great demand.
- Many agency files may be obsolete because they don't reflect the cultural and ethnic diversity of the United States. This does create opportunity for photographers.
- The sweeping and constant change in styles—dress, business equipment, etc.—creates a constant demand for images.
- It's going to be harder for the generalist to make a living. Much of the general or generic material is now available on CD-ROM clip art discs.

In later sections the intricacies of doing business in stock are detailed, and photographers interested in either getting into the field or learning more about working in the field should read carefully the sections on working through agencies and marketing your own stock. That information will give you a greater appreciation of what is involved. To reiterate what is stated elsewhere in this publication: stock is not for the faint of heart nor the noncommitted. It's a tough business.

This table represents a photographer whose marketability is average; half of what he/she shoots will be accepted. He/she is shooting scenic and travel images. Half of his/her production expenses is film.

AVERAGE % OF SALABLE FRAMES PRODUCED	TOTAL NUMBER OF FRAMES NEEDED TO PRODUCE 25,000	ROLLS OF FILM	COST OF FILM	OTHER COSTS
70%	35,715	993	$14,895	?
65	38,462	1,069	16,035	?
60	41,667	1,158	17,370	?
55	45,455	1,263	18,945	?
50	50,000	1,389	20,835	?
45	55,556	1,544	23,160	?
40	62,500	1,737	26,055	?
35	71,429	1,985	29,775	?
30	83,334	2,315	34,725	?
25	100,000	2,778	41,670	?
20	125,000	3,473	52,095	?
15	166,667	4,630	69,450	?
10	250,000	6,945	104,175	?

Producing Stock

The making and marketing of stock photographs has grown to such a prominent role in photography today that an understanding of stock is essential for the professional. *A stock photograph is by definition one that already exists and is available for licensing by the copyright owner or an authorized agent.*

The copyright owner of a stock photograph, under the Copyright Law of 1976, is the creator of that image unless it was made in collaboration with others and an agreement to that effect was made in writing. The agent is generally an established stock photo library or occasionally the photographer's professional "rep." The term "to license" (the casual term used in the trade is "to sell") a stock photograph means to grant specific and limited rights to the licensee or user (the trade term is "buyer") in return for an agreed on fee ("price"). The picture remains the property of the copyright owner and, after the necessary time for use by the buyer, is returned to the stock files where it is again available to be licensed.

The typical stock file of a photographer contains material from three primary sources: (1) photos that originate as assignments and have been returned after fulfilling the original client's needs; (2) photos that the photographer has financed, usually with the intention of putting them on the market as stock; and (3) photos generated through cooperation between the photographer and photo agency under varying financial arrangements. Submissions to stock agencies have shown a decided shift away from assignment outtakes toward the second type, photographs produced specifically for stock.

The subjects in assignment photos are selected for, and sometimes by, the client and are photographed in a style and format consistent with the client's purposes. The creativity and energy of the photographer are channeled to that end. It is only secondarily that these photos are later adapted to a different role—that of stock photographs. The photographer or agency selects from the existing "take" those images that will sell to stock buyers.

Self-assigned photos on the other hand enjoy the advantage of being custom-made expressly for the stock file. Here the photographer has the opportunity to incorporate all the qualities of subject, style, and format that go into making a superior-selling stock image. The advantage to the photographer, of course, is complete freedom of creation, but it must be weighed against the burden of working without a fee.

What Makes a Good Stock Photo?

In actual practice, a top-selling stock photo can come from either source: custom-made for stock or simply edited from an assignment. What determines its success is the photographer's understanding and awareness of what makes a good stock photograph. Certain stock images definitely sell better than others. Experienced stock agents agree that some photographers are able to produce these images more consistently than other photographers. There are photographers who simply seem to be "naturals" when it comes to pictures that sell well from a stock file, but more often their success is the result of deliberate study and knowledge of the market. There is a shift toward photographs made for stock due to their higher volume of sales. There is no single formula that can be applied to all the variations of good stock photos, but there are common ingredients. Among those qualities are the following:

Universality: The "ideal" stock photograph may well be one that shows a classic subject or concept in such a clear and graphic way that it triggers a common emotional response in the widest variety of viewers. Ideally, this message would transcend differences in age, sex, race, or ethnic background. Like a classic actor, the photograph would be capable of playing any number of roles and, as a consequence, would enjoy steady employment.

For example, a warm and intimate photograph of an attractive mother and young daughter reading a book by the soft glow of a lamp in a comfortable living room might well be used to illustrate the theme of "security" in an ad for a utility company, "education" in a direct-mail brochure for an encyclopedia, "single parenting" in a magazine article, or "togetherness" in a mural hung in the headquarters lobby of a corporation that makes fine papers for books. The photograph should carefully exclude anything that would limit the universality of the image, such as a distracting eye-catching name brand.

Information: The unique ability of photographs to convey accurate and believable information is a quality highly valued by stock photo buyers such as textbook publishers as well as users outside the educational field. The adages, "A picture is worth a thousand words" and "Seeing is believing" still ring true.

When the purpose of a photograph is to impart information, the camera approach should usually be straightforward and direct with broad, even lighting and sharp, understandable details best described as "photographic reality." Anything that distracts from the subject itself, such as an overly artistic style that shouts the presence of the photographer, interferes with the purpose and effectiveness of the image. For example, a photographer visiting the temples of Thailand might well be fascinated by the abstract patterns made by tropical vines trailing up a temple wall, but the straight shots of monks in saffron robes going about their daily routine would probably be more successful as stock pictures.

Flexibility: A stock photograph that takes into account the requirements of a wide variety of buyers has the obvious potential for repeat sales. The market for stock is diverse and expanding rapidly. Buyers such as advertising agencies and producers of annual reports appreciate the high quality of stock photos and they may, for example, need empty space in a photo where they can drop in a product picture, company logo, or advertising copy. Photographers who keep up-to-date and follow the market automatically tend to produce images with flexibility. They also know their photos must be "released" and that they should not be readily identifiable as to location.

Technical excellence: There is no room in today's stock photo file for anything less than images of professional quality. The competition is fierce and buyers insist on technical excellence—in lighting, exposure, and sharpness.

Many of the world's hottest photographers are making their photos available as stock and, knowing their name is on each image, guard their reputation by editing tightly. They also know that the art director buying a stock photo today could well be the same one making an assignment tomorrow. And they are aware that stock photos that receive a credit line, as in books and magazines, also become a sort of extended portfolio, leaving no place in the portfolio for technically flawed photographs.

The above qualities—universality, information, flexibility, and technical excellence—are all pretty much within the control of the photographer. There are countless photographers who can produce a successful photograph; the end result of good photographic skill, visual imagination, and personal taste. But in the commercial world of stock photography, producing a fine picture is only half the equation. The other half—and this is essential—is that the photograph must be of a subject that is wanted by buyers: the magazine editors, textbook publishers, and advertising agencies who phone in with their "want lists" of subjects they need and are willing to buy. "What sells" is primarily a factor of the market, but for the photographer interested in stock photography, it is vital.

Subjects that Sell

Producing stock images can be approached from almost opposite viewpoints. One photographer may analyze the market for stock photos and tailor images to fit this knowledge. Another photographer may be deeply involved in specialized assignment, and view "stock" as a residual use of the work. For this photographer, knowledge of the market for stock photographs would be a low priority.

Stock agencies vary just as widely in their philosophies. A number of well-known agencies feel that photographers produce their strongest, and therefore most salable work, by concentrating on subjects they personally find compelling. Their attitude is that "good photographs sell." Typical of the kind of photographer who might follow this advice is the one who sets aside a week or so of intense shooting of what they like, in their own style, to create images that reflect their style. It might not be typical stock, but can, and often does, find its way into markets. It also provides the photographer the opportunity to shoot for himself/herself rather than be dictated by the commercial requirements of stock. Be warned though; there are few photographers with the talent and style to make a success of this approach. Other equally successful agencies are continually advising their photographers about what photo subjects potential buyers are requesting. The assumption is that the photographers are willing to shoot specifically for the market. There is no right or wrong, but the photographer who is intrigued with the concept of stock photographs and who is exploring ways to fit stock photography into his or her career will almost always have a corresponding interest in what sells.

"What should I shoot—what topics will sell?" used to be the first question asked by a photographer entering the stock business. Stock has reached a level of sophistication where it is no longer enough to ask what to shoot and expect a list of surefire, money-making answers. Trends change fast. Today it is essential for the photographer to do some homework, to research the market, and to know what's happening. You must keep current on trends in business, society, and the world. Clues to changing trends are all around you—in news magazines, in business journals, on television, and even in the streets.

As an example, when the film *Jurassic Park* came out, dinosaurs were a hot topic. Some smart stock shooters capitalized on this and created many images with children interacting with anything related to dinosaurs.

Also, changing attitudes affect the salability of pictures. Stock photography reflects our culture and with the cultural diversity of the population in the United States, and indeed many European countries, there is demand for pictures which illustrate this diversity. To put it simply, agencies need pictures of ethnic groups.

Styles and props change. The photograph of a businessperson using a laptop computer is outdated almost as soon as new generation of smaller laptop computers hits the market. Clothing and hairstyles change. This sweeping and constant change in the world around us creates a constant and changing demand for pictures.

Concept: Subject matter is only one, relatively unimportant, aspect of a photograph—concept may be the most important, according to some industry experts. When shooting for stock, figure out what idea you want to convey, what thought or emotion the photograph might symbolize. Relationships among people are very important to the message of the photograph. What can you convey by their gestures? Intimacy, power, caring, anxiety?

Watch the style of what's being published. You need to know the ways in which to shoot as well as the subjects themselves. If you're interested in selling to the advertising market, collect current ads and analyze the photographs used. Understand the lighting style, use of color, and look of the models. But a word of caution: don't try to duplicate these images as they appear or you will be guilty of copyright infringement. Rather, do a new interpretation of the concept in your own style.

Be aware that information on what sells can also steer you down the wrong path. Learning that model-released people pictures generate the most money might tempt you into thinking that your best opportunities lie there. What you might not know is that you would be competing with some of the top photo-illustrators in the business, photographers who have been doing this type of stylized assignment work for years. And this style might not be natural to you. Be true to yourself. Don't ask what's the most lucrative area. Ask what it is that you do best, what excites you.

With current trends, find the area where your style is most applicable and create concepts that you want to communicate. Then consider the actual subject that will convey the concept. Remember: concept first, then subject matter.

The market for stock photos, ranging from typical family situations to the exotic or erotic, seems to be almost unlimited. To get just an inkling of its breadth, study the magazines in the periodical room of a public library, leaf through a current set of encyclopedias, or examine the photos used on packages in a supermarket or drugstore and ask yourself if these photos might have come from someone's stock file. Or, for a preview of what you will see in the immediate future, read the "want lists" that come into the stock agencies: "people taking inventory in a health food store," "a horizontal color of a small town scene with a lonely dog," "a haunted house," "sonar equipment," "Las Vegas at night," "released camping scene using a pyramidal-shaped tent," "pretty girl rowing on still water," or "classic American doorways."

The market for stock photographs is indeed diverse and at times delightfully unpredictable. But experienced photographers and stock agents, who receive thousands of requests annually, find that the following picture categories are requested more often than others.

Travel: Travel and candid shots of indigenous people top the list. A picture showing the dress of the women in Madras, India, for example, might be needed for a book on clothing fashions, or an airline advertising its new service to Chicago might want a dramatic view of the city's skyline. These are expected uses, but travel images are also frequently used to symbolize mystery and adventure or perhaps the well-deserved good life for the retired. They can be used for their explicit subject content or the dreams they conjure up in the imagination of the viewers. Classic images of New York, Paris, the South Sea islands, or the ruins of Greece have obvious use as illustrations of appealing travel destinations, but they can also be used to provoke an emotion.

For buyers of travel photos, it makes unusually good economic sense to seek out stock images. Financing an assignment to another country or even just another state can be extremely expensive, especially when only a single or limited number of photos is going to be used. The high cost of travel, plus the fact that even when you are on location outstanding travel photographs are dependent on weather, seasons, and other elements of chance, makes stock files the source of first choice.

At the same time, travel photographs are the category in largest supply—almost every photographer visiting Paris makes a version of the Eiffel Tower. An art director needing this subject can make a few phone calls and within a day or two be able to select from a hundred different angles under almost every weather condition.

Industrial: This category can be thought of as pictures of the world at work—manufacturing, building, harvesting, or servicing. As stock, industrial pictures are most salable if they are generic rather than specific to either a location or a corporation; for example, a dramatic picture of blast furnaces will be usable to more buyers if it reads as "heavy industry U.S.A.," rather than "U.S. Steel, Pittsburgh." The assembly line at a particular computer plant in California might be photographed so it symbolizes all "high-tech manufacturing," thereby expanding the market for the photo beyond that particular company.

Also in heavy demand in the industrial category are pictures of people at work: engineers, safety directors, and industrial scientists, as well as farmers, fishermen, and heavy-equipment operators. These pictures, too, should lean toward the symbolic and, of course, be model-released.

People: The emphasis here is on human relationships—people relating to each other, to their environment, or directly to the viewer. As human beings, we are intensely interested in other people, and the most successful of these pictures will cause an immediate recognition and emotional response from the viewer. The "people" pictures most in demand show usual everyday situations, which, strangely enough, are often overlooked. Stock agents consistently report that good, current, model-released people pictures are in short supply.

Family: These are people pictures made in such a way that the viewer automatically assumes the subjects are members of the same family. There is a demand for both the pleasant and the stressful and for all nationalities and ethnic backgrounds.

School and education: This subject category not only consists of structured classroom and campus situations from elementary school through and beyond college, but also includes informal learning in the home, playground, or museum.

Careers: This overlaps with industrial subjects but emphasizes the people who work in occupations and professions ranging from medical/scientific, to marketing and media, to banking and government.

Leisure time: Upbeat photographs of the many ways we use our discretionary time and spend our discretionary income are in constant demand. Pictures of the world at play are used in magazines to report on current interests and lifestyles and in the commercial market to sell products related to a leisure activity.

Sports: This is yet another subject category where the stock photo is used to project a message other than the sport itself. Sunday's newspaper sports section may show the winners of Saturday's sporting events, but on Monday stock photo buyers want sports pictures because they can graphically illustrate themes such as "fast start," power, speed, grace, teamwork, endurance, elation, or risk. Thanks to television, people of all ages and economic classes are knowledgeable, even expert, on sports they have never played or even seen live. Sports appeal to all elements of society, and images of sports have become something of a universal language. Stock photographers who realize the thematic possibilities will not limit themselves to pictures of winners.

Backgrounds: In packaging and advertising especially, there is a constant demand for mood-setting background photographs against which product pictures and printed copy can be displayed. These pictures—sunsets, oceans, rolling mountains, fields of wildflowers—are like background music in that they create a mood but don't compete with the main message, the product. The proliferation of CD-ROM clip art has affected the generic image market and backgrounds definitely fall into this category. However, photographers continue to report sales in this area, but it's not a market that experts advise new photographers to spend a lot of time on.

Fads and trends: These pictures are of the latest fashions, activities, or ideas to capture the imagination of the public. The CB radios of the past, for example, have given way to the cellular phones, laptop and handheld computers of the present. The photographer who is interested in, and sensitive to, the passing fancies of society has to be nimble in getting photos into the stock picture pipeline while interest is on the rise.

The above list of most popular stock photo subjects is informative and interesting as a guide, but it must be remembered that it is only a summation of the total market of hundreds of thousands of sales by thousands of photographers annually. At best, the individual photographer is capable of supplying only a very small percentage of this total. To be successful you don't have to follow the market. You can, and probably should, stick with the photo subjects that interest you most.

Future trends: In planning stock shooting, it is important to consider future trends that will affect social and economic aspects of our society. These changes will influence the need for and selection of stock photographic subject matter. To be able to project, even in a general way, changes in demographics, trends, and markets is a valuable boost to any stock producer.

For example, the population of people aged over fifty has risen dramatically. This should translate into an increased demand for good stock photographs of people in that age category. At the same time, the country is going through a mini baby boom, with a growing population of children. The young adult as the ideal market target is giving way to the child and the elder. Obviously, as products and services are created to reach this expanding consumer market, there will be a corresponding demand for good stock photographs of appropriate subjects.

Studies of demographics can be used to project future trends in geographic population density and may therefore help in predicting which type of regional environment will be a popular subject in the future. For example, if the population of reclaimed desert areas is growing at a significant rate, then it may be wise to add photographs of that environment to your file.

Demographics of the United States have changed the situation dramatically. For instance, the number of different languages spoken in this country—some 112 in New York, and 59 in New Jersey alone—indicate the cultural mix of people who read magazines published in languages other than English and who watch TV broadcast in those same different languages. This indicates that photographs of people with different ethnic backgrounds will be in demand.

Technology is also changing at a faster rate than ever before, and the demand for photographs of users of the new technologies will probably increase. Whether you photograph technology directly as your subject or use it as background material, thus staying "up to date," an awareness of the current and future popular technologies is important.

Projecting future trends is not always so simple. But information on demographics and age distribution is easily obtained through government and academic reports. Newspapers, news magazines, scientific journals, and business and literary magazines can also be meaningful keys to shooting for the future. An informed photographer stays current, which adds greatly to the value of his or her stock file.

Shooting for Stock

Learning not just which subjects sell but how to shoot for stock may be the most critical aspect of the process for today's stock photographer to consider. Many photographers whose major stock experience has been in channeling assignment outtakes to their agencies have a transition to make if they wish to maintain a competitive edge in today's market. They need to understand what's involved in shooting just for stock and to develop their own style for doing so.

A commitment to excellence is one ingredient for success. Assignment shooters starting to produce stock on their own sometimes fail to realize that anything less than an all-out effort will cripple their ability to succeed.

There is an ongoing debate about shooting for stock. Some maintain that shooting just for stock, with only the dollar value in mind, can be deadening to the photographs produced. They bemoan the sausage-factory mentality that turns photographs into a product. Others, who promote stock production as the wave of the future, state that shooting for stock can be challenging and even more demanding on the photographer's creativity and intellect than assignment photography—that it can produce imaginative, lively, and salable photographs.

Speak with any agency and you will be told that there is constant demand for fresh imagery which exudes a new approach to old subject matter.

The answer seems to be to choose for yourself among the touted best-selling concepts (or the advice given by your agency) to find subjects that excite you visually and intellectually. By creating stock as if it were a portfolio piece, you can accomplish both goals.

Many photo agents state that what they are looking for in addition to talent is the photographer's brain; they seek intelligent, aware photographers who watch the market trends. They advise that if you plan to produce stock, first "think" stock. Understand the needs of the market, use the most current research, and analyze the current successful stock seen in ads, brochures, and magazines.

It can be useful to study a particular photo and, by decoding its message, learn what made it successful. Be careful of being too strongly influenced by the actual execution of a photograph or of inadvertently "copying" it. You could be open to charges of copyright infringement if you make a version that is substantially similar to the original. Assignment photographers are aware that they may not replicate a photograph in an art director's layout for the same reasons. Besides running into ethical and legal questions, the photographer who does derivative work is also short-changing his or her own creativity. A useful exercise when analyzing a good stock photograph is to identify the concept and find a better, more imaginative way to express this concept.

Shooting and editing overlap, and knowledge of the market affects both phases of stock photography. Mental editing is a continuous process that goes on even as the photographer shoots. As you gain experience, you will develop your own insights, but there are some common maxims:

- The adage of placing empty areas in a photo, especially at the top and bottom, to allow an art director to superimpose type or product pictures effectively, is no longer universally true. It depends to a large extent on the picture. Some leading photographers use out of focus areas in the background as "open space" design elements. The empty area rule still has its place, but for many subjects "Shoot tight!" has become the advice. Let the area of central focus carry the message.

- Whenever possible, make both horizontal and vertical views of your subject. Stock photos often have to fit preconceived layouts rather than the other way around. Vertical pictures are particularly useful. It may not be the most natural way to hold a camera, but magazines, books, and posters are usually in a vertical format.

- Whenever possible, vary the focal length of the lens, or move in and out, giving the art director a choice. The photo that "works" best in a given application is the one chosen for purchase.

- Be careful not to date the photos by dress, cars, and the like.

- Use "real" people who are attractive. Look at published images and get an idea of the people being used in them. For example, unattractive people do not sell travel destinations or some products, but weather-beaten, craggy faces could be perfect for some uses.

- Keep backgrounds simple and generic, compositions straightforward and graphic.

- Always get model and property releases. They greatly expand the marketability and profitability of a stock photo.

- Make "similars" in the camera when possible; that is, shoot several identical frames. Dupes are particularly valuable in stock photography, especially if you are using several agencies in different parts of the world. Also remember that chromes are fragile and cannot survive many trips to the separator without suffering wear and tear.

In addition to creating in-camera "similars" whenever the subject lends itself, some stock photographers make lab dupes on their most salable stock. By sending out these dupes instead of originals, they hope to cut down on the problems arising from loss or damage. Some leading photographers make 70mm duplicates of their top images and send these out to clients and to agencies. The impact of a high quality, larger image can be effective. Also, electronic transmission of images either via modem or on disk can replace sending dupes. However, there are photographers who believe that the clients who demand top quality still require originals.

Be sure to inquire about your lab's policy on copy work. Materials marked with a proper copyright notice should never be copied without proper permission but, in practice, unauthorized copies are often made. These "copies" include duplicate slides and larger duplicate transparencies, copy slides and larger copy transparencies, and copy prints made from original slides or transparencies and from various forms of flat art. Some labs are unaware of copyright law and its importance to photographers. Others know about copyright law but are reluctant to risk offending a customer by asking about permission to copy. Some professional labs will require a release to be signed by the customer authorizing the lab to copy the material and absolving it of legal responsibility if an infringement occurs. Often this "reproduction release" is the customer's first experience with copyright concerns and may cause further inquiry into the subject. The best way to protect yourself is to make sure your lab is fully informed about copyright problems and considerations. Protecting the photographer is ultimately in the best interest of the lab. Many labs now display the common "when-it's-created-it's-copyrighted" signs and also are enforcing a policy of requiring authorization before copying a photographer's work.

The following ASMP-created *Authorization to Reproduce Copyrighted Photography* can be used to give the lab permission.

Authorization to Reproduce Copyrighted Photography

Granted to: _____ (Laboratory)

As copyright owner of the photographic material described herein, I hereby authorize the above named laboratory to reproduce the following materials:

The authorization is granted for the sole purpose of allowing the laboratory to deliver the authorized reproductions to the following client:

No reproduction rights are granted to said client by this authorization. Such rights are granted only by separate written license in accord with the terms and conditions contained therein.

Signature of Copyright Owner: _____

Date: _____

Another consideration in shooting for stock is the type of color exposure most satisfactory for reproduction. Until recently the advice given by Norman Sanders, and followed by most of us, was that film underexposed by about a one-third stop gave rich saturated color that was preferable to an overexposed washed-out chrome. New printing techniques, however, are raising questions about this. The "Guidelines for Photographers" put out by National Geographic's *Traveler* suggests: "Because modern electronic scanners can produce better results for reproduction working from a lighter exposure, the long-standing tendency to go for strong shadow areas and rich color saturation with darker exposures should be abandoned. When bracketing, think over rather than under. The printed result will be much better and more satisfying to all." As more clients begin to use electronic printing methods, it will be important to rethink old preferences and determine the type of exposure most widely requested.

Editing Stock

Editing—eliminating unsuitable images—is a two-step procedure, one following the other. The first step—and the photographer should be decisive and ruthless here—is to discard images that are technically deficient—poorly exposed, not sharp, badly lighted. Buyers of stock photography today, more than ever, expect top professional quality.

The second editing step, which is much more subjective, is selecting those images that in your judgment belong in a stock file. This is especially important when editing assignment outtakes for stock. You must judge the content and composition of each photo from the viewpoint of a wide variety of buyers; editorial art director, annual report designer, or sales director of a hotel chain. You can improve your skill at editing by consciously studying stock photos that have already been used. In each case, imagine yourself in the position of the art director/buyer. What were the needs? Why was this particular photo selected? What had the photographer done to produce an image that satisfied those needs?

Captioning

If the stock photography maxim is true, "The more complete the caption, the more salable the picture," then many photographers are guilty of limiting their income by not captioning their pictures fully. Buyers differ in the type and amount of information they need, but a single word like "Rome" or "sailing" or "grandmother" is rarely enough. Since you don't know who the eventual buyer is going to be, it stands to reason that you should caption for the type of buyer who needs the most. Generally, this is the editorial user who, in turn, is going to need a caption for the magazine, book, or newspaper.

Journalism schools teach that a well-written newspaper story always answers the questions of who, what, where, when, why, and how. Answering the same questions with your picture caption (unless the answer is self-evident from looking at the picture) is sound advice. Put yourself in the position of various buyers and provide answers to the questions they might ask. The first question is usually "where?" and if your files or those of your stock agency carry a lot of travel pictures you might start with the country then narrow down to the exact location, as in USA, Texas, Midland, Lazy Cow Ranch, corral. Location is a common method of specifying picture requests and a common method by which stock photos are filed. It may also be useful to include a "concept" title, if that's applicable. In any event, common sense will dictate what and how much information is desirable. The thing to remember is that is pays (in dollars) to do the job properly.

Photojournalists who are old hands in providing this type of information usually write a detailed master caption sheet as soon as they return from an assignment, using notes they have made on location and the maps, calling cards, telephone directories, brochures, and other reminders they have collected. This master caption sheet is then referred to when the time comes to write captions on photographs selected for the stock files. It is filed and available should a buyer need more or different information from that included on the mount. For a master-caption file system to operate smoothly, an accurate numbering system is necessary and particularly helpful if a chrome is returned from the separator mismounted, unmounted, or in such condition that the original caption has been destroyed or obscured.

Other photographers use a tape recorder for making in-the-field voice notes for each photograph, or series of photographs and keep a cross-reference notebook for the counter number on the tape recorder. Obviously, when you return from a trip, it will take time to go through the tape and transfer the information onto paper.

You or your agency will develop a system of labeling the photograph with such information as caption, copyright notice, agency name, file number, and model release information. Well-designed and legible rubber stamps and the easily typed peel-off labels are two of the most common methods. Since stock photographs are usually sold as individual pictures, it is necessary to caption each individual image and each look alike fully and completely.

These days, the best solution for many photographers is to use computer-generated caption labels. There are programs available that offer several lines of information front and back so there is no excuse for badly labeled slides. Computer-generated labels are a great help when multiple captions with slight variations are needed on each chrome—saving the time of retyping (or writing) each one. On the label you can include such additional information as availability of model or property releases and your copyright notice, eliminating the extra step of stamping your name and the copyright date. Also, professional labs often offer a labeling service so standard information such as your copyright notice, year, name, address, phone and fax number can be printed onto your slide mount. Inquire if your lab has this capability.

Another reason for taking special pains with your captions is to minimize exposure to a claim of libel. Briefly, libel is injury to one's reputation. An accurate caption on a photograph is one of your best protections against such liability. If the ultimate user of the photograph changes your caption or deletes it and inserts his or her own, chances are good that the user, not you, will bear any resulting liability.

Photographers who do not think of themselves as journalists dread captioning and view it as a tedious bore. Yet it can be very beneficial to your growth as a photographer, for the very process of captioning gives you the opportunity to examine your work critically, two weeks or two months after a shoot, when you can be more objective about its merits or see angles that might have been missed or techniques that might have made for a better photograph. Being forced to take a good second look at your work is one of the hidden benefits or preparing stock photographs.

A related issue is protection. The majority of experienced professionals use cardboard mounts and archival plastic twenty-pocket sleeves. Individual "Kimac" plastic sleeves are added to any transparencies leaving the studio to a client. Larger formats are similarly protected with plastic sleeves.

Shooting, editing, and captioning are only a fraction of the job in stock photography. What has become obvious in today's competitive environment is that marketing makes up the lion's share of the job. You must set up an effective system that will lead to getting your stock photos before the eyes of prospective buyers. The principal systems used by photographers to market their stock photographs—selling stock photos themselves, using a stock agency, or setting up a personalized combination of both—are discussed elsewhere in the chapter.

There are certain basic elements to be included on all photo labels. Many photographers consider the following to be essential:

- Copyright notice: © year of first publication and photographer's name*
- "All Rights Reserved" (for protection outside the U.S.)
- Identification (can be incorporated with caption)
- Caption information/identification (who, what, when, where, and how)
- Model release on file or MR**
- Model release file number or MR#
- Property release on file or PR
- Property release file number or PR#
- No release or NR
- Photo file ID number, serial number, or bar code number. (If slide is going to an agency, they will provide their number.)

Additional information that many photographers consider important for their labels:

- Assignment client (Mobil)
- Restrictions on client (no permission, oil industry) or time limit
- "Over" (for two-sided captions, so information on reverse is seen)
- "Model release possible" or "Property release possible" (used by some photographers to indicate that they can be in touch with subject to get a release)

Semiotics and Advertising Photography

Semiotics, which has been called the "science of the sign," offers a way of analyzing nonverbal signs. Semiotics does not tell you what to think, only how to think and how to probe beneath the surface. It tells you what things signify.

Advertising today has become less overtly product-oriented and more emotional and nonverbal in its approach. Ads rely heavily on visual images as emotional triggers to bond the consumer to the client's product or service. An emotional impact is thought to be more persuasive than attribute arguments.

A photographer who wants to create successful advertising photographs needs to read, interpret, and master the "signs" used in the advertising world to stimulate consumption. This type of analysis has been called "psychological semiotics," or iconology, or simply image decoding.

For the stock photographer, the purpose of all this is to help create more effective

---

* All information with legal significance should appear on the front of the slide. This includes ©, date, name, and property and model release information. Some photographers, especially when using a computer or typewriter, use parentheses instead of a circle around the "c" in the copyright notice. While this style may be adequate, it is best to either hand-draw a circle or to type or print out the word "copyright."

** The abbreviation "MR" is widely used to save space on slide mounts and is understood by experienced photo buyers, but it is safer to write out the full "model release on file."

selling messages. To be truly effective, images should have a strong association with values and attitudes already held by consumers. The images should contain symbols that evoke a strong positive "resonance"—the feeling that a particular object or place in a particular context can acquire a universal significance.

Techniques in Nonverbal Communication

1. Color coding. Every color has meaning and symbolism. Experience has shown that color has psychological meanings and associations for everyone and can affect human behavior and response. Mental associations with a color can trigger deep physiological responses and psychological changes in attitude and behavior. (See chart on color associations.) Something to be kept in mind though is that colors can mean different things to different cultures. Colors signifying bravery or strength in one culture could mean cowardice or weakness in another. With the global market of stock today, this aspect could affect your sales.

2. Styling: perceptive propping and dress. By putting objects or clothing into the photograph that are recognized as powerful symbols—icons that resonate and connect with values, attitudes, and associations already held by viewers—the photographer will be rewarded by a favorable reaction to the image.

3. Gestures/body language. A great deal can be read into a photograph by reading the gestures of the players in the picture. We can sense caring, loving, victory, defeat, anger, and the like by observing people's facial cues and body positions. This is an area too often neglected by photographers. Photographers need to concentrate more on directing their subjects to deliver emotionally charged performances. It is important to note that inanimate objects such as trees, old sagging barns, or skyscrapers, have a quality of gesture that gives them meaning beyond their physical existence.

4. Proxemics. How close are people when they interact socially? Control of this spatial relationship can enhance the expression and emotional meaning of photographs, but is widely overlooked. Photographers should make it a habit to look at ads featuring people interacting and notice the position of their heads, hands, and bodies. Drawing a circle around the action area that encompasses the heads and hands of the players will call attention to the dynamics of the spatial relationships. In short, get your people in close. Get them to touch. Pack the shot with emotion.

5. Cinema verité. Grain and black-and-white photography are much in evidence today. These techniques are supposed to evoke feelings of integrity, sincerity, and reality in the consumer—the concept that journalism doesn't lie. The idea is to give the selling message the look and feel of the real thing, as a slice of everyday life.

In addition to understanding techniques for nonverbal communication, you need to be aware of certain concepts that have emerged as important in the stock market:

- Togetherness
- Wholesomeness
- Family
- Friendship
- Caring
- Sincerity

- Integrity
- Teamwork
- Self-pride
- Patriotism/pride in America
- Emotion and sentiment

An understanding of semiotics and these traditional values will strengthen your visual vocabulary. (The information on semiotics and color coding is based on research provided by Richard Steedman of The Stock Market.)

Color Associations

1. High illumination implies hot, active, and comic situations.
2. Low illumination implies emotional, tense, tragic, melodramatic, and romantic situations.
3. High chroma implies emotional, tense, hot, comic, and melodramatic situations.
4. Warm hues (red, orange, and yellow) imply active, comic situations, leisure, recreation, and the like.
5. Cool hues (green, blue, violet, purple, and gray) imply tragic and romantic situations, efficiency, work, etc.
6. Warm colors refer to action, response required, spatial closeness.
7. Cool colors refer to status, background information, spatial remoteness.
8. Gray, white, and blue refer to neutrality.
9. Pink has the effect of decreasing aggression and reducing physical strength. It reflects the new romanticism—we look through rose-colored glasses when we want to feel optimistic.

Red: the color of extremes in human nature

POSITIVE ASSOCIATIONS (love and courage)

Engenders a sense of warmth

Courage, valor, bravery

Love, passion (Valentine's Day)

The heart

Emotions (extreme)

Joy and happiness

Tried manhood and prowess (*The Red Badge of Courage*)

Symbol of revolution

Color of aristocracy

Red Letter Day

Red Cross

Hot line (red telephone)

NEGATIVE ASSOCIATIONS (extreme passions and vice)

War (Mars: God of War)

Lust (scarlet women)

Rage/anger

Revenge/hatred

Anarchy (negative view of revolution)

Hot/fire

High anxiety/immediate action required

Murder/blood

Red-handed

Stop/danger

To see "red"

ADDITIONAL COMMENTS

Top color in rainbow

Exposure quickens the heart rate/enrages the
body

Color thought to hold the key to all knowledge (the Philosopher's Stone)

Green: the color of life and love

POSITIVE ASSOCIATIONS

Life/love (planet Venus)

Spring (rebirth of new life)

Vegetation (green planet Earth)

Nature/fresh

Vigor

Immortality

Faith/hope

Plenty

Victory

Fertility

Money/stability

Emotional balance

Go; safe; okay

Gullible

Green hands

Youth/inexperience

Green thumb

Green berets

Irish national color

Refreshing (mint cool)

Playing fields

Lawns (status symbol)

NEGATIVE ASSOCIATIONS

Mold/decay/rot

Poison (arsenic)

Nausea

Envy/jealousy

ADDITIONAL COMMENTS

Ambivalent hue (decay, life)

Most restful color on the eyes (surgeon's gowns)

Used in most camouflage (Robin Hood)

Represents tranquil, quiet lifestyle (being in
nature and rural areas)

Blue: the color of infinity and tranquillity

POSITIVE ASSOCIATIONS

Royalty (blue blood)

Blue ribbon (winners)

Blue chip (secure)

Soothing/tranquil

Spiritual/heaven/cosmos

Infinity

Sky (blue skies)

Ocean

Vast exposure

Optimism

Ford corporate color

IBM corporate color

Tranquillity to isolation

Boy child

Bluebird of happiness

Tenderness

Music (the blues)

Fashion (denim)

Blue suede shoes

Labor (blue collar)

NEGATIVE ASSOCIATIONS

Blue mood/sadness/sorrow

Blue gown; blue humor; blue movies

Cool; cold (blue with cold)

ADDITIONAL COMMENTS

Calming effect/lowers blood pressure

Corporate qualities of reliability

Yellow: the color of hope, joy, wealth, and enlightenment

POSITIVE ASSOCIATIONS

The sun/life-giving

Gold/earthly wealth

Wheat fields

Cheerful/joyful

Richness/splendor

Glory/power

Spring flowers

Yellow pages

Hertz corporate color

Sunflowers (Vincent van Gogh)

Kodak corporate color

NEGATIVE ASSOCIATIONS

Sickness (yellow fever, color of quarantine
flag at sea)

Cowardice

Yellow journalism

Caution: warning, slow, test

Age (yellowing with age)

ADDITIONAL COMMENTS

Young children choose yellow to represent
"happy"

Quickly perceived

Makes people feel optimistic

White: the color of truth, purity, and peace

POSITIVE ASSOCIATIONS

Light/airiness/space

Truth

Innocence

Peace (white dove)

Purity/virginity (white weddings)

White magic (for good)

Modesty

Clean/ultra-clean (clean rooms)

Unadulterated

Ivory soap (99% pure)

The White House

White smoke (election of new pope)

NEGATIVE ASSOCIATIONS

Cowardice (white feather)

Surrender (white flag)

Fear of hospitals and doctors

White elephant (burdensome possession)

ADDITIONAL COMMENTS

Often paired with black to create tension
between opposite forces, such as good
(white) and evil (black)

Black: the color of mystery and power

POSITIVE ASSOCIATIONS

Elegance

High fashion (basic black)

Formal (black tie)

Classic

Expensive

Black Label scotch

Professional cameras and equipment

Power/powerful

Authoritative

Night (rest from day's labors, beauty of the
night)

NEGATIVE ASSOCIATIONS

Ominous/gloom

The unknown/mystery/void

Night/darkness (fear of)

Death/mourning

Depression of mood, mind, spirit

Black magic (for evil)

Black knight

Blacklist

Blackmail

Blackball

Black market

Black sheep

ADDITIONAL COMMENTS

One of the colorless colors; it is the negation
of color;

a powerful force in the world of high-fashion
chic;

used by adolescents to express defiance of
society (rockers, punks, and Hell's Angels).

Keys to Success in Production Stock Photography

Jon Feingersh

Rockville, Maryland, photographer Jon Feingersh is one of the growing number of specialists who shoot stock exclusively, foregoing the constraints of assignments and yet treating the majority of work as an assignment. Several years ago Feingersh formulated what he calls a nebulous plan for shooting stock, photographing virtually everything to see which subjects sold. He also began to produce shoots at the rate of about one every two weeks, increasing that as he could. Gradually he found his niche and has become a people specialist. In addition to photographing exclusively for stock, he is also exclusive with one agency, The Stock Market. Many leading stock producers are favoring agency exclusivity although there are arguments for and against this arrangement.

Many photographers have been called by the siren song of stock. Some become fabulously successful, eventually becoming free of the tyranny of constantly searching for assignment work. Others bomb out, frustrated after a few months or a couple of years. What separates the successful stock shooter from the one who quits after just a few months? The following are just a few keys to becoming a success in producing stock photography:

1. Start today. The journey of one thousand miles begins with the first step. Put a shoot date on the calendar and keep to it! Treat it as you would an assignment from your best customer. Put another on the board two weeks from now, and keep doing the same. Try to work up to 50 self-assignments per year.

2. Invest in yourself. When you attended college, you were prepared to make an investment in yourself. Do the same now. Plan to invest at least $5,000 the first year, double that next year, and keep increasing as you can. Pretty soon you won't be spending those large sums for self-promotion anymore.

3. Put it in writing. Write yourself a business plan and stick to it. Note what you intend to shoot, how often, how much you can invest, etc. If you feel you're losing your way, refer back to your plan. Set high standards and goals. When you achieve them, set higher ones.

4. Be patient. It takes a long time to see results. At the very least, a year. Often much more than that! Be prepared to work without any feedback, compliments, income for at least two years before judging results. Ninety-nine percent of the photographers who think they want to pursue stock will bail out within the first two years.

5. Study the market. Become aware of current media trends and what they tell you about the future. Don't copy others' work, but realize that if you have seen a concept in a national ad, it has probably gone through many layers of agency approval, focus groups, test marketing, etc.

6. Start a concept file. Clip magazine ads religiously and add to your files constantly. On those slow days when you can't get jump-started go to your file and find inspiration. Look at the ads for clues as to trends, stylistic changes, and cultural movements which should be mirrored in your stock photography.

7. Observe current media for trends and themes. Study the ads which are on block-

buster TV shows as these have the highest production values and should indicate what the print advertising market also needs. Become aware of gesture, proxemics, and symbols. Watch TV and movies with special attention to how people relate and interact. Think of yourself as a film director, not just the cameraman. Your best frames should look as if they've been taken out of a film, with equally good action in frames on either side.

8. Shoot model-released people. The photography which is most in demand is the best way to make your fortune in product stock. Get model releases . . . every time.

9. Don't copy other photographers' work. Be true to yourself and your own vision. Don't try to obtain every stock agency catalog and use them as shooting scripts. Those photos have been in the files for years and the researchers and clients are already tired of them. The stock photography market and the country's demographics change so rapidly that those photos are way out of date. The best way to be successful is to be original.

10. Shoot verticals. Okay, sounds silly, but few photographers will do so unless forced. Many sales are lost because the subject wasn't shot both as a horizontal and vertical.

11. Aim for the top. Set your sights high. Do enough great work that you will be accepted by an agency with national and international significance. Even if you are not successful, your work will be good enough to dominate a smaller agency's files.

12. Read contracts carefully. Don't get caught in a situation which will make you unhappy. Don't get stuck in an agency which doesn't deal fairly with its photographers. Make sure you control your images. Make sure you have the ability to extricate yourself if necessary.

13. Listen to your agency. Become a creative partner with your agency. Study their want lists, talk to the researchers and editors about what they need and what is current. Styles and needs change, be prepared to change with them. Ask them how you can improve your work.

14. Specialize. Learn what your strengths are and develop them, all the while keeping in mind what the market needs. Target the market accurately. The best way to become significant in your agency is to be a specialist.

15. Stress quality. You're now competing against photographers who are used to shooting big-budget campaigns and annual reports. Only the highest production values will do. The best way to fail is to scrimp on costs. If you can't afford to make your photographers big-budget, just be sure to style and construct them so they look as if they were.

16. Volume, volume, volume. The most successful stock photographers do it on a production basis, and have tens of thousands of images in the files. Commit yourself to produce continuously. It will take a few years before your earnings catch up to your efforts. The payoff will begin when you have a critical mass of photos on file.

17. Hire help. If you can't do it yourself, hire people such as a production coordinator, a stylist, or extra assistants. They will help you do a better job and lead to

better sales. Get a good computer program to label slides, and an assistant to slap them on.

18. Forget money. After taking a businesslike approach, remember that being concerned with money will only stultify your images. Think about your hopes, your craft, your vision, your particular viewpoint on our culture. Try to remember those creative impulses which made you wish to enter photography in the first place, and photograph accordingly.

19. Choose the right agency. Choose the wrong one and it's professional death! The right agency will treat you fairly, pay you on a timely basis, feed you ideas, grow with the field. The wrong one will not be a player on the playing field of the future, will cheat you on sales (or not be able to pay you at all), tell you untruths which won't further your career, or will take in your work and then never sell it.

20. Plan and review your shoots. Preproduction story boarding, or listing the shots you want to accomplish will enable you to be more productive on your shoots. A postproduction review lets you see where you can improve.

21. Know who is buying your work. Realize you are no longer shooting for yourself. The photo buying client doesn't care in the slightest about your beautiful photo. All they care about is advancing their product or service. Although your work must be desirable and worthwhile to all of the various decision-makers in between, the ultimate buyers are the consumers, and your work must be tailored to be acceptable to them.

22. Look for niche markets. By now our country's changing demographics have made most agencies' files obsolete. This is especially true for the ethnic markets. These markets need a constant supply of fresh imagery, well shot and well targeted.

Marketing Your Own Stock

The decision to undertake the day-to-day licensing of reproduction rights to your own photos (informally called "selling stock") rather than using a stock agency should not be taken lightly. Selling stock yourself can be financially productive and an enhancement to your professional life, but only if you are well prepared and go into it for the right reasons. Some industry analysts say that those who benefit from marketing their own stock are the exception and that the photographers who go farthest are those who concentrate on what they do best: shooting. However, it is an important alternative today, now that there are fewer openings for photographers in the established photo agencies. Still you should consider the pros and cons carefully to find out if you have the inclination or the personality for such an undertaking.

Almost all photographers, during the first year or two of business, experience the incidental sale of one of their existing photographs for an unexpectedly nice fee. They then realize that the photographs in their files are very valuable if made available to buyers at the right time. The idea of more such sales is very appealing and the natural inclination is to think about setting up some way to consistently exploit picture files in this way.

There are decided advantages in making a deliberate, rather than casual, business decision to sell your own stock rather than work through a photo agency. Many photographers do it, but don't be misled into thinking it is going to result in quick or easy money. A worthwhile stock operation—which means satisfied buyers, repeat business, significant volume, and continuing income—requires the investment of a lot of time and energy, not to mention a solid file of first-rate images. It also requires patience and a meticulous mind. By its very nature, marketing your own stock is a long-term investment and a business of details that doesn't lend itself to halfway measures.

Selling stock efficiently requires setting up well-thought-out, well-organized systems and then maintaining them with careful and constant attention. It really entails setting up another business in addition to your assignment work. Many established assignment photographers have an assistant, partner, or spouse whose primary business function is just to run the stock business. Other photographers, with flexible shooting schedules, are able to see to it themselves between jobs. Whatever your situation and your personality, give the decision careful and serious consideration.

Perhaps the first thing to do is to make an accurate assessment of your files and examine your expectations. If they are unrealistically high or your images not suitable to the stock market, you could end up wasting your time; if your expectations are reasonable and you succeed, you might be able to choose between assignment photography and producing and selling just stock.

Advantages

Aside from some current difficulties in finding agency representation, many photographers who sell their own stock have made that choice for a variety of reasons. They have said that they:

- have found that the contacts they develop in selling stock often lead to assignments
- like selling and marketing and feel they are in a better position than anyone else to develop the right selling strategy for their own material
- believe that even after expenses they will net more money selling stock themselves than by splitting fees with an agency
- believe that the best way to learn how to shoot successful stock photos is to become involved in selling them
- have learned that their personal involvement in submitting photos and dealing with buyers results in a higher percentage of sales than when they rely on an agency or third party
- believe (especially if they are specialists or have high-profile reputations) that buyers who want their work will come to them directly
- believe, if they are specialists, that they have a better idea of their market than any agency would
- want to control where their images will be reproduced, and where their credit line will appear; they are not comfortable delegating this responsibility to the staff of a stock agency
- fear that if they join a stock agency, they—and their images—will get lost in the crowd

- think that the four- to five-year standard agency contract plus the one- to two-year picture retrieval period is too long a commitment
- simply enjoy the tasks that are part and parcel of selling stock photos themselves.

Disadvantages

There are decided disadvantages in selling your own stock photography, due primarily to the endless details inherent in the job. Unfortunately, these don't hit home until a year or two into the career of most starting photographers. Typically, they sell their own material while establishing their assignment business. It's only if they're successful in both areas—assignment and selling stock—that they run headlong into the drawback of:

- erosion of shooting and personal time
- concentration on business and administration
- the need for meticulous organization
- the need for investment in additional equipment, space, and staff
- time involved in training others to handle stock files
- the need to keep replenishing stock rather than experimenting with new photographic ideas (these are sometimes mutually exclusive)
- uncertain financial return.

The last point is especially critical. You must accurately assess the real financial return from the stock side of your business. In recent years, many photographers have rushed headlong into selling their own stock without determining whether they can actually make money at it. A high turnover and large volume of business do not indicate that you are making a profit. The photographer who does not carefully calculate the costs involved in selling stock could end up being no more than a conduit of funds.

The key is that in selling stock you never "catch up." The process is ongoing: an active and successful stock photo business is like an endless conveyor belt. On any given day there can be a dozen or more submissions at one or another stage in the progress toward a potential sale and each stage requires monitoring, decision, and action. The more successful you are, the more requests will come in and start their demanding journey along the belt. To get an idea of how demanding, consider the following review of the steps in the process.

Steps in a Stock Sale

1. The request. You may receive requests for stock pictures over the phone, in personal visits from buyers who may select directly from you file, or in writing, via a "want list" sent through the mail, by fax or over a computer network. For phone inquiries, a form is often used to record and confirm details, and the skill and experience of the person taking the request can decisively affect the appropriateness of the photos selected for submission. This person can also prevent wasted effort by inquiring first about budgets, describing the photographer's general fee structure, stating delivery terms, and explaining research and holding fees and how they are applied.

2. The "pull." After the request—which will sometimes be quick, simple, and specific and other times subjective and more complex— is analyzed, the photo files are searched, and a selection of possibilities is pulled. These are winnowed to a reasonable number and "logged out" in your record keeping system. (If you don't have dupes and wish to send them out instead of originals, this is the time to have them made.)

3. The delivery memo. Each photo in the submission is then listed on a consignment or delivery memo that goes out with the pictures and a duplicate is kept in your files. Many photographers (and agencies) have a light box/photocopying setup that they use to make a visual record of each submission. Two photocopies are routinely made—one for the client, which accompanies the submission, and the other for the photographer's (or agency's) file. These records are invaluable if a loss occurs.

4. Invoicing the research fee. If the buyer has called to request a specific image for purchase, the bill is usually sent along with the submission. Otherwise, many established photographers enclose a bill for a research fee along with the delivery memo and pictures—usually for about $75 per submission, which helps cover administrative costs (and discourages buyers who are not serious). This fee is sometimes deducted if a sale above a minimum amount (often $200 to $250) results. Be aware that many agencies do not charge research fees, a trend started by a major agency which others followed.

5. Packing. Protection of your pictures is a priority, along with making sure all the correct images and paperwork are enclosed. Most photographers sandwich their photos in corrugated cardboard, then put the package in a padded envelope for further protection. Others use professionally designed labels and preprinted outer containers to show that they value their work and ensure well-packed returns.

6. Delivery. How the package of submissions is delivered to the buyer (in person, by messenger, by mail, or by courier) will depend on deadline, location, and cost, but the number one concern is the safety of your images. Choose a system that allows tracking the package, and always get a receipt. Most photographers have worked out preferences for various situations, but occasionally buyers will specify a service, sometimes even giving an air-courier charge number so that delivery charges will be billed directly to them.

7. Record keeping. All records covering each submission must be carefully entered in your system which might include a log book, a chronological register to facilitate follow-ups, an alphabetical file by buyer's name, or any other system that can tell you the exact status of each picture in your files or out on submission.

8. Returns. When the first group of rejected pictures, or "returns," comes back, they are checked off on your copy of the delivery memo, inspected for damage, and logged back into your photo files. Some photographers discourage unauthorized use by sealing mount edges with labels that read, "layout fee charged if mount has been cut."

9. Additional returns and holding fees. As additional reject pictures are received, the same procedure is followed. It is not unusual for art directors to go through

several picture-editing meetings before making a final selection. If holding fees are warranted, they are billed immediately.

10. The negotiation. Once one or more photographs are selected for use, the exact price and rights—if not already determined—are agreed on, after a discussion covering size, print run, distribution, format, time of usage, and other factors. Remember that there is no need to rush into quoting a price. Take your time, get all the information, consult with colleagues if necessary, calculate your price, and call back with a figure and a range—including the minimum—in mind. Negotiation is key to your financial success in stock.

11. The buy. The client sends a billing request or formal purchase order, which you check against your negotiation notes, resolving any discrepancies.

12. The invoice. You prepare and mail an invoice specifying licensing rights, payment terms, copyright credit line, and other terms and conditions, and requesting tearsheets of the published image.

13. The payment. When you receive payment, examine the check for any "fine print" conditions, mark it off against your invoice, enter it in your bookkeeping system, and deposit it in the bank, making sure that any holding and research fees have also been paid.

14. The final return. When your photographs are returned after use, inspect each carefully for damage (see box) and check them off on the original delivery memo, which has remained in your "pending" file.

15. Cleaning and remounting. A transparency is usually removed from its mount in the reproduction process, so make sure it has been returned to its own mount, that the mount is in reusable condition, that the transparency is clean, and that the caption and file information on the mount has not been obliterated by art director's or printer's instructions.

16. Refiling. Return the image to its proper place in your photo file, ready for another stock submission.

Setting Up a Filing System

The need for organization at every step along the route to a stock sale is obvious. The first step—the foundation of any stock business and important for estate purposes too—is the organizing, editing, and filing of the photographs themselves. Without a workable system, you won't be able to put your hands on an image when you want it, you won't be able to return it to its proper place, and you will certainly lose track of who has which photograph. The first rule, therefore, is to know for certain where every image is at all times.

There are various approaches to setting up a system, but it is probably wise to study the systems that other successful photographers have developed. Experience is the best proof of a system's workability. If you file your pictures under one system for even a couple of years and then find it unwieldy, you face a formidable and discouraging task in switching to another. So it is worth the time spent to be sure your system will work the first time around, or to adjust or change it as soon as you see a better way.

A stock photographer's filing system consists of three parts: (1) housing—the physical bins, drawers, dividers, folders, mounts, and other materials in which photos are kept; (2) identification—the system under which they are filed and identified, both with marks on each photo and in separate written or computer listings and/or descriptions; and (3) paperwork—the record keeping files that include a photographer's model release file, caption information file, promotion materials, stock photo lists, delivery memos, correspondence and billings with clients, copies of expense receipts, and so on.

A good filing setup should provide a number of benefits:

- Quick and easy classification for identifying and filing each photograph
- Safe storage
- Easy entry and retrieval of images
- Flexibility, to allow for expansion and contraction as subjects change over the years
- Simplicity, so others can understand and use it quickly
- Adaptability, so it can be transferred to a computer.

Choosing a Classification System

This is first and most important since the decision you make will to a certain extent determine the physical equipment you'll need for housing your files as well as the logging effort you'll make in keeping track of it thereafter.

Some photographers use a numbering or coding (combinations of numbers and letters) system. A well-designed system can identify every image individually, providing accurate traffic control to and from buyers; it can ensure quick and accurate return of the image to its assigned place in the photo files; and it can tell you the subject matter, the date the photo was made, who the original client was, whether there is a model or location release, or almost any other bit of information you might want to incorporate.

A good numbering system can also save your sanity when it comes to retrieving pictures. There is nothing more maddening or disheartening than getting a request, knowing you have the ideal picture, and then spending hours locating it. Aside from the emotional fatigue the loss of money is staggering if you go through this futile activity many times a year. Your numbering/coding system is critical.

Although many professionals and photo agencies believe that a good numbering system is the most accurate way to keep track of your images, there are a few successful stock photographers who function well without any numbering system. It will be necessary for you to analyze your business needs and style to determine how best to set up your files.

In making a decision regarding a numbering system, consider the size of your file. Is it small enough at this stage to adapt easily to a numbering system? Or is it so large that beginning the process of numbering would be a staggering affair? If the latter is true, then you might consider random numbering (bar codes work well here) for images being logged out. That numbering would be used just for tracking and record keeping. In this way the photographer who has a file so large that it would be prohibitive to number can still reap the benefits of tracking by number. Under this system, however, a coding device or method for refiling would still be needed.

As you'll see from the examples that follow, creating a system is just a matter of analyzing your needs and developing codes to fit them. If a computer is in your future, and it should be if you're selling stock, make sure your system is adaptable to computerizing: numbers and number sequences should read left to right, and the information these numbers represent should progress from the general to the specific. Not to be overlooked if you're planning to computerize are bar codes, which are more error free than writing or typing numbers by hand.

Numbering by subject category: This is a handy and versatile system that allows for a large variety of subjects and great depth of coverage. You begin by assigning numbers to broad general categories like People (1), Travel (2), Technology (3), Transportation (4), Sports (5), and so on. You can do this even if you don't yet have material in some of the areas. You can also be more specific, using Men (1), Women (2), Children (3), Crowds (4), and so on.

Keep in mind that your filing and numbering system should accommodate "concept" categories (such as cooperation, teamwork, pride, or trust). This can be handled through a cross-reference system, but if you have a significant number of photographs that fit the concept approach, it is a good idea to design them into your main file.

There are many sources of file categories—some in computer programs designed by photographers—that you can adapt for your needs, and there's no need to set up lots of empty categories until you have images to put in them. A computer program for photographers may save you a lot of energy if you find one that works with your subject file. If so, it's one wheel you won't need to reinvent.

The point now is simply to start a system that has room in it for growth. You do have to establish categories for the images you have. One simple way is to make piles on a large table putting "like with like." Those become your categories.

Assign easy-to-remember low numbers to categories in which you specialize or expect to do a lot of shooting. Then create a second rung of number codes, this time more specific, so that under Travel (2), for instance, #1 could be India, #2 China, #3 Southeast Asia, and so on. You could add another rung, if you have an extensive travel file, perhaps using letters for the names of cities or states, such as (for India) Calcutta (A), Bombay (B), Delhi (C), Madras (D), Bangalore (E), and so on. Or you may prefer a rung by subject matter, such as Religious Festivals (A), Street Scenes (B), Architecture (C), Transportation (D). This is how you set up your file drawers and what you mark on each photo. Finally, you can also note on the photo the date of the shoot and the number of the photo in the shoot, to get a complete code like 2-1-B-3996-20, which translates as Travel/India/Bombay (alternatively, Street Scene)/shot March 9, 1996/ 20th photo in set. Or to put it another way:

Subject category for Travel	2	General
Subcategory for India	1	Specific
Sub-subcategory for Bombay	B	More specific
Date of shoot	3996	Even more specific
Individual photo in set	20	Unique

You can also add a rung for clients, especially if you do most of your work for a few of them.

Work out your categories this way on paper and see what makes the most sense for you. The trick is to assign numbers according to where your material will fit on the "ladder." Then if you have 200 photographs edited from a trip to the Yucatan, but have no other scenics in your file, you can still assign accurate numbers simply by putting your material in the right place on the ladder:

Scenics	9	No scenics in file but number assigned anyway
Subsection for Mexico	1	No other Mexico in file but number assigned
Sub-subsection for Yucatan	1	Your new photos
Date of shoot	5396	
Individual photo in set	1–200	Number of each photo

Thus the numbers for your Yucatan pictures are 9-1-1-5396-1 (through 200).

To use this system, you need to keep a separate "code bible" listing each number and what category it represents (see example). A loose-leaf binder is probably the best choice, or a set of files in your computer, with a page assigned to each general category on which you can add subcategories as you shoot them or as the category becomes too large and you separate it into two smaller ones (Indian Religious Festivals, for example, could be subdivided into Hindu and Buddhist).

The system really shows its advantages in the file drawers. You can easily put both the name and the number on the drawer and folder labels; for example, a drawer for Sports (5) and inside a section for NFL Football (5-1) and folders for Dallas Cowboys (5-1-B), and so on. No matter what words are written out, each folder must bear the full number code for its category. This allows it to easily be replaced by a new assistant, who can simply follow the numbers. However tempting it may be, don't overload your system with codes. Keep it simple, or you may end up with dozens of folders in your files and one photo in each. Remember that every category you add to your code is another number that has to be written on each image and typed onto delivery memos and other records relating to it.

Numbering by date: This is a system that provides an exact chronological reference plus a unique, never-repeated number: 32396-18, for instance, would stand for the date the picture was made (March 23, 1996) plus the number of the individual photo in the set (18). Additional digits or letters can be added for more information. Basically, this system is the reverse of the subject-category system above, which always concludes rather than starts with the date and photo number.

Using a Job Book

If you're creating a stock file out of assignment work and use one of the systems above, your code will tell you where to put the picture in your files and the day it was shot, but unless you include a client code—which adds to the already long number—it won't tell you who the client was, where the scene was shot, circumstances that might be important for captioning, or restrictions that might affect submissions. Many assignment photographers keep a chronological job book. A typical entry might read: 6/20/96 Maimonides Hospital, Div. of parapsychology, ESP research, Pfizer. Since the date in the photo's code number leads straight to this reference, anyone having access to the code bible, the photo files, and this book has a complete history of every image in the files.

Model and Property Release Coding

The letters MR and/or PR should be added to a picture's code or otherwise marked on the mount or computerized label or black-and-white print to indicate there is a model or property release on file. The releases are usually kept separately (see "Supporting paperwork" below).

Cross-Referencing

A single photograph can show a wide range of subject matter and at the same time illustrate a mood, theme, or concept. Such images make very good stock because they can fill a variety of stock requests, but they're a problem to classify since they can only be in one file at a time. The solution is to follow your instincts and file the image under the most obvious heading, the one that comes most immediately to mind. Then if you have a photocopier, put a copy (marked with the original's code number) in each of the other possible files so that researchers looking there can see it and know where to find the original. Another system is to use a sheet of $8\frac{1}{2} \times 11$ paper in a color you won't use for anything else, print up a stack with the bold legend "See also: _____," fill in the number of the original, and put the sheets in the alternate files. This same cross-referencing approach is well suited to the computer.

Take, for instance, a photo of a woman eating a taco on San Antonio's famous River Walk. If you're a general editorial photographer, you might file it under USA, Texas, San Antonio, the Southwest, or another designation for that area. You could then put "See also" sheets into Street Scenes, Ethnic Food, Urban Redevelopment, or other categories you have already established. But if you're a food specialist, you might immediately put the photo into your Food, Mexican category and place "See also" sheets into the Texas, Southwest, Lifestyles, Street Scenes, or other folders. If within the take you have a few closeups of the woman gazing pensively at the river, you could cross-reference them under Mood. In any case, when time to retrieve, you'll unconsciously know where to look for the picture and its code will tell you where to refile it.

The key to a valuable cross-reference system is follow through. It's worthless if not kept up-to-date.

Supporting Paperwork and Record Keeping Files

Model releases, property releases, and other documentation relating to photographs are critical—you can lose picture sales without them. They are usually kept in a release file of their own filed by the code number you've assigned to the shoot or the individual photo; or, like some photographers, you may prefer to use a sequential MR numbering system. You're far more likely to be able to find the model release for a photo you took three years ago under the photo file number or the MR number than under the name of an individual model. Caption information and other materials relating to the picture can be kept in a "Backup Information" file, also by code number.

The other paperwork files specific to stock are the logging in/logging out records that must be kept every time a photo leaves your file or returns to it. Photographers with a large volume of business usually assign a consignment number to the delivery memo and enter it in a log book. When a photograph goes out, these are the only records that show where in the file it came from and where it went, so they are vital. (This is also the tedious part of stock selling and one reason for the increasing popularity of computers and bar codes.)

You automatically log out any photos you send to clients when you fill out the delivery or consignment memo that accompanies them, keeping a copy for yourself, and log them back in as they return. Keep your copy of the delivery memo in your client account file. If you have a photocopier, this is when you would make a visual record to go in your files and to accompany the delivery memo. A popular method is to place a very strong light (gooseneck lamp works well) above the machine and copy with the copier top open, which will yield a record of the information on the slide mount plus a recognizable black-and-white image of the slide. If you don't have a photocopier, simply photograph your images on a light table, overexposing 1½ stops from what your camera meter indicates. This way you will be able to see the image on the film as well as read the caption on the mount. (However, this convenience must be weighed against the possible damage to transparencies over a long period time. Those knowledgeable about archival storage warn against the repeated use of strong lights in projectors or photocopiers. A piece of ¼-inch-thick Plexiglas over the surface of the copier will reduce the potential damage.)

It's also smart to create a "photos out" folder (or box or three-ring binder), and keep it handy for constant review. In it, put a second copy of all your delivery memos; keep them together this way, and you'll have an ongoing, up-to-date record of everything that's out, where it is, and how long it's been out. You can even use an accordion file with slots for the months of the year; put your delivery memos in it and you can see at a glance how many months old they are. (Even after the photos come back and you've logged them in, you might find it interesting to save the delivery memos and at the end of the year do an analysis of how many photos you sent out and how many you sold.)

If you want a record in the photo files as well as the logging files, make place holders as recommended in the method for cross-referencing. For large-format pictures, pick a different color paper, print a stack with the bold legend "photo out" fill in the code number of any picture you remove from a folder, note the number (or date) of your consignment memo or the client's name, and put the sheet in its place. When you refile the picture, destroy the place holder. For 35mm slides, 2-inch square cards serve the same purpose by holding the slide's place in the pocket of the plastic slide sheet. This system, used by many agencies, gives a quick visual check on where each slide is—through client name listed or the consignment number. The cards can be ordered from most small printers, who will cut card stock to size for a modest fee.

In addition, you'll have the same files as other businesses: active client files for jobs on submission or awaiting payment or the return of photos; other client files for your completed jobs; and the business's own financial files (bank, expense, insurance, equipment, tax, and other records). Your accountant or financial specialist can advise you on how to set these up, and there are also business software programs for photographers if you have a computer.

Tax Records

In order to comply with tax record–keeping requirements, particularly when faced with an audit, it is essential to keep accurate and detailed expense records. These thorough records are also essential in order to run a sound business. Without good records to track your costs and sales, you will find it impossible to assess the profitability of your stock operation. Careful records will enable you to analyze which types of stock are selling best so that future stock shots can be planned on an economic as well as aesthetic basis.

Physical Filing Setup

Your stock-selling setup equipment should include, besides file cabinets and folders, a computer, a copier, fax machine, light boxes, plastic filing sheets, and all the stationery, labels, forms, and packing materials you need for taking stock requests and sending out submissions.

Price is not the only factor to consider, even at this stage. "Safe storage" is a prime benefit your system needs to offer, along with ease of retrieval. These are directly related to the quality of your equipment. You'll be in and out of file drawers hundreds of times a month. Don't get anything that's unstable or cumbersome to use. There are other considerations as well.

If you, as an active professional, have chosen to sell your own stock, it means that you are going to spend a good portion of your working time among your file cabinets, light boxes, office machines, telephone, desk, and packing table. Photographers tend to appreciate and want quality equipment and it therefore seems wise to buy the highest quality materials and equipment you can afford; to go first class for your own pleasure and to support both your personal image and your stored images. What you acquire now should literally last a lifetime.

Temperature and humidity are extremely important to the health and longevity of your photographic images. Photo storage areas should be cool, dry, and free from dust and harmful light, especially the overexposure of color materials to sunlight. Individual image sleeves or 20-per-page slide holders should be archival quality—made of material free of impurities. You can also store 35mm color in metal boxes with a baked-on enamel finish (as wood leaches acid). Boxes work particularly well for photographers who file by number—slide pages commit you to categories, while boxes are convenient for numerical retrieval. If you had a card/computer file with key words such as "Santa Barbara, beach, California," the computer would show which numbers fit and retrieval could easily be made from the numbered boxes. As long as you set up a storage system that respects the fragility of color transparencies, twenty years from now you'll have the pleasure—and profitable business—of selling pictures that are just as rich and color saturated as they are today.

With all its parts in place your photo filing system will be free-standing and offer the flexibility, adaptability, ease of retrieval and replacement, and other virtues you need. To make it really work for you, you must now respond with good work habits; your filing system, no matter how well designed, will stutter badly if you don't promptly refile pictures that return from a submission. Returned photographs that are "temporarily" stored in desk drawers are as good as lost when it comes to filling an urgent phone request from an ad agency.

As you work with your photo file over a period of years, it will expand here, contract there, and possibly take on for you some of the characteristics of a living and friendly organism. The file will no doubt need some modification and fine-tuning, but if it is well designed and both you and it are flexible, it will be a pleasure to work with.

Marketing

Somewhere out there an art director is pacing up and down in a small cubicle wondering where to find the classic chrome showing a man in a red flannel shirt who is trout fishing in New England. At the same time you are sorting through the latest film from the lab and you pause at some photos you made from a covered bridge showing a red-shirted man lifting a fish into his net. The problem is you don't know that the art director in the cubicle wants to use that photo in a major ad campaign, and he or she doesn't know you have just the picture that's needed. The solution to this dilemma is called marketing—letting buyers know what is in your files and getting it out to them.

Finding Buyers

Established assignment photographers just starting a stock file may use their assignment clients as a base for their stock marketing efforts. However, the way to find a wide range of buyers is to reach them by mail. This extends your possible market as far as courier services—or the post office—will take it. There are established lists of photo buyers and source books that you can use to develop your mailing list. Assembling and maintaining it will be a continuous process.

You will probably want to start with a small mailing list, and build it as you increase your capability to handle additional clients. You should begin your mailing list with local clients, ad agencies, designers, and other photo buyers in your area. As your business grows, you can increase your list. Your list should not grow to the point where you become unable to maintain contact with your clients. You will probably want to review your list every year or so, deleting names that don't show activity, and adding new clients that do. Your goal should be to send a promotion or mailing to your list at least four times a year. From the start, your choice of names should follow a deliberate marketing strategy of aiming at buyer groups, industries, or geographic areas that interest you the most or to which your work is suited.

Once your stock business is established, you may choose to advertise in one of the source books or directories available that are distributed to photo buyers. Make very careful comparisons of the page or space rates of the books being considered to be certain that you are spending your advertising budget wisely. Compare the cost per column inch among the books, as well as that charged to your colleagues for similar space in their photo agencies' catalogs to determine the going rates.

Some promotional book publishers seek to market your images directly to photo buyers. If they ask you to sign a contract, have it checked by your lawyer. Be wary of any agreement that would limit your ability to offer exclusivity to a client or prevent you from joining a photo agency that has exclusivity as a requirement. You should also be concerned about your copyright and make sure that it can be protected under any such marketing program.

If possible, check the mailing lists for these books before signing up, to find out how many photo buyers they reach and whether those buyers are the market for the kind of work you do. Also keep track of the new business this or any other kind of advertising or promotion brings in so that you can evaluate the return on your investment and determine the best places to spend your promotional budget.

Every avenue of making contacts or finding buyers should be explored. You may have the most desirable—and salable—photographs in the world, but unless you put energy into marketing them, they may never reach that art director in the cubicle.

Niche Marketing

If you decide that selling your own stock is for you, niche marketing is well worth exploring. Niche, or micro, marketing operates on the principle that it is more productive to identify and serve the potential buyers of a specific and limited range of interest than to try to sell a wide range of material to a wide market. And if you are a specialist, niche marketing makes even more sense.

For instance, if you specialize in a segment of a sport, say fishing, you might have a great deal of excellent fly-fishing material. By making an effort to identify potential buyers of these pictures—calendar publishers, fishing magazines, advertising agencies that represent manufacturers of fly-fishing equipment—the niche marketer is on the way to finding outlets for their work. The information can be found in most public libraries reference sections.

The next step would be to make an inexpensive promotional mailer with impact and send it to the identified buyers. Initial impact—to get the message across that this source of images is something special—is essential. The mailer must stand out. Such an approach identifies the photographer as a specialist in an area of interest to the recipient. That is a nice position to be in when trying to make a sale. It also leads to quick recognition as a source of relevant images and assures continuing consideration and the chance to build a relationship. Good niche marketing is an excellent way to build long-term relationships between client and stock photographer, which leads to better retention of clients. Retaining satisfied clients is easier than trying to find new ones.

And if you decide that you don't want to sell your own stock, the niche marketing approach can also be a successful way of getting into an agency and filling a need within that agency—provided there is assurance that the agency will actively market your specialty. A drawback to having a small specialty in an agency is that the agency might concentrate more on promoting its files of more popular subjects. Of course you could start to shoot the more profitable subjects, but that would make a crowded market even more crowded.

The message is simple: is niche marketing for you? If it is, you might want to consider whether greater control over the marketing and sales of your work is called for. If not, you might want to consider whether the traditional stock agency is best suited to your needs.

Using the Internet and CD-ROMs

Many photographers are exploring the Internet and creating sites on the World Wide Web to promote their work. This new marketing medium is still in its infancy but worth exploring. More information about the Internet and Web sites is available in the section on Stock and the New Technologies.

And while exchange of pictures and on-line delivery systems will increase, some industry authorities maintain that the usage of digital media such as Photo CDs will increase stock usage because of the proliferation of CD-ROM–based, multimedia products. Similarly, photographers are able to make their own Photo CDs for promotion and niche marketing. Traditional print materials such as brochures, flyers, and catalogs for direct-mail marketing are here for the foreseeable future, but as more buyers become fluent in the new technologies, so will photographers be able to use floppy disks and CD-ROMs to send out.

The Photographers' Cooperative

Cooperatives can be a viable method of marketing stock and generating assignments for a small group of photographers. There are several advantages inherent with a general pooling of resources including sharing administrative costs, office equipment, and marketing materials as well as having a local support group of like-minded photographers.

Depending on the scope of its operation, a cooperative can market story ideas to magazines, target specific clients, notify potential clients if any of its members are traveling to a certain country(ies) or region(s), and work in collaboration with photographers to generate work or market ideas. In essence, it's structured to help the photographers who are the principal shareholders. Members are able to travel on assignment knowing that a system is in place to take care of business in the photographers' absence.

A cooperative is not for everyone and many photographers probably would prefer to work on their own, especially younger photographers who want the experience of dealing with editors, marketing their own ideas and stock, and getting more involved with the intricacies of doing business. Established photographers, who have a large collection of work whose re-licensing potential has not been fully exploited, might see a cooperative as an ideal way of selling stock and creating assignments within the intimacy of a small business with friends and colleagues.

One of the most successful small photographers' cooperatives is Photographers Aspen, founded in 1984 by a trio of leading editorial assignment shooters Paul Chesley, David Hiser, and Nicholas DeVore III who had become aware of the value of stock and wanted to combine their resources to market their work.

While the modus operandi of cooperatives will vary depending on its member photographers, their specialties, and location, the guidelines used by Photographers Aspen provide a model for others. ASMP thanks Janie Bennett, Photographers Aspen's director, who helped found the cooperative and has steered it from inception to its current status as a leader in its field, for supplying this information.

The most important ingredient, and without this there's little to be gained by pursuing the idea, is a spirit of cooperation. The personalities involved must be compatible. This is not something which can be defined by a contract. It's an intangible, a factor which the cooperative's founders will recognize if it exists in them initially, and then with new photographers who join. The founders of Photographers Aspen were motivated by wanting to market their images for stock and were eager to cooperate to achieve that goal. Fortunately, about the time they wanted to explore the possibilities of doing this, Janie Bennett, who would become the founding director, arrived in Aspen. This highlights the importance of another vital ingredient—a capable individual who is not a contributing photographer, but who understands and enjoys the business and has marketing skills.

Photographers Aspen, hereafter referred to as PA, has five member photographers and four to six office staff, most of them part-timers. When started, PA was funded by a quarterly contribution from each photographer to cover expenses. Income from sales went independently to the photographers. Currently photographers receive 50 percent with the other 50 percent used to run the operation. Janie Bennett points out that 50 percent is necessary for administrative and marketing functions. In this business the profit margin is slim, especially if the cooperative reinvests in technology and marketing.

Based on PA's experience, and appreciating the aforementioned essential components, here are some guidelines for a photographers' cooperative:

- The member photographers must have a collection of work that can be accessed.
- Establish guidelines for funding the operation.
- Consult an attorney but leave your options open. Don't be in a rush to draw up legal agreements until there is indication the cooperative will get off the ground. In PA's case, Bennett feels that launching into legal aspects too soon could have created a lot of extra pressure and stress, diverting the PA founders from their main objective. Based on a strong desire to get stock images into the market, PA evolved without a formal business plan or legal agreement among its founders. Eventually, when the operation matured—and because of liability issues—PA became a corporation. However, the principals of a cooperative are advised to determine this facet of their business based on their own situation and personalities. Although the above approach worked for PA, it might not be appropriate for others.
- Have a photographers' admission and dismissal policy. Criteria for admitting new photographers could include such things as their collection of work, their willingness to contribute material regularly, and their being in sync with the spirit of the cooperative. Everyone must agree to their admission. PA has not set a limit on the number of photographers.
- Dismissal could be based on such factors as lack of work contributed and person-

ality conflicts. Ensure that the possible reasons for dismissal are clearly outlined and agreed to in writing.

• Establish procedure for ending a business relationship, whether it's dissolution of the cooperative or for "paying out" a departing photographer based on their share value or other criteria. Get legal advice on establishing this procedure. Also have guidelines for a reasonable time to return a member's work if they leave the co-op.

Creating Mini Catalogs and Portfolios

The new technologies have given photographers the ability to customize letterheads, invoices, and other stationery by importing images into word processing and printing the text and pictures on desktop color printers. In the same way, photographers can create short-run promo sheets, even mini catalogs, to send to clients. The quality depends on the resolution at which the photographs are scanned and the printer, but the results can be excellent and very suitable for target marketing of stock.

Preparing a Mailing

The photo market is like any other supply-and-demand situation, once you've located the potential buyers and let them know what you have to sell. The first step in marketing your stock is sending out a list of your stock photo subjects—an inventory of the types of images you have available to license. List your subjects by category, in alphabetical order, and be reasonably detailed. Don't list every shot, but don't list just "Sports" either. Under "Sports" put "NFL football" or categories like "Training: Dallas Cowboys, New York Giants," "Playoffs, 1995: San Francisco 49ers, Dallas Cowboys," etc. This will let buyers, who are rarely looking for just a picture of a football game, know exactly what you have for them. It's also important to include concept categories on your list, so you can attract buyers who may not need a subject-specific picture, but rather a symbolic photo for a brochure, ad, or poster.

Print your list in an attractive readable format and use good-quality paper since it may be kept on file by buyers and referred to when they are seeking pictures in your subject areas. Prepare your list carefully and accurately. It can serve you in many ways as a promotion piece, a constant reminder that you exist, a notice of your areas of interest and specialization, an overall picture of you as a photographer, and a timesaver for both you and the buyer when it comes to picture requests.

Prepare a cover letter highlighting your career accomplishments, awards, and published credits to accompany the mailing of your list. Include tearsheets or reprints as examples of your photographic style and ability. As your business grows, consider printing special promotional mailers showing recent additions to your stock file or highlights from it. These periodic mailings are just as important as the self-promotion you do for the assignment side of your business. Remember that you are competing with the glossy catalogs and other high-powered marketing techniques of the major photo agencies.

Ask buyers to send their "want lists." If they are anywhere near you, invite them to make personal visits and inspect your files, or ask for an appointment to show them your work.

Shipping Photographs

It's always been a dilemma: what is the best, most economical way to send your valuable images to an agent or a client? When shipping to a client, the solution is usually to obtain from them their delivery service number and charge it to them, making sure that it be signed by a recipient.

A delivery service, such as Federal Express, is the preferred method of delivery in most cases, but it can get expensive and there are other alternatives.

Insurance is always a concern and photographers are advised to ask the delivery service what options are available. Some services will insure irreplaceable items, such as original slides, up to a maximum $500 per shipment.

One veteran stock producer ships virtually everything to his agencies via registered mail. The important thing is registered, as distinct from certified. Registered mail is signed for by everyone who handles it and in the event of loss, a trace to the last signatory is possible. With certified mail, a receipt of delivery is sent to the sender but no tracking en route is possible.

This same photographer, who has numerous international agents, sends overseas material as registered small packets marked as "Press Material, No Commercial Value" (to avoid duties if any value is stated on customs forms). Also, it is wise to send only dupes internationally unless there is a specific demand for originals. If shipping registered small packages internationally, ask the post office what is the maximum weight or size of a small packet that can be sent to the recipient's country. Some nations have different regulations concerning this.

Of course, digital transfer of images might one day replace traditional shipping of images, but at present most photographers will ship slides by either U.S. Postal Service or by delivery service.

Updating

As you add new images to your files, you should update your stock list—or completely revise it if necessary—and send out new mailings. Some photographers prepare a series of shorter subject lists, each customized to the needs of a different client group. These more sharply targeted lists, especially if sent frequently, project an image of vitality by keeping your buyers informed of your latest photographic ventures while sparing them the necessity of reading through a long list of subjects they may never be able to use.

Other Marketing Techniques

In addition to the traditional stock lists and photographic mailers, some photographers are making imaginative use of their marketing budget by sending buyers everything from personalized tote bags to calendars featuring their work. One specialist in aerial photography sent out miniature balsa plane models for art directors to assemble—with his name emblazoned, of course. Consider what items might suit your style of photography and your marketing budget.

Learning by Doing

As stock requests come in by phone, mail, computer network, or personal visits, you will develop your own sales skills and techniques. You will learn to listen carefully, ask the right questions, understand the needs and practices peculiar to the various sections of the market, and become efficient with your own and the buyers' time. You will learn that buyers respond to interest in their needs, appreciate your efforts to help, and respect honesty and professionalism. You will learn to negotiate a fair price and to say no without offense. You will learn that as an individual photographer you can rarely match the volume or the range of the files of a good stock agency, but can offer instead a photographer's eye and experience in the field, and a proprietor's personal interest. You will learn that experienced buyers are quick to size up the quality of a photo file, and that it pays for you to be forthright. You will learn that buyers generally love photography, appreciate photographers, and make good friends. And you will probably learn to be a better and more professional photographer.

Meeting Buyers' Needs

Experienced photo researchers and art buyers do most of their business with photographers and stock agencies that fulfill the following five broadly defined needs:

1. Technically excellent photographs. The day when stock files could comprise "seconds" and pictures with flaws is long gone. Success in today's market requires top aesthetic and reproduction quality. Even if its subject matter is just what is needed, a picture won't sell if it is under- or overexposed, soft in focus, scratched, or dirty.

2. Continuous flow of a variety of subjects. Picture buyers need continuing sources of wide varieties of images they can call on for a steady flow of material. Occasional one-shot transactions don't keep them, or you, in business.

3. Deep coverage in one or two areas of specialization. Some photographers specialize in one or two subjects or photographic techniques, and their expertise and reputation attract a narrow but faithful range of buyers who need that specialty. Such photographers may not do a large stock business, but their specialization ensures a certain income as well as prestige as a source for a rare type of image.

4. Convenient location or easy access. No photo buyer has the time to walk through the wilderness or leave twelve phone messages to reach you and your file. Stock requests are often part of the "hurry up and wait" syndrome, and buyers want to know immediately if you have the image they want. If you are not in a metropolitan area populated by buyers you must be very easy to reach by phone and be able to offer overnight delivery.

5. Professionalism and good service. Buyers will not return to a photographer who is habitually late in delivery or doesn't follow up on requests. They just can't

afford to chase after photographers who don't provide good service. This is what professionalism is all about. You can also show it in other ways, from prompt paperwork to making things easier for your client whenever possible. For instance, if you're responding to a long "want list" where the buyer will be getting a volume of pictures from many sources, organize yours so that they are keyed directly and logically to the want list. This courtesy will be appreciated and may give you an edge when it comes to picture selection and future requests.

Using Forms

Form agreements are essential to the running of a good business. Written documentation has the advantage of spelling out the respective obligations and responsibilities of the client and the photographer. Forms provide accurate written records and go a long way toward eliminating misunderstandings.

The forms in the "Formalizing Agreements" chapter cover the basic form agreements used in the industry: model and property releases, delivery and delivery/invoice memos. These are only examples and, if used, should be modified to suit your own business needs.

Selling your own stock photographs can be an interesting, productive, and effective way of getting your work into the market—or it can be a tedious and wasteful experience that drains away your money, time, and enthusiasm. Your skill in setting up a file and marketing system, plus your tolerance for the necessary detail work, can make the difference between success and failure.

The steps and information outlined here give just a small indication of what is involved in the daily practice of selling stock. For some photographers, it is an exciting challenge; for others, a bore. If the idea intrigues you, talk with other photographers, as much about the problems and satisfactions as about the filing systems and money to be made. Talk to those who tried selling, gave it up, and are now with stock agencies. Visit and talk with agencies. In other words, don't just drift into it; know exactly what you face before making a commitment.

Determining the Value of Your Photos

Under the law, customers will be held liable for materials they receive that they had asked to be sent, since they have had an opportunity to reject the materials or the document that may have been attached to the same, but instead chose to keep them. In determining value, recent New York cases have taken into account a broad spectrum of factors, described as "including technical excellence, the selective eye of the photographer, his prestige and earning level, the uniqueness of the subject matter, established sales or use prices, group value of individual images and frequency of acceptance by users" (Hoffman v. Portogallo, Inc., Index No. 1910/85, Supreme Court, New York County [1987]). This broad-based approach has resulted in recoveries for photographers in the range of $1,000 to $1,500 per transparency.

Photographers can provide in their paperwork for a stipulated valuation of each photograph. Such valuation can and should be an amount that the parties agree is fair and reasonable—the figure of $1,500 is often cited for this purpose. It must be understood, of course, that whatever the amount stipulated, it will ordinarily be necessary for the photographer in litigation to establish that such amount bears a reasonable relationship to the provable value of the photograph—in the manner described in the preceding paragraph.

Care and Handling of Transparencies

A New York stock agency sends out a version of this sheet to new clients. You might consider modifying it for use with your delivery memo.

Transparencies are extremely vulnerable, and the fee for irreparable damage is the same as for loss and can be $1,500 to $2,000 each. The following preventive measures will reduce the incidence of damage.

1. Transparencies are very vulnerable to: heat (which melts them), light (which fades them), liquid (one spill could ruin dozens), cigarettes (whoosh!), fingernails and pencil/pen points (which can scratch), and fingerprints (which can remain forever, impossible to remove).
2. So please always keep them in their plastic "Kimac" sleeves. Never remove them.
3. Keep them in "color" envelopes to alert staff that valuable originals are inside, or in envelopes with cardboard, but no sharp closures.
4. Never put coffee or any other beverage on the same surface where you examine transparencies. Beware of falling cigarette ashes as well.
5. When viewing transparencies on a light box, don't lean on them with your elbows.
6. Resist pointing out your favorites with a fingernail or sharp pencil.
7. Don't mark or stick anything onto or over the cardboard mounts, which could obscure critical caption information.
8. Don't leave transparencies on a light box, in a projector, in direct sunlight, or near a radiator, and when possible don't photocopy them without putting a ¼-inch Plexiglas shield over the glass first.

The life expectancy of a transparency is affected by heat and humidity. In an air-conditioned building, it should enjoy considerable longevity, but one drop of coffee or touch of a fingernail could bring an untimely end. Many thanks for your consideration, awareness, and protection of those in your care.

Rules for Returns

Your transparencies are your stock in trade, just as cars are for a rental company. They can go out and come back, but unlike cars, once damaged they cannot be repaired but are gone forever. Your photographs are more than the product of your labors—they are your aesthetic and intellectual property—so you must do everything you can to protect them while they are in your care, and inspect them carefully when they are returned to you. Here are the things to watch for and guard against.

1. Set up a returns box. You must set aside one place, such as a "returns box," in your studio where all returned slides go until they are properly checked in. If you leave them lying around, you can forget to check them in and file them or even

send them out again. And if you don't have a foolproof system ensuring that you will always check in all slides every time, you won't be able to be absolutely positive you don't have a picture when the client claims they have returned it. And you need to be certain in order to press the issue.

2. Check for mixed mounts. This is a recurring problem. Printers remove slides from mounts in order to make color separations, then sometimes return them to the client in the wrong mounts. Often clients don't catch the mistake (nor do some agencies) but simply count the number of returns and log them in without actually looking at the images. They return or refile them according to the caption or code on the mounts, and the mismounted slide is virtually lost until or unless someone wants what the mount says it is and discovers the error. So always check returns visually as well as by ID number. When submitting photos, send a photocopy if you can—and keep one yourself—showing the images as well as the information on their mounts. Use your copy to check the images when they are returned.

3. Inspect for scratches and damages. Do not sign any delivery memos from clients, printers, agencies, or anyone else sending or returning your slides to you until you have inspected the slides carefully. Here's how to check for scratches: At first glance, an image may look fine. To double-check for quality, place a black card about 2 × 3 inches in size on your light box. Hold the slide about a foot above it and position the image to line up with the card. This "dark field" illumination technique will bring to light serious damage that you might have overlooked. (There has been an increase in damage because in some laser-scanning separation processes an oil is used that stays on the transparency and makes it extremely vulnerable to damage by attracting dust onto an image already softened by the oil. Eventually the oil is rinsed off chemically but often too late to prevent damage.)

Storage of Slides

When you consider the amount of time and money you have invested in your stock files it becomes obvious that the images deserve special treatment, handling, and storage.

Most photographers store their slides in archival slide pages, hung in file cabinets for the bulk of their file. Some keep their most valuable images in fireproof cabinets, which will prevent fire damage up to a certain temperature.

The longevity of films, that is the age at which colors fade, used to be a major concern but new and improved films and digital storage have alleviated some of that concern. Some photographers suggest making copies of highly prized images—either duplicate transparencies or scan them —and store the originals in archival conditions.

There are steps you should take to preserve your images. The two major concerns are temperature and humidity. The colder and dryer the storage area, the better for your film. At freezer temperatures, fading is almost arrested.

For day-to-day working, and where there is constant access to files, here are some suggestions:

• Store slides in archival pages.

- Store the pages vertically in hanging file folders in baked-enamel steel cabinets.
- Keep room temperature and humidity moderate. Air conditioning is desirable, especially during warm, humid periods.
- Avoid strong paint fumes, raw wood surfaces, and high-sulfur content industrial gases.
- Don't smoke in your slide storage area. Tobacco smoke stains surfaces it touches, including photographs.
- Avoid slide pages made of PVC, and other unstable plastics.
- Don't stack pages in piles—the heavy pressure can cause images to stick to pages.
- Keep slides away from excessive light, especially sunlight but also projectors or light boxes.
- If you intend to project slides, have dupes made and use them in your slide presentations.

For long-term archival storage, put slides in a freezer at 0°F (–18°C). Low relative humidity, in the 30 to 35 percent range, is recommended. Low relative humidity can be maintained by using moisture-proof storage envelopes.

A comprehensive book on the subject is *The Permanence and Care of Color Photographs: Traditional and Digital Color Prints, Color Negatives, Slides and Motion Pictures*, by Henry Wilhelm and Carol Brower (Preservation Publishing Co. Ph: 515-236-5575; ISBN: 0-911515-00-3). The hardbound book costs $69.95.

Also available free from Eastman Kodak is *Storage and Care of Kodak Photographic Materials*. The document's code number is 390403. To obtain a copy, call 1-800-242-2424. While this is a Kodak publication, the information can be used for any film.

Choosing a Stock Agency

Many photographers have made the decision to market their stock images through an established stock agency rather than to deal with all the paperwork and follow-up. For them, using an agency has proven to be a successful way to realize financial rewards for pictures that might not otherwise reach the marketplace.

The decision to pursue agency representation is an important one and requires considerable thought and research. There are, of course, advantages and disadvantages to using a stock agency. Also keep in mind that it is not as easy as it once was to find and get into the agency that is right for you and your pictures. There is increasing competition among photographers as overcrowded agencies are becoming more selective.

In this section are many factors to consider when choosing an agency and a question which should be asked is: Is it realistic to expect all the information you request of an agency? This was posed to several leading agencies and the consensus is yes; if the agency is interested in representing you. As is mentioned in the section "How to Choose an Agency," don't expect to walk into an agency without their having any knowledge of you or your work and have every question you ask answered. They simply don't have the time to do this. However, once an agency is interested in you, you deserve, and can expect, honest answers. And will these answers really be indicative of the relationship once it starts? Time will tell, but before signing any contract be fully aware that a bad contract can be disruptive to your business. It may even put you out of business. A good agency, a good contract, and a good relationship based on a creative and business partnership can be wonderful for a stock photographer. There are many successful stock photographers who will attest to that.

Read the Picture Agency Council of America's Code of Ethics (at the end of this section) and the joint ASMP/PACA statement of working with photographers. Study the model ASMP stock photography contract and the MP©A agreement, and before signing anything, ask if your intended agency's contract is similar. Signing a contract is a major commitment, and the majority of problems concerning agencies that photographers bring to ASMP could have been avoided at the contract stage. Most of the agency contracts which ASMP sees don't meet the minimum standards of the model ASMP contract.

How an Agency Benefits You

- Increased earnings: A stock agency is in constant touch with a wider range of market contacts than you are likely to reach on your own. More important, photo buyers know each agency and call regularly with photo requests. What the agency offers you is an established reputation in the marketplace and a range of contacts it might take you years to develop.
- Full-time availability: A stock photo agency is always available for client requests. While you may be out on a photo assignment or business trip, it is there to answer calls and sell pictures for you.
- Clerical service: The agency handles the tiresome paperwork, freeing you to shoot new photographs. Logging, filing, remounting, and invoicing are extraordinarily time-consuming, as well as costly.
- Partnership in the stock business: A good agency can help you develop your direction in shooting for stock and can guide you in needed photo topics and salable style. Most provide "want lists" and share valuable market research so you can be aware of current requests and gear your shooting accordingly. Additionally, good agencies are able to stay current with their marketing and electronic distribution efforts.
- Higher prices: Professional staff at good stock agencies use information gleaned from continuous daily contact with clients to maximize licensing prices. They know what different usages are worth to their clients and they can be more objective than photographers in the negotiation process, since the photos are not their own. Even considering the percentage paid to the agency in commission costs, many photographers find that their share of the license fee is often higher than what they would have charged had they been making the deal.

Drawbacks to Using an Agency

- Commission costs: Most agencies keep 50 percent of the reproduction fee. It's important to remember, however, that the work the agency saves you and the overhead it carries to be in a location convenient to clients. Of course, you may prefer to keep 100 percent of the sale income and do all the work, including all the marketing. It is sometimes possible to use an agency and sell stock yourself if you are scrupulous about any conflict—although today more agencies are requiring exclusive contracts.

- Exclusive agency contract: This kind of contract limits your options to sell stock in other geographic areas with additional agencies and could limit your ability to sell your own images.
- Loss of control: Once a photo is entrusted to the agency, you leave the decision-making to them. With few exceptions you no longer have a say in where your work is sent and how it is used. The agency selects which pictures are sent out, negotiates the deal, and agrees on the price. You learn the results when you get the sales report.
- Volume sales: Photographers often complain that their agencies give discounts on volume sales which reduces the amount per photograph the photographers receive. Ask your agency if they give volume discounts.

If you decide that using a stock agency is the route for you, the most important step you will take is the first one: finding the most suitable stock agency. It is not so easy or casual as it once was. There are so many photographers looking for agencies that the agencies have become very selective, and you may not be accepted by your first few choices. You must then consider whether to wait until your collection and reputation grow or look carefully at some of the newer agencies, many of which are doing an excellent job.

How to Choose an Agency

In one sense, when you put your pictures in the hands of a stock agency, you are putting your children out for foster care. You want to feel that they'll be tended carefully, sent out into the right part of the world, nurtured to realize their greatest potential, and finally to be able to support you in your old age.

Naturally, as a businessperson you want to reach agreement with the foster parent about your children's importance and potential. You're aware that this is a process that may take years. For these reasons, you want to discover an agency where there is an atmosphere of shared interests, of free exchange of information, of trust in both financial honesty and marketing judgment, and of collaboration. Your own personal needs and market targets are going to make a difference in your final choice, but the best indicator is that indefinable but very real sense of being at home, in a place that's right for you. How do you find this place?

Choosing a stock photography agency to represent you is a process of research that combines self-understanding and knowledge of the field. Because the relationship is so much like a partnership, a "marriage" if you will, you should go into it with your eyes open and a full understanding of your own and the agency's needs, wants, and conditions. Anything less could result in problems later on.

The first step is to begin with self-examination. Edit the selection of images that you plan to submit for evaluation, grouping them by subject and eliminating any that have technical flaws or need excuses. Often, as editors are looking at a prospective photographer's work, they are barraged with a steady stream of explanations of the work, including comments such as, "I couldn't shoot from the position I wanted because there was a wall, a tree, etc.," or "The light wasn't great that day, but isn't that an interesting shot?," or "The models brought their own clothes. I would've dressed them in. . . ." Your submission should need no explanation or excuses.

Make sure that what you show is your best work. There is no reason to show more than one frame of a particular shoot unless the shots make up a definitive editorial series. Even when you are visiting an agency in person, select your work as if you were dropping off your stock portfolio or delivering it by courier. Just as selecting work for an assignment portfolio, include only your very best work. Then, once you have captivated the interest of the editor looking at your work, you can set up an appointment for a more in-depth review.

Use brand-new, clear viewing sheets for presenting your samples. Remember that as editors make their first impression of your transparencies with their professional, sharp, loupes, any dirt or hair on your chromes or in the sheets will be magnified as well. Absolutely, do not send old transparencies, no matter how beautiful the subject matter, if there is any fungus growing on the film. Make a reproduction quality dupe instead and show that. Agencies must be on guard for fungus, as it can spread and infect an entire collection.

Make sure that your entire package is professional looking and don't forget to include your name and address. Every agency has a place where they store submissions that were received without a return address, and sometimes the photographer's name. Stamping your slide © Smith is not enough identification.

Finally, wait until you know that a stock agency is specifically interested in you before you submit them to your stock agency "questionnaire." While you have every right to know what to expect from an agency, keep in mind that busy editors do not have the time to answer a general questionnaire from every photographer, but will be happy to discuss every detail with the photographer they would like to represent.

The next step is finding out where you fit. What do you want the stock agency to do for you—what "image" do you want to project to the world? Agencies have distinct characters, and the one you choose can have as much to do with your career as your style of photography. Remember, you're dealing with your professional reputation, your pictures, and your "eye." Where do you want to see your work? What kind of photography—and other photographers—do you want to be associated with? These factors should be weighed when determining which agency to join—in many cases, it may come down to a question of style, and the choice you make may color how the world views you and your work.

How do you discover the agency that matches your needs? First, you should realize that although stock agencies are all in the same business, they each go about it in a fairly distinct way. It is no understatement to say that agencies have personalities and that these personalities are, in large part, determined by the individuals who run the business. Their particular styles—and the real distinction between different agencies—should become apparent as you do your research.

There is a great diversity of sizes among agencies. There are big, small, and mid-sized agencies. Some have forty employees and others only two. It's said that larger stock houses, which have salespeople on the road and printed catalogs, will bring in more cash faster. It's also said that smaller agencies take a more personal interest in their photographers and promote them harder. Another view is that a photographer starting out should go and grow with a new agency. As you can see, the choice depends on your personal needs and requires investigation, not assumptions like "bigger is better" or "smaller is more intimate."

There are agencies that accept 35mm color only, while others welcome black-and-white in addition to color or prefer large-format style and size.

Comparing your work to published samples of stock agencies' files is an excellent way to narrow down the list of agencies you intend to approach. One such stock agency directory is *The Stock Workbook*, published by Scott & Daughters.

Agencies are located all over the country and serve a variety of markets. Some have a long-standing reputation in the field, while others are just beginning with aggressive marketing and the latest in sales technology. Keep in mind that despite the increased competition to get into any agency, there is always demand for new talent—the picture—buying market is in a growth period and requires a constant flow of fresh material.

Certain information will help you narrow your field of choice of stock agencies, such as:

1. Agencies that are in your geographical area: You might want to start with agencies that are close to home, although in this day of overnight express services it's certainly less important than it once was to have an agency right around the corner. Clients visit agencies in person less and less, and once digital transmissions become the standard method of submission, the location of the agency will not matter. Regional agencies used to market only within a set boundary. This is no longer the case for most agencies. With courier services and telecommunications, it's possible for every agency to operate worldwide from any location. This also presents a new set of problems for U.S. agencies who do not have exclusive arrangements with their photographers. Sometimes, foreign agencies start selling work in the U.S. by photographers who have signed with U.S. agencies. More of this back-door marketing could result in more conflicts.

   A point to keep in mind is that the most important part of searching for an agency is not location, and it's not even subject matter. Probably the most important element is the creative partnership. Can you talk to someone in the agency to get feedback on your work? Do they give you ideas about what to shoot? Will they help you explore your own ideas so you can produce more marketable stock? Each agency has its own personality. Find one that suits you best.

2. Agencies that market pictures in your specialty: Agencies can be eliminated from consideration if they don't accept the type pictures you have to sell. For example, if your stock is weighted toward the recreational-leisure market, you won't be right for an agency that specializes in industrial pictures.

3. Agencies that serve the particular markets you want to sell to: There are agencies

that concentrate on supplying images to specific markets such as educational, medical, hi-tech, news, or celebrity accounts. If you have a substantial number of people pictures, but none of them are released, you should check out editorial-type agencies. Released people pictures, on the other hand, might make more money for you with a stock house interested in the advertising markets.

4. Agencies that serve the geographical area where you want representation: Some smaller agencies serve only a limited geographical area and don't mind if you have contracts with other agencies outside that area. If your files consist mostly of local subjects: skylines, local architecture and points of interest, then a local agency, large or small, is the best way to go. However, keep in mind that acceptance will depend on your material being up-to-date and more interesting than what they already have on file.

5. Agencies that are newer versus older, established agencies: You have a better chance of having more pictures selected by a new agency that hasn't filled its files than with an older established agency. However, if you sign with a new agency that does not have a track record of success, you cannot know how long they will stay in business, thus putting at risk everything you have invested. If you do sign with a beginning agency, be sure you know the owners and feel confident that they understand the stock business.

Observing the photographer/agency credit lines on pictures in publications in which you would like to see your work is another way of possibly pinpointing the agency for you. It can also be an indication of the style of picture the agency keeps on file and sells. A trip to a library to leaf through different kinds of periodicals can be very informative.

Perhaps one of the most important sources of information is your peers. The experiences that other photographers, art directors, and picture buyers have had with various agencies are firsthand pieces of information that can help round out your research on an agency. When you attend photographic meetings and seminars, or just in the course of your daily business, put the word out that you're considering X, Y, or Z agency and then listen. You might be pleasantly surprised, or you might hear stories that make your hair stand up. Ask the picture buyers in your field which agencies are their first three choices when they need a particular shot and why. Although some tales might need to be taken with a grain of salt, you'll begin to get an impression of how different agencies do business.

The most valuable information may come from your own assignment clients. Ask them which photo agencies they use and why. If their reasons for naming an agency are top quality and good service, you've gained an important insight. In fact, your clients should top your list of best sources for information about a photo agency, which are:
- Clients
- Other photographers
- ASMP publications and meetings
- Photo credits and tearsheets

Keep in mind that the reputation of an agency is important not only because it affects sales, but also because it reflects on you as a member photographer. Your name becomes associated with that of the agency. The realities of what occurs after the initial agency-photographer courtship are what should interest you. The way an agency really deals with photographers and their pictures is of vital importance. A disregard for either could affect your entire career.

List your needs and check them against the agency information provided in these pages.

Do you want an agency with a highly targeted market focus, or one that serves general markets? Do you need monthly rather than quarterly payments? Do you require tearsheets? Do you expect reports on exactly where the pictures are used? Do you value regular "want lists" notifying you of pictures wanted immediately by the agency? Do you desire a consulting type of relationship with the agency, or one that leaves you alone to follow your own instincts?

What you're doing is narrowing your focus, finding the dozen or so agencies closest to your "ideal" profile. Once you've arrived at a broad list, try to narrow it again to five or six. You might discover new factors as you go through the process. For instance, does the agency have foreign sales connections? Do they refuse dupes? Do they have special buyers for your work?

Once you've compiled a list of prospective agencies, make preparations to visit them. Contact them first to learn about their interview procedures, and before you go prepare your questions and portfolio as these visits are very important. Put together a fair and representative selection of your work in the style and numbers preferred by each agency. Caption your photos as if they were going right into the agency files that day. Don't show anything you wouldn't want published—don't lead the agency, and ultimately yourself, down the wrong path. You are going in as a professional, and your portfolio should reflect that fact.

Your first visits might be to the agencies closest to you; the next, to those on your list that have the best recommendations and where your specialties or favorite subjects seem to fit best. At the time you make an appointment with an agency, put in a request for a tour of the operation. Don't arrive assuming they'll usher you around if you haven't advised them of your desire beforehand.

When you make your initial contact, be frank about the fact that you're researching agencies. Ask for and discuss a sample contract; take it home and study it. Compare its provisions with the ASMP prototype in this book. Consult a lawyer. Talk it over with other photographers who have stock agency experience. If there are clauses that are offensive, get the help of your lawyer to work out alternatives that will satisfy your needs. Be realistic and be prepared to negotiate, even to compromise. For each agency, measure for yourself what you stand to lose as well as to gain.

If you are prepared and businesslike, you should expect each agency to be as frank with you as you are with them. But remember, no businessperson can afford to spend an enormous amount of time interviewing you. Follow-up appointments will give you time to digest the information obtained on your first visit. And remember that the research you do while trying to find the right agency is just the beginning. Once you have signed with an agency it's important to continue a careful analysis of their performance and yours.

Your knowledge about an agency will be greatly enhanced by giving it a good look-ing-over on your tour. You are a photographer and should know how to use your eyes. Refer to the "What to look for" list provided in this section and make mental notes of what you see. A large stock house dealing mostly with advertising clients might have an impressive reception room, and an agency serving the lower-paying editorial mar-kets might have more modest premises but those are not necessarily indicators of the volume of business. You have to look closer to gauge the prosperity of an agency and the care with which it handles images.

The answers to the questions you ask should confirm your research and assump-tions as well as fill in the gaps in your knowledge of the agency. It can be helpful (especially in agencies with large, departmentalized staffs) to talk with the editor of incoming material and the picture researcher who chooses pictures to send out. They can be specific about the image of the business.

On the business side of the operation, the watchword is communication—the ex-change of information. Remember, you are investigating an enterprise that may be quite new to you, one to which you might be entrusting your valuable images. Don't be hesitant—make straightforward and vigorous inquiries. At the same time, the agency wants information about you: how you work, what subjects you like to photograph most, your plans and aspirations for the future.

The way a stock agency looks at your samples may be quite unlike what you're used to in assignment work. In general, don't expect much comment. The agent is trying to figure out whether the work you are offering, or seem capable of producing in the future, will make money for the agency over a period of time. If the answer is in doubt, some alternative directions might be pointed out to you; perhaps another agency will be recommended.

One very selective agency has a submission guideline that puts its position quite succinctly: "Unfortunately we are also unable to give free critiques, career guidance or commiseration on the financial woes of photography. We urge photographers not to take rejection by us as any kind of comment on the merits of the work, but solely on its usefulness to us right now." Some of the top producers in stock photography have occasionally been turned down by agencies and have gone on to be very successful with other agencies.

Another very selective agency lists the qualities they look for in a photographer and includes originality, a quality that should not have to be spelled out, and commitment, which is every agency's continuing problem with photographers. Big promises. Little delivery!

So, for a good long-term relationship in the stock business, each party needs to understand the other's needs and accept them. Listen to your instincts—if you find yourself uncomfortable with any part of the setup, say your polite good-byes and go on to the next agency on your list.

When you arrive at the point in your search where you feel a sincere interest in working with a particular agency, it's quite proper to ask for the names and phone numbers of one or more of its photographers. When you call these other photographers, be straightforward and clear about why you are calling, stick to the business at hand, and respect their confidences. In the final analysis, the stock agency is a go-between matching photographers and buyers, and your queries about a particular agency will help you in making a decision.

The ultimate question you should be asking yourself is, do I want this agency to handle my pictures? A good agency-photographer relationship is based on trust, and this sense of trust should ideally run deep. If problems arise, a photographer's first recourse is likely to be his or her personal relationship with the agency. This is especially true in terms of intangibles such as the agency's aggressiveness in pushing its photographers' work, its efforts to keep its photographers up-to-date on the needs of the market, and its care in physically handling irreplaceable originals.

You should feel confident that the agency will support your career plans and goals, and that it will go to bat for you in other ways, such as going to court to sue for damages to chromes or for infringement of copyright.

At the same time you should realize that you, the photographer, are accepting what can only be described as a "calculated risk" when you physically deposit your photographs in the files of a stock agency. Insurance against loss or damage, even if it were available, would be prohibitive in cost for either of you. Consequently, in typical contracts, "gross negligence" is the only basis of agency responsibility, and it behooves you, before deciding on an agency, to satisfy yourself that reasonable and professional care is being taken in the handling of images.

An interesting dilemma is surfacing as more working photographers become involved in the ownership of stock agencies. On the one hand, all the photographers contributing to the agency benefit if, as a consequence of ownership by a photographer, the agency's philosophy and procedures reflect the love and respect of photographs that a photographer is bound to have. On the other hand, the realization that the owner's photographs are in the same stock file as yours can leave a little nagging doubt, if the owner has a substantial percentage of sales. The question then is, "what percentage of sales are by the owner of the agency or members of the staff?" When the number is relatively small or inconsequential, there is no cause for concern. Even if the percentage is as high as 25 to 50 percent, the degree of risk (of favoritism to insiders) is reduced by the professionalism and quality of the agency. The policy of the agency should always be to send appropriate selections which answer the client's request and which are the agency's best offering, so that they can make the sale. Certainly, agencies can't stay in business on research fees (many don't even charge those anymore either), nor will they stay in favor if they send their clients stacked submissions using work of favored photographers if the work is not appropriate to the client's request. Another important question is whether the agency offers any of their photographers contracts with "guarantees." If they do, then they may succumb to pressure to license the work of those photographers at the expense of the rest. Any agency that pushes the work of a particular photographer, be it the owner or otherwise, risks its reputation with clients. The only solution, if this situation exists in an agency that interests you, is an open and aboveboard discussion before any contract signing. The agency too will welcome it.

It is also important to find out how much competition within the agency you'll face from other photographers who have a specialty similar to yours. Will you be one of two or three specialists in aerial photography, or does the agency plan to take the work of every good aerial photographer it can, thus diluting the strength of your work within the file?

Another area to investigate is foreign representation. Numerous U.S. agencies work directly with foreign agencies and thus can offer an expanded potential market for your work. If an agency does offer this service, find out what checks they have on the foreign agencies and how they handle foreign sales. It is also possible to deal with foreign agencies directly yourself, but it is important to find out as much as you can about these agencies before you enter into any agreements.

After you've done all the research, take some time to consider the best course. Presumably, you've explored more than one agency and have a basis for comparison. In the end, you should want to work with the agency and have a real feeling of support and enthusiasm for, and from, them.

Some photographers choose to go with more than one stock agency, citing geographical and specialty considerations. Such a decision needs to be discussed openly with all concerned. It's important to avoid conflict of interest especially when it comes to the selling of certain rights. It's important to nourish a sound relationship with a primary stock house, and the issue of giving material to one agency after signing with another is a touchy one that is best resolved through communication before the fact.

It is definitely not permissible, and in fact it is unethical, to offer a second agency material using a pseudonym even if you think that the work does not conflict. Discovery of such dealings could result in public exposure and difficulty in obtaining representation with any reputable agency in the future. If you want to work with more than one agent, be frank with each of them, up front.

Keep in mind that exclusivity in agency representation seems to be the wave of the future. Agencies that insist on having an exclusive contract cite the various difficulties in negotiating complex and lucrative photo sales without being able to guarantee the media or time restrictions that the photo buyer requests. Additionally, some authorities maintain that electronic media such as CD-ROM and digital transmission of images make representation by more than one agency redundant. Imagine a client calling several agencies only to receive the same material by electronic transmission (at his expense) or searching a CD-ROM catalog only to find the same photo popping up based on his search criteria. The result would be he/she would get prices from each and license from the cheapest. This is not a good situation for the photographer. Nonexclusive contracts can also hamper the agency's ability to make deals with foreign agents, some of which would be breaking the laws of their country if they claimed exclusive representation when, in fact, the photographer had photos in several other agencies. Also keep in mind that Europe, considering the European Union, and in fact the world, is becoming a more united market, especially because of the advent of electronic media and transmission.

In addition, some agencies spend time and money helping their photographers develop a stock career and in the process share valuable market research that, they argue, might benefit a second or third agency if their photographers were not under an exclusive contract. Hitch your wagon to one star is their advice.

However, not all photographers choose to put all their eggs in one basket or can get representation by one of the large agencies offering the advantages of exclusivity and career development. The "star" agencies can handle only so many wagons. So each photographer must find a workable solution for his or her own business circumstances.

Some photographers have said that finding the right stock agency is like finding a good doctor. Some stock agents liken the intimacy of the relationship to marriage. Whatever the analogy, it's clear that a common thread to the arrangement is trust. What makes photographer-agency relationships work is personal compatibility, confidence that all parties are working toward shared goals, and agreement about professional standards and ways of working.

Remember, when you give your images over to a stock agency, they'll probably be in its files for many years. Take your time, and keep searching until you find an agency that gives you the feeling of trust as well as professionalism and good marketing skills. Then, go into the relationship with the idea of making it one of mutual satisfaction and profitability.

What to Look for When Visiting Prospective Agencies

1. Is the location of the agency convenient to visits by buyers? Is business conducted by mail and messenger?
2. Is there a reception area? a receptionist? Are photographs on the walls?
3. Is your first impression entering the premises one of professionalism?
4. Do visiting buyers have direct access to the photo files? Are there separate viewing rooms for clients, and are buyers serviced on a one-to-one basis?
5. Is the file area bright and cheerful?
6. Are there signs of food and liquids in the picture-handling area? Is it clean?
7. Are good image-preservation practices observed? Is the photo-file area dry and cool? Are color transparencies unnecessarily exposed to sunlight? Are archival-quality materials used?
8. Are the furniture and equipment of good quality and in good repair?
9. What kind of protective packing is used to protect photos leaving the agency by mail, by messenger, or by researcher? Does the finished package look professional?
10. Does the agency use registered and express mail and bonded couriers?
11. Do you get the impression that the agency staff members are talented and respect photographs? Do they act and talk as though they were committed to the agency?

What to Ask

1. Do you publish a catalog? What do I have to pay to have my work included? Are my catalog costs deducted from commissions? Are the deductions from the specific image sale or from my total catalog costs? In other words, if a catalog image doesn't sell, am I charged for its inclusion in the catalog?
2. Will I be required to participate in advertising sponsored by the agency?

3. Are photo buyers charged a research fee? Is it deductible from the reproduction fee, and in the event of a sale, is the photographer's commission calculated on the total amount the buyer paid?

4. Are "holding fees" charged when buyers keep material beyond a specified time, and does the photographer get a share?

5. Do you secure assignments? How much is your commission?

6. How much do you charge buyers for lost or damaged chromes? What percentage goes to the photographer?

7. If dupes are made of my chromes, who pays for them? How much? Are these the actual costs? Do you charge subagents for dupes? What happens to the dupes if I leave the agency?

8. What happens to my photographs if there is a change in agency ownership? Bankruptcy? Death of the owner?

9. Is my permission required before you agree to a buy-out?

10. If you sell in foreign countries, what copyright protection do I have? Also, are tax credits from foreign sales passed on to photographers? Some countries have a tax credit agreement with the U.S. to avoid double taxation. What bookkeeping procedures are in place to ensure that these credits benefit the photographers as well as the agency? (Given the global market for stock photography, this is an important issue.)

11. How do you maintain contact with photographers?

12. How many photographers do you represent? How many are major contributors? Will you supply their names to me?

13. How many color images do you have on file? How many black-and-white? How often do you edit the files for outdated material?

14. How many images does the most successful photographer have on file? Approximately how much money does this photographer net per year?

15. What market area (advertising, editorial, books, magazines, etc.) are you strongest in?

16. Which agencies are your strongest competitors?

17. Do your files contain photos by agency staff or owners?

18. Do you work with foreign agencies? If so, how often do you visit them? What are your accounting procedures for foreign sales? Are funds from foreign agencies kept in a separate escrow account?

19. How many years is your contract?

20. Does your contract contain a "first in/first out" provision? (This means that the time-period provision of the contract applies to each picture individually, starting on the date each photo actually enters the agency files.)

21. Is the renewal provision in the contract an automatic one, binding the photographer to an additional contract period automatically unless the agency is legally notified within a certain time period?

22. Can I see a typical sales statement? Does it specify the rights that are granted and the fee for each sale? Is the buyer identified? Is the photograph identified? Is one person responsible for bookkeeping?

23. May I have a copy of your delivery/invoice form? Are the terms comparable to those on sample ASMP forms?
24. Does the agency have a photographer relations group to represent photographers' concerns and suggestions to agency management?
25. What fees, apart from agency commissions, does the agency take from its photographers?
26. Is the agency involved in producing royalty-free, clip art CD-ROMs?
27. Does the agency produce CD-ROM catalogs, and if so, what protection devices are used to prevent infringement?
28. What agency reports are regularly available for review.
29. Does the agency provide regular want lists?
30. Are volume discounts given, and are they a normal part of doing business?
31. Do you send photographers their money monthly or quarterly? Are sales reported when they are made, or paid for?

Questions to Ask about Catalogs

Because catalogs represent such a high percentage of sales, as much as 50 percent, photographers should know about the agency's catalogs. The following questions are suggested in the *International Report on Stock Photography.*

- Size of the catalog in pages.
- Frequency of publication.
- Print run and circulation. Average low to high circulations are:

United States	25,000–50,000
Europe	25,000–60,000
Asia and Pacific	5,000–30,000
Other regions	3,000–10,000
World total	58,000–150,000

- Types of secondary uses with the same page, if any; for example, inserts, image directories, direct mailings.
- Quality of printing reproduction, paper (grade and weight), separations (colors and color balance), inks (brightness), and cover style.
- Unique features that help the catalog have lasting power or memorability.
- How the catalogs are being delivered to clients.
- Quality and quantity of dupes, their format and cost, and how they will be captioned and mounted. (This applies to the dupes the agency makes of images which are in the catalog).
- Whether any photographers have an advantage in the catalog.

The following DOs and DON'Ts, provided by Susan Turnau, president of the stock agency SharpShooters Inc., constitute valuable advice:

DO have a realistic ideas of your work.

DO your homework—research which agencies are most likely to file your work.

DO send for submission guidelines first.

DO follow instructions to the letter.

DO send reprints from trade directories or other printed promotion pieces as a first "teaser" with a letter.

DO present only your very best photos. (Remember the old advertising slogan, "The quality goes in before the name goes on.")

DO make sure your presentation is clean, orderly, and attractively packaged.

DO make sure your name and return address are included, as well as return postage or courier account number as required.

DO ask clients, as well as peers, which agencies they prefer for material like yours.

DO find out about the agency's payment records—are they up to date in payments?

DO make sure you understand the contract. If you don't, or if it is in "legalese," take it to your attorney.

DON'T send unsolicited material to agencies unless you don't care to have it returned.

DON'T promise to send a new stock shoot each week if you aren't set up to produce it.

DON'T promise to send new submissions only to have your agency call ten times to get you to send the package.

DON'T ask your agency to help you with what you should shoot only to ignore their advice and shoot something entirely different than what was discussed.

DON'T call your agency to see what's out to clients and then keep bugging them to see if the clients have decided yet.

DON'T call continually to see how much money is on the books so far for this payment period.

DON'T expect miracles. If your work isn't good enough to get assignments, chances are stock buyers won't want it either. Aim for constant improvement. Even photographers at the top can't afford to just get by with shots that are "okay for stock."

DON'T spend all your income from stock for living expenses or vacations. Put some of it aside to bankroll future shoots.

Where to Start Looking for an Agency

In addition to asking fellow photographers, clients, editors, and others in the industry about agencies, there is another valuable source: trade associations established by agencies. In the U.S., the principal group is PACA, the Picture Agency Council of America, whose goal is to develop uniform business practices within the stock photography industry based upon ethical standards established by PACA. The organization serves member agencies, their clients, and their contributing photographers. PACA publishes a directory of its more than 100 member agencies and from this can be gleaned some basic information about each agency, their specialty, and principal contacts. (At the end of this section are listed several international agency associations.)

Being with an agency which is a member of PACA does have its advantages, not the least of which is photographers having an authority through whom to channel grievances. PACA can mediate between photographers and their agencies if the need arises.

The following was written for this publication by Paul Henning, director of Third Coast Stock Source, Milwaukee, Wisconsin, and a past president of PACA:

Being a professional photographer can be one of the loneliest jobs imaginable. For some, it's a simple matter of distance: you may spend a good deal of your life on location, away from family, friends, and support services. At other times, this isolation factor manifests itself even when photographers are working in a studio, surrounded by models and assistants, and realize that ultimately it is they and they alone who are responsible for the creative and technical decisions which will determine the success or failure of a shoot.

It's no wonder then that photographers seek the benefits which membership in a professional trade organization like ASMP can provide: by joining and no longer working in a vacuum, ASMP instantly connects the photographer with an array of supporting services, the most important of which may be inclusion in a network of colleagues facing similar challenges.

There is another professional trade organization, however, with which ASMP members should also become familiar. Since stock sales have become an important part of many photographers' business plans, it is good to know that the Picture Agency Council of America (PACA) exists. PACA's roots go back to the 1950s, and its membership consists of over 100 of the most important stock picture agencies doing business in North America today. While there are many facets to PACA's mission, perhaps the most important to photographers is the organization's commitment to upholding a solid ethical foundation for the stock picture business.

This commitment begins with the membership process itself. Potential PACA member agencies must satisfactorily demonstrate their adherence to sound business practices by supplying samples of their delivery contracts, invoices, photographers' sales statements, and other paperwork. In addition, they must provide references in the form of the names and phone numbers of at least six of their contributing photographers, and be sponsored by an existing PACA member. These references and examples of business practices are scrutinized by PACA's membership committee and shortcomings in any one area may result in rejection of the agency's application.

Once accepted into PACA, member agencies sign a commitment to adhere to PACA's Code of Ethics, a three-part document stating an agency's ethical responsibilities to clients, other agencies, and, most importantly, to the photographers it represents. Included in this section is a commitment to standards for ethical and equal treatment of photographers including open discussion of various areas of the agency's operations, use of a fair and straightforward written contract, reminders to provide photographers with payment in accordance with the agency's contract terms and to take all reasonable steps to assure copyright protection, and more.

Further demonstrating PACA's belief that good ethics make for good business, the organization has an Ethics and Grievance committee devoted to resolving problems between agencies and photographers. In an ideal world, agency-photographer disputes would be worked out between both parties in a rational, amicable manner which would leave them satisfied with the result. Unfortunately, in the real world there are those occasions when a dispute simply reaches an impasse and additional action is required.

This is when the Ethics and Grievance committee can be the photographer's greatest resource, as it provides a neutral deliberative body whose mission is to find solutions to controversies.

PACA and its member agencies have demonstrated an ongoing commitment to doing business in a manner which reflects the highest standards of fairness and professionalism. For that reason, the PACA membership directory is probably the best place to start when searching for agency representation. For details on obtaining a copy, or for any additional information about PACA and its members, simply call 1-800-457-7222.

ASMP's Board of Directors Approved a Joint Statement with PACA which Follows.

1. Photographer's funds—Since the agency collects reproduction fees generated by the photographer's work, and since a contractually agreed-to percentage of such collections is the photographer's share, photo agencies agree not to use the photographer's share for operational expenses, or any other expenses, without the photographer's permission. Agencies are encouraged to establish separate accounts for the photographer's share of all fees except when payments are issued on a monthly (or even more frequent) schedule.

2. Right to audit—Since the photographer vests control of the leasing of photographs with the agency, the photographer should have the right to audit all agency records which pertain to the reproduction fees for his or her work. This right to audit should be conditional upon reasonable notice to the agency, and agreement upon a mutually acceptable time. The right to audit should be covered in photographer-agency agreements.

3. Reports of licensing—Since the photographer owns copyright to the images being licensed on his or her behalf by the agency, the agency should be willing to provide reasonable details regarding client usage of the photographer's images. Minimum details include: (1) End user of the image(s); (2) Duration; (3) Geographic limits; (4) Reproduction size of licensed image; (5) Identification and description of licensed image; (6) Press run or circulation of media; and (7) Number of insertions or uses. It is recognized that certain of these details are not required with all licenses (i.e., duration is not often discussed when an agency grants one-time reproduction rights to a photo used in a capabilities brochure, but it is typically discussed when rights are granted for billboard usage).

4. Equal terms—Contracts between photographers and photo agencies should contain terms of renewal and termination which are the same for both parties. Contracts which automatically renew themselves are discouraged.

5. Assessments—Since agencies often pass a share of certain costs along to photographers (such as promotion expenses or duping costs), and since it might be possible for photographers to incur a level of debt that exceeds stock income, it is agreed that photographers should be entitled to set the levels of debt to which he or she will allow the agency to commit. (All potential deductions from photographers' accounts should be explained in photographer-agency agreements.) In the event the photographer or agency terminates the contract while such debts exist,

the photographer's images and/or copyright licensing authority should not be held by the agency as collateral for such debts.

Finding an Agency (Domestic or International)

In the U.S., stock agencies can be located through PACA, and while not every agency in the country is a member of PACA, more than 100 are. *The Stock Workbook* also lists numerous agencies, including some international. Another source of agents, and buyers, is the *Photographer's Market,* published by Writer's Digest Books, 1507 Dana Avenue, Cincinnati, Ohio 45207.

Several countries also have agency associations, and to make contact with a foreign agency get in touch with the association and request a list of their member agencies.

A very useful European group is CEPIC which is an umbrella organization for about eleven national associations in eight European countries including France, Germany, Great Britain, Italy, Norway, Spain, Sweden, and Switzerland. CEPIC represents the interests of more than 600 photo agencies and libraries and some 30,000 photographers. Lists of their member associations and agencies can be obtained by contacting CEPIC (see below).

The following will help photographers reach a large number of agents.
* Picture Agency Council of America (PACA)
  P.O. Box 308, Northfield, MN 55057-0308
  Ph: 800-457-7222; fax: 507-645-7066
* Japan Photo Agency Association
  Orion Press, 1-13, Kanda Jimbocho, Chiyoda-ku, Tokyo, 101, Japan
  Ph: 3 3295-1402; fax: 3 3295-1430
* Coordination of European Picture Agencies (CEPIC)
  Teutonenstr. 22, D-14129 Berlin, Germany
  Ph: 49 30/816 994-29; fax: 49-30/816 994-35

Internet Stock Photography Information

Think of a topic on stock photography, including agencies, and the chances are you can find it on the Internet.

Elsewhere in this publication is more information about stock and the Internet (See Stock and the New Technologies), but photographers should be aware that learning to use the search engines on the Internet (Yahoo, as an example, is one such search engine) is the key to accessing information.

There are many excellent stock photography sites but because Internet addresses change, and because sites are continually being updated, we have not listed specific addresses (URLs) here.

Most pages have links to other sites and accessing the page of a major corporation—film or camera manufacturer—will invariably provide links to other sites, including those specializing in stock photography. Another starting point could be Web sites of leading schools of photography. Try searching for "stock photography" and undoubtedly you will have a multitude of options.

Once a good site is located it will probably have links to other sites so you can cruise endlessly if you want to. To save time, and to make efficient use of the Internet as a resource, it's advised that you be as specific as possible in your search.

PACA Code of Ethics

Picture Agency Council of America members will at all times endeavor to promote policies and practices that serve to elevate the stock photography industry, rigorously maintaining the highest standards of honesty and fair play with clients, photographers, and each other.

Picture Agency Council of America members commit themselves to the highest standard of services and products.

Picture Agency Council of America members will comply with all applicable laws, rules, and regulations.

Picture Agency Council of America members will provide each employee of their respective agencies with a copy of this Code of Ethics and will encourage distribution of same to their photographers.

In addition, Picture Agency Council of America members commit themselves to the following standards in the following areas:

Stock Agency with photographer

PACA members will:

1. Be ethical in dealing with photographers.
2. Give all photographers equal treatment in representing their work.
3. Be mindful of the trust placed in them by photographers and always endeavor to promote the interest of the photographers they represent in tandem with their own.
4. Be willing to discuss the following items openly and honestly with their photographers:
   - Ownership of agency and/or change thereof.
   - Assignment policies, if applicable.
   - Editing, inventory, and refiling procedures.
   - Disposition of any suit or settlement pertaining to a specific photographer's work, including documentation if requested.
   - Policies concerning photographer guarantees, if applicable.
   - International representation policies.
   - Policies regarding free or reduced rate usages for charitable organizations.
   - Subagency and franchise representation and policies.
5. Offer photographers a fair and straightforward written contract. Contract should address such items as:
   - Payment schedule.
   - Right to inspect agency records as they pertain to the individual photographer involved.
   - Procedure for handling lost and damaged photographs.
   - Contract period and renewal.
   - Charges, deductions, or assessments related to the photographer's account.

- Procedure and schedule for return of photographs upon termination of contract.
6. Scrupulously fulfill their contracts with photographers.
7. Provide photographers with payment in accordance with the Photographer/ Agency contract. Statements should be sufficient for the photographer to correlate the end usage with the photograph in all domestic sales and every effort should be made to do the same in foreign sales. Statement should include:
  - An adequate photo description as agreed upon between photographer and agency.
  - A description or code for the usage.
  - A description of the photographer's share.
  - An itemization of any deductions that are made.
8. Take all reasonable steps to ensure copyright protection.
9. Use every reasonable effort to protect the physical safety of photographs.
10. Make every reasonable effort to secure proper photo credits where possible and appropriate, according to the terms of the delivery memos in use.
11. Make reasonable efforts to secure samples for photographers' portfolios.
12. Refrain from deceptive advertising.
13. Maintain confidentiality of records and information pertaining to individual photographers, except as required by law, or by terms of the Bylaws of Picture Agency Council of America.

Working with an Agency

Perhaps the most important aspect of cementing a long-term relationship with an agency is to treat the alliance as a creative partnership. Among the main complaints most agents have about their photographers is they don't listen to what the agency needs. Agents send out want lists which go unheeded. Those photographers who do take the lists, create shooting scripts that not only encompass the subject matter but also reflect the photographer's own vision and style, and then produce the wanted images, are on the way to successfully working with their agents—and making money.

Most successful stock photographers who use an agency work closely with that agency. They update their files regularly and they listen carefully to suggestions from agency personnel. A successful relationship takes commitment and concentration.

Another usually overlooked facet of working with an agency is to promote your association with the agency. For instance, one leading agent comments that when photographers have articles written about them they fail to mention their agencies. Agencies are always looking for ways to promote their photographers but they cannot reach everyone. To have an agency mentioned in an article can help sales.

Helping Your Agency Help You

Here are some tips provided by prominent stock agency owners and managers.
- Be as businesslike with your agency as you are with your own clients.
- Organize your submissions as your agency photo files are organized to speed your material into the pipeline—and earn more money sooner.

- Add new material consistently. You can trigger a sharp increase in sales this way.
- Edit your shoot before submitting. Your work will get into files faster. (And the editor in charge of reviewing your submission will love you for it.)
- Include complete and accurate captions. They can double the value of your stock photos.
- Provide model and property releases. They are money in the bank.
- Work with your agency. This should be a creative business alliance with equal partners and equal responsibilities.
- Pay attention to the agency's shooting advice. They are in touch with the market every day.
- Stick to your strengths and apply them to the agency's want lists.
- Be realistic about your expectations.
- Listen.

The photographers who make top money follow the above advice. There is no magic formula for success in stock; rather it is a combination of many factors including commitment and working closely with the agency personnel who have great insight into what the market needs.

Stock agency personnel work with dozens, sometimes hundreds, of photographers. And they work with stock images and buyers all day, every day. Most are actively in touch with colleagues throughout the industry and the world. The following advice is based on the extensive experience of leading agency personnel. Heed this advice, apply it to your situation, and your chances of succeeding in a very competitive field are enhanced.

Expectations: One of the frequent questions photographers ask is how much annual income to expect from a stock file. Your agency can help you arrive at a realistic estimate, but keep in mind that it's an estimate. If you are new to the agency, allow at least twelve months for a tentative evaluation and two years or more for a dependable assessment. Not even the best agent can guarantee exactly how your stock will sell in the future. There are too many unpredictable variables: market trends, the popularity of a particular shooting style, hot subjects, social trends, big individual sales, a recession, and so on. Over a few years these variables can cancel each other out—but you never know for sure.

Your agency can, however, evaluate your competition. They know how many other photographers within the agency or within the field have material similar to yours. They can also help you analyze your work. Do you have sufficient images of subjects currently in demand? Does your style fit contemporary market requirements? One agent comments: "A big downfall of many stock photographers is not analyzing their own work realistically. They seem to lack an overall perspective of the field."

Another criticism is that photographers do not really understand stock and lack the insight that agencies have, based on thousands of photo requests. True, photographers can see in catalogs and major advertising examples of thousands of stock photographs, but what they don't see are the brochures and trade publications where most stock is sold. This can lead to both a misunderstanding of what will sell and unrealistic sales expectations of their own work.

So, let your agent help. Don't be defensive when submissions are rejected. Listen and learn; it can influence how successfully you shoot stock in future. You and your agent are, or should be, a team, and if a photographer shows a willingness to learn and shoot images based on the agent's input, the agent will be more willing to work closely with you. You should analyze your stock before choosing an agency, but it's an ongoing process. Set goals. If they are realistic, your energy can be spent in meeting them, not in quibbling with the agency.

Shared responsibilities: Attitude plays a key role in maintaining positive ongoing relationships. If you and your agency acknowledge that you are equal partners, you will accept equal responsibilities. For instance, you will appreciate that a "wait-and-see" attitude after an initial submission of 500 images is not the way to enhance the alliance. It is not a one-way street. You must continue to contribute and build your files if you want a productive relationship.

It's imperative that you work with your agency. It is not an adversarial relationship. Make sure your agency is doing its best to sell your work, but also ensure that you are doing all you can to help your agency. You should have, and should expect, close contact, honesty, and openness with your agency.

Good agencies are open to photographers' grievances and complaints, and at one agency a photographer is asked to act as a "photographer liaison" each year. He or she is part safety valve/part ombudsman, passing on photographers' concerns to the agent. Informal mediation is accomplished, doors are left open, and a climate for creative ideas is produced. When seeking out an agency, you should inquire if such a mechanism exists.

Professionalism: Treat your agent as you would your client. One agency complains that some photographers wouldn't stay in business if they treated their clients the way they treat the agency. And with today's competitiveness, slipshod business methods just won't cut it. Don't expect agency staff to do "the drudge work" of sorting through a bag of unedited, uncaptioned images. Agency staff time spent redoing photographers' work benefits no one. In fact, most agencies would probably return the work as is and request that it be submitted in a more professional way.

Editing and organizing: An intelligent edit, organized by categories similar to the agency's system, will simplify the agent's job and get your pictures into the market faster. The less energy the agency has to put into organizing a chaotic submission, the more time that can be spent on marketing the work. Also, it's preferable to send new material that gives in-depth coverage of each subject. Include different views of the same subject, with verticals, horizontals, closeups, and details. Although single shots that are excellent will always sell, a mixed bag of subjects is less valuable for an agency file than good coverage of one topic.

Captioning: Agents say that photographers who have not worked in the selling end of the business don't understand the value of captions. They maintain that a full and accurate caption can often be the deciding factor in selling a picture competing with an equally good shot that is vaguely captioned. One successful stock photographer stresses that with the computerized captioning and labeling systems available today, there is no excuse for captions not to be professional and complete. There is no question about the tedium involved, but the photographer who wants to compete should make every effort to caption images accurately and completely. When on location, keep notes which you can refer to later—don't rely on memory. And, agents urge, don't be a one-word caption writer, trusting your memory when and if the picture is sold. There might not be time to contact you, especially if you are on an assignment, and the client has a tight deadline. In captioning, follow the journalism guide of who, what, where, when, and why for each picture. Trying to piece together the information of a long stock-shooting trip after the event can be difficult; important information can slip through the cracks. Some photographers keep track of where they've been by noting the route information in color on a map of the area; specific subjects shot (e.g., monuments, icons) are noted on the map in another color. The details are cross-referenced in a notebook and at the end of the trip all the information is there, including film numbers. The systems used are individual choices, but the message is this: support your images with detailed captions.

Model and property releases: Releases dramatically increase the sales potential and value of your stock. Without a release, images which have identifiable people cannot be used for advertising, which pays better than editorial. Even if you are in a foreign country it's advisable to obtain a release if you can. Veteran stock shooters who travel frequently will often take releases in the language of the country they're visiting, or have a translator or guide explain to people the reason for the release they're signing. It can be difficult to have an English-language release signed in a foreign country. If your agent has a subagent in the country(ies) you're visiting, have the agent translate your releases and take a supply with you. At a time when stock is being used globally, releases are more important than ever. Of course, if your material is intended for editorial purposes only, generally a release is not needed. Agents agree that photographers should get them, file them, mark MR or PR on the mount and, above all, be truthful. To falsely state you have a release could land you, and the agency, in legal hot water. Each agency has its own system for recording and confirming the existence of model releases. The ideal, from the agency viewpoint, is to submit a photocopy of the release with the picture.

Fresh material: It is not uncommon for photographers to run hot then cold. They start by submitting an exciting selection of work, promising more to come, but then leave the agency waiting. If you think of your agency file as an investment portfolio to which you add consistently, you'll keep your agent happy and see better sales results. Although practitioners agree that in today's market the best stock comprises powerful, unique imagery, the business is still essentially a numbers game, especially over the long haul. The larger the number of pictures on file, the larger the numbers on your sales reports. Part of the photographer's responsibility is to keep supplying fresh material, and a steady flow is preferable to one major deluge. The agency wants a constant influx of new material. Keep in touch with the agency, request want lists, pick out needed subjects, and request guidelines. Most agencies supply want lists periodically. Ask your agent what sells and what doesn't. But don't just talk—follow up! Agents insist that if you supply the photographs requested, your chances of selling are increased.

Work that doesn't sell: If you think your sales are off, don't hesitate to ask your agent why. But raise the issue in a positive way. Don't go on the offensive, grumble, or complain. There's a good chance the agency will be able to analyze the problem. Keep in mind that it's in the agency's interests to sell your work. And it costs them money to file your material too. Here are some reasons that your work is not selling. Be honest, and ask yourself if they apply to you, especially if you've been with an agency a few years.

Sparse coverage: Do you send a broad coverage of a subject? Random good shots from all over the world seldom do as well as images which cover a topic in depth. That good single image could be out when a buyer is looking, and without backup there's no sale. Most agencies maintain that the broader your coverage of a subject, the higher your odds of selling.

Second-rate transparencies: Do you send your agency your seconds, thirds, or dupes? If you keep those precious firsts at home, just remember that you're competing against many photographers who shoot just for stock and who put first-quality work in the files. One leading agent comments: "If you are not willing to give your agency quantities of originals you are shortchanging yourself. Agencies cannot afford to make multiple dupes of your originals, and perhaps you can't afford to pay them to do it or do it yourself. The solution is to shoot more in-camera originals. If your agency has foreign offices or affiliates and distributes sixty frames of a shot, you could plan to shoot enough film to give them two rolls of similars of each situation. It's less expensive and less trouble than making dupes, and better quality to boot. This is commercial photography. If you can't stand the idea of letting clients use your original transparencies, your work doesn't belong at a stock agency, it belongs in a gallery or museum. Certainly, sometimes there is clearly one frame that works best, and if that is the case, reproduction dupes, while costly, must be made."

Atypical photographs: Once it could've been argued that if images were so original or unusual that they didn't fit easily into generic categories they were hard to sell. But agents now stress the importance of breaking out of molds. "Our clients want to see classic subjects shot in new ways," said one. And another used travel photography as an example, encouraging travel photographers to work with models, guides and translators to create new icons of familiar subjects. "The good travel photographer does not look at the location just for what it shows, but works to make it an icon, using either talent brought in for the shoot or sets up a situation with local people," said the agent. The highest moneymakers, agents say, are pictures in the mainstream of market trends. Currently released people pictures, especially those with ethnic mixes, are much in demand.

All these factors are usually discussed at the beginning of a relationship with an agency, but somehow the idea does not sink in until they start to affect the photographer's pocketbook. Once the realization hits that the photographer's participation can definitely affect the success of stock sales through an agency, cooperation can blossom.

Most agencies and photographers work together toward a productive relationship that is mutually beneficial. To ensure that success, remember that agents are human; treat them with respect and they'll work hard for you. Don't waste their time with special demands. Instead, listen to what they need and follow through on their advice. Help them and you help yourself.

Keeping Tabs on Your Agency

The first step to evaluating if an agency is doing its best for you is to be sure your expectations are realistic. Placing stock photographs with an agency is a long-term investment (perhaps thinking of it as a mutual fund without expecting immediate results is a good analogy). Most photographers agree that it takes at least two to three years to evaluate how well an agency is working for you. And that's provided you are doing all you can to help your agency.

Just as there are questions to ask about an agency before you join it, there are questions about its ongoing performance. The points outlined in "What to Ask an Agency" suggest what to look for. But remember, it's almost impossible to check everything in an agency. Trust has to be the underpinning of a relationship. Just remember it's a creative and business partnership. If you supply the agency with good material, it will work to sell it.

Combining Stock Agencies with Direct Selling

Many photographers do sell their own work as well as having it represented through agencies. There are advantages to this approach and some photographers are very successful using it. Those who do, and have multiple agencies, say they've never experienced a conflict of having a client see the same image in two different sources and pit one against the other in a price war. How photographers apportion what goes to whom varies. The problem of whether an agency gets originals or dupes also arises and some have solved this by providing high quality 70mm dupes of 35mm originals.

Here are some of the advantages to selling stock directly as well as using one or more agencies for stock sales:

1. Increasing your income. Combined selling can be a way of fully exploiting your stock. It provides a way to increase the potential market for your images, including clients you have developed yourself, as well as those developed by the agency. It also allows you to be a stock entrepreneur, which can be challenging and a satisfying part of your overall business.
2. Stabilizing your income. Many photographers feel that as a stock agency grows, increasing the number of its photographers, an individual photographer's sales suffer because their pictures become a smaller percentage of the agency's total file. Selling directly gives a photographer the opportunity to stabilize the total stock income by increasing his or her own efforts in areas where the agency's sale of work has diminished.
3. Retaining house accounts. In some cases, photographers have built up contacts before getting involved with an agency, and it may make good economic sense not to surrender these accounts to an agency that will fulfill the same function. It's not easy to give up a settled relationship with a house account, or turn it over to someone else.
4. Keeping up contact with the client. Stock sales can generate assignments simply because you have direct contact with the picture buyer, something which rarely happens when your stock is sold through an agency. In some cases, you may be able to provide a shot from your files when an assignment is subject to bad weather

or seasonal conditions. Also, you may pick up information that could lead to a lucrative assignment.

As a direct stock supplier you can keep in touch with a client generating sales, sending out stock updates and making appointments to show new stock images. Additionally, you can offer different images or formats, such as black and white, that your agency may not handle.

5. Maintaining image control. Many photographers feel that certain special pictures should be protected and want the control that direct selling affords. They choose to market these selected pictures themselves, some of them portfolio pieces, and only to markets they deem appropriate.

Photographers who work with more than one agency maintain there are additional advantages to this arrangement.

6. Covering diverse markets. Multiple agency affiliations can provide specialized representation in different markets. For example, some agencies might concentrate on editorial, some on corporate. By being with several agencies, a photographer can get a spread of agencies.

You might choose a specialty agent to handle sports, animals, or feature stories plus another more general agency. Or you might divide the country into geographical areas and guarantee your West Coast agent exclusivity in that area, and make similar arrangements with agents in New York, the Midwest, and the South. Most large agencies, and many smaller ones, have relationships with foreign stock agents, but you can arrange separately with an agent of your choice in Tokyo, Paris, or London, thereby gaining more direct control as well as a larger percentage of revenue.

However, one agent urges photographers to keep in mind that if your agency has a catalog which it distributes to its foreign affiliates, it won't include your work since there would be conflicts in those countries where you have made your own arrangements. Unless you can print and distribute your own catalog, or you are included in each of your foreign agent's catalogs, you will lose income. Additionally, you will lose the U.S. sales you would have made had you been included in the agency's catalog.

7. Diluting any problems. With multiple agency affiliation, if a problem arises with one agency, it doesn't affect the photographer's relationship with other agencies. If you're with one agency only, and become dissatisfied, you have to break off the entire relationship.

8. Clarifying an agency's strengths. According to some photographers, using several agencies can enable you to make clearer judgments about how your work fits into the marketplace. When talking with agencies, it might be difficult to determine exactly what their strengths are and how these dovetail with your strengths. With more than one agency, certain patterns might emerge. If your pictures don't sell with any of your agencies, your photography might not be up to par, and, if this is the case, it behooves the agencies to let you know why. But if your pictures do better with one agency than another, it could be the agency, or it could be that your pictures fit its area of concentration.

Disadvantages: One of the reasons you put your work in an agency is to remove all the paperwork attendant to stock sales. By doing both, you're presented with the problems of both: satisfying an agent and your own clients can be an emotional drain.

And as one leading agent points out, you are also placing clients in a position to call your agency for a shot, and if they don't like the price, to call you as well. Unless you and your agency have very firm positions about who can handle the deal, and unless you both charge the same price, you will be opening the door to a steady stream of "beggar" clients who want to improve the deal in their favor, with an end result of less money for you.

Of course, some photographers who have multiple agencies and sell their own work maintain that the above situation is unlikely to occur, but the possibility exists and is worth taking into consideration.

A major danger of selling stock yourself is that it can become an obsession, stealing time and energy from your primary role—shooting photographs. This is one reason many leading stock specialists have chosen to sell only through agencies, and in many cases having exclusive contracts with a major agency with an international network. That way the photographer can concentrate solely on producing photographs that the agency knows are in demand. One photographer in this category, who several years ago was a staunch proponent of multiple agencies, said that selling direct could also mean diluting the quality of your submission to the agent by keeping back images for your primary files which might otherwise sell if they were with the agency.

Selling stock through more than one stock agency presents special problems. There is the added office work of pulling selections and preparing slides for various agents. Although your income may increase, you need to calculate how much you really gain after you deduct such hidden costs as your own valuable time.

Perhaps one of the major disadvantages of multiple agency relationships is characterized by the analogy to the person who is "playing the field" and, in the course of dating many people at the same time, never gets close to anyone.

Another major problem with multiple affiliations is that many agents now require an exclusive contract. They will not take you on unless you give them exclusive rights to market your work. These agents believe that without an exclusivity clause their hands are tied from a negotiating standpoint. They can't, for example, guarantee a client that the image isn't being used elsewhere. Additionally, these agents are reluctant to share their hard-earned market research information with someone who may take this knowledge to a competitor.

From a client's point of view, there is also a disadvantage to multiple representation. A client who sees the same image from three or four agencies—and pays a research fee to each—is bound to resent it. As many agencies now don't charge research fees, that aspect might not be the problem it once was. However, for whatever reason, a client might resent seeing the same image from different sources, which could result in loss of a sale.

If you do decide to use several agencies, be certain that each agent understands your arrangements and concurs. Negotiate a degree of exclusivity that satisfies you both. If you submit duplicates to more than one agency, be sure that each is aware of this in order to avoid a conflict if a client wants to buy rights of exclusivity beyond the standard "one-time only."

Making it work: Combined selling requires a certain degree of sensitivity to and awareness of the needs of your agency(ies). It's important to be frank and open about your situation with whomever you do business in the stock field. Conflicts can arise and there should be an open channel for their resolution.

Here's an example of multiple affiliations that works: Photographer X has a split personality. Her usual assignment is shooting sports, covering professional football and basketball games as a stringer for several sports magazines. She gets stock rights to this material and has developed extensive files of sport personalities in action. But her real passion is nature photography and she spends every spare moment out in the wilds, shooting animals, especially small baby animals, about whom she intends to make a book. What does she do about stock? She signs contracts with two agencies, each with its own specialties. The sports photos go to an agency that specializes in that field, and the animal shots to another. There is no conflict at either agency; in fact, with each one she has a "subject exclusive" contract.

To one degree or another most stock photographers have experienced selling stock themselves, even if it's only the occasional sale of a specifically requested picture. Combination selling on a committed and professional level means duplicating the services offered and the selling steps followed by your agency. What first appears tempting should be examined carefully and honestly. Ask yourself if you really want to be involved in both producing and selling stock or concentrate on being a prolific and successful producer, leaving the selling to someone you trust.

Pricing Stock Photography and Negotiating Fees

Stock photography is primarily a commercial business. As with any business it requires organization, production, marketing, filing, and ultimately, pricing, with which many photographers feel uncomfortable. But while negotiating prices might not be the photographer's forte, the health of any business depends on sales at prices sufficient to keep the operation profitable. After all, that's what you're in business for—to make a profit.

The keys to successful negotiating and the principles of pricing stock are covered in the chapter "Negotiating Fees and Agreements," and you are advised to read that chapter thoroughly. Additionally, the chapter "The Art of Pricing and Estimating" includes much valuable information on all the facets of estimating fees which can be applied to pricing stock. Also, refer to the chapter "Rights and Value in Traditional and Electronic Media," which contains much information on value and pricing structures. Electronic media should be regarded as new markets for publication and, as such, should be based on industry standards of usage, volume, and other accepted practices. In "Rights and Value in Traditional and Electronic Media," examples of the pricing system developed by the Media Photographers' Copyright Agency (MP©A) are given, and these can be used as a guideline.

A prime consideration in pricing stock is to appreciate the value of the image(s) to the client's project. As part of the information gathering process, prepare yourself to understand a client's advertising budget for media buying. If you know what media or magazine your clients advertise in, you can obtain their rate cards. Since the effectiveness of an ad may depend on the impact of your photograph, you should know how much the client is prepared to pay for the ad space. Keep in mind that the client may be looking at a media buy of about $250,000 for a double-page spread in four-color. Knowing the cost of media will help you charge a fair fee.

A basic principle in pricing is: the larger the total budget of the entire project, the more the buyer should be able and willing to spend for the photograph.

The stock market has three broad categories, each with a developed price range of its own.

Advertising: This is usually the highest paying use of stock photos because of the high cost of buying media space, the immediate profits realized, and the revenues the photograph will help create if the advertising is successful.

Corporate/Industrial: The use of photography in company annual reports, promotional trade shows, public relations, recruitment booklets, and the like is a less direct form of advertising and promotion than consumer advertising, thus it usually has a more moderate budget.

Editorial: This use is defined as photographs that run in magazines, books, or on TV for their illustrative or informational value. The budget of an entire project may be large but a large number of pictures might be required, so the per-page budget is relatively modest.

Determine your bottom price. Once you have established this, never, never go below it. That way you not only are taking steps to maintain your own business's profitability, you are also contributing to the health of the stock industry. Don't be afraid to say "No" if the price offered does not meet your minimum.

Before arriving at a price, ask the client every conceivable question about the usage and take detailed notes. (Refer to "The Art of Pricing and Estimating," which lists questions you should ask.) Above all, don't give a price immediately. Get all the facts, evaluate them, and determine an equitable price.

If you are inexperienced in pricing stock photos, there are several sources of advice. These include:

- Photographers who specialize in stock. Experienced colleagues are usually happy to share their knowledge of the business, especially when it comes to maintaining equitable prices. It's in all photographers' interests to maintain fair prices.
- Your stock agency. Ask the person who specializes in the agency's sales for the market you need information about, e.g., if it is a potential advertising sale, ask that person's advice.
- Consult pricing guides or use software (see the Bibliography for potential sources).
- Surf the Net. There are several stock photography forums on the Internet and also numerous Web pages featuring stock photography. The Internet, if used intelligently, can be an excellent source of information on a multitude of subjects, including stock photography.

Stock and the New Technologies

Many experts see the Internet as the one single development that will have the biggest impact on stock photography. This massive and far-reaching communications system has potential so great that it could revolutionize the way business is done in stock. What is happening and what will ultimately happen are open to conjecture, but the tremendous interest in the Internet, the thousands of people worldwide who daily are connecting to the system, and the huge amounts of money being spent by large corporations in developing a presence on the Net and the World Wide Web, highlight the value major high-tech players and individuals alike are placing on it.

And how do stock photographers take advantage of the Internet? Opinions are divided on that. Some see it as a hole in cyberspace, with the majority of interest in marketing stock being shown by sellers, not buyers. As with the advent of most technology, that will probably change as more people become comfortable using it. The traditional ways of finding images—calling for submissions from photographers and agencies, and searching through printed catalogs—will remain firmly entrenched in the foreseeable future. On-line searching and requesting images will accelerate.

However, advertising on the Internet is here and it will grow. And advertisers are licensing images for use in Web pages. This is a new market for stock, albeit a small one by comparison with traditional print markets, but one which commands good prices. Refer to "Rights and Value in Traditional and Electronic Media."

Photographers are advised to base pricing for electronic media on the same criteria as for print. Such factors as size, duration of license, and distribution, which are criteria for traditional usage, are applicable. Also, keep in mind that publishers who have sites on the World Wide Web are charging high advertising rates. So, photographers should not discount the value of their work used commercially on the Internet.

The Computer in Business

Refer to chapter eight, "Electronic Technology," as this explores the importance of using computers in your business. The computer is a valuable business tool for tracking sales, maintaining records, invoicing, customizing forms, e-mail communicating, and a multitude of other uses. Harnessing computer technology can help business people be more efficient and profitable. It's hard to imagine any business today running without assistance from computers.

Some excellent software programs written specifically for photographers are now available, and if used efficiently these can make your business more orderly. As a business-person you need to take advantage of any tool which can make you more profitable.

Key Areas for Applying Technology
- Creation of stock images
- Image correction—alteration, manipulation
- Storage of digital information
- Research and delivery
- Licensing and protection

Creating and Correcting Images

Some stock photographers shoot images specifically for combining with other photographs, using one or more elements to create entirely new pictures. They shoot subjects such as city skylines or clouds with specific final computerized images in mind.

Before buying expensive imaging equipment ask yourself if sitting in front of a computer, possibly for long stretches, manipulating stock images is what you really want to do. It might be more efficient and profitable to hire an expert in this field to handle image manipulation for you. If you liked darkroom work and all the intricacies of dodging and burning on paper, the chances of your adapting to computerized manipulation probably are greater. If you'd rather make photographs with a camera, then computerized manipulation might not be for you.

Here are some advantages to computer manipulation:
- Flaws can be removed, retouched
- Color can be corrected
- Colors of models' clothing can be changed
- Elements from different images can be combined
- Fantasy photos can be created

Storage of Digital Information *by James Cook, chair, ASMP technology committee*

Images are converted to digital form by scanning. The scanning can be done by a service bureau (used to be lab), or you can purchase your own scanner and digitize images for yourself. Either has benefits and disadvantages.

Having scans done by a service bureau means letting someone else invest in the rapidly changing technology. You also leave it for them to commit the time and effort required to develop the necessary skills for creating high-quality scans. The downside is much like having a lab printing your photographs; the results are subject to their interpretation of what you want, and the delivery time is pretty much determined by their schedules.

To do it yourself means you need to buy a scanner that is likely to become old technology sooner than many of your other computer components. Then you have to not only put in the time to learn and master the scanning process, but also the time to do each and every scan. Of course, you get your scans when you want them and looking the way you want them.

If you have scans done by a service bureau you need a medium to physically transport your digitized images. Even doing your own scans usually requires expandable storage to satisfy the voracious space appetite of images. Typically, this is satisfied using "ejectable" media versus hard disks. Ejectable media refers to disks or cartridges that slip in and out of a special drive much like a floppy disk does, but with much greater capacities. A film quality scan of a 35mm image requires 60 megabytes of storage capacity so you can see that storage requirements mushroom as you accumulate digital images. (Which, by the way, also demonstrates the efficiency and the incredible amount of information stored on a piece of film.)

Ejectable media come in a few basic types; compact discs (CDs), magnetic cartridges, and magneto-optical disks. It's important to talk to your service bureau, and anyone else with whom you expect to be exchanging files, to see what they're using. You can't trade files with them if you're not using compatible formats. It's worse than trying to print 4 × 5 negs using a 35mm carrier in your enlarger.

Many computers now come with CD drives built in and ready to read Kodak Photo CD and other compact discs. Usually Photo CD provides a very economical means of getting images scanned and into your computer. However, getting them back out again in digital form requires a CD writer or one of the other types of ejectable media. Magnetic media are the most commonly used ejectables. They won widespread acceptance because they appeared first on the market with the most appealing prices for drives and cartridges. Magnetic disks come in a wide variety of sizes and capacities. Although well suited for transferring images from one place to another, they're relatively unstable, making them undesirable for long-term storage. Magneto-optical is considerably more stable, enjoying claims of twenty years or more. Optical disks and drives were originally much more expensive than their magnetic counterparts, but prices have come down sharply to the point that they're competitive and possibly preferable. These too come in an ever-expanding variety of sizes and capacities.

And therein lies the final rub. No matter what you choose as your medium, it will be eventually replaced with another. Our information age is in jeopardy of becoming the lost information age as more and more information gets locked into past technologies. Have you ever tried to find a player for your old 8-track tapes? It's important to keep an eye on the changes and be sure your images don't get caught in an orphaned medium. Film may still be our best long-term storage solution.

Research and Delivery

The keywords you have applied to your images determine how easy it will be for someone to find your images on a large database, Photo CD, or CD-ROM. Agencies that have created CD-ROM catalogs use special keywording software, which standardizes a tedious task. Don't overlook the importance of thorough keywording. Although time consuming, comprehensive, appropriate keywording will pay dividends. When buyers start searching through thousands of images, they rely on the keywords they use to narrow the hunt. A standard keywording system has been suggested, along the lines of the Dewey Decimal System used by libraries. But until such a standard is developed, be as thorough as you can. Agencies are responsible for keywording photographs in their files, but if you store your own images in any digital form, you have that task.

Keywording Theory

What keywords should you create? That's impossible for us to say. Everyone's needs are different and what's right for us may be terribly wrong for you.

A good keywording system takes time and thought and cannot be constructed in haphazard fashion with expectations of great results. If you build keywords well, the result is faster, more fruitful file searches. Keywording is not so much for data entry as it is for searching later on.

Whether you call it cross-referencing, keywording, or indexing, there are two basic methods for choosing index words.

First, and probably most common though not always the best, is the open vocabulary. If you look at an image and use whatever words it inspires in the keywords, you're using an open vocabulary. One day you may cross-reference an image as "ship, harbor." Entered on another day, you might have cross-referenced the very same image as "boat, port." Later, when the search is on for this image, who knows what you'll find or overlook because of inconsistencies in open vocabulary. Of course, you can look for all entries that contain harbor or port or anchorage or boat or ship or vessel, but this requires a vast patience or a good memory.

Using keywords with a controlled vocabulary, your selections for entering image keywords and later for searching are limited to a specific set of words. Try using an open vocabulary in searching for that image we mentioned above as an example. It's a hit or miss proposition. If you find no entry for "boat," you must keep looking, trying other words in your keywords. When you discover "ship," you select it and move on to the next word. Failing to find "port" or "anchorage" you keep digging among the terms available until you make a hit. "Harbor" turns up the image and you're on your way.

As you make entries in your closed vocabulary system you should have the option to add a new keyword. If you fail to find a satisfactory keyword for an image, add a new one to fill the hole. This way the keywords build slowly and thoughtfully as need arises. You are spared the monstrous task of building an entire keywording system before you know what you might need.

Suppose your files contain many animal images. Start with a general category, Animals or Nature or Wildlife. Now, let's say you have numerous bears among your animals. Try a subcategory, Bear. Use yet another level for details to get down to the fine points, Brown, Grizzly, Kodiak, Polar, and so on. These details are hardly suitable for another category or subcategory.

A category, Bird, could have subcategories of types of birds; maybe Eagle is one. Details for Eagle might be Bald, Golden, and *haliaeetus leucocephalus*. If you're tempted to include details such as Flying, Egg, Hunting and the like, remember, these details apply to many birds. Flying, Egg, Hunting might be better as subcategories.

For efficiency, use the most basic, generic terms, usually singular versus plural. Use terms that can absorb several others. Fuzzy logic is still stronger in humans than in computers. Reduce synonyms to the single most suitable word for a category or subcategory. This narrows rather than expands your search vocabulary list. For instance, here is a list of synonyms: precipitation, condensation, downpour, deluge, cloudburst, torrent, rainfall, shower, drizzle, sprinkle, monsoon, plus all their plurals. Rather than create a category, or even a subcategory for each and every one, use a broader term, such as Rain.

Limiting the number of choices increases the accuracy of new entries and expedites searches. In the next breath we say, "Don't go overboard." Don't be so extreme in avoiding new terms that you diminish coverage. A happy medium exists, but it's up to you to decide where it is.

Licensing and Protection

Photographs have always been susceptible to theft if someone wants to steal them. With sophisticated scanning equipment, it's now easier than ever for someone to scan a photograph from any publication. To some degree, honesty and people's willingness to be honest will always have a role in this. But there are ways to protect images. One is electronic watermarks that can be imbedded in a photograph and cannot be detected until the photograph is reproduced, rendering it useless. A code must be used to remove the watermark. (Refer to "Image Protection Standards for the Digital Era," written by Roger Ressmeyer at the end of the chapter "Electronic Technology.")

The Internet

Not too long ago, relatively few photographers had e-mail addresses, communicated by modem, or surfed the Net. Things have changed and will continue to change. How stock photographers adapt and harness the new technologies needs to be addressed. Communicating with fellow photographers and asking questions is a start. Ask photographers who have Web pages how their business has been affected. Explore the Web and look at other photographers' pages and also search for forums which address stock issues. There is a wealth of information generated on the Internet, but to access it you will need a computer with a modem (the fastest you can afford is highly recommended). Once you start browsing you will find information on any subject you can think of, including stock photography.

Elsewhere in this section is an article by Thom Bunting, which explores the possibilities and mechanics of publishing and marketing on the World Wide Web. Additionally, photographers interested in creating Web pages have a plethora of designers eager to help, authoritative books for reference (any good bookstore will carry an array of titles on the subject) and within ASMP, colleagues who are already promoting their work on the Web.

Going On-Line

If you are considering going on-line, here are ten important things to do. They were provided by courtesy of John Uppgren, chief information officer for Gage Marketing Group.

1. Take time to explore the current offerings. Buy or obtain for free a trial subscription to America Online, CompuServe, Prodigy, or other access providers.
2. If possible, get to a school or university that has direct access to the Internet and spend time "surfing the Net."
3. Read at least a couple of books on the Internet and the digital age. Three magazines worth looking at are: *Wired* (for the front-edge thinking), *Interactive Age*, and *Interactive Week*.
4. Consider any partnerships or cooperative efforts that will make your message a little bigger. Cooperative efforts have a higher viewership.
5. Establish a budget in the same manner that you would consider media buys for newspaper or magazine publications. The budget should include ongoing administrative and support costs for making periodic changes to your page(s).

6. Take some time to think about your presence on the Net. Do you want a "here I am" approach, a focused look that identifies you as a specialist, or a mix? Consider using mail to stay in touch with people browsing your pages. Also, solicit comments on your page.

7. Select a good example of your work, digitize in two resolutions (100 dpi and 2,400 dpi) for use in the pages. Watermark your images. If you are capable, caption the work in its digital form using an image editor.

8. Lay out the rules of engagement for potential buyers in a low key but clear language. Develop other copy that will accompany your images.

9. Find a home page designer. Every college campus in the U.S. has a group of students who can build HTML pages. Alternatively, you can find agencies that will do the work. Costs will vary accordingly, perhaps from about $500 and up to $1,000 even $50,000 depending on the scope of the page.

10. Once you have all the pieces in place, look for a provider to post and maintain your home page. System reliability, bandwidth of the access, and pricing are all key elements to consider. Make certain that you or your provider notifies all of the relevant listing services so that subject, name and word searches list your home page.

Accessing the Web

The Web can be accessed through networks such as AOL and CompuServe, but generally access and working your way through linked pages is quicker if you have an Internet address. This may change as the networks streamline their systems.

When considering service providers keep in mind that while local service providers might be less expensive than national organizations, they will probably have fewer phone lines. In theory, unlimited access is good. But if other subscribers tie up lines for hours you might not get access at convenient times. Ask about the number of lines and what plans there are for expansion before signing onto a provider.

At present, marketing stock on the Web is in its infancy and it's going to take time—and no one knows how much for sure—before buyers become comfortable and adept at searching for images via the Internet. Letting people know you have a home page is one way to facilitate the process because with the multitude of choices out there, and growing, there's few chances a buyer will stumble on your page.

How do you, the photographer, let people know you have a Web page(s)? Put your home page address on printed literature—in print ads, on your letterhead, promo sheets, and anything else you send clients. The fact that you have established a home page on the World Wide Web is a reason to contact clients. In short, use traditional marketing techniques to promote your Web presence.

Developing and maintaining a Web site is not something every photographer will want to do. There are agencies promoting the work of groups of photographers, and there are advantages in being involved. For one thing, it does provide a central source for potential buyers to look and your page will be linked to others. Being linked to other sites is a definite advantage.

The ASMP Home Page

For example, as a service to members and to buyers, ASMP has created a home page on the Web with a searchable on-line membership directory. Buyers can find member photographers by name, city, state, and specialty. Links are also being established to members' home pages to allow potential buyers to view members' work. **The ASMP home page also contains much other information about the Society. The address is: www.ASMP.org.**

How Photographers Can Explore New Territory on the Internet *by Thom Bunting, Ph.D.*

New opportunities for doing business on the Internet:

Today, many millions of people are using the Internet worldwide. It's predicted that in three years there will be over 100 million people using the Internet. Because of the Net's virtually endless possibilities for connecting people to resources, businesses of all sizes are finding the Net's potential value to them, whether as sellers or buyers, increasingly difficult to ignore.

According to studies such as those performed by the Graphics, Visualization, and Usability Center, Internet users are typically well-educated, affluent professionals with far-ranging interests and backgrounds. While experts cannot determine precisely how many people use the Internet, no one disputes its astonishing growth. Whether it's the 5.8 million users confirmed recently by O'Reilly and Associates (in a survey conducted in the United States), or the 30 million users estimated last year by Matrix Information and Directory Services (MIDS), the Internet currently provides an expansive world-wide market. By all counts, the numbers of Internet users are increasing dramatically; they will continue to expand for many years.

For many potential users, though, the Internet has loomed as unknown territory—the kind of place where old maps used to say "Here There Be Dragons." Because it developed from military sites and scientific research institutions, behind most of our backs, until recently you had to be at some special place and needed to possess some technical prowess to gain access to the Net. Unless you had a specific research project and a lot of time to hunt for the answer, you might conquer the dragons only to get into the Cave of Winds—or a gigantic jumble room. Until recently, only the most adept Internet users could hope to locate useful information stored every which way amidst thousands of computer sites.

Fortunately, recent developments in the computer technology called World Wide Web ("the Web," "WWW," or "W3") have enormously upgraded and accelerated the management of information on the Internet. At last, the Net's vast resources are becoming easily accessible to nontechies via the Web. This fast-developing computer technology offers many opportunities still at the pioneer stage of being explored.

It is now relatively easy for the smallest business to develop a dynamic Internet presence—a Web site—as effectively as a large corporation. Stock agencies and photographers, already working in a visual medium and thinking in design terms, have become especially active in exploring the Web's appealing capabilities. Along with many other businesspeople, photography professionals can use the Web's multifaceted resources (text, graphics, sound, and video) to promote and market their work.

After reviewing some background, this article will focus on some practical ways in which photography businesses can use Web technology. Some examples do relate to specific conditions in the United States at the time this article is being written, yet the main lines of discussion encompass general trends of WWW development. As you read, the most important things to keep in mind are how quickly the Web can make what you offer available worldwide and how interactive with your target audience it can allow you to be. Whatever your publishing or marketing objectives, it is likely that the Web can expand the quality, immediacy, and effectiveness of your outreach.

Understanding the rush toward commercializing the Internet:

To understand why businesses are moving so quickly to develop Web sites, it's important to have some background. The Internet began with relatively small computer networks established in the United States during the 1970s to serve the needs of scientific research institutions and the military services. For decades, this set of computer networks was funded primarily by the United States government and by large universities, with strict prohibitions against commercial use. Eventually these research-oriented networks expanded worldwide into what is known today as the Internet. Except for sectors restricted to secret military-industrial projects, these networks developed largely in a spirit of cooperative development, free interchange, and open access—pursuant to a shared, academically oriented vision of international collaboration.

In 1990, fundamental changes were made to the Internet's "Acceptable Use Policy"; most significantly, these made the Net's resources hospitable to business for the first time. Since then, businesses of all types have been striving to establish favorable positions in the expansive international marketplace developing on the Net.

For some time, however, that marketplace continued to be limited by the degree of technical knowledge required of users and by the lack of protection for sensitive financial transactions. Recently, much energy has been devoted to making the Net both more convenient and more secure.

Government-supported consortia (such as CommerceNet) as well as high-tech corporations (such as Sprint, MCI, AT&T, Microsoft, and Netscape) have been persistently working to develop convenient and secure methods for transferring proprietary data and financial information over the Internet. With these new methods, it may soon be commonplace to order and pay for business products directly via the Net. On-line publishers, storefronts, shopping malls, and banks before long may offer Internet users as many or more products as their "real" counterparts do today—all with greater convenience and efficiency.

Because of strong competition among Internet Service Providers (including cable companies and major telephone companies such as AT&T and, soon, MCI and Sprint), it is becoming easier and less expensive for a wide range of people to access the Net's expansive marketplace. Many experts see this as the prevailing direction of future development.

Given this background, all businesses today have strong incentives to keep up with emerging trends of Internet commercialization. Photography businesses need to be particularly attentive, because the fortunes of the industry are so intertwined with emerging trends of marketing, publishing, and advertising.

Overview of evolving Web technology:

Over the past five years, Web technology has become immensely popular for its exceptionally user-friendly and versatile combinations of text, graphics, audio, video, interactive forms, and more. Originally developed to serve the needs of high-level physics researchers (at CERN, the European Center for Nuclear Research based in Switzerland), this new technology combines many useful features of previous Internet technologies such as Gopher, FTP (File Transfer Protocol), news (Usenet), WAIS (Wide Area Information Systems), and e-mail.

Most important, Web technology adds one key innovation: HyperText Transfer Protocol (HTTP). Because of this remarkably efficient new means of linking and transferring resources across the Internet (technically speaking, it depends upon "stateless" connections), a user can easily access electronic text, graphics, and multimedia from any Web site in a matter of seconds. By means of simple mouse clicks, one can almost instantaneously move between photography-related Web sites in the United States, Australia, Europe, Japan—or anywhere else. Without needing to know technical details, one can easily locate, download, print, or review information from any of the countless Web sites across the world.

Another element in the Web's ease of use is a special code/language called HyperText Markup Language (HTML). Once this HTML coding has been placed into a document, it can be displayed on any computer that uses Internet-capable software to browse the Web.

Also important to Web technology is a codified address named the Uniform Resource Locator (URL); this tells any computer on the Internet the specific location of a Web document. By including URLs that point to other Web resources, one Web document can link itself to a nearly unlimited number of other resources. By recording chains of URLs, newly invented Web robots tirelessly work to create linkages between virtually all Web documents available on any given topic.

How does one know what's on the Web? Extremely powerful search mechanisms have become useful Web features. Thanks to ceaseless work performed by Web robots (and the human beings who interpret their findings), Web users can easily perform interactive searches on any topic. For instance, suppose that you wish to find whatever is currently available on "Ansel Adams"—or on "medical photography." By entering search terms such as these into an interactive Web form, within seconds you can review lists of hundreds of resources matching your criteria.

Another possibility is to review Web directories, which offer well-organized pointers to resources on nearly all conceivable subjects. For example, review of the popular Web directory called "Yahoo" shows (at the time this article is being written) a broad range of photography resources on the Web: in addition to photography museums (5), galleries (11), exhibits (244), and magazines (12), there are many sites created by photographers (196), stock agencies (33), studios and labs (56), and purveyors of supplies and equipment (27). New sites are added nearly every day, so these Web directories reflect the constantly developing nature of Web resources.

As you find especially interesting and noteworthy resources, Web technology also lets you make personal "bookmarks" that record their exact locations. In effect, you thereby create your own Web directories listing resources most directly relevant to your specific interests.

Designed to be more efficient and comprehensive than previous networking technologies, the Web is also designed for continual synergism. Steadily becoming the de facto standard for Internet use, WWW technology promises to develop into a universally adaptable means of electronic communication. It lets virtually any computer system (PC, Mac, UNIX, etc.) gain access to Internet resources. In effect, the Web has restored something like a pre-Babelized state of a common language for all computers.

Web technology is developing extremely fast, with many high-tech corporations (Netscape, Sun Microsystems, Microsoft, etc.) devoting massive resources to enhancing its twofold development: (1) Web servers that "publish" electronic documents; (2) Web browsers (client software) that let Internet users connect to Web servers and obtain published documents. Even though Web browsers and servers have varied capabilities, and people using various types of browser software have diverse visual experiences, it's remarkable that so many people using such fundamentally different assortments of hardware and software can easily share vast ranges of resources in common.

Most significant for Internet novices, Web technology provides a remarkably easy-to-use interface. When reviewing Web pages, users simply click on selected words or images to connect to other relevant documents. Liberated from remembering tedious commands and keystroke combinations, users can focus directly on the content of Web publishing and marketing.

Some practical applications of Web technology to stock photography:

Because of its user-friendliness and power to represent information dynamically (with limitless combinations of text, graphics, or multimedia), Web technology offers stock photography professionals many useful possibilities.

For instance, photographers may wish to create Web pages for publicity and marketing—to describe their background and work, and to provide Net users with a convenient way to contact them on-line. Web pages may offer sample images (with resolution sufficient to look good on-screen but not of such high quality they can be downloaded by theft for commercial use). Of course, these images can be changed at will. Internet users will find text passages to click on to get further information, buttons to click to send e-mail to the photographer, and interactive forms to order images (either directly via the Net or by traditional means). Internet users who access a photographer's Web site can easily view all text and images on-screen, print what they like on their own printers, or capture text to files on their own hard disks. Photographers can also set up on-line "address books" for anyone interested in registering for follow-up; if desired, they can also review data automatically recorded by every Net user connecting to their Web pages.

Other examples of ways to apply Web technology include on-line newsletters and database listings. Formatted and well designed, a Web version of a newsletter could be revised and expanded whenever news comes in. Subscribers to the newsletter can be given access to complete articles; others could be provided simply with tables of contents or with selected highlights. Many benefits also come from bringing databases on-line via WWW. Data can be updated continuously, and users can see the updates immediately. Mistakes can be quickly corrected, changes instantaneously incorporated, and Net users can easily give feedback. An enormous amount of duplicative and wasteful cost can be saved by not having to print an immediately obsolescing directory.

These uses of Web technology can be commercially viable because restrictive security can be varied. Access to publicity documents, for example, can be open to everyone on the Internet. By contrast, access to proprietary products and services can be restricted solely to qualified Internet users who pay required fees.

Given that Web technology is developing rapidly in many exciting ways, there are clearly many other possibilities for applying it effectively to meet specific needs. In comparison to previous technologies for obtaining and disseminating electronic information such as computer bulletin boards, the Web has unmistakable advantages in reach and adaptability.

Practical requirements for accessing the Web:

The best way to understand what the Web offers is to browse some of its resources. Three basic components are required for accessing Web resources: (1) a suitable Internet connection; (2) Internet-capable software; (3) appropriately configured hardware (computer and modem). Nearly everyone will be pleased to discover that expenses related to each factor are steadily falling.

Internet connection options:

Currently, there are two basic kinds of providers of Internet connections: (1) long-established proprietary networks, such as CompuServe or America Online, which offer Net access through "pay systems" charging hourly (and sometimes flat) rates; (2) flat-rate "Internet Service Providers" (ISPs), which in many locations are now actively competing for business. Many telephone companies and cable systems now offer their customers access to the Internet as well.

Members of "pay systems" such as CompuServe or America Online may already have access to Internet resources. To date, members of these proprietary networks have found the interfaces and Internet gateways provided by pay systems to be sometimes as much in the way as helpful. In any case, the cost of sustained Internet access can become quite significant when billed at hourly rates.

In many locations, flat-rate Internet Service Providers offer full access to all the resources on the Internet at $20 per month, with no additional network-usage or telephone charges. Even in small towns or suburban areas, users can now often set up accounts with flat-rate ISPs within their local telephone zones; with this arrangement, they do not have to pay telephone company unit charges for using the phone line. Such arrangements make it possible to access the Web and all Internet resources on a remarkably economical and flexible basis. To identify flat-rate ISPs within your area, check with nearby computer stores or look for advertisements in computer magazines or local newspapers.

In evaluating options for Internet connections, it's important to compare several factors in addition to costs of hourly or monthly rates:

- Graphical interface is absolutely necessary for photographers and for everyone wishing to make optimal use of the Web's graphical resources. A few providers of Internet connections, both pay system and flat rate, offer only a command-line interface.
- Convenience of access, without annoying delays or restrictions, is important. It's frustrating to encounter too many busy signals when trying to connect by modem. Once connected to the Internet (via SLIP or PPP connection), you should have full access to all Internet resources.

Whenever possible, evaluate your options carefully by checking reviews or discussing the reliability of the ISPs with their customers.

Internet-capable software:

Here is a list of key software needed for a full connection to the Internet:
- TCP/IP software (e.g., Winsock, MacTCP)
- SLIP or PPP software (e.g., InterSLIP, MacSLIP)
- WWW browser software (e.g., Netscape Navigator, Mosaic)

Especially for Internet novices, the most convenient software option may be to use all-in-one packages such as Netscape's "Navigator Personal Edition" (800-528-6292), SPRY's "Internet in a Box" (800-777-9638), or Netcom's "NetCruiser" (800-353-6600). Such packages typically cost less than $100 and they are designed to set up Internet connections quickly (advertisements claim within five to thirty minutes) at reasonable rates. Normally, these packages allow users to choose from a range of pay system or flat-rate ISPs. All basic software required for an Internet connection should be included in each of these packages, and everything should be configured automatically upon installation.

If you are inclined to put together a system yourself, it is possible for technically advanced users to do so at little expense. As makes sense in the context of the Internet's cooperative spirit, most of the software you need can be obtained free or at low cost. Whenever there's a need to upgrade or expand software, the Net is full of resources for software and helpful advice.

At this point, Netscape has developed the most popular and versatile software used to browse the Net; its many advanced features related to visual design and display make Netscape Navigator the favorite software of photographers and everyone concerned with Web aesthetics. Because of strong competition and great demand for new features, however, all Web browser software is steadily developing enhanced capabilities while prices remain quite reasonable.

Hardware options:

Because hardware requirements are modest, it's possible to access Web resources with most computer equipment in use today. Here's an overview of recommended hardware configurations:
- Computer: any PC running Windows 3.1 or higher (33 MHz 486 recommended;

66 to 100 MHz 486 or Pentium preferred); any Macintosh (faster Performa or
PowerMac preferred); any UNIX workstation

- Memory: 6 to 8 Megabytes RAM officially recommended (8 to 32 MB preferred)
- Hard Disk Free Space: 6 Megabytes recommended (20 to 60 MB preferred)
- Monitor: 256 colors or greater
- Modem: 9600 baud acceptable (14.4 or 28.8 baud or faster preferred)
- Pointing Device: standard mouse (ergonomic mouse preferred)

Those planning to upgrade their computer hardware soon would be wise to match
the highest preference guidelines feasible. For those upgrading to new operating systems such as Windows 95, it of course would be necessary to make allowances for the
new system's particular memory and disk-space requirements.

Options for developing Web Sites:

A business wishing to develop a Web site needs to: (1) establish space on Web
server; (2) register a domain name; (3) design effective sets of Web pages. Each of
these tasks involves considerations that can be difficult to work through independently,
and it may be useful to hire a consultant skilled at creating and maintaining customized
Web sites.

Establishing space on a Web server:

Web servers are like printing presses in the electronic age; by establishing space on
a Web server, businesses are in effect setting up mechanisms for delivering electronic
documents (text, images, multimedia) on demand to a virtually unlimited number of
Internet users. Technically advanced business owners may have the ability to construct
their own Web servers on dedicated computers using high-volume, leased lines. In
most cases, however, the considerable time and expense required for this construction
project usually make other options preferable.

One option is to use a comprehensive "WWW Service Center" that can design, test,
and place Web pages on a server. Typically, such service centers require high per-page
fees for their work, often with additional monthly charges for storing Web pages on a
server.

Another option, usually the most economical, is for a business to rent space on a
Web server operated by a flat-rate Internet Service Provider. At present, it's possible to
make such arrangements with ISPs charging flat rates around $20 per month (plus
reasonable extra charges for storing large quantities of files, or for supporting extra
high-volume traffic generated by extensive use of graphics or multimedia).

Registering a domain name:

To help Net users locate its Web site, a business needs to register a domain name.
This unique name, which identifies a specific Internet address, should be easy to remember and somehow associated with the business identity. A consultant should be
able to help a business identify and register a suitable domain name.

Designing effective Web pages:

The most important goals for a business developing a Web site are the effective presentation of information in text and graphics as well as effectual communication with the business's target audience. Being in sync with the culture of the Internet is critical. As a result of its special history, the Net's culture favors more informal, cooperative, and dynamic communication than what businesses typically produce in traditional forms such as advertisements, business letters, and press releases. Consultants experienced in working on the Internet can help a business develop appropriate strategies for publishing and marketing in the interactive computer age.

In many cases, the most economical and reliable option for designing customized Web pages is to have a consultant work on a time/cost basis. Many Web sites are being developed effectively with that arrangement, which enables a business to keep costs to a minimum while getting well-focused assistance on those points that require consultation. Consultants can offer any of a range of services, from assistance with technical details of setting up a Web site to advice on elements of design and strategies for publicizing and facilitating use of the site's offerings.

Conclusion:

Stock photo professionals currently have a great variety of possibilities for developing Web sites, from the simplest publicity-oriented presentations to constantly changing or highly interactive sites that feature updatable newsletters, database/indexes, and interactive marketing. Different objectives require different approaches, and businesses should explore various options carefully.

In any case, it's prudent for businesses of all types to consider the present and future benefits of publishing and doing business on the Web. Given the fast-expanding numbers of Net users and the steadily improving support for commercial activities, the Internet clearly has much to offer.

Photographers and photo agencies have a wide range of opportunities for using the Web to promote business. At this point, the Web does remain in many ways a new frontier—one that eventually could transcend many traditional limitations of doing business within geographical boundaries. As typical of new frontiers, there are uncertainties regarding future development. While experts cannot predict exactly how businesses will develop on the Web, those establishing sites now are breaking new ground and creating new frameworks for doing business in the future.

Thom Bunting and Consulting Associates specialize in developing Internet sites. They can be reached via e-mail: thom@tcb-consulting.com Tel/fax: 607-277-0336 (U.S.) 0181-543-1226 (U.K.)

Negotiating Agency Contracts

While some might dispute the contention that picking a stock agency should be done with the same care as choosing a spouse, photographers who have fallen out with their agencies would probably agree. They know full well the ramifications of that happening. The divorce can be messy.

So entering into any partnership should not be done without careful research, and an appreciation that at some stage a parting of the ways is a distinct possibility. And the photographer's contract with an agency is indeed akin to a prenuptial agreement—an understanding of who owns what, the partners' responsibilities, and how the assets will be protected in a breakup.

Most businessmen know that nothing lasts forever and photographers should be aware that some day, almost surely, either they or their estate will part company with an agency. So this makes the stock contract—the prenuptial agreement—even more important in protecting the photographer's assets during the relationship and if or when it ends.

Photographers are advised to read carefully the section "Choosing a Stock Agency" in this chapter, which reinforces the information here.

The contract presented by agencies is usually the same for all photographers, but the contract form is not set in stone—if you have a special concern, the contract should reflect that. While most agencies have form contracts, many will alter them for individual photographers if the request is reasonable.

Look over these agreements with an open mind, but never forget that the agency's contract probably was written by the agency's lawyer. It could be a balanced agreement you might be happy to sign, but in some cases you might find points not in your interests.

Certainly, the rights of the agency have to be respected, but most definitely the agreement must protect your own interests. Don't be intimidated by something that is presented to you. Modifications can be added. There are photographers who have created agreements that are signed by the agencies.

Some agencies, like some publishers, may adopt a "take it or leave it attitude" but, when pressed, will agree to modify contracts. Look at the PACA Code of Ethics. (See "Choosing a Stock Agency".) Compare the code with the agency contract to ensure it embodies those principles. If it doesn't, ask why.

Determine your needs and whether you can give them up. Understand the agency's perspective, but never give up anything which is a fundamental need. Ask yourself: Is my request for a change in the contract reasonable, and is there a sound reason for requesting it?

It's not easy to extricate yourself from an agency after you've been there a few years. If the contract is not working for you, you have to make a business judgment: Do you make a stand and be prepared to terminate the agreement? If you do, try to position yourself so you are not dependent on that contract and can make a living if you terminate it. There are photographers who have all their work with one agency and who want to terminate, but can't because of losing income.

Return of work after leaving an agency can be a problem. It's suggested to have a provision on the contract for return of work in a relatively short time, such as thirty days from the agent, sixty days from subagents. Any of your work out with agency submissions should be returned to you as soon as possible. Ensure this aspect is covered to your satisfaction.

Determine how long the agency holds money before paying the photographer. Don't lose sight of the fact that the agency owes you your money. Try to get paid monthly or in a timely fashion.

Obtain the right to audit the accounts involved in the production of your work. This will enable you to inspect the agency's books if you have any doubts about getting paid.

When you give the agency the right to sign agreements with subagents, it should be stated that the subagents abide by the terms of the contract the principal agency has with you. This includes the right to audit the subagent's accounts related to your work. ASMP is beginning to see more problems associated with subagents not abiding by the terms of the principal agency's contract with their photographers.

When an agency licenses the use of an image, the copyright owner should know: who is the end user of the image, the duration of the license, geographic limits, reproduction size, identification of the photograph used, the print run, and the number of uses.

Contracts should not automatically renew. Some have a window of ninety days after a five-year period—if you miss that window, the contract is automatically renewed. You should have the same rights to terminate as the agency.

Inquire what is deducted from photographers' earnings. You should have the right to set limits on what is deducted from your income, and the contract should guard against this. Nor should agencies be able to hold photographs as collateral if the photographer leaves the agency.

If there's a law suit on your behalf, be able to have a say. This could avoid situations like the one where a stock agency filed a claim against the photographer's best assignment client without consulting the photographer.

Also, if the photographer believes there is an infringement and the agency does not want to take action, the photographer should have the right to proceed. At that point, the agency should have the right to determine if it wants to be involved and share costs. And the person bearing the costs should call the shots.

Determine who should be paying for duping and catalog costs. And are there volume and bulk sales? If so, the photographer should be able to allow the number of images used and their duration of use for that purpose.

More agencies are seeking exclusivity. Ask what the benefits of exclusivity are to you. Does it guarantee more images in catalogs; if you are a specialist, will the agency limit the number of other photographers who do similar work? And if the agency changes its slant and your images are no longer their forte, do you have any recourse? Is it in your best interests to have an exclusive contract? If you are dubious, limiting the contract's duration could be advantageous.

Ask what constitutes a gross sale and request that sales statements show both the gross amount and the net to the agent.

Clear up such things as: what the service charges are; what say do you have in catalog selection; are there filing fees?

Is the agency involved with on-line services and other electronic imaging outlets? Avoid agencies which offer CD-ROM clip art discs. And if images are digitized, ensure that there is language in the contract to make sure you are made aware of any digitizing of your images before it can be done. Permission is not automatically granted for your images to be digitized. There are numerous questions to be answered before you enter into a contract with a stock agency. Ask those questions before the marriage. Or you might have to forever hold your peace.

The following examples of contracts are what ASMP considers the ideal for photographers. One is a suggested contract between a photographer and a stock agency, and the other is the contract the Media Photographers' Copyright Agency (MP©A) offers its members. Both are based on fairness and equitability.

Contract Between Photographer and Stock Picture Agency

AGREEMENT made this _____ day of _____, year_____, by and between (name and address of Photographer) _____

_____

(hereinafter referred to as "Photographer") and (name and address of agency)_____

_____

(hereinafter referred to as "Agency").

RECITALS

Photographer is engaged in the business of creating photographic images (hereinafter referred to as "Images"). Agency is in the business of arranging for the license of such Images to interested clients (hereinafter referred to as "Clients"). Photographer and Agency have determined that it is in their mutual best interest to enter into this Agreement whereby Agency shall represent certain Images of Photographer for license to Clients upon the terms and conditions which are set forth herein.

1. Grant of Authority

(a) Photographer hereby appoints Agency, and Agency hereby accepts such appointment as Photographer's agent in respect of the license of Photographer's Images. As used herein, the term "Images" shall be limited to those Images created by the Photographer as shall be delivered by Photographer to Agency and accepted by Agency pursuant to Paragraph 3, below.

(b) Agency is granted limited exclusivity hereunder as follows (check appropriate limitations):

(i) Regional U.S. as follows _____

(ii) B&W _____ Color _____ Both B&W and Color _____

(iii) Stock _____ Assignment _____ Both Stock & Assignment _____

(iv) May Agency employ Subagents? Yes _____ No _____

If yes, list permissible Subagents_____

(c) The obligation of exclusivity set forth in subparagraph (b) shall consist solely of Photographer's covenant not to place the Images with any other stock picture agency, picture library, or other similar selling medium of Images as limited by subparagraph (b). Unless otherwise provided, nothing contained herein shall in any way be deemed to prevent Photographer from engaging in assignment photography for Photographer's own account or from engaging in the sale or license of Images directly to Clients. The accounts listed on Exhibit A, attached hereto, shall be deemed "House Accounts" and serviced exclusively by Photographer for all purposes, and all fees attributable to "House Accounts" shall be Photographer's sole and exclusive property.

(d) Except as may otherwise be provided herein, Agency shall have discretion regarding the terms and conditions of any license of the Images, delivered to it by Photographer. Notwithstanding the foregoing, any license of rights in and to the Images, on a "buy-out" (i.e,. a transfer of all or substantially all rights in and to an Image) or "exclusive" basis, shall require Photographer's prior written approval, not to be unreasonably withheld. Agency shall have no authority to transfer to any client any underlying rights in the Images.

(e) Agency acknowledges that it will not license the use of any of the Images for less than _____ Dollars ($_____) without Photographer's prior written approval.

2. Term

(a) This Agreement shall commence as of the date first set forth above and shall continue for a period of three (3) years thereafter (the "Initial Period"). Agency shall have the right, at least thirty (30) days prior to the expiration of the Initial Period, to notify Photographer of its desire to renew the Agreement for an additional period of one (1) year commencing upon the expiration of the Initial Period. Agency shall thereafter have a continuing right, upon thirty (30) days' written notice prior to the expiration of each successive renewal period, to elect to extend the term of the Agreement for a one (1)-year period. Notwithstanding the foregoing, Photographer may, upon receipt of any such thirty (30) days' notice, notify Agency of its desire to terminate this Agreement, and the Agreement shall thereafter terminate at the expiration of the then current Term. The Initial Period and each renewal period are collectively referred to herein as the "Term."

(b) In the event Agency has failed to derive gross billings from Photographer's Images for a period of one (1) year, Photographer shall have the right to terminate this Agreement on thirty (30) days' prior written notice to Agency.

3. Delivery of Images

(a) Promptly after the execution of this Agreement, Photographer shall deliver to Agency such Images as Photographer deems will further the purposes of this Agreement. Promptly upon receipt of such material, Agency shall review same and within thirty (30) days thereafter return to Photographer all Images, designating those Images which Agency deems appropriate for license pursuant to its Agency obligations hereunder. Images so designated shall be redelivered to Agency, and the use of same shall be governed by this Agreement. Images not selected and not representing so-called "dupes" or "similars" to Images designated by Agency may be sold, licensed, or used by Photographer at Photographer's sole discretion.

(b) Images redelivered to Agency for use pursuant to the terms of this Agreement shall at all times be and remain the exclusive property of Photographer, to be held in trust by Agency solely for the limited licensing purposes described herein.

(c) All references herein to "Images" shall be deemed to refer to those Images accepted by Agency.

4. Obligations of Photographer

Photographer shall use all reasonable efforts to accurately caption all Images and affix proper copyright notice in Photographer's name to such Images. Photographer shall indicate those Images for which a "model release" has been obtained. Upon Agency's request, Photographer will deliver a copy of any release to Agency. In the event an Image does not contain a notation concerning the existence of a model release, Agency acknowledges that no such release shall be deemed to exist and Agency assumes full responsibility for the subsequent use of such Images, and releases and indemnifies Photographer from any and all damages incurred by Agency, Photographer, or third parties in connection with such uses.

5. Warranties of Photographer

Photographer represents and warrants to Agency as follows:

(a) Photographer is the sole and exclusive owner of the Images and of the right to license such Images.

(b) The Images do not knowingly infringe copyright, trademark, right of privacy or publicity, and do not knowingly defame any third party.

(c) Photographer has the right to enter into this Agreement and perform Photographer's obligations hereunder.

6. Obligations of Agency

(a) Agency shall supply a suitable environment for long-term storage, care, and retrieval of Images, including protection from dust, heat, damp, and overexposure to light.

(b) Agency shall use its best efforts to license the Images and to maximize the prices received by Agency for same.

(c) Agency shall diligently and carefully process all Images so as to avoid loss or damages thereto, and index the Images with reference in each case to Photographer's name. The method of indexing the Images shall be at the Agency's sole discretion, provided such method must permit location of any Image within two (2) weeks and return to Photographer within one (1) month after request for same by Photographer, subject to Paragraph 8, below. Upon the return of any Image to Agency from a Client, Agency shall promptly cause such Image to be refiled so as to insure ready access for subsequent licensing and/or retrieval.

(d) All Images licensed by Agency shall contain copyright notice in Photographer's name as such notice has been indicated by Photographer on the face of the Images. In the event no notice is so affixed, Agency agrees to affix notice in Photographer's name before license of any Images to the Clients as follows: year_____ [Photographer's name], and Agency in each such case shall determine from Photographer and shall utilize the correct year to be included in said notice. Agency shall require, in all agreements with Clients, that the Images shall be protected by copyright in all uses, pursuant to applicable law or regulation.

(e) Agency shall promptly notify Photographer in the event it discovers unauthorized or infringing use of or the loss of or damage to any of the Images. Upon receipt of such notice, Photographer shall control any legal action and shall notify Agency as to the manner in which Photographer wishes to proceed in respect of such infringement, loss, or damage. Photographer shall have the right to cause Agency to be joined as a party in any litigation concerning the Images. Any recovery from such action shall, after payment of all costs (including reasonable attorney's fees), be divided between Photographer and Agency on the same basis as revenue is to be divided, as set forth in Paragraph 7, below.

(f) Agency agrees to conduct itself in all its dealing with Clients in an ethical and reputable fashion.

(g) Agency acknowledges that the Images are of a unique, fragile, and extraordinary artistic nature which cannot be easily duplicated and the loss or damage to any such material will result in irreparable harm to Photographer, not readily compensable by monetary reimbursement. Accordingly, Agent will use its best efforts to protect and preserve the Images, and exercise all due care in the handling of the Images.

(h) To the extent information supplied to Clients by Agency in respect of an Image differs from the information supplied to Agency by Photographer, the accuracy of such information shall be Agency's sole responsibility.

(i) All obligations of Agency under this Agreement apply as well to all permissible subagents.

7. Compensation

(a) In consideration of the services furnished by Agency hereunder and the performance of its obligations hereunder. Agency shall be permitted to retain: _____ percent (____%) of gross billings in connection with the license of the Images. "Gross billings" shall be defined as all revenue, of whatever nature and from whatever source, derived from license of the Images, and shall include, without limitation, holding fees and interest assessed, but shall not be deemed to include so-called "service fees." The only permissible deductions from gross billings are the following:

(i) bad debts and other uncollectible sums actually incurred.

(ii) reasonable currency conversion costs.

Agency acknowledges that all sums received as gross billings from the license of the Images are held in trust for Photographer, subject only to the retention by Agency of its commission as set forth above.

(b) Agency shall remit payment and provide Photographer with a detailed statement setting forth the licensing by Agency of the Images on the following basis [select one]:

(i) Every thirty (30) days on or before the 25th day of each month.

(ii) Every sixty (60) days on or before the last day of each odd ☐ /even ☐ numbered calendar month.

(iii) Every ninety (90) days on or before fifteen (15) days after the close of each calendar quarter.

(c) Such statement shall include the following information:

(i) Identity of Image.

(ii) Identity of Client.

(iii) Rights granted.

(iv) Date payment received.

(v) Gross billings.

(vi) Deductions from gross billings.

(d) If, during any reporting period, gross billings derived from Photographer's Images do not exceed One Hundred Dollars ($100), payment of such sums to Photographer may be deferred until the next reporting period. In no event, however, shall royalties be paid any less frequently than annually, and notwithstanding any deferral of payment, regular statements shall continue to be sent to Photographer.

(e) Photographer or a designated representative shall have the right, upon reasonable notice and during regular business hours, to inspect Agency's books and records and to make extracts thereof as same relate to Photographer's Images. In the event, as a result of such an audit, it is determined that Agency has underpaid Photographer by an amount equal to or in excess of five percent (5%) of all monies due to Photographer, then Agency shall bear all costs and expenses of such audit as well as remitting to Photographer all past due sums with interest to date. The foregoing shall not be deemed to be a waiver of or limitation upon Photographer's other rights or remedies in the event of such underpayment.

8. Retrieval of Images

(a) Upon the expiration or termination of this Agreement, Agency shall use all reasonable efforts to promptly retrieve and turn over to Photographer all the Images then in Agency's possession, no matter where such Images may be located. In no event shall such retrieval and delivery to Photographer require more than a period of: (i) three (3) months after termination, in respect of Images in Agency's files; or (ii) one (1) year after expiration or termination in respect of Images in the possession of Clients or Subagencies at the time of such expiration or termination.

(b) Photographer shall have direct access to Agency's files, upon reasonable prior notice, for purposes of furtherance of Photographer's professional interests (e.g., exhibitions), or in the event Agency does not comply with its retrieval and return obligations pursuant to this paragraph.

(c) During the retrieval period after termination or expiration, Agency shall diligently return to Photographer all Images returned by Clients. If Images are still outstanding one (1) year after termination or expiration, Agency shall provide Photographer with written notification specifically setting forth: (i) identification of Image; (ii) name of Client in whose possession Image is being held; and (iii) address of Client.

9. Dupes

(a) For purposes of this paragraph, "Dupes" shall be defined as duplicates, facsimiles, or other reproductions of Images, whether created by Photographer, Agency, permissible Subagents, or Clients.

(b) Agency [select one] shall___ shall not___ be authorized to license the use of "Dupes" to clients.

(c) In the event licensing of "Dupes" has been authorized, Agency shall not permit clients to create "Dupes" without Photographer's prior written approval.

(d) All "Dupes," regardless of which party has caused such "Dupes" to be created, shall be and remain, from the moment of creation, the sole and exclusive property of Photographer, subject only to permissible licenses.

(e) Agency shall account to Photographer for "Dupes" in all respects as if they were Images licensed under this Agreement and all provisions of this Agreement shall apply to such "Dupes."

10. Default

(a) Agency shall be deemed to be in default of its obligations upon any of the following occurrences:

(i) Breach of any of its representations or warranties contained herein or any other undertaking on its part to be performed hereunder and failure by Agency to cure such breach within ten (10) days after receipt of notice from Photographer specifying same.

(ii) Any activity by Agency outside the limited scope of the authorization issued to Agency hereunder.

(iii) If a petition in bankruptcy or for reorganization is filed by or against Agency; or if Agency makes an assignment for the benefit of its creditors; or if Agency fails to timely pay its general creditors; or if a receiver, trustee, liquidator, or custodian is appointed for all or a substantial part of Agency's property, and the order of appointment is not vacated within thirty (30) days; or if Agency assigns or encumbers this Agreement contrary to the terms hereof.

(iv) If Agency ceases to conduct its business or sells or merges substantially all of its assets.

(b) In the event of any act of default as set forth above, in addition to any other remedy Photographer may have, Photographer shall be entitled to immediately terminate Agency's authorization under this Agreement and shall thereupon be relieved of any continuing obligation it may have to Agency. Upon such termination, all business activity in respect of the Images shall immediately cease, and Agency will promptly retrieve and deliver to Photographer all Images as required pursuant to Paragraph 8, above.

11. Foreign Subagents

In the event Photographer permits Agency to employ the services of any foreign subagents in connection with the license of the Images, Agency may do so, subject to the prior written approval of the Photographer first having been obtained after notification to Photographer of the name and address of the proposed subagent. In no event shall Agency commission or fees, including the fees of Agency and all permissible subagents, exceed that percentage of gross billings specifically stated as Agency's compensation in Paragraph 7, above.

12. Death or Disability of Photographer

In the event Photographer shall die during the Term hereof or shall become disabled or incompetent, Photographer or, in the case of death or incompetency, Photographer's personal representative, shall have the right, exercisable by sixty (60) days' prior written notice to Agency, to cause this agreement and Agency's authorization hereunder to terminate.

13. Taxes

As between Photographer and Agency, Agency shall be solely responsible for the collection and payment of any and all taxes whether in the nature of a sales, personal property, remittance, excise, or other tax which is or may become due and payable in connection with any license of the Images pursuant to the terms of this Agreement.

14. Inability to Locate Photographer

(a) Agency shall use all reasonable efforts (including inquiries with appropriate trade associations) to locate Photographer in the event statements are returned unclaimed. To assist Agency in this endeavor, Photographer shall provide Agency with an alternate address for notice purposes on the signature page of this Agreement.

(b) In the event that, notwithstanding Agency's efforts, Photographer cannot be located, Agency shall deposit any portion of gross billings due to Photographer in a separate interest-bearing account (into which account Agency may deposit sums due to other Photographers whom Agency is unable to locate). Such sums shall remain on deposit for a period of five (5) years or such longer period of time as may be permissible by law. Six (6) months prior to the expiration of such time period, Agency shall provide the American Society of Media Photographers, 14 Washington Road, Suite 502, Princeton Junction, NJ 08550-1033, or its successor organization, with written notice of the name and last known address of Photographer. Such notice shall be sent to the executive director by certified mail.

(c) If Agency is not contacted by Photographer or his/her personal representative before the expiration of such time period, the sums on deposit with Agency shall be treated according to the laws of the State of _____ concerning abandoned property.

15. Indemnity

(a) Each of the parties hereto agrees to indemnify and hold the other party harmless from and against all final judgments and settlements with consent (hereafter collectively referred to as "claims") which may arise as a result of a breach or alleged breach of the party granting the indemnity (hereinafter the "Indemnitor") of any representation, warranty, or undertaking to be performed by such Indemnitor. The party being indemnified (hereinafter the "Indemnitee") shall promptly notify the Indemnitor of any such claim, and the Indemnitor shall thereupon have the right to undertake the defense of such claim. The Indemnitee shall have the right, but not the obligation, to be represented by counsel of its choice and participate in such defense at its sole cost and expense. The Indemnitee shall not settle any such claim without the prior written approval of the Indemnitor.

(b) Anything to the contrary containing herein notwithstanding, in the event Photographer is called upon to indemnify Agency pursuant to the foregoing indemnity, Photographer shall not be liable for any monetary sums in excess of the share of gross billings heretofore received by Photographer from Agency pursuant to this Agreement.

16. Miscellaneous

The parties hereto acknowledge that this Agreement is one of agency only and does not constitute an employment agreement and that Agency is acting in the limited capacity of an independently retained agent on Photographer's behalf. Agency may not set itself out or bind Photographer contrary to the terms hereof.

17. Miscellaneous

(a) Agency may not assign this Agreement without the prior written consent of Photographer. Any assignment in contravention of the foregoing prohibition shall be deemed null and void. Photographer shall have the right to assign this Agreement to any corporation in which Photographer is a principal stockholder, and to assign Photographer's share of gross billings earned hereunder.

(b) Except as may otherwise be provided herein, this Agreement shall be binding upon and shall inure to the benefit of the respective heirs, executors, administrators, successors and assigns of the parties hereto.

(c) This Agreement incorporates the entire understanding of the parties concerning the subject matter contained herein and may not be modified, amended, or otherwise changed in any respect except by a separate writing signed by the party to be charged therewith.

(d) This Agreement and all matters collateral thereto shall be construed according to the laws of the State of _____ and any jurisdiction of such state.

IN WITNESS WHEREOF, the parties have executed this Agreement on the day and date first set forth above.

Agency _____

Photographer _____

Principal Address _____

_____

_____

Alternate Address _____

_____

_____

Business Telephone _____

Media Photographers' Copyright Agency, Inc./ Photographer Full Service Agreement

This Agreement is made this _____ day of _____ year_____, by and between _____ (hereinafter referred to as the "Photographer") and the Media Photographers' Copyright Agency, Inc. (hereinafter referred to as the "Agency").

RECITALS

The Photographer is a member of the American Society of Media Photographers, Inc. ("ASMP") and is engaged in the business of creating photographic images for publication.

The Agency is a wholly owned subsidiary of ASMP and is engaged in the business of licensing the photographic images created by ASMP members, under terms and conditions established by them, to interested third parties for their use, reproduction, distribution, and/or publication.

1. Grant of Authority.

(a) The Photographer designates the Agency as the Photographer's nonexclusive agent for the purpose of negotiating the licensing of all images which are authorized by the Photographer to be licensed by the Agency on the Photographer's behalf (the "Images") as provided in Paragraph 3, below. The Agency is authorized to solicit licensing opportunities on behalf of the Photographer with respect to the Images and to enter into negotiations for the licensing of the Photographer's Images. The Photographer retains the authority to make all final decisions with respect to the terms and conditions to be incorporated into any such license, including but not limited to the amount of compensation to be paid by the party granted rights to use the Images (the "Licensee"). For purposes of this Agreement, the "Licensees" shall include all actual and prospective licensees of the Photographer's Images.

(b) The geographic scope of the Agency's licensing authority shall be worldwide unless otherwise limited in writing by the Photographer.

(c) The Agency is authorized to use or employ such subagents as may be necessary to carry out the purposes of this Agreement.

(d) The Agency shall not have the right to sell or assign any of the Photographer's copyright rights in the Images unless specifically authorized to do so in writing by the Photographer.

2. Custody of and Rights in the Images.

(a) All the Images delivered to the Agency for licensing under this Agreement shall at all times be and remain the exclusive property of the Photographer and shall be held in trust by the Agency for the purposes of this Agreement.

(b) The copyright and other rights in and to the Images shall remain the exclusive property of the Photographer, and nothing in this Agreement shall be interpreted as a conveyance of any such rights from the Photographer to the Agency, other than the rights specifically enumerated in this Agreement.

(c) The Agency shall have the right to record any Images on or in any storage, delivery, and/or catalog system, regardless of whether such system is digital, analog, print, or photographic (the "Recorded Images").

(d) Upon the termination of this Agreement, the Agency shall _____ shall not _____ continue to have the right to license the Recorded Images pursuant to the terms thereof. In the event the Agency is granted such a right, its authority shall be revoked upon receiving thirty (30) days advance written notice of revocation from the Photographer.

(e) Not withstanding the termination of this Agreement or of the Agency's right to license the Recorded Images following termination of this Agreement, the Agency shall not be required to remove the Recorded Images from a storage, delivery, and/or catalog system referred to in Subparagraph c, above.

3. Images Eligible for Licensing by the Agency.

Unless otherwise specifically designated by the Photographer as ineligible for licensing, the Agency is authorized to license, subject to the Photographer's approval of the terms and conditions thereof as provided in Paragraph 1, all the Images created by the Photographer and in which he or she retains sole ownership of the copyrights.

4. Obligations of the Photographer.

(a) The Photographer shall affix a proper copyright notice consisting of the symbol ©, the name of the Photographer, and the year of first publication or if unpublished the year of creation, to all copies of any Images delivered to the Agency or to the Licensees for purposes of this Agreement.

(b) The Photographer shall be responsible for accurately captioning all the Images delivered to the Agency or to the Licensees pursuant to this Agreement.

(c) The Photographer shall be responsible for obtaining all model and/or property releases that are necessary to enable the Agency to lawfully license the Images to the Licensees and shall provide the Agency with copies of such releases upon request of the Agency. The Photographer shall specifically identify each Image for which all necessary releases have been obtained.

5. Warranties of the Photographer.

The Photographer represents and warrants the Agency as follows:

(a) The Photographer is the sole owner of the copyrights in the Images and has the right to license the use, reproduction, distribution, and publication of the Images to others.

(b) To the best of the Photographer's knowledge, the Images do not infringe the copyright, trademark, privacy, publicity, or other rights of any third party, nor do the Images defame any third party.

(c) The Photographer has obtained all necessary model and/or property releases with respect to the Images that the Photographer has identified as necessary to be released.

(d) The Photographer has the right to enter into this Agreement, and the performance of the obligations established by this Agreement will not violate any other contract or agreement to which the Photographer may be a party.

6. Indemnification by the Photographer.

The Photographer indemnifies and holds harmless the Agency from any and all claims and liabilities, including but not limited to the costs of defending such claims, arising from or related to breach of the Photographer's warranties set forth in Paragraph 5, above.

7. Obligations of the Agency.

(a) The Agency will attempt in good faith to license the Images on terms and conditions that maximize the benefits to the Photographer. The Agency does not guarantee or promise that its licensing efforts with respect to the Photographer's Images will be successful. The Agency represents only that it will use its best efforts on the Photographer's behalf and will communicate to the Photographer for his or her acceptance or rejection the terms and conditions of any licensing arrangement that may be entered into with a Licensee. The Agency will not, however, enter into any licensing agreement with a Licensee on the Photographer's behalf without first obtaining the approval of the Photographer of all terms and conditions contained in such licensing agreement.

(b) The Agency shall promptly notify the Photographer upon discovery of any potentially infringing use of the Images or of the loss or damage to the Images. Upon receipt of such notice, the Photographer shall be responsible for undertaking any enforcement or other legal action necessary to protect his or her rights, but the Photographer may engage the Agency, upon its agreement, to undertake appropriate legal action on his or her behalf as provided below in Subparagraph f.

(c) The Agency shall collect all monies paid to the Photographer by the Licensees that enter into agreements with the Agency for the use of the Photographer's Images and shall deposit all monies in a single separate account maintained for all funds collected for the Photographers who engage the Agency as their nonexclusive licensing agent.

(d) The Agency shall remit payments due to the Photographer under this Agreement on a monthly basis, unless such payments are less than One Hundred Dollars ($100), in which event payment may be deferred no longer than six (6) months or until such time as the amounts due to the Photographer exceed that amount.

(e) Each monthly payment by the Agency to the Photographer shall be accompanied by a detailed statement containing the following information:

(i) The identities of the Image(s) generating the revenues.

(ii) The identity of the Licensee(s) paying the revenues.

(iii) A reference to the licensing agreement(s) (by number, date, or other appropriate designation selected by the Agency) pursuant to which the Licensee(s) made payment.

(iv) The date the payment(s) was received by the Agency.

(v) The gross revenues collected by the Agency for the period in the form of licensing fees paid for use of the Photographer's Image(s).

(vi) The deductions from gross revenues made by the Agency pursuant to the terms of this Agreement.

(f) If requested to undertake the enforcement of the Photographer's copyright rights against one or more infringers and if the Agency agrees to undertake such enforcement action on the Photographer's behalf, the Photographer and the Agency shall enter into a separate written agreement specifying each party's rights and obligations with respect to the action to be taken against the infringer(s).

8. Compensation of the Agency.

(a) In exchange for the licensing services provided to the Photographer under this Agreement, the Agency will be entitled to be paid thirty percent (30%) of the gross revenues (as defined below) earned from the Agency's licensing of the Photographer's Image(s). Such payments to the Agency shall be made by deducting thirty percent (30%) of the gross revenues received by the Agency for the preceding month from the licensing of Photographer's Image(s). The balance of the gross revenues, or seventy percent (70%) of those amounts, shall be paid to the Photographer in accordance with Paragraph 7, above.

(b) For purposes of this Agreement, "gross revenues" shall consist of all revenues received by the Agency from the licensing of the Photographer's Images. "Gross revenues" shall include, but shall not be limited to, all holding fees, "comp" fees, and lost transparency charges attributable to the Photographer's Images.

9. Term

This Agreement shall commence as of the date written above and shall continue until such time as either party gives thirty (30) days advance notice of intent to terminate the Agreement to the other party. Both the Photographer and the Agency shall have the unrestricted right to terminate this Agreement for any reason.

10. Notices

All notices given under this Agreement shall be delivered to the following addresses unless otherwise stated in writing:

For the Photographer: _____

For the Agency: 14 Washington Road, Suite 502, Princeton Junction, NJ 08550-1033

11. Governing Law

This Agreement shall be interpreted in accordance with the law of the State of Delaware.

12. Amendment

This Agreement can be amended only in writing signed by both parties.

13. Assignment

The rights, benefits, and obligations under the Agreement cannot be assigned to others by the Photographer or the Agency without the prior written consent of the nonassigning party.

14. Complete Agreement

This Agreement contains the entire understanding of the parties with respect to their licensing arrangement and supersedes any prior written or oral understanding between the parties related to that subject.

WHEREFORE, the parties have evidenced their assent to the terms and conditions of this Agreement by the signatures set forth below.

_____   MEDIA PHOTOGRAPHERS' COPYRIGHT AGENCY, INC.

Signature of the photographer

_____   By: _____

Printed name of the photographer

Title: _____

Ethics and the Photographer's Responsibilities

Today, photographers are working in an increasingly complex and competitive arena. Rights are being eroded and obstacles encountered at every turn—corporate takeovers, tightened budgets, work-for-hire, and the proliferation of CD-ROM clip art. It's important to fight vigorously to protect those rights. Our battlefield is the classic one of a free marketplace, where unfair practices abound.

It's also important to remember, however, that rights are not a one-sided issue. When we make a business deal, we also assume certain obligations. Many of these are spelled out in a contract, but others are a matter of ethics and good business sense.

The market for stock photography is intensely competitive. In this crowded field a few photographers may be tempted to cut corners to make a sale.

There are two sound reasons not to bend the rules. One is purely ethical—it's wrong. If that's not enough to deter you, consider the practical reason—it's bad business. Even though you may not always face legal repercussions, if you burn a client or stock agent through questionable practices, they will not do business with you again. Furthermore, bad news travels fast, and in a short time others will be wary of dealing with you. Even if your mistake is the result of sloppiness rather than intention (for example, your assistant sends out a photo before its time restriction is up), your reputation may still be damaged. Worse, your action brings disrepute to the industry and makes the fight for protection of rights all the more difficult for the thousands of photographers who are stringently upholding ethical standards.

ASMP believes it is in the best interests of the photographic community to examine these issues closely. In its efforts to promote good business practices and protect photographers' rights, the Society emphasizes the highest level of professional and ethical standards. The following are some of the areas in which photographers would be well advised to be meticulous in their business dealings.

Responsibility to Assignment Clients

Whether your contract is written or oral, honor its content. Keep to the spirit as well as the letter of the deal.

1. Time restrictions. Don't release pictures to your stock agency or put them in your own stock file until any time limit agreed upon with the assigning client has expired. This requires that you set up safeguards in your logging system so that photos are not inadvertently sent out ahead of time.

2. Non-compete clauses. Honor any non-compete restrictions you have agreed to and alert your agency to them by placing a warning label on the slide mount (for example, "no permission liquor ads" or "restricted construction industry use"). Even when there is no contract, use good judgment by avoiding the use of photographs by a competing client. Although you may legally be free to sell an assignment outtake to a client's competitor, you may be on very shaky ground if you do. At the very least you'd be wise to discuss the move with the assigning client.

3. Piggybacking. When you're on location for an assignment client, how much of your time, creative thinking, and energy should be spent on that job? The ethical

photographer would say "all of it." Depending on the terms of the job and the understanding with the client, shooting stock on assignment time is cheating. Just because the assignment has been "adequately" fulfilled doesn't mean the photographer has license to stop short of an all-out effort in order to skim some time—or a sunset—for personal use. Of course there are many exceptions to this rule and there are occasions when you can shoot your own pictures without short-changing the client in any way, such as stopping for a skyline picture on the way to the airport. What is important to remember is that your first responsibility is to fulfill your obligation to the client. Your pride and self-respect as a professional require it.

Staying in Touch

Delivery memos spell out the responsibilities of clients for handling photographs with care and returning them in a timely manner. And it is a valid business practice for a photographer to charge a holding fee when clients retain photographs too long; after all, they are keeping them out of circulation. But what about the responsibility of the photographer to retrieve his or her work when a client or photo agency is finished with it?

In one case, a photographer left a large number of slides with a client to review for a project. When the client called to have the photographer pick up his slides, they found he was away. His phone number was an answering service and his mailing address a post office box. After two months of leaving messages and sending notices, the client still had received no reply. They felt responsible for the slides in their custody and knew that their liability was increasing every day. Mailing the slides back, even via registered mail, was not a viable option without the photographer's knowledge and assent. Obviously the photographer assumed that the client would hold onto his slides until he returned.

Photo agencies more frequently complain of this problem when they want to return photographs. Not only are some photographers casual about picking up their work, but many fail to inform their agencies when they move or change phone numbers.

The professional photographer must also work in a professional manner. Remember that regardless of what your delivery memo says, you share in the responsibility of ensuring a safe and businesslike return of your materials. You must provide an avenue for a client or photo agency to return your photographs. That means, if you are away, you need to arrange for someone to check your answering machine or service and open your mail, and you need to check in with that person periodically or leave word of where you can be reached. And, of course, maintaining a good relationship with your photo agency requires that you keep your status with them current.

Responsibility to Stock Photo Buyers

1. Accurate captioning. Nearly every photographer has been tempted, at one time or another, to "adjust" a caption to make a picture a little bit more salable. However, there is no justification for modifying information—either you're lying or you're not. Let's say you've got good pictures of a celebrity mayor. Maybe they

were taken when he was running for city council and later he ran for mayor. A buyer wants them and your agent calls to ask if you know exactly when they were taken. The sale may depend on the date and the mayor still looks to same, so what do you do?

These are the kinds of questions that every photographer is confronted with. We are honorable people, but there are those moments when some of us may think, "What harm could there be?" That's the first step on the road to self-destruction.

2. Model releases. If you don't have a model release, then you must say so. If you do have a model release, you must determine if it is valid. Let's say you take a picture of kids playing in a park and their grandmother signs the release. She's not the legal guardian, but who's going to know? Do you wait until you get sued, or do you follow up and get valid releases from the parent or guardian? It's all too easy to "adjust reality," but sooner or later it's going to backfire.

3. Exclusivity. The temptation to make a big advertising stock sale has occasionally caused photographers to mislead a buyer about their ability to guarantee exclusive usage in the buyer's market. If you have dupes of a "great" photograph in four agencies, how can you promise that they won't come head to head with the exclusive you've just sold? And checking with the agencies on the status of the picture after the sale may leave you and them in a very embarrassing position.

Responsibility to Your Stock Agent

1. Accurate captioning. This is important to your agent for the same reasons it is important to the buyer. The additional point to be made here is that your agent is your representative and should not be put in the position of lying for you. If he or she finds out that your captions are misleading or just plain deceitful, you will have ruined not only a sale but an important relationship and may incur legal liability in the bargain.

2. Exclusive contract. If your contract with an agency is exclusive, don't go around the corner putting your pictures in other agencies. Some photographers have been known to use pseudonyms on photos in secondary agencies in order to circumvent their exclusive contract, which can be described as shabby behavior as well as breach of contract. If you agree to an exclusive contract, stick to it. How can an agency represent you if you are undercutting it at every turn? And the end result could be to put all your agency relationships in jeopardy.

Responsibility to Your Models

Whether you are using professional or nonprofessional models, don't misrepresent what the project is and how the pictures will be used. It is especially important to make clear what a stock photo file is. Pay agreed-upon model fees on time and follow up on any other promises you have made, such as sending complimentary prints or tearsheets. Relationships with models are frequently ongoing ones, and it makes good business sense to keep them well maintained.

Responsibility to Other Photographers

Every creative photographer has a personal responsibility to push his or her ability to the limits in order to make the best photographs possible. Your responsibility to other photographers is to avoid plagiarism of their work. This pernicious practice seems to have become more prevalent with the proliferation of stock agency catalogs and photography sourcebooks. These are tempting easy sources for creative ideas, but they are not yours for the taking.

"Rip-offs" of other people's photographs usually fall into two categories—those that are actual infringements of copyright, and those that technically may not infringe but still present problems. Whether or not a photograph can be considered a legal infringement can only be decided in a court of law. Proving copyright infringement can be a long, painful, and expensive task. Even if the author of a work (in this case a photograph) and others think it is clear that another photographer has violated copyright, proving it in court is difficult. The photograph has to be "substantially similar" to the work that is plagiarized. What does "substantially similar" mean? Although each case must be decided on its own merits, generally it means that an ordinary observer would think the two photographs are one and the same.

If a photographer wants to create a photograph that substantially derives from an existing copyrighted photograph, or other work, he or she is then creating what copyright law calls a "derivative work"—which is perfectly legal so long as he or she obtains permission form the copyright holder of the original work.

Even if a photograph is not found by a court to infringe on copyright, it can be so imitative as to financially hurt the original creator and harm the reputation of both the copier and the originator. Imitative photography hurts the original photographer in two ways: it deprives that person of money from selling the original and it hurts his or her reputation. After all, if the imitative photograph is not as good, an undiscerning viewer may attribute the inferior work to the original photographer and make a subconscious judgment about the photographer's ability.

Imitative photography hurts the copying photographer too, in a subtle but pervasive way. While the imitator may be able to derive some income from this type of work, his or her career will suffer because of lack of creativity.

Many young artists at the start of their careers copy the works of predecessors they admire. It is a time-honored tradition for painters to copy the old masters to gain understanding of their techniques. So, too, photographers copy old and new masters to learn how they make their pictures. It is difficult to find a personal style. Style doesn't happen suddenly but evolves over a period of time. For that reason it may be acceptable to copy as an exercise, as long as you understand that you are doing it as a study and don't have the right to any remuneration for the copied work.

To put your name on a work, that work must be fully yours. It must be yours in conception and in execution. Copying another photographer's concept is unethical, even if it is not legally actionable (under copyright law, it is basically the "expression" rather than the "idea" that is copyrightable). When the copying is discovered, it generally lowers the reputation of the photographer who has done it. We have all seen photographs that were well executed but not original and said, "I've seen that one before."

Even without knowing exactly who made the original photograph, we know that whoever made the copy did something wrong.

Some photographers copy because they think that if a certain style or technique works for someone else it will work for them. Good art directors tell us, however, that if they want a certain style they will hire the original photographer, not a cut-rate imitator. Of course, there are art directors who are unsure of their own creativity and who see hiring a copycat as a sure way of getting an acceptable job done. While this happens all the time, it does not enhance the reputation of the copycat or the art director.

One photograph widely copied shows a vacationing couple in beach hats, sitting side by side on white chairs at the edge of the ocean. Their backs are to the camera and their sense of joy and relaxation is displayed by their posture: hands folded behind their necks, elbows out, basking in the sun. Since this photograph was originally published, numerous plagiaristic copies have been made. Sometimes the copy is exact down to the size of the beach hats. Sometimes the color or the material of the chairs is changed to make it "different." In many cases, the new photograph is so similar to the original that they must be compared side by side to distinguish which is the copy.

Another classic subject for copying is the executive at a desk with blinds (or maps or windows) behind. One photo agency reports having received a batch of photo returns from a client who by mistake included eight or nine virtually identical "executive" pictures—from three different agencies. Who ripped off whom—and when?

Does this mean you can't ever photograph an executive as a desk in front of a window? Of course not. Under the law you cannot copyright an idea—only the tangible expression of an idea. Therefore the idea—an executive at a desk—is still up for grabs, but the tangible expression you make must be substantially different from what's been done before. That's the creative challenge.

All too often we hear the plaintive refrain: "What about the art director who sends me a layout with a sketch showing what he wants me to shoot? Then what am I to do?" In fact, some art directors are even so bold as to include a photocopy of a photograph they want imitated.

The answer is to "just say no" to plagiarism. Tell the art director that you recognize the work as someone else's and that you cannot legally or ethically copy it. Explain that if you do copy it, you could be sued for copyright infringement and so could the art director and his or her agency. Your tactful explanation will show that you are on the art director's side by protecting both of you from a potentially nasty situation. Suggest a new approach to the same concept. The photographer should be a creative asset to the art director and help in creating a new work for the client.

Remember that, in the final analysis, copying is detrimental to your creative growth as a photographer. You become like the student who cheats on an exam and passes the test without learning how to solve the problem.

Creating a Good Impression

Photographers, like many other professionals, often have a pressing need and an inflexible deadline and sometimes are guilty of barging into a location, promising the moon to get cooperation, and then disappearing in a wake of broken promises and strained tempers.

We have a responsibility to clean up after ourselves, to return a location to its original condition—whether that means picking up stray Polaroid papers from the floor, removing gaffer tape from furniture, putting pictures back on the wall, or anything else that's necessary, no matter how troublesome.

Creativity and good business sense aren't the only ingredients to success in photography. Attitude is just as important. Every time you photograph in a location and leave a pleasant feeling among those who helped you, you create a better climate for the next photographer who comes along. If altruism isn't your strong suit, consider that you may be that next photographer, grateful for the good will engendered by colleagues who came before you.

And so we come back to our original point: good ethics are good business. Adhering to the spirit as well as the letter of a contract makes for a happy client, one who will want to work with you again. The benefits far outweigh any loss of what you might gain by cheating, and reach far beyond yourself.

These days we are so caught up in a crushingly competitive environment that we may not take time for introspection, for examining our own attitudes and practices. A common attitude in our profession is, "We photographers against the world." We seldom stop to see if we are doing our part—living up not just to the performance part of the bargain but to the trust as well.

Sometimes it's hard to see beyond our own needs, but it is essential that we do—that we look outward and see the needs of others as well. Ethical behavior is not just the right thing to do. It instills the pride in work that is the hallmark of a professional.

All photographers are urged to abide by the ASMP Code of Ethics, reprinted below.

ASMP Code of Ethics
A guide for ethical business dealings, protecting the profession, the photographer, vendors, employees, subjects, clients, and colleagues.

Responsibility to colleagues and the profession:
1. Maintain a high quality of service and a reputation for honesty and fairness.
2. Oppose censorship and protect the copyrights and moral rights of other creators.
3. Never advance one's own interests at the expense of the profession.
4. Foster fair competition based on professional qualification and merit.
5. Never deliberately exaggerate one's qualifications, nor misrepresent the authorship of work presented in self-promotion.
6. Never engage in malicious or deliberately inaccurate criticism of the reputation or work of another photographer.
7. Negotiate licensing agreements that protect the historical balance between usage fees and rights granted.
8. Never offer nor accept bribes, kickbacks, or other unethical inducements.
9. Never conspire with others to fix prices, organize illegal boycotts, nor engage in other unfair competitive practices.

10. Refuse agreements that are unfair to the photographer.
11. Never undertake assignments in competition with others for which payment will be received only if the work is accepted.
12. Never enter commercial competitions in which usage rights are transferred without reasonable fees.
13. Donate time for the betterment of the profession and to advise entry-level photographers.

Responsibility to subjects:
14. Respect the privacy and property rights of one's subjects.
15. Never use deceit in obtaining model or property releases.

Responsibility to clients:
16. Conduct oneself in a professional manner, and represent a client's best interests within the limits of one's professional responsibility.
17. Protect a client's confidential information; assistants should likewise maintain confidentiality of the photographer's proprietary information.
18. Accurately represent to clients the existence of model and property releases for photographs.
19. Stipulate a fair and reasonable value for lost or damaged photographs.
20. Use written contracts and delivery memos with a client, stock agency, or assignment representative.
21. Consider an original assignment client's interests with regard to allowing subsequent stock use of that work by the client's direct competition, absent an agreement allowing such use.

Responsibility to employees and suppliers:
22. Honor one's legal, financial, and ethical obligations toward employees and suppliers.
23. Never take unfair advantage of one's position as employer of models, assistants, employees, or contract labor.

Responsibility of the photojournalist:
24. Photograph as honestly as possible, provide accurate captions, and never intentionally distort the truth in news photographs.
25. Never alter the content or meaning of a news photograph and prohibit subsequent alteration.
26. Disclose any alteration or manipulation of content or meaning in editorial feature or illustrative photographs and require the publisher to disclose that distortion or any further alteration.

The Photographer's Estate: Annuity and Asset

One of the attractions of your stock file is that, if managed and exploited properly, it can earn money on its own—today while you're building it, in the future if you retire, and after your death for your heirs and beneficiaries. So no matter what your age, you should view your stock file as a potential asset and plan for its disposition after your death.

Two conditions support this: first, the Copyright Act of 1976 grants you ownership of the copyright to your images for your lifetime plus fifty years. Second, the result of building a stock file over the course of your photographic career could be an asset that produces income for many years after your death.

How to manage your file effectively and have it produce the most income possible— and avoid creating a tax burden for your heirs (like any other asset, the file can be taxed when bequeathed, sold, or otherwise transferred)—is where financial and estate planning can help. Only recently have photographers recognized the stock file as a valuable asset, and so there are no long-established procedures for handling this asset in estate planning. However, when general guidelines for estate planning are combined with those for managing a stock file, you can get an idea of what you need to do, and the few hours you spend considering this now can be worth a lot of money later.

The Need for Estate Planning

First, take a look at the "Estate Planning Primer" at the end of this section, which explains the terms and some of the processes involved. Quite simply, your estate is the property you own. In terms of estate law, it is generally the property you own at the time of your death. What happens to that property is determined by your will, which spells out what you want done with it upon your death and also names the person who is to handle it—your executor or personal representative. In the absence of a will, state law determines who will be appointed to dispose of your estate, and how it will be disposed of, which may be very different from what you would have wished.

The estate is an entity, a "taxpayer" like any other, and it pays estate and other taxes. The Internal Revenue Service and/or the state taxing authority will come in and value the property in the estate if you have not done this prior to your death, or it may contest the value you have placed on the property. In either case, the executor is going to have to take a position on the value of the property. If there is not enough money in the estate to pay tax, property may have to be liquidated or your beneficiaries may have to pay taxes out of their own pockets. That's why estate planning is so critical. Without it, you may be leaving your heirs a tax burden instead of an income-producing asset.

Making a Stock File an Asset

Once you understand what can happen to your estate after your death you'll see that, unlike stocks and bonds, your photo file requires unique handling in order to produce income for your heirs. Your attorney can interpret the laws for you, and your attorney, accountant, and/or financial adviser can recommend procedures to maximize the value of your files and minimize the tax liabilities for your heirs. However, it's up to you to take the necessary steps—you're the one who knows the photographic business—and these are the steps to take:

- Enriching the file,
- Organizing the file,
- Valuing the file,
- Deciding on its disposition,
- Providing for its management.

Many variables can affect your decision. In creating a file, your interest may be determined by how old you are, how many dependents you have, whether your specialties lend themselves to long-term income, and similar influences. In arranging for its management, whether you're incorporated or a sole proprietor, or whether family members are involved who know your stock and can market it, can all play a role in your decisions.

Enrichment of the file

What is the present contribution to your income from stock versus assignment or other photography work? More important, what type of photography do you do? Are the subject specialties strong enough to produce income without your adding to them constantly? During your later years, consider adding topics that have a longer market life.

Organization of the file

If the file is in disarray, it's almost not an asset, and in fact can create a tax crisis for your heirs because it could be taxed as if all the photographs had the same value (see below). Certainly no one else coming to the files will have a prayer of licensing anything from it unless it's properly catalogued and captioned.

Valuation of the file

This is probably the most critical step you can take in planning your estate. To begin with, if your executor sells the entire stock file before the death tax returns are filed, the sale price will generally be the value used on the death tax return. If you direct that the file be sold, or if your beneficiaries do not instruct him or her to hold the file, your executor is legally bound to liquidate that asset, which means selling the entire stock file and turning it into cash to be distributed under the will. If no buyer is found, or if you have stipulated that the file not be sold, the IRS will require that the file be valued in some other way.

A variety of approaches to valuation can be taken, but a crucial factor is the tax impact of valuation. The tax authorities typically want to maximize the file's value, and hence the taxes generated by your estate. Your executor has to decide whether to minimize the value (within justifiable limits)—and the estate taxes—or to maximize it so as to reduce the income taxes that may be paid later. If you leave valuation to the tax authorities, they may take their own figure, perhaps the same $1,500 lost transparency sum often cited in the industry as a fair valuation figure, and simply multiply it by every slide in your studio—the rejects, the dupes, everything. So you must first clean house and throw out or clearly label and separate dupes, test shots, and extras from those that are bona fide salable stock. If you're a fine-art photographer, this means separating work prints from exhibition prints and, further, the signed ones from the unsigned.

The real value of your file to you is the income it has actually earned for you. But so far no consistent estate tax approach to valuing in this way has been established. One formula looks at use value, based on the idea that an image's value is determined by its actual use, and that a yearly average of five years' past income performance from stock would give a fair picture of the file's value. A factor here is depreciation. (Note that some stock agencies believe that an inactive stock file—to which the photographer has not contributed new material—depreciates approximately 20 percent per year for five years until it reaches a certain level of sales, depending of course on the type of subjects in the files and current trends.)

You can also get an expert appraiser to come in during your lifetime and appraise your work. These are private individuals used by attorneys and the IRS to determine the value of stock files. You might consider a general consultation if your files aren't in apple-pie order, to identify those areas that are likely to have more long-term value and therefore benefit most from the time invested in cataloguing and captioning. If your files are in good shape, you can get a definitive estimate of value as of the time the appraisal is done, which can be a guideline for future work and can also be updated. An appraisal can be of inestimable value if you want the file sold outright or if your beneficiaries should want to sell it.

Disposition of the file

This is simply deciding what will happen to the file—who will get it—which should be dealt with by a will and/or trust instrument. You stipulate whether the file should go to a beneficiary, whether it should be sold and the proceeds given to a beneficiary, or whether it should be held by a trustee.

Providing management

No matter how you choose to dispose of the file, you should appoint someone who knows how to manage, exploit, and protect it, since amateurs simply cannot be expected to handle this very specialized task. If the file is not managed, it may be of little or no real value, just as when it isn't catalogued. There are specific options for this, including using your executors, using an agency, or using a paid private manager.

Using an executor and/or a photographic executor

First of all, remember that the job of executor can be burdensome and thankless, especially on a large or complicated estate. Although executors, like trustees, are entitled to commissions specified by law, you should nevertheless make sure that anyone you name is willing to take on the work. If your executor is not familiar with photography and the business of making images produce income, you should give him or her as much direction as possible concerning how you want your files treated: sold outright as a single asset, sold gradually over a period of time, distributed to your beneficiaries to manage for themselves or through a stock agency, held in trust for a period of time, and so on.

Since you can have more than one executor, you can pool multiple talents by choosing people and/or entities who can contribute in different areas. If you do, consider a provision in your will dividing the responsibilities (and perhaps also the liabilities), so that the photographic executor has one role and the primary executor another. Your photographic executor could go through the "firsts" in your portfolio and any other unfiled material, to select those images that will add even more value to your stock files. This person, or another you stipulate, could also see to the liquidation of your equipment on behalf of your heirs.

Using a stock agency

If you already have a good relationship with an agency, you may want to continue the arrangement in your will. The obvious advantage for your beneficiaries is that they won't have the headache of managing your file. The disadvantage is that they may have less income and very limited control over what happens to the images. You should make your beneficiaries (if they're not knowledgeable about this) aware of the procedures of the agency or agencies that handle your work, and also provide the name of an expert adviser to help them decide the questions that come up and to guide them if the agency closes or decides against continuing to handle the file some time in the future. If you want these procedures to be mandatory, you should include them in your will; if they are only suggestions, they can be in your will or in a separate letter of instruction. At the same time, let your agency know the names of your beneficiaries and instruct them as to how payments are to be made.

If you aren't using an agency and want to make provision to transfer the file to one, you should plan ahead for that too, again informing all parties and naming expert helpers. Many agencies are becoming overloaded and less receptive to new materials, especially if the file has been on its own and they cannot expect new material from a photographer who can be promoted in an increasingly competitive market. If you don't make advance provision, and the agency you stipulate rejects the file, your beneficiaries could be left to fend for themselves after all.

Using a private manager

If you sell your own stock, you may want to have your file in the hands of a knowledgeable manager who can either continue the business or place it with an agency.

Using a trust

Your lawyer may recommend the creation of a trust—established during your lifetime or under your will—for tax reasons and/or in order to keep control in the hands of a trustee other than a beneficiary. You can create a trust, either under your will or in a separate document. The stock file is then held by the trustee, as legal owner, who manages the files, collects the income, and pays the net income to your beneficiaries. This provides the benefits of the files to your beneficiaries while imposing the management and fiscal burdens on the trustee. Like the executor, the trustee may be given the power or the instructions to hire an agency or other outside manager. Also like the executor, and like the stock agency and private manager, the trustee is entitled to be paid for his or her services.

Other options and tax strategies

There are other options, and the following may serve as a starting point for you and your legal and tax advisers.

1. You can give the stock file, or a portion of it, to your children while you're still alive. You can make a gift to your children, or others, tax-free to a certain value per year. A number of photographers have followed this method in order to stave off income taxes now and estate and inheritance taxes later.

2. You can spin off and incorporate the stock part of the business. Some photographers place their stock business in a separate corporation with those whom they wish to benefit as owners. The revenues realized from the stock come into the corporation and are disbursed as income or dividends. Upon your death, the corporation will continue to exist and will continue to disburse dividends and income to these owners, who are now your beneficiaries. In this way, the corporation may not be an asset of your estate and may not be subject to estate or inheritance taxes.

3. You can take a portion of your stock files and donate it, under your will or otherwise, to a nonprofit organization such as a museum. (But check with the institution first to be sure it is willing to accept the bequest, or you'll create a headache for your heirs. Some institutions require a fund for maintenance of a collection.) You or your estate may then qualify for a charitable deduction. Many stock photographs can be considered to have historical value, particularly if a photographer has established a reputation or has specialized in one field of endeavor.

Keep in mind, however, that devices like these are governed by highly technical rules, so it is essential to seek professional advice in these areas.

In any case, it's important to take the matter of the handling of your photographic estate into account now; to begin to think ahead and make all the necessary arrangements. When you consider all the effort you've put into amassing a valuable stock file, you'll realize that planning for the future should be a natural extension of that energy and time.

This section touches on some of the issues you should be thinking about, for your sake and for your beneficiaries. Remember that estate planning is a highly complex business, requiring the professional services of lawyers and tax accountants.

Make the transition period for your beneficiaries an easy one. In many ways, every image that a photographer makes is an extension of himself or herself, and the legacy of those images should be organized in a meaningful way. Allowing stock files to fall into disuse or to become a burden to those who survive you will only tarnish what can be a beautiful legacy.

Estate planning primer

- An estate has two kinds of personal assets: tangible (such as jewelry, car, photographs) and intangible (such as copyrights, bank accounts, contracts).
- When estate assets pass into the hands of another, they are ordinarily subject to tax (although there can be exceptions, such as for contributions to nonprofit institutions).
- There is currently a federal provision that gives each estate the ability to transfer up to $600,000 in assets to beneficiaries without being taxed. In addition, assets that go to a surviving spouse generally pass free of federal estate tax.

An estate plan is recommended by many lawyers and financial advisers because you can reach and pass that $600,000 exemption equivalent surprisingly quickly, especially if the Internal Revenue Service is doing the valuation. Estate planning is a process that includes a number of aspects, such as:

1. A will. This is the document describing what you're leaving to whom. In it you can pass assets directly to beneficiaries or use a trust or other form of transfer. It also specifies whom you want to be in charge of various responsibilities, such as your executor.

2. An inventory of assets. This is a thorough list based on documented appraisals of the value of the assets.

3. Fiduciaries. These are defined as follows:

   a. An executor, sometimes called a personal representative, is one or more persons and/or entities (such as a bank with fiduciary powers) that you name as being responsible for seeing that the terms of your will are carried out, including winding up your affairs, paying various taxes, and collecting and distributing your property. You may also name additional parties as literary or photographic executors to handle those special assets.

   b. A trustee is one or more persons and/or entities (such as a bank with fiduciary powers) that you name as being responsible for carrying out the terms of your trust, including investing trust assets and paying income from the trust as well as the trust property, to beneficiaries.

   c. The executors, administrators (appointed by the court in the absence of a will), guardians (who you may name to manage any property passing to beneficiaries who can't manage their own affairs because of age or other condition), and trustees, are your fiduciaries, held to the highest, strictest standards of conduct for the protection of your beneficiaries. Being a fiduciary is a responsibility that carries with it the risk of being sued and significant potential liability.

4. Letters of instruction. These are sometimes used to convey requests or suggestions to executors regarding particular wishes, such as who should be consulted about liquidating photographic equipment. However, such letters are usually not legally binding, and if you wish to require—rather than merely suggest—certain procedures, you should deal with such matters in your will.

5. Trusts. Trusts can be created by wills or by separate written documents, usually

referred to as agreements or deeds of trust. They are devices to provide management of assets over a period of time by separating the responsibilities for property from the benefits of that property. The trustee bears the responsibilities, and the beneficiaries receive the benefits. Except for trusts created to support beneficiaries, all trusts must end after a period of time.

Future Stock: Gazing into Their Crystal Balls

In researching and updating the information for this publication on stock photography, one question kept arising: what is the future of stock? Or worded another way: what does the future hold for the stock photographer?

To shed some light on the topic, ASMP approached several authorities in the business and posed a variety of questions on which to base the following essays.

The questions covered topics such as: do you think the industry is going to expand or contract within the next five years? What effects will new, emerging niche markets have on the volume of stock used? Are CD-ROM clip art discs here to stay? What is the agency of the future going to look like—will it be all or principally electronic? How are photographers going to have to change the way they shoot? Is there still room in the industry for new photographers? What's going to happen to the price of stock in the immediate future (say three to five years) and in the long term?

We asked the principals of major agencies on both sides of the country, and photographers, to write the following short essays expressing their views of the future of stock photography.

ASMP thanks the authors: Craig Aurness, president, Westlight, Los Angeles; David Barnes, stock photographer, ASMP member; Barbara B. Roberts, president, FPG International Corp., New York; Vince Streano, stock photographer and past president of ASMP; and Susan Turnau, president, SharpShooters Premium Stock Photography, Miami, Florida, and at writing, president of PACA, Picture Agency Council of America.

Craig Aurness

The year 2000 represents many things to many people. Some look to the millennium with fear, others see the year 2000 as just another year. Photographers need to look to 2000 as the year when more images will be sold for digital applications than print.

In the past, the majority of money made in photography required print media publishers with months and years of advance notice before images were seen by the public. Ultimately, the public was paying for the images. Technology is bringing the public in closer contact with the photographers. On-line surveys and studies can instantly spot what a client wants to see. An image usage can be personalized to the client. Single image advertising will be replaced by groups of images, but we'll still be able to compete because of the requirement to conserve digital space and deliver information quickly.

The use of photography in the year 2000 will dramatically increase, but the number of suppliers may be reduced. Buyer's time is valuable and many prefer to view only very well-edited collections. Many photographers hope technology will open direct buyer access which is likely but randomly constructed files will discourage buyers. In addition, regional sales will be replaced by global sources. The net result being that a few very well-managed collections could dominate the global photo market.

Stock photography pricing is going to drop because too many talented, world-recognized photographers have released their images to clip art. Only a few specialized areas will hold up pricing.

The largest issue facing photography is attitude. The trend today is that most photographers are giving up or quitting. There is a trend for photographers to fear the future. The real winners will be photographers who are practical, highly self-motivated, and who study current trends and seek to produce unique images. These photographers will succeed, even against clip art.

Smart photographers need to be digitizing and keywording their best images. Once an image is transferred to electronic format, it can be easily and economically moved down a number of electronic marketing pathways.

David Barnes

The need for photographs has been steadily growing for many years and I can only see this continuing, and probably expanding. The percentage of these pictures has been increasingly coming from stock. This trend, I believe, will continue as well. The sources of those photos is another question.

The future of my own stock sales is much harder to predict. For starters, I must continue to produce material which the market place needs and for which it is willing to pay enough to cover my costs and leave me with a profit. With increasing competition from photographers around the world this means I must continue to hone my skills as a photographic communicator; the level of both the form and content of my work must continue to rise.

Another critical part of this equation is how to position oneself in the market; which photographic subjects will I concentrate on, and how will they be marketed. The first part is easy for me: I have always followed my interests and will continue to do so. The marketing side is not as obvious. There are many major changes in the marketing of stock and it is only a guess where things are going. Stock agencies, large and small, are being sold regularly. New breeds of agencies such as Corbis are evolving and changing the operating standards for photographers. And, of course, clip art discs are an ever-present factor.

If I were starting out in the stock photo business today, I'm not sure which course I would take. However, since I have been involved in stock sales to an ever-increasing degree for over twenty years, I have much from the past which must be integrated into the present and future. This has made for some hard decisions in the past couple of years. I have worked with many different agencies over the years and continue to work with several around the world. This gives me the stability of a broad base. Many years ago I had the unpleasant experience of being strongly dependent on one agency, only to have them go out of business. On the other hand, as the world market place comes closer together it is ever harder to work closely with agencies who are in close competition with each other. There is mounting pressure to work exclusively with one agency. As long as that agency remains healthy and works hard for you, you can do well. As soon as that agency gets in trouble, or is sold to a buyer who doesn't suit your needs, you've got a big problem.

Many stock photographers are marketing their own work quite successfully. Personally, I prefer having the large amount of time this takes to be photographing. Also I am away from home for long periods of time, thus I am not always around to fill clients' needs when required.

I am sure that there will be a continuing need for good photographs. As long as photographers as a group don't give up too many of their rights, or undersell their own work, I should be able to make a decent living as a photographer.

Currently, I see the biggest impact on stock sales as the globalization of the market. No longer can each of us sell into our own regional market as an exclusive reserve. It is easy for picture buyers to have access to photos of the subject they are interested in from many parts of the world. That puts me in direct competition with photographers from around the world. Another change which worries me is the continued concentration of power with some of the largest agencies. Power corrupts and photographers could be the losers, especially if they do not keep informed and have the courage to say no at the appropriate time.

Selling into niche markets is probably one of the best places to be. A good niche is when one has the small supply where a larger demand exists.

I can't add anything to the volumes already written about how changing demographics are influencing the look of images.

Yes, clip art discs are here to stay. Yes, stock will survive them.

If CD-ROM catalogs do become more popular than print catalogs, it won't be for a while. Print is still far more user friendly, and just plain more enjoyable. I find thumbing through a catalog a relaxing pleasure, whereas skipping around on a monitor to find a given image is tedious work. Many of my own images have been put on CD catalogs, with little result to this point.

In time I would expect electronic delivery to become the norm. That will still be several years away, however.

In the foreseeable future, agencies will continue to have most of their material on traditional film. It will take a long time to switch over to an electronic standard.

Yes, there is still room for more photographers in the industry but only the determined, flexible, imaginative, self-motivated, talented, smart, risk takers need apply, at least if one wishes to be independent, which is the best part of this business for me.

In the future, agencies will expect what they have always expected: photographs which will make them money.

Part of the fun of photography for me is that I never know how I will change the way I shoot. I don't think of photos as widgets, but rather as some expression of how I view the world. As I evolve and change, so does my work. I personally feel that once one knows the tools of photography, the best way to improve one's work is to learn and grow within oneself. The more a photographer has going on inside, the more he or she has to communicate and express.

Yes, I expect the World Wide Web to be a viable part of marketing stock, but I have no firsthand experience.

What will happen to the price of stock? I wish I had a crystal ball. There are many forces pushing the prices of stock photos down. If they go down too much, photographers will start to go out of business. If too many producers of a product disappear and there is still a strong need, more producers will reappear, but only if they can sell their product or skill at a price which makes it worth their while. Only time will tell how this will sort itself out.

Barbara B. Roberts

We would conclude that the three big forces that have been affecting stock photography in the last five years will continue to do so in a most positive way.

First, the technological forces. Yes, clip art has arrived and is here to stay and does take some of our sales, and yes, scanners have made it much easier to scan photography. But countering these trends is the fact that clip art introduces many new users to the advantage of incorporating photography into their presentations and products. In our experience, many of these new photography users quickly come to realize the shortcomings of clip photography, i.e., that the photo they choose will also be chosen by their competitor and that not all the legal work, such as trademark clearance, has been done well by the clip art companies. Once they realize this, they quickly find their way to traditional stock suppliers.

Second, the advent of scanners has forced many of us traditional agencies to improve two things that we probably should have improved for the last fifty years. That is, it has lead us at FPG to start bounty hunting programs where money is paid to anyone who helps us capture "infringers." Of the hundreds of infringements that have been brought to our attention since this program was inaugurated, over 90 percent are from traditional uses and printing technology. One must conclude that this has probably been going on for a long time and would have continued undetected if not for procedures put in place in fear of the new technology.

The second positive thing that scanners have done for the photography world is to pull us together in seeing a need for stronger copyright law. This must become a major priority for the industry and with stronger laws one could become even more optimistic.

Another major point about our new world is that computers can make a traditional stock agency more efficient, market driven, and profitable. Some examples of this is how the new technology helps agencies save money on catalog production which lets us distribute more books at the same costs. It also has enabled us to track uses on our photography which allows us to sell our photographs for major exclusive uses often at over $10,000 prices. (This in fact has lead to our average price at FPG going up every month for the last two years, a trend that we very much expect to continue.)

The second big trend affecting the stock photography world is the changing demographics and the very positive trend in America and many other nations to become truly multicultural. The majority of FPG and most traditional agencies' sales are in lifestyle photography. Up until 1990, the vast majority of these photographs were of white people. One cannot stress enough the continuing and escalating demand for multicultural stock photography. Also, this change in demographics has led to a greater dependence on multifaceted and highly targeted advertising and marketing campaigns.

This also probably will continue to lead to a decrease in assignment shoots and a continued increased demand for lifestyle stock photography.

The last big trend for stock is the repercussions of the extraordinary changes in the international arena in the last five years. There are major opportunities for growth for stock photography as the former Communist countries develop "consumerism" and advertising and as the idea of private intellectual property flourishes in place of public property. We have seen phenomenal growth in our international business in the last five years and have opened up a new relationship in a new country just about quarterly. We believe this trend will accelerate. For photographers this probably does mean the best approach with agents is to make an exclusive agreement with one that has a very strong international marketing network.

So these are some comments on the business outlook for stock. But the trend which makes us most bullish is the explosion in quality and personal aesthetic vision in the stock photography submitted to FPG and many other agencies. This is just beginning. We have no doubts that agencies and photographers who clearly understand what they are uniquely about and act on that vision in a quality, friendly, client-oriented way will be assured great success in the next five years.

Vince Streano

The stock photography industry is in the middle of a very volatile period. On the one hand, the industry as a whole is still rapidly expanding. More and more uses are being created for stock images, especially in small desktop printing jobs, and of course the new exploding area of electronic uses.

On the other hand, this expansion is being noticed by very large investors who suddenly see the value of our images, and they want a piece of the pie. Stock agencies are now owned by Bill Gates and the Getty Investment Group. In addition, you have agencies such as PNI, KPX, and The Image Bank owned by large corporations. All of these agencies are trying to win market share, and some are doing so by slashing prices. Stock photography is no longer the trusting partner relationship that existed in the past. It is now big business.

Mix into this equation the explosion of clip art discs and you have the formula for a very volatile market for the next three to five years.

Traditional stock agencies and stock photographers are doing their best to maintain pricing standards that have been established in the marketplace. However, it is becoming increasingly difficult because of the assault of clip art discs and low-priced Internet images.

What the future holds is anyone's guess, but these are my views. In the next five years, the stock industry will go through a major consolidation. Larger agencies will buy up smaller agencies, and the smaller ones that are not purchased will find it difficult to remain in business.

Stock prices are going to continue to erode. Clip art discs and low-priced Internet images will find increasing favor as more and more stock buyers get familiar with the technology. And once we have a downturn in the economy, these low-priced alternatives will become most buyer's first choice.

The one bright spot in the stock pricing equation is for unique images. Stock photography pricing has to follow the same principles as other industries, that is the law of supply and demand. If the photo buyer needs a unique image to fulfill his or her needs, then they should have to pay a premium price. And that price should increase as the price for more common images continue to fall. This is a lesson anyone selling stock will have to learn well if he or she intends to survive.

The only way smaller agencies will be able to remain competitive will be to specialize in a particular subject area, and offer unique images that can't be found at other sources.

Stock agencies will continue to offer both digital and paper catalogs, with digital catalogs replacing paper in five to seven years. I also believe the timing is the same for digital transmission of images. Traditional image delivery systems will continue to co-exist with digital delivery systems, but digital systems will slowly replace the more traditional methods now being used.

The stock shooter is also going to have to adjust during this period. It will be increasingly difficult to earn a living in stock from simply shooting general stock images. Stock agencies are going to demand more and more unique and specialized images from their photographers. Those who don't adjust will be pushed aside for other photographers who will shoot to a specialized agency formula.

Some stock shooters may respond by going back into assignment work, others may find an area of stock specialization that works for them. A third option will be a change of careers.

I can't even speculate what will be the best way for photographers to market their stock for the next five years. Marketing decisions will depend on the subjects and the type of images a photographer shoots. If, for instance, a photographer shoots a specialty that is very much in demand, and that photographer makes good money from a large agency with an international marketing network, then the photographer should work exclusively with that agency.

If, on the other hand, one agency cannot sell enough of a photographer's work to support that photographer, then the photographer will have to look to other avenues for marketing and sales. This could include signing nonexclusive contracts with multiple agencies, self-promoting, Internet marketing, and other avenues yet to be developed.

Stock photography will definitely survive and flourish in the foreseeable future. The big question I have is whether photographers will get a large enough piece of the pie to be able to continue making a living.

Susan Turnau

During the last ten years, the licensing of stock photography has evolved from an adjunct sideline of professional assignment photography to an international industry which stands on its own merit. The demand for images of all kinds continues to increase exponentially: photography, illustration, animation, video, as well as composites and combinations of all of the above. The continuing population explosion (unfortunately) assures that the number of consumers worldwide will increase and that they will have widely varied and expanded needs for visual, rather than verbal, information. This is good for photographers.

Parallel to the increase in the market are the changes in how the image is delivered to the potential end user. We are at the first step of The Digital Age. Within the next five to ten years we will see major changes in the way that the stock industry works. The stock image agency (not limited to actual photos) of the future will be entirely electronic. Images which are presented by photographers in the traditional (read "old") mediums of film or print will be digitized at the photographer's expense before they are included in the library. Clients will place requests and receive images by transmission through telephone or satellite. CDs will go into the same graveyard where 8-track tapes and cassettes are memorialized.

The transmission of images across the world through the Internet or other channels of communication will make the market truly global. Regional representation and multi-listing will no longer be possible when someone in Rome can call an image provider in Argentina, or someone in Los Angeles feels just as comfortable with calling North Carolina as Melbourne, Australia. Rather, we may see niche marketing of hard-to-find specialties which can be accessed by anyone around the world. The agencies or photographers who provide these hard-to-find images will be able to charge decent prices for their work, while large, general libraries of easy-to-obtain material may find prices extremely competitive and spiraling downward.

So, think about who has control over transmission.

Big business is moving in. The media industry, which is now marrying into the communications industry, is taking a long, hard look at "content providers." You have already heard about the investors who have bought into our industry. Whether or not they continue to take an interest in acquiring stock agencies remains a very interesting question. There is some speculation about whether all of the acquisitions which have already been made have ended in happy results, and that some big players may not want to be tied so tightly to their information providers.

Scott Donaton, executive editor of interactive and new media at *Advertising Age*, wrote that what's driving all the frantic search for "synergy" is fear. "Information providers fear they won't have a place to distribute their products in digital form, while communications networks fear they'll build a vast infrastructure reaching into millions of homes and businesses and then have nothing to pour through it."

The fear in our industry is that a few large companies will control all of the images and that prices will go into the toilet. It doesn't have to be that way. The cost of the technology to compete with the megacompanies is coming down continually and may eventually even out the playing field. Companies which have acquired multimillions of images will not necessarily have the edge unless they can also offer quality which can compete with the specialists. The bottom line is that quality will prevail, not quantity, and quality is generally found by searching a variety of sources. Those sources will continue to exist and to compete for the client's business. In fact, the number of sources will grow rather than diminish, overturning the prophecies of doom that have fed the fear of the future of stock photography.

Stock agencies will expect greater quality from photographers. In the last fifteen years, automatic cameras have given every person who has the money to own one the possibility of becoming a photographer, just because, by definition, he or she can make an image appear on film.

Now, photographers will have to accept the challenge to emerge from the pack and bring art to the table. There is always room for talent.

Chapter 3

The Art of Pricing and Estimating

Annette Laabs Paajanen (estimating), Stephen Seeger (pricing and estimating), Emily Vickers (estimating), Richard Weisgrau (pricing)

Fundamentals of Pricing

The pricing of photography assignments has always presented a dilemma for many photographers. Worrying about whether their pricing might be too high or too low, many advertising and corporate photographers turn to surveys of photographers' fees as a guide. Many editorial photographers simply accept the "established day rate," interestingly enough, set by their clients, the magazines.

These methods of determining the pricing structure are almost unheard of in other types of businesses. If they served photographers well, it is only by accident, not by purpose or design. These methods of pricing offer no assurance that they will provide a level of revenue that is sufficient for your business. These methods are badly flawed and should be avoided. Here are the reasons why.

Using a survey result to determine your price is dangerous for several reasons. First, you must have information as to how the survey respondent arrived at his or her response. Is it fact or fiction? Was the statistical base carefully determined? Were the results carefully analyzed? Was the survey weighted by a disproportionate geographical response? Was it weighted with photographers that carry a similar set of capabilities, services, and overhead as yours? Was it weighted reflecting photographic operations such as yours, or lesser than?

In a survey conducted by ASMP, photographers were asked to prepare estimates on certain hypothetical assignments. Some of the test cases used a range of prices that boggle the mind. For example, the range between the high and the low on one advertising illustration placed the low price at 15 percent of the high figure (or the high as six-and-a-half times the low price!). Is there a range of prices in between these two? Which is the "real price?" Which one was right? Which one should you accept as suitable? Would an average of the high and low be acceptable? Let us explore this concept.

Pricing by survey is like allowing your competition to determine what you should charge. Taking an average of all the figures in a survey may well not be a true reflection of what your price should be. There are too many parameters and variables coupled with each project, and each photographer, to rely on a templated price structure. Each project is individual, one of a kind, a custom problem to be solved with your own unique vision and skill, individual problem solving and solutions provided for that individual client. If priced by survey, the unique variables of the project, and your unique capabilities have been ignored. Also, the individual concerns and needs of your client have been passed by. Most important, your own unique set of services (aka overhead structure) and the ultimate value of your work to your client (usage), have both been totally thrown out of the equation. Follow along, and we will take what may be a new view of "pricing."

In a study of editorial photographers' costs in 1987, ASMP learned that the rising costs of business would make it necessary for an editorial photographer to charge $550 in 1987 for the same type of work he would have done for $185 in 1969. At that time, the "day rate" offered by major magazines had climbed to only $350. Now in 1997, with the same cost formulae applied, that base "day rate" survival figure for editorial photographers could top $700.

Years ago, photographers could earn their living solely from editorial photography. With a guaranteed base "day rate" plus fees paid for each placement of their photographs, photographers shooting editorial work could make a reasonably decent living and survive. That changed, attributed to the demise of many magazines, and a change in the pricing structures of those that remained. "Day rate" became a standalone fee, as placement rates at many publications either diminished or disappeared. As photographers moved on to more financially rewarding areas of the profession, the term "day rate" followed, and was misapplied to other forms of work other than editorial.

Now there are more magazines and venues for photography than ever before, and more photography is being used now than at any time in history. Why have prices not followed in an upward trend with use? The answer is multifaceted. One problem seems to be that the magazines have determined what photographers will make by artificially placing a price structure on top of the industry. Another variable has been the use of stock photography to fill the need for content, and with the growth of the stock photography niche of the industry, some agents and clients have treated the photography more as a commodity than as a valuable individualized asset, reducing the price and perceived value of the medium in general. Also, unlimited rights stock CD-ROMs have infiltrated the market, leaving the impression by proxy and misnomer that the value of content is minimal. Nowhere has the increasing cost of business been addressed. In fact, it is being ignored.

Unfortunately, many professional photographers never receive any business training other than what they learn from other photographers as they grow up and travel down the road of their profession. Great photographs are the goal of many photographers, at the sacrifice of all else, and in the quest for these amazing images, many lose sight of the need for fair compensation in order to survive, and for the survival of the entire industry.

The message in this chapter has already been learned by many successful photographers, but for those who don't feel comfortable with their ability to determine their prices, the following material should offer some help. It should be tailored to the individual circumstances of each individual photographer. Each photographer should make an independent, informed, intelligent decision regarding the terms and conditions, and the very survivability of the circumstances under which he or she works, and the fees that should be charged to both survive and prosper.

The Objective of a Business

Just as each photographer has his or her own style that leads to better photographs, each successful businessperson has his or her own formula that leads to better profits. In business, the fundamental equation in every circumstance is:

$$Income = Revenue - Expenses$$

It doesn't take a Ph.D. in economics to understand that your income is dependent upon the balance of revenues and expenses, and exceeding expenses being the key to profit!

Every business has expenses. For photographers, these expenses are centered in three areas. First, there are those that flow from the constant and ongoing operation of the business (administrative and overhead costs). These costs exist even if the photographer never takes a single photograph. The second set of expenses is closely coupled with and flow from each assignment that the photographer takes on (billable job expenses). The third set of expenses covers the impact of doing the volume or type of work required by your clients (an extra large studio space, specialized equipment, equipment wear, extra support needed to perform special services for your clients, and the costs to carry the extra overhead). All of these variables and various types of expenses should be considered when determining how to price an assignment.

Let's take a look at two types of small photography businesses. The examples presented here are not built on factual models, rather, they are designed to offer illustrations of possibility. Each one would have similarly categorized, but variable fixed costs. Example A operates out of an office or home. Example B has an average-sized studio space in a moderately priced city.

Basic annual administrative and overhead costs

	A	B
Rent, office	$6,000	
Rent, studio		$19,500
Electricity	900	4,100
Gas	300	900
Insurance (liability and equipment)	2,000	3,500
Telephone(s) and long distance	3,900	4,200
Advertising and promotion	3,000	9,000

Portfolio samples	2,500	2,500
Office supplies, etc.	800	1,500
Accounting	2,000	4,800
Legal	300	500
Postage (basic and promomotion)	500	2,000
Stationery (letterhead, etc.)	500	1,500
SUBTOTAL: OVERHEAD	$22,700	$54,000
Depreciation		
Office equipment	$500	$500
Computer equipment	800	1,500
Cameras and lighting equipment	1,500	4,500
SUBTOTAL: DEPRECIATION	$2,800	$6,500
Staff expenses		
Owner's salary	$25,000	$45,000
Clerical salary	9,000	17,000
Employee benefits	5,000	8,500
Employment taxes	5,500	9,000
SUBTOTAL: SALARIES AND BENEFITS	$44,500	$79,500
TOTAL BASE EXPENSES	$70,000	$140,000

The previous examples could obviously have things added to them, such as entertainment, professional dues, etc. Some cities require business licenses, personal property taxes, or mercantile taxes. There are workmen's compensation premiums and unemployment taxes to consider, key person and overhead insurance policies to protect you from exposure should you become incapacitated for a short (or long) period. There are regional variables in space, utility costs, state regulations, etc. Each business has unique needs, from the type of equipment to the number of phones. The list could go on and on . . . All these items will differ—from case to case, from studio to studio, and have been purposely left out to simplify the example.

The $70,000 total is the minimum amount of money that photographer A will need to run his operation, maintain his slim staff, and pay himself a basic salary (which every business owner should do). To run her studio, photographer B needs $140,000. Hers is a totally different operation from photographer A, with different capabilities and costs. Each is attempting to meet the minimal expenses to keep his or her business open, to look for business, and to operate routinely. Of course, in each example, no direct assignment expenses have been included. The totals are there even if they never shot a job. We will refer back to these basic costs throughout this section.

Applying the basic costs

We can now see how much it costs to run a basic business, but what should we do with the information? Let's review and consider that fundamental formula:

Income = Revenue – Expenses

Taking the basic costs of being in business, remember that these are a part of the expenses that will be incurred. The remaining expenses will be attributable to specific assignments, and will (or should) be passed along to the clients that commission those assignments. Knowing your basic costs, and adding assignment-related expenses to your totals will provide you with figures that will approximate your gross annual expenses. You will not know your business taxes until you determine your revenues each year, so you will need to estimate them to make a provision.

To accommodate these basic costs in your pricing, which you must do if you are following the fundamental formula, you will have to estimate the number of assignments that you will perform and what type of business you are pursuing for the coming year. Of course, this is an unknown figure for any photographer, but based upon experience in prior years, and projected sales quotas for coming years, a target budget can be originated. Every business should set some sort of budget with accompanying target sales quotas for each year.

If you expect to shoot one project each and every week (except during your vacation period and seasonal holiday slow time), you would pick an average figure of forty assignments per year, shooting for example, fifty days per year. Many photographers will do more, many will do less. Projects might last but one day, others may be more lengthy. Each of these "shooting days" become billable days, the lifeblood of the business.

Dividing the basic costs, we have found for our photographers A and B ($70,000 and $140,000, respectively), by the "average" number of productive days in our year, we come up with a "base rate" of $1,000 for photographer A and $1,400 for photographer B. This "base rate" is the floor, the least that each can accept, and a figure that each will not want to accept less than to avoid taking an annual loss. This, however, does not equate to profit for the business.

There will be some projects each year that will demand extra effort, specialized skills, or expanded visibility that will increase potential revenue. At the same time, there will be assignments that have lesser visibility and "value" to the client, that will decrease potential revenues. Rather than charging this "base rate" on each and every project, fluctuating your rates to the project at hand, while maintaining focus on your annual needs, should provide the annual vision toward stability and providing for your business. However, since basic costs are integral to the overall business structure, a more even application of the "base rate" is a more accurate and realistic view of your business needs.

You could apply the costs to each assignment alone, and not spread them across the number of shooting days. In that case, photographers A and B would divide the base costs by 40 (per projected assignment), and charge $1,750 and $3,500 per assignment, respectively. The problem with this approach is that it makes one-day assignments very expensive compared to multiple-day projects, and is not a true reflection of the value granted to each client. It would very probably hurt your competitiveness in the market. Assignment photography is service oriented and time intensive. But often snippets of your time are spent providing nonphotographic services, e.g., discussing a layout or checking a travel detail. To be compensated, you must figure that time into pricing your shooting days.

Valuation of Photography

Before you can go forward with calculations of assignment fees, and fee structure in general, the concept of the value of photography must be explored. To each photographer and to each client, there is a diverse view as to the actual value of the photograph. The only way to quantify this valuation of the photograph is to create a context through its use.

Years ago, the quantity of the print run was a good barometer of the client's perceived value granted the project. Millions of printed pieces meant commitment by the client to a major campaign, and an ease of negotiating higher fees for the "visibility" of the image. Now, with greater computer power, and more information about consumer demographics and buying habits, a shorter run, targeted specifically by buying habits, could garner the same net results for the advertiser at far less cost but at a greater impact per piece. A short run of a few thousand well-targeted pieces can do better than a blindly massed mailer. Does this reduce the value of the photograph? On the contrary, it increases it!

We must all be educators as to our perceived value of our work, while being good listeners as to the clients' needs, and their perceived value. We must all be good investigators and understand the industry and related costs, to create that context of value for our clients. Use equals value. Context equals value. Perception equals value as well. The balance of context-to-perceived value is a strong determiner of price in the free market.

Calculating Your Base Rate or Assignment Fees

Now it is time to establish the revenue figure in the equation. Revenues come from the fees you charge on the invoices you collect from your clients. Your "base rate" or "assignment fees" may take into account several key variables. Each of these is discussed below:

- Basic factor. This is the share of basic costs that has to be absorbed by each assignment you are shooting or producing, which was addressed in the previous exercise.
- Creative factor. This is the fee for your services as a photographer. It will vary from project to project, depending on the degree of talent that you need to bring to a particular assignment (and your client's appreciation of it), and the uniqueness of the talent supplied. For example, let's say the assignment is to take public relations portraits. This is a job that many of your competitors can do, so you charge for your talent accordingly, and in balance with the market. On another project, the specialized needs are more unique. If the job is to photograph skydivers while jumping with them, there are fewer specialists working in this niche, and the differences between these specialists may be more marked. With less competition and more specialization, a photographer competing for this project may ask for a creative fee much higher than when competing for a more pedestrian assignment. Different projects require different capabilities and call for different levels of talent, expertise, and innovation.
- Usage factor. This is a multiplier which may be applied when licensing usage

rights. Usage rights can be described as the granting of limited rights for those particular applications the client has indicated. Under this variable, the governing principle is: The more the photograph is used, or the higher its exposure, or the more valuable its target niche, the higher the factor. If, for example, the client wants "one-time rights," the factor might be zero. If the client wants "first publication rights," the factor might be 0.5. If a client wants "exclusive rights" (no one else can use the photograph), the factor might be 1.0 per year. If the client wants an unlimited use for one year, the factor might be 2.0 for the first year. Additional years mean additional value, and an increased factor; five years of use might call for a factor of 3.0 or 4.0. Finally, a transfer of the copyright might call for a factor of 5.0 or greater.

There are no hard-and-fast rules for these factors. They are a starting point for negotiating value from your perspective. Business after all involves judgment calls, but it is judgment based upon information, not guesswork. The usage factor may be based on anticipated loss of residual revenue from limiting your right to use the work, or it could be based on the loss of billing revenue from not limiting your client's right to use the work, or finally, it could be based on the true value your client is receiving for every dollar paid.

Preproduction Fees

Along with the fees for each day of shooting and the usage and creative factors, there are other opportunities to earn remuneration from your client for value given and service performed. While each project is unique, all have some form of "preproduction" involved, which is an integral part of guaranteeing the client a quality result and insuring your own product.

For instance, if the project calls for the use of talent, you could either book talent over the phone at the advice of the booker at the talent agency, or you could expend the extra effort and have a casting session with the talent coming by the studio to make certain that the talent actually looks something like the head shot on the composite in the file, or to make certain that the hair is the same length or color.

Or, if the project is on location, checking out the color temperature of the various lights at the factory would help with the problem solving, making the day of the shoot go smoother and quicker, or seeing if those electrical sockets are really live, and not just there to look good—again, guaranteeing the results of the session before it happens.

Or, if the project demands travel, making sure that there is a minivan confirmed at the destination, rather than a "request" through the 800 number that leaves you, your assistant, your equipment, and your client high and dry without a vehicle at midnight.

Preproduction is actually organization and planning taken to a physical level. It is the concentration on details as a means to guarantee your work before it is too late. Categories of preproduction vary by photographic specialty. They could include testing, casting, packing, location scouting, location checks, travel coordination, permit coordination, production meetings, and more. The value given the client is tangible. The photographer is assuming responsibility and exercising control over areas that will affect the outcome of the project. While some preproduction service may be expected by clients, it does take time to perform, and time has value. This service has value and should be charged for in addition to the fees more directly related to the day of the shoot.

Markup Factor

Many photographers charge an additional percentage above cost for the supplies and services that they must purchase for an assignment. This is referred to as a "markup." For each transaction that a business makes, there is time, energy, and capital expended and invested.

The concept of markup is not restricted to the photographic industry. Retail establishments habitually mark up their inventory from 200 to 400 percent, but then again they do not charge fees. Advertising agencies may mark up the invoices from photographers and other suppliers, and most mark up printing and advertising placement rates 15 to 20 percent.

In photography, let's look at film, which has to be purchased, held in inventory, tested and retested, processed, mounted, edited, sleeved, and packaged. Each of these steps adds value to the end product, or ensures its quality. Some film is lost in process through testing, accidents while loading cameras too fast, or by going out of date. Having too much film on hand has never been the reason for missing that perfect last shot. The risk of holding perishable items demands reward. Clients rarely pay for film before it is purchased, so the cost of financing the investment until you are reimbursed must also be considered.

All of the expenses tied to a project may be marked up, as they have all been found, tested, qualified, delivered, and financed. All have experienced "added value." While there are no rules as to which expenses may or may not be marked up, or rules regarding what percentage, it is applied industry wide, and varying from 10 to 20 percent, and from item to item.

If "markup" is listed as a separate line item on a final invoice, it may be objected to by clients, who may perceive it as an unjustified expense, which cannot be justified with presentation of receipts, which some clients require with the photographer's billing. It is ironic that the same client does not require the restaurateur to present his receipts for the side of beef and case of onions when paying his restaurant bill, or the printer to present his receipts for the ink.

Markup is a business practice that must be calculated rather than applied blindly. It involves decisions that each businessperson must make. Indeed, every photographer does not mark up his or her expenses. Some simply absorb the loss for the services rendered, or some prefer to make it up by charging a higher fee.

As an exercise, track the time, capital investment, and other added items needed to add value to a particular job expense. Seeing how much time, energy, and capital are expended to improve or guarantee or finance that expense through the process may convince you of the added value, and provide the information to educate your client to the efficacy of marking up the expense.

Calculating Your Fees

From the theories presented here, you can see that an assignment fee might be calculated using the following factors and formulas:

BASE RATE	the basic overhead you must meet
× CREATIVE FACTOR	the specialty that sets you apart or project difficulty
× USAGE FEE	the added value per the client's needs and use
+ PREPRODUCTION	additional values added to particular job demands
= FEE	for that particular assignment and use

When you consider the amount of organization, calculating, planning, and research that go into garnering a price based upon facts, you can see why some photographers and their clients rely on the staid and improper phrase "What's your day rate?" You can also see that with all the varying structures in each individual business, the diversity of talent in the marketplace, the unique challenges of each project and individual needs of each client, that the term "day rate" means very little, and applying the term does all a disservice. It is far better to base a price upon research and fact, than to rely on guesswork, surveys, or hearsay.

Calculating Your Price

Although we deal with the calculation of the fees first in this section, normally a photographer should determine and calculate all expenses that will be billable on each particular project. Expenses range from film and processing, crew, props, talent, set design, set construction, set materials, construction, historical research, location fees, permits, to travel costs, and more.

Each project will demand a different set of variables to be researched and quantified. Different solutions to the same creative challenge will bring different prices. Variations in problem solving, and the various prices offered, can help to win the job. Over time a body of research can reside in your computer database, providing a template both for price and for thought, reminding you of details in each category of expense as you put together an estimate.

The "Production Report" at the end of this chapter is an excellent way to pin down some of these variable expense items and attributable costs. By doing this first, it will help you determine the complexity of the job, attribute correct costs to each item, and in fact, aid in helping solve the creative problem at hand. It will also be helpful in determining the creative fee portion of your estimate, and allow you to see the ratio of fees to expenses.

After these exercises are complete, you are ready to fill out your "Estimate Form" and send it to your client for approval. Examples of this form can be found at the end of this chapter.

Conclusion

Take one last look at that fundamental business equation.

Income = Revenue − Expenses

As you can see, if you follow the system presented here, all of your basic business expenses should be calculated to formulate your base fee, which is the total projected expenses, divided by the number of days of projected shooting production per year. Shooting this number of days per year (or more) will give the business revenue, which if greater than the total expenses, will grant you business income. If you calculate and incorporate the proper share of administrative and overhead expenses in your base fee, and accurately calculate all of your assignment expenses accurately (including the markups for values added), it is mathematically impossible to take a loss.

Be aware that income is for the business, and is not your personal salary. You pay yourself a salary on a regular basis. There is a difference between business income and your personal income. Profit within your business provides growth potential for the future, and cushion for the lean times, and should stay within the business until you have both enough cushion to spare, and growth to maintain the energetic nature of your business.

If you achieve the goals of making money for your business and yourself, you can spend more energy on the reason you became a photographer— to make great images!

Fundamentals of Estimating

Knowing how to produce rapidly an accurate, detailed job estimate is no longer an option for the professional photographer; it is a matter of economic survival! Projecting assignment fees and expenses within a narrow margin of error can mean the difference between getting the job, making a profit and continuing in business, or going broke.

In all of the following forms of presentation, good research and estimating habits are rewarded, and sloppy preparation is penalized, as each should be.

When requesting a cost projection for an assignment, the buyer may ask for an estimate, a bid, or a quote. These terms are not interchangeable, and it is important to understand the subtle differences between these terms. Each is very different, both in understanding and expectation. Each has a different expression of risk, and a different assignment of that risk. By definition, they are as follows:

The Estimate

An estimate is an advanced calculation, supported by research, of the fees and expenses necessary to perform a particular assignment. An estimate is presented with all variables and contingencies covered, and with the idea that "this is what it would take" to do a top flight job. All fees and detailed expenses are broken down for explanation and the client's perusal.

With an estimate, if the project is received, all prudence and caution will (and should) be exercised in the execution of the job, but (delineated in your terms and conditions) it is understood that there is a 10 percent cap on expenses in excess of the estimate. At the same time, if the expenses are less than expected the savings remain with the client.

The estimate is an expression of confidence and shared risk. Each partner, the client, and the photographer have a shared interest in maintaining a high level of quality while exercising fiscal prudence. There is also built-in flexibility to perform and adjust your performance to the opportunities at hand.

The Competitive Estimate

This is a term that is rarely, if ever, used. It must be discovered through diligent research. An estimate may or may not be competitive. The photographer should always ask if there is anyone else estimating on the project, and if so, then who they might be. This information is extremely valuable, and lets the photographer know the level of his or her competition, allowing him to see if the playing field is level, or if the client is shopping for ideas and solutions, or merely using him or her for a high number. Photographers all know who is who in their market, and their competition's pricing habits. If there are others in the hunt, ask the client what the determining factors may be, whether they are style, problem solving, other capabilities, personality (it counts too), or merely price. This will give you a good read on the client's motivations for calling you in the first place.

If the estimate is competitive, a looser presentation of fees and expenses should be the norm. Too much detail allows an unscrupulous client to pick the photographer's brain, and then pass along ideas, suppliers, and solutions to lesser priced photographers. Detail can always be revealed and discussed after the project is awarded. The "competitive estimate" still should have the same financial characteristics of the estimate, with shared risk and reward.

The Bid

The term "bid" is useful, if at the same time overused and abused. In its true sense, it is an expression of risk taken on solely by the photographer, in a very competitive situation. Here the primary focus of the client is the budget, and the "low bid" usually is awarded the project.

To perform for a client requesting a bid, extremely diligent research is paramount. Knowing exactly what your bottom line is, from actual costs of base overhead expenses to the exact percentage of markup being used, can give the photographer the insight to realize their margin of profit (or loss) on that particular project.

Here, many photographers eliminate details from their estimate presentation, submitting simply a solid number. This is an important concept. A bid is a solid figure, in and by itself, that cannot be exceeded. It is also an expression of profit margin on the project, that cannot and should not be reduced. A bid is the purest form of accepted risk. If the bid is too low, and expenses exceed the margins of profit, then the photographer gracefully absorbs the loss. On the other hand, should the photographer be accurate, efficient (and sometimes even lucky), and the expenses come in less than expected, then the photographer should silently, and gracefully accept the additional profit. All the risk was his or hers. The client was unwilling to share risk or liability, or maybe even show flexibility in approach and execution, and is therefore undeserving of sharing the reward.

All these types of presentations have the same elements (fees and expenses), and it is easy to see how the terms may be used interchangeably. The differences lie in both flexibility and assumption of risk. It is imperative that the photographer spell out what is being submitted. Always use the term "estimate" when discussing a job with the client unless your research shows that the estimate is "competitive," or unless they insist you make a firm "quote," or it is realized that you are competing in a bidding situation. With each of these exercises, treat each differently and be certain to delineate the difference on your paperwork.

The Quote

The quote has similarities to both the estimate and the bid. The major difference is that it may or may not include a process of competition.

The same estimating process is used, but instead of cushioned flexibility and shared risk on the expenses, there is a solid "cap" placed on the entire shoot and a firm bottom line. The figure provided to the client should be round and solid, with fees and expenses lumped together as it is in the bid. Here, as in the bid, the risk and rewards both lie with the photographer.

Once you're being considered for an assignment, you begin a five-part process which ends with submitting a completed estimate. The steps are:
1. Information gathering,
2. Reconciliation,
3. Visualization,
4. Research, and
5. Getting it in writing.

Information Gathering

Asking questions is essential to preparing a concise calculation of job costs. Get used to it. You need two kinds of information, creative and financial. Invariably you will be talking to two different information providers, and often it might sound as if they're talking about two entirely different projects.

Speak with the creative decision maker first. From the outset, you must balance the client's artistic goals with their financial constraints. However, as a creative consultant you must first understand the art director's ideal, and convey your desire to fulfill that ideal.

All creative questions spring from the layout or shot list. Ask to see it, have it faxed, or, ideally, collect it and discuss it with the creatives. Some questions will be self-evident when you see the layout, but also refer to the creative questions list later in this section. Essential questions are: What is the underlying concept of the shot? How is it to be used and for what type of client? Is there a headline? What is the message to be conveyed and to which market? Consumers? The trade? Their own stockholders? Is the shot in studio or on location? Black and white? Color? What format? Does the art director have a regional location preference? Do they want to use professional models or "real people"?

The more specific your questions, the better your understanding of the creative concept, and the easier it will be to provide insightful creative solutions, identify technical possibilities and options, qualify expenses, identify risks, and create a quantifiable, explainable, and accurate expense estimate. At the same time, the time investments, preproduction options and difficulty factors and the creative factors (outlined in the pricing section) can be quantified and applied to the fee portion of the estimate as multipliers of your base creative fee.

From exciting creative concepts and artistic goals, you must now delve into the more mundane but very important realm of finances. Those concerns must be directed to a "money person." Occasionally, the creative person will deal also with financial matters, but more often you will be speaking to an art buyer, an account executive, or a client representative responsible for the budget.

This is the most critical portion of the estimating process. Detailed questions and detailed answers about the creative process make for wonderful, insightful, and unique images but insight to the context of use and value to the client are what will make or break your business financially. Great ideas and dreams of "art" can get inflated. Budgets are not unlimited, and photographers are squeezed often between their desire to create wonderful images and their need to operate a fiscally sound business.

Research with that "money person" can help the photographer to determine the perceived value the client places on the images and the campaign. Understanding how, and in what context the images will be used can help the photographer place a dollar figure on the client's investment. Knowing this, the photographer can appreciate that the images being created are now much more than pretty photographs, they are an integral, if not primary, part of a larger picture.

It is this exercise that will allow you to use the "multipliers" described in the pricing section where the usage and placement questions can be answered and then quantified in the fee portion of the estimate.

Usage is probably the most powerful tool a photographer has to garner revenue. By understanding the value of the placement and the value to the client a context can be created, linking dollar amounts and values transferred, giving the photographer a negotiating tool par excellence.

The following questions are the beginning. The layout will present specific questions. Get the answers!

Creative and logistical questions:
- Is there a layout or shot list? When can I see it (them)? Who is the client? What is their market? Consumer? Trade? Stockholders?
- What is the concept of the photo? The message/feeling/flavor?
- What is the quality of the light? Directional? Diffused? Overcast? "Golden hour"?
- How "tight" is the layout? How much flexibility is allowed?
- What is the headline?
- Is there to be copy or text superimposed on the photo, i.e., does the photographer have to consider type in his or her composition?
- Has the copy been written or will it come from the photo?
- Is this color or black and white?

- Is there a format preference?
- Is this a studio or location shot?
- Any location area preference?
- Studio set building?
- Models—pros or "real people"? Age? Ethnicity? Hair color? Size? Type?
- Casting—who will do it? Photographer? Agency? Client? All three?
- Wardrobe? Who gets it?
- Props? Special effects? Rain? Smoke? Wind?
- Who will have final approval of the casting, props, etc.?
- What's the vantage point? Aerial? Bird's eye? Overland?

Usage questions: Who is the client?

Advertising:

1. Print advertising: What market? Consumer or trade? International, national, regional, or local distribution? Which magazines? Number of insertions? Period of use? 12 months? 18? 24? Size of ad? Proportion of photo within ad? Number of photos in ad?
2. Point of sale: Posters? In-store display cards? Hang tags? Number of items printed? Distribution?
3. Transit posters and billboards: Display context? Transportation terminals? Bus shelters? Subways? Numbers of posters? Size of boards (standard is 24 sheet) Distribution? National or regional?
4. Direct mail and catalogue: Size of piece? Number of photos involved? Where will photos appear on piece? Print run?
5. Collateral: Brochure? Sales aid? Size of piece and print run? Does the client seek a package of multiple uses?

Corporate/institutional (collateral): What is the project?

Annual report? Capabilities brochure? Recruitment brochure? Corporate magazine/newsletter? Executive portraiture? Internal/corporate communications? Public relations? How many pages? How many photographs? What is the print run? What type of printing? Web? Sheet? How will book be bound? Color or black and white? Will other photographers be involved in the project or will the piece be exclusively yours? Will client coordinate or will photographer make contacts? Will client representative travel with photo crew?

General questions:

- What other photographers are being asked to submit estimates?
- Who will be issuing the purchase order and therefore be responsible for paying your invoice? The client? Agency? Design firm?
- What expenses will the client pay for directly? (i.e., some advertising agencies prefer to negotiate terms with and make payment directly to professional models.)
- What is the timetable, timeline, shoot dates, schedule? The drop-dead deadline for delivery of edited film?

- How many agency/client representatives will be on the shoot? What expenses (if any) for these people should be included in the photographer's estimate figures?

Reconciliation

Give the art buyer a detailed summary of your discussions with the art director. If discrepancies exist between creative goals and what the client has in mind, reconcile them before going any further. Suggest a meeting to resolve the issues. This is the ideal solution to avoid misunderstandings, but scheduling problems might prevent it. A conference call is the next best thing to clarify the situation.

In a perfect world, all interested parties including other photographers in a competitive bid would meet, review the layout, and receive the same information simultaneously. Such meetings are rare. However, insist on knowing who else is bidding. An accurate estimate is tedious and time-consuming, and photographers seldom charge a service fee. Knowing your competition will tell you what ballpark you're playing in. If the buyer tells you the client has a low budget and you know your competitors are hungry newcomers, or notorious low-ballers, ask, "Is the job going to be rewarded on a creative basis or is the bottom line the deciding issue?" Usually the answer will be a combination of both. However, if you've been asked to bid as an example of a high-end-range shooter, and know you have little chance of getting the job, you may not wish to devote time developing a realistic cost projection.

Visualization

Once you've gathered all your creative and financial information and reconciled disparities between the two, you're ready for the most important step in the estimating process: visualization. Think through the assignment thoroughly beforehand and try to anticipate every possible contingency in producing a photo shoot. The success of your estimate depends on it.

Imagine being in the studio or on location doing the job from start to finish. The supplies, equipment, and support you will need all appear in this scenario. Make an outline or sketch and ask yourself questions. How many days will this take? How many shots? How much film? Where will I stand to get the shot? Will there be an adjacent rooftop or must I rent a cherry picker? How long will the shoot last? Is the location remote? Are there models and client representatives at the shoot? How will they get there? Where will they go to the bathroom? Will we need a location van or meal caterers?

During this phase, it's helpful to use a preprinted estimate form listing categories of possible expenses or the "Production Report" at the end of this chapter. Even if you don't submit this form as your estimate, it reminds you of details you might forget.

Research

Once you decide what's needed, you must research where to find it and what it will cost. Your most important source of information for job estimates is another professional photographer (ASMP members are ideal sources), who has done similar types of jobs. Don't hesitate to use this source. Most professional photographers, contrary to popular misconceptions, will share information with less experienced shooters who want to present fair estimates. It's in everyone's best interests to share information to help prevent the further decline of fees. Photographers "low-ball" out of insecurity and ignorance. It's up to the more experienced shooters to educate and encourage newcomers. Smart professionals know that they have less to fear from an informed competitor than from those who haven't a clue about the value of their work. There is nothing illegal or immoral about speaking with other members of your profession about any aspect of the business. As long as there is no attempt to fix prices, no collusion to establish fees that eliminate competition, communication among professional peers is normal, healthy, and should be encouraged.

In addition to photographers, consult with other professionals who can provide information in determining your estimate. Early in your career, develop a network of people to work with; it can save time and make your estimates more accurate. A good reliable travel agent is essential, as is an independent location scout/production coordinator. Interview assistants, stylists, prop managers, and hair/makeup artists during your slow periods so you can assemble a crew quickly when required. Film commissions exist now in almost every state and are a rich source of information about local talent, locations, and other support you'll need away from home. Source books which are available in most major markets are quick guides to everything from model agencies to lift truck rentals. Become familiar with your local source books or contact other photographers who will probably be familiar with them.

It is even possible (and recommended) to call the competition, if only to see if the information that was passed along from the client was the same for all. Projects change from conception through execution and, depending upon at which point of evolution each competitor was "enlightened" with the details of the project, the specifications might have changed drastically. Discussions with the honored competition about creative direction, style, shot count, backgrounds, schedule, projected placements, and usages of the images do not constitute collusion to set price. Far from it. Details can be missed by all of us, or not relayed by the client, skewing the accuracy of the set of estimates. These conversations better serve the client who can then compare "apples to apples" rather than just an assortment of fruit. A blown estimate being awarded to an unaware and unprepared photographer is a recipe for disaster for the client, and the entire industry. As long as there is no discussion of, or attempt to fix prices, and no collusion to establish fees, this communication should be encouraged.

Getting It in Writing

Finally, you're ready to prepare the hard-copy estimate. The format may vary from pre-printed to computer-generated or customized-on-your-letterhead versions. The format matters less than the necessary components which must be included. They are:

- Heading
- Job/rights description
- Creative fee
- Expenses
- Schedule of optional future uses (if necessary)
- Terms and conditions

Always date your estimate. If you must revise the figures, which happens often, the dates will identify quickly the original and subsequent revisions. Address the estimate to the person who will approve it and issue the purchase order if you get the job. It's important to have a signed estimate and purchase order from the person ultimately responsible for paying you. Also limit the estimate as valid for thirty, sixty, or ninety days.

The crucial elements of the job description are: what kind, where, for whom, when, how many, how used, for how long? (see sample "Job Estimate Form"). These detail the estimated job and what rights the client has to the final product, your photographs. Each is important to clarify what your estimated figures represent. For instance, by designating New York as the area for which you're estimating travel figures, you've protected yourself in case there's a last minute change to a California location. Clearly, the travel costs must be revised in that case. The same is true for each element—especially the usage information. You must be explicit in the number of photographs, the exact usage, and the length of usage time before further usage must be renegotiated.

In some cases, clients don't know exactly how the photograph might be used in the future, but have learned to apply an overused and misunderstood term to gain ultimate flexibility, and ask for a "buyout." The term "buyout" might, at stretch of the imagination, be termed "an unlimited use, for an unlimited time" meaning "here, there, anywhere, everywhere, nowhere, and forever." In reality, and legally, it means nothing.

Unfortunately, the clients' perceptions of value are lost on this ultimate flexibility; their thinking may be locked into the project and they may be unwilling to expand their thinking beyond the budget at hand. By applying the term "buyout," the client may be avoiding the real questions about researching anticipated needs, or may be attempting to avoid any future negotiations, or, because of a bad experience—such as being sandbagged exorbitantly for a use after the fact—may merely be protecting themselves.

If faced with the buyout phrase, see if the clients can define their needs or their fears and negotiate them, or assuage them. Ask if they really desire a "complete transfer of rights," and then if they are willing to pay in multiples of five or ten. If the client demands flexibility, then educate them as to the value and get them to pay you gladly. If the client is afraid of being sandbagged, offer a schedule list of uses and time for them to pay as they go. Help your clients understand that you are dealing with a transfer of values, not just a hollow catch phrase. (See the "Schedule of Optional Future Use Fees," of the sample "Job Estimate Form").

Following the heading and job description, the body of the estimate includes fees, expenses, and the bottom line. The fee may be described in a number of ways, depending on the type of job you're estimating. Many photographers have replaced the outmoded term "day rate" with the more precise "creative fee" when estimating. This reflects more accurately the role of the photographer as a creative collaborator and not simply a day laborer. The creative fee represents the time a photographer spends on the shoot plus the fee for licensing the rights to use the photograph. Ancillary fees for time alone, such as travel, casting, scouting and prep should be separate line items on the estimate form.

Calculating a fair creative fee is one of the most perplexing jobs in estimating. Since most estimates contain little if any "markup" on expenses, the photographer must remember that the fee total, and not the bottom line, represents the total gross income for the time to be spent on this job. Few freelance photographers shoot every day, and every job entails some time and effort for which the photographer is not reimbursed, such as postproduction editing time. The fee must pay for the photographer's overhead and equipment, insurance and taxes—all costs of staying in business. The photographer must establish a threshold fee for time which covers these fixed costs, then determine the value-added and licensing fees from a number of factors directly related to the photograph's usage. These factors include context, exposure, and time. A photograph used in a company newsletter has less value than the same photograph splashed across a double-page spread ad in *Newsweek*. Twenty-four-months' usage should cost the client more than three-months' usage. To reiterate, your most important source of advice for fee determination is a photographer who has done the kind of assignment for which you're preparing your estimate. Talk to other professionals, but do your own homework as well.

Research your client's budget. Advertising space rates are available directly from magazines or in *Standard Rates and Data,* a resource book in your public library's business reference section. Average costs for copywriting, typesetting, separations, retouching, and printing should be within a body of information you employ when negotiating the relative value of your contribution to the finished piece.

Expenses include everything from film and processing to taxicabs. Whether you're filling in a form or creating a customized letterhead estimate, refer to your visualized job model to insure that you don't leave anything out. Add it all up for the bottom line, which should stress that this is an estimate, not a guaranteed price.

Misunderstandings in business arise when the needs and concerns of each party aren't spelled out clearly from the beginning of the relationship. The terms and conditions portion of your estimate, whether stated on the reverse of a preprinted form or on a separate page should be explicit. Many photographers, especially when dealing with a new client, are reluctant to present the boiler-plate legalese on some printed forms. A less intimidating approach is to use a form, or letter of agreement, covering the major points of rights and obligations.

At last, you're ready to mail, fax, or deliver the estimate to your client.

In some cases, it's advisable to include a cover letter that explains the necessity for some of the line items in your expenses. The letter also gives you one more chance to express your desire to collaborate with the client and agency on your mutual goal—a successful photo shoot.

The crucial determinant of your creative fee is how the photograph will be used. There should be a direct correlation between the value of your contribution to the client's project and the overall budget needed to bring it to final publication. If the end use of your photograph is a full-bleed double-page spread ad destined for multiple insertions in national consumer magazines, the client will be spending many hundreds of thousands of dollars to buy space. Your creative fee should reflect fairly the relative value of your contribution to the overall success of that ad. Don't be afraid to ask in-depth, detailed questions about end usage. Insist on answers before submitting your final figures.

The Creative Fee

The photographer's creative fee for advertising photography assignments may reflect several elements:

Shoot time: This is the number of days required of the photographer to complete the shoot. It reflects the scope and complexity of the assignment.

Media use: When major national advertising campaigns involve hundreds of thousands of dollars in media purchases, the photography gets extensive exposure. The quality of the photograph is expected to be high, the value of the image to the client is high and, therefore, the photographer's fees may reflect these facts. On the other hand, if the media buy is limited—for regional, special interest, or trade publications—the photography costs may reflect a more modest budget overall. The exceptions are specialty areas such as medical/pharmaceutical media advertising—known for especially exacting requirements—or technologically innovative illustrations, regardless of the limited circulation of publications involved.

Overhead: Advertising photographers, as a result of client demands, have typically sustained larger overheads than many other photographic professionals because they have greater requirements for full-time staffing, studio space, and special equipment to complete the job satisfactorily.

Billable Expenses/Production Charges

These expenses and production charges are often billable to the client, if mutually agreed to between photographer and client. The "Production Report" at the end of this chapter provides a convenient way to keep track of these expenses:

1. Casting: A fee, plus charges for research, equipment, Polaroid shots, and a casting director when the photographer has to be involved in model selection.
2. Crew. Includes all personnel required to complete an assignment, such as assistants, stylists, hairdressers, etc. (overtime to be included as necessary).
3. Film and prints. Including Polaroids, tests, and final film or prints.
4. Insurance. Includes liability and insurance specifically required for a particular job, and coverage against faulty stock or camera malfunction. Many photographers consider this a part of their overhead, and show it as a separate line item only when a special rider is required.
5. Location. Includes scouting costs, research expenses, transportation costs, location fees, and permit fees.
6. Props. Includes all inanimate objects mutually agreed to be necessary, such as furnishings, surfaces, food, and wardrobe. These objects may be purchased or rented depending on the situation.
7. Rentals. A studio and/or special equipment may be rented as needed for certain assignments.
8. Sets. Includes all costs and labor for building a set: carpenters, painters, hardware, lumber, paint, set design and research, backgrounds, surfaces, and studio materials.
9. Shipping. Includes messengers and trucking.
10. Travel. Includes airfares, baggage transport, cabs, car and van rental, lodging,

hotel, and meals. Compensation for time spent traveling to and from location may also be billed.

11. Miscellaneous. Includes gratuities, telephone calls, postage, and working meals.

12. Talent. Usually talent (including animals) booked through a professional talent agency are billable directly to the client rather than the photographer.

13. Weather days. When the client has requested specific weather conditions for a shoot or when inclement weather prevents a shoot. Some photographers opt for rescheduling after a restricted number of weather days.

Production Fee Markup

A pre- or postproduction fee, markup, or handling charge may be added to the photographer's invoice, particularly for complex illustration assignments. It covers studio staff time to handle specific arrangements such as phone calls and other myriad details related to the job. It also covers any time lag in payment of advance expenses that the photographer may have incurred.

Some photographers include markup as part of their creative fee, others incorporate it into the price of each individual item that is marked up. Some actually show it as a line item, but this method is more likely to be challenged by clients as an unnecessary expense.

Other Business Practices

Return of photographs: All prints or slides from the take (or the photographer's selection) are customarily returned to the photographer for safekeeping after the client's use. Usually, the photographer's files are the most secure place for this material. Many photographers provide and retain a photocopy of all slides to help clients keep track of them and to ensure their return.

Postponements: A "postponement" is normally defined as a rescheduling of a shoot to a mutually agreeable date within the next thirty days, specified in and guaranteed by, a signed purchase order or assignment confirmation.

To compensate for time lost to the photographer, and possibly lost assignments, a postponement penalty (plus all expenses and postponement fees of crew members) usually equals a percentage of the agreed fee.

Cancellations: A cancellation fee represents compensation for time and effort spent organizing a shoot and for lost booking time. The photographer will probably not be able to substitute another assignment on the shoot day if given notice of only a few days (or less).

A cancellation fee (plus all expenses and cancellation fees of crew members) may be negotiated between the parties and the amount of that fee may take into consideration the cancellation notice given and the duration of the shoot, e.g., within forty-eight hours or seventy-two hours of a three-day shoot or within forty-eight hours or seventy-two hours of a longer shoot.

Reshoots: Spell out, in writing, areas of responsibility for reshoots. Photographers customarily reserve the right to reshoot without fee when they are dissatisfied with the quality of the photography. Ethically, and in routine situations, they often reshoot without fee when they are clearly at fault as a result of, for example, darkroom errors or equipment failures. However, if production costs are high, photographers may consider taking special reshoot insurance. Let the client know up front what your reshoot responsibilities will be.

Changes or variation of any kind for items previously approved (props, layout, location, model, etc.) by the client are billed as full-fee reshoots, minus the usage fee. An appropriate purchase order is furnished to the photographer before the reshoot begins. In addition, a first option to accept or reject a reshoot assignment is usually granted to the original photographer.

In some cases, there may be genuine ambiguity as to whether the reshoot is due to unacceptability of the film quality, or it may be impossible to offer the original photographer the option of reshooting (for example, if the subject is in another location or the ad deadline would be missed). In such cases, it is considered fair and equitable business practice for the client to pay, and for the photographer to accept payment, for all expenses and a discounted fee for the original usage.

Most reshoots are avoidable if the client or representative is at the shoot to approve—with a signature—Polaroids.

The fees, prices, charges, percentages, and terms and conditions on the following forms are provided for illustrative purposes only. Photographers must determine their own fees and charges for each assignment, and the terms and conditions of each assignment must be determined by agreement between the photographer and client. ASMP stresses that all figures are to illustrate a hypothetical assignment.

Job Estimate Form

The following form is a three part, on-your-letterhead form that is an estimate for an imaginary job to produce a photograph for a national consumer magazine ad. Please note the language of the job description on Page One limiting the usage covered by the Creative Fee to one picture, in a specific format, context, and period of time. Page Two is a partial list of optional future uses for the photograph, and Page Three lists the terms and conditions under which the assignment is accepted and will be executed. Note the guarantee against unethical stock sales of job outtakes. *Any fees, prices, charges, percentages, and terms and conditions are provided for illustrative purposes only.*

To: XYZ Advertising

On-location color photography in the New York/New Jersey area for CLIENT Corp. One photograph of "Family at Picket Fence" for use as a double-page spread advertisement to run in national consumer magazines for a period of twelve months from date of first insertion. Optional future uses available as indicated on attached "Schedule of Fees."

Creative Fee $10,000.00
Based on up to two shoot days and the usage described above.
Additional shoot days billed at $3,500.00.

Casting/prep/scout (2 days @ $2,500.00/day) .... $ 5,000.00

Total Fee $15,000.00

ESTIMATED EXPENSES
Film and processing $1,750.00
Assistant's fee 350.00
Location scout 900.00
Scout expenses 200.00
Location fee 750.00
Casting expense 250.00
Model fees 1,500.00
Location van 1,000.00
Stylist 900.00
Props and wardrobe 200.00
Hotel (if necessary) 500.00
Food 300.00
Rental car 250.00
Gasoline and tolls 40.00
Weather forecast service 90.00
Miscellaneous phone, messengers, cabs, etc. 150.00
SUBTOTAL EXPENSES $9,130.00

Insurance $720.90
Liability, negative and co-insurance calculated as 3% of total fee and expenses

Total Fee and Estimated Expenses (without sales tax) $24,750.90

Page one of three

To: XYZ Advertising

Schedule of Fees

The following are fees for OPTIONAL future uses. These fees are guaranteed available when and if you request additional usage of the photograph described on Page One of the Job Estimate.

Extension of original use:
Additional 12 months: + 50% of Creative fee.
+ 30% of Creative fee per year thereafter.

Single page/National Consumer Advertising/12 months .... $ 3,000.00
Double page/National trade advertising/12 months .... $ 2,500.00
Single page/National trade advertising/12 months .... $ 2,000.00
Newspaper/National/12 months .... $ 2,500.00
Collateral usage/12 months .... $ 2,000.00
Point of Sale/National/12 months .... $ 1,750.00
Out of Home/National/12 months .... $ 1,500.00
Outdoor/32 sheet billboard .... $ 1,500.00
Direct Mail .... $ 2,000.00
Packaging/hang-tags .... upon request
Broadcast rights .... upon request

Regional usage: 25% of National per region

Any usage not mentioned above may be negotiated in advance or at time of usage.

Page two of three

To: XYZ Advertising

This is an Estimate only. The final cost may be different. All expenses will be passed on at cost with backup, except film and processing which is a service charge.

Some line item costs may be higher and others lower as we attempt to produce the job within the projected budget.

Any unusual cost will be cleared with a representative of the Client/Agency, if one is available. This is NOT "work made for hire."

All work is Copyrighted by PHOTOGRAPHER'S NAME and all rights not specifically assigned in writing are reserved, including broadcast rights. All transparencies remain the property of PHOTOGRAPHER'S NAME and must be returned no later than three months from date of final usage.

PHOTOGRAPHER'S NAME will not permit outtakes of photographs taken for this assignment to be used by third parties before twenty-four months from final usage date or another date agreed upon by Client and Photographer, whichever is sooner. In addition, PHOTOGRAPHER'S NAME agrees to withhold in perpetuity usage of outtakes by direct or indirect competitors of Client.

No third-party usage of the photographs actually chosen for Client usage will be permitted, ever.

It is understood that this assignment will be to interpret creatively the idea, and not to re-create literally the layout(s).

A Purchase Order and an advance of 50% of _____(expenses) (fee and expenses) are required for an assignment to be scheduled.

Kill Fee (within 48 hours of scheduled start) is 50% of Fee and 100% of all INCURRED expenses.

Weather days on location billed at _____ per day.

_____   _____
PHOTOGRAPHER'S NAME   XYZ Advertising

_____   _____
Date   Date

Page three of three

Production Report

Photography _____ _____

_____

_____ _____ $ _____

Preproduction _____ _____

_____ _____ $ _____

Travel _____ _____

_____ _____ $ _____

Weather delays _____ _____

_____ _____ $ _____

Other _____ _____

_____ _____ $ _____

Casting   Fee _____

     Film _____

     Casting from files _____

_____ _____ $ _____

Crew   Assistants _____

     Home economist _____

     Prod. coordinator _____

     Stylists: hair _____

           props _____

           wardrobe _____

     Trainer/animals _____

     Welfare/teacher _____

_____ _____ $ _____

Film   Editing _____ $ _____

Lab charges   Polaroid _____

     Prints _____

     Roll film _____

     Sheet film _____

_____ _____ $ _____

Page one of three

Production Report

Insurance	Liability	_____
	Photo Pac	_____
	Riders/binders	_____
	_____	_____ $ _____
Location	Scout	_____
	Film	_____
	Research	_____
	Location Fee	_____
	Permits	_____
	Travel	_____
	_____	_____ $ _____
Messenger/	Messenger	_____
Shipping	Out-of-town	_____
	Trucking	_____
	_____	_____ $ _____
Props	Purchase	_____
	Rental	_____
	Food	_____
	_____	_____ $ _____
Rental	Camera	_____
	Grip truck	_____
	Lenses	_____
	Lighting	_____
	Special Effects	_____
	Special Equipment	_____
	_____	_____ $ _____
Sets	Carpenter/painter	_____
	Hardware/lumber	_____
	Paint/wallpaper	_____
	Set design/research	_____
	Backgrounds/backdrops	_____
	Studio materials	_____
	Surfaces	_____
	_____	_____
	_____	_____ $ _____

Page two of three

Production Report

Studio	Build days	_____	
	Shoot days	_____	
	Overtime	_____	
	Strike	_____	
	_____	_____	$ _____

Travel	Airfares	_____	
	Excess baggage	_____	
	Cabs	_____	
	Car rental/mileage	_____	
	Truck/car rental	_____	
	Motor home/dressing room	_____	
	Parking tolls/gas	_____	
	_____	_____	
	Lodging, per diems (est.)	_____	
	Hotel	_____	
	Meals	_____	
	_____	_____	$ _____

Wardrobe	Costume design	_____	
	Seamstress	_____	
	Purchase	_____	
	Rental	_____	
	Special makeup/wigs	_____	
	_____	_____	$ _____

Miscellaneous	Gratuities	_____	
	Long-distance phone	_____	
	Nonprofessional talent	_____	
	Working meals	_____	
	_____	_____	
	_____	_____	$ _____

Model details		NUMBER	HOURS	TOTAL TIME
	Adults	_____	_____	_____
	Children	_____	_____	_____
	Extras	_____	_____	_____

Page three of three

Emily Vickers is a partner in Mason Vickers Productions, which offers full production services to location photographers. Ms. Vickers also provides individual negotiation representation to photographers on an assignment case-by-case basis. She can be reached at (609) 466-0911.

Chapter 4

Negotiating

Richard Weisgrau

Simply stated, negotiation is the process of balancing the interests of two or more parties in a way that is acceptable to all of them.

Photographers and their clients have both complementary and competitive interests. Both parties need a photograph or series of photographs that fulfill a need, yet are likely to have different views on compensation and rights.

Disagreements over such matters have ended many photographer/client relationships and, in a business sense, that is costly. It is more expensive and time consuming to acquire a new client than it is to retain an existing one. To retain clients, you must be able to preserve the relationship by settling disagreements whenever possible.

Disagreements can be resolved through reasonable and appropriate communication—or negotiation—between you and your clients. Through proper negotiation you can reach agreement, enhancing the complementary interests you have with your clients, while reducing the competitive interests.

The Skill of Negotiation

Good skills are the key to a successful negotiation. A good self-image is important. A confident negotiator can communicate verbally, organize thoughts, and visualize outcomes. Photographers visualize outcomes for a living, so visualizing a negotiation taking place and the desired outcome of that negotiation shouldn't be difficult.

- Negotiation involves making important decisions. Some photographers have trouble making decisions when they get into business situations, but the process is the same whether you're trying to solve a photographic problem or a negotiation problem. Just as important is being able to live with your decisions. Even if you make a bad decision, you must make good on the agreement in order to maintain your reputation as a negotiator and a businessperson.

- Good negotiators try to keep harmony. It's much easier to negotiate in a friendly atmosphere than in an adversarial one. Negotiations become more adversarial when resolving a disagreement after the fact. Try to avoid that by having good harmonious relations and negotiations up front, before the work is started.

- Good negotiators are reflective. Try to be analytical in your negotiations. Look deeply into the issue, because what you hear at first is not always correct. Explore the "if-then" possibilities. If you do this, then what will they do? Try to anticipate all the alternatives.

- Good negotiators are flexible. Be ready to shift your position without changing your principles. Be flexible on those items where there is room for discussion. Fees, general range of rights, timing of the shoot, and the terms and conditions under which you will shoot are some issues where you can be flexible as long as you don't jeopardize the fundamental policies of your business.

- Good negotiators are empathetic. Try to relate to what the other side is feeling. You have to understand the other party's problems before you can deal with them.

- Good negotiators are fair-minded and option-oriented. If you try to get the best of every deal, eventually you will lose your clients because they always feel beaten down. Basically, a negotiation is simply presenting options until there are enough on the table to resolve the disagreement.

- Good negotiators are good listeners. Most people think of good negotiators as simply good speakers, but more often they are good listeners. It is from understanding the other party's position that you create options to settle any impasse. Also, with good listening come good questions. Answers to properly asked questions give you insight into what options might solve a disagreement.

- Good negotiators know the value of what they do. This is most important. If you do not know or believe in the value of your work, then you can never obtain it. You must believe that what you do has value, understand that value, and be able to justify it.

Around the world, photographers are one of the most valuable links in the communication system. If photographers started saying "no" to bad deals, would clients stop buying photographs? Of course not. They are extremely important to them. Therein lies the photographer's strength and value.

Consider that in some major magazines a double-page spread is about $200,000 for a four-color page. Even with frequent insertion discounts, the amounts are staggering compared with the reproduction fee charged by a photographer for that same space. If, when you're asked to quote a price for an ad in a major magazine, you know just what it's costing the client for the space, you'll feel more comfortable negotiating a fair fee.

The Necessities of Negotiation

An absolute necessity for any negotiation is that the person on the other side be willing and able to negotiate. Some people are incompetent at the process or simply refuse to negotiate. You cannot negotiate without a willing and capable counterpart.

You must be a bit of a salesperson when negotiating in a business environment. Sales is the most important division in your company, even if you are a one-person operation. If there are no sales, there is no work, no invoices, no revenues, and no income. If there is no income, you are out of business.

Two of the most vital and universal steps in sales are answering objections and closing the deal. When you consider negotiations as an extension of your sales effort, those two steps become more than necessities. They are absolutely critical.

The Wants and Needs of Negotiation

Disagreement destroys relationships. If you destroy enough of them, you're out of business. Disagreement results from having different wants, and can be resolved only through negotiations aimed at satisfying needs. Wants and needs can be demonstrated simply. I want a Leica. I need a camera. I want a Mercedes. I need a car. There is a spread between wants and needs. Your wants may be the price you ask for your services. Your needs are your bottom-line price, the one beyond which you cannot go. The spread between wants and needs is the negotiable range of any issue.

When you identify the wants, identify the needs, and move the wants closer to the needs; that's the process of negotiation.

The Stages of Negotiation

There are four stages in a negotiation. The first is the analytical stage, when you assess the ramifications of the problem or disagreement. The second is the alternative stage, when you develop and present alternatives to solve the problem. The third is the acceptance stage, the process of looking at alternatives and coming up with those that are acceptable to solve the problem. Finally, the fourth step is agreement, where you sign off on the deal.

Even though a negotiation might take five minutes on the phone, all of this happens. You may not realize it because it can happen with great speed. After you've done it many times it becomes almost routine.

Within the entire process are three aspects to a negotiation: the methodical, the psychological, and the substantive. They will be discussed in detail throughout the rest of this chapter.

The Methodology of Negotiation

The methodical aspect includes things that a negotiator has to know and the tactics to be used. It centers on asking questions—who, what, where, when, why, and how.

Who will be the negotiators? You? An art director? An art buyer? A communications director? Can you clearly identify the person with whom you're going to negotiate? Are they authorized to negotiate, or are they simply carrying your message to another person who is the behind-the-scenes negotiator making all the decisions?

When will you negotiate? Right now? Next week? Choosing the time you negotiate has a great deal to do with your ability to get your needs met. Many negotiations for photography occur immediately after some creative discussion. You sit down with the buyers of the photography, talk about the assignment and, together, build a photo shoot or sequence of images. Your creative juices are flowing. You're feeling very giving. Then it's time to talk about money and rights. But now is the wrong time. You're in the right frame of mind to create, but the worst frame of mind to negotiate. You need to change hats, be more analytical and think about your needs. It's very easy to "give away the store" when you negotiate immediately after a creative session.

Buy some time. Try saying, "This is great. I'm glad we have arrived at what we want to do. I know it's time to talk about how much this job is going to cost and how we're going to approach this whole deal, but before we do that I'd like to have a couple minutes to get my thoughts in order."

Get psyched up for the negotiation. That doesn't mean getting angry or mean. It means getting determined that since you're trying to make a living, you need to meet your own needs.

Where will you negotiate? Many negotiations happen on the phone. The nice thing about a phone is you have the other person's undivided attention. You're talking right in their ear.

If you're going to negotiate in person, be sure to get the client away from possible distractions. Imagine this setting. You're in an art director's office or cubicle, with other offices all around you. As you talk, there is a lot of hustle and bustle. You're about to close a good deal when someone sticks their head in the door and says, "Listen, we just got a call from the photographer who shot that job last week. All the film is ruined. You're going to have to reshoot." The art director is crushed. He's desperate, and has totally lost contact with everything you've said. He doesn't give a damn about this job for the moment. You've lost all your momentum, simply because the art director was accessible to other people.

If you want to sell somebody in a negotiation, isolate them. Take them across the street to the park and buy them a hot dog. Ask if there is a conference room where you can meet. Do whatever it takes to avoid interruptions.

Why are you going to negotiate? What do you want out of this negotiation? You know you'll negotiate fees and rights. You can also negotiate money, usage, time, advances, and purchases. In fact, anything of value is fair game in a negotiation.

How can you negotiate time? Time has a value. You're booked on Wednesday and you're not about to cancel that job. You say, "Well, I'll tell you what. I'm already booked into another job on Wednesday. If I can do it on Tuesday or Thursday, it'll cost $2,000. If you really need this on Wednesday, it's going to cost $3,000. The reason is, I've got to keep everyone working for sixteen or eighteen hours. I have to bring in extra help or go into overtime. Everything costs more at that point. If you can do it a day earlier or a day later I don't incur those extra fees." You're not negotiating the fee, you're negotiating for a different day, for time.

What do you know about the agency or firm? Do they make unreasonable demands? Do they negotiate? Are they a "take-it-or-leave-it" company? If you haven't worked with the firm, try to find people that have and ask them what they know about the art director, art buyer, or communications director. What is their style? Are they tough on certain issues? Chances are, if they are tough on others, they'll be tough with you. The more you know about the job and the client, the better your position in dealing with them.

What do you know about the budget? Every job in the world has a budget. Try to find out what they have projected the photography will cost. Don't ask, "What's the budget on this?" That indicates you accept their budget as a limit. Maybe they have done their homework wrong. Their budget may not be adequate. Try asking, "What kind of money have you projected for the photography costs on this project?" Projections are not budgets, only educated guesses. A budget is a target, but it's their target, not yours.

As you accumulate this information, whether it's over a period of minutes or days, keep notes on it. There are many details you need to know, especially if you're talking about a production shoot. Be thorough. For a checklist of production details, refer to the "Production Report" form at the end of "The Art of Pricing and Estimating" chapter.

What is the worst-case scenario? Ask yourself, what is the worst thing that can happen if you don't get this job? Will you be out of business or simply have lost a job? Can you find other work? Once you know the worst-case scenario, you can see if the next best alternative—finding other work—makes the loss less painful.

The bottom line is this: There is no such thing as a free lunch. You're not going to get anything of value from the client unless you perform for it, and you're not going to give up anything of value unless they pay for it. That's a fundamental concept of good business.

After you go through this process of analyzing what the job is about and what your wants and needs are, set some goals for the negotiation. These are:
- Envision the outcome.
- You're going to get X-number of dollars for so many days of shooting.
- You're going to get so much money in advance.
- You're going to grant certain rights.

Write those goals on a piece of paper. That will prevent you from changing your goals too early. Any goal that is not in some fixed form can change instantly and at will. Any goal that is written down has to be actively changed. If you change it, know why and change it on the paper.

Developing Mindset and Techniques

The psychological aspect is one of the most important factors in negotiation. Basically, there are two types of negotiators: hard and soft. Hard negotiators stare you in the face and intimidate you. They're tough. They make demands and don't cut you a break. Soft negotiators are laid back, talk softly, are friendly, accommodating, and understanding. Many people fall between those two extremes. A good negotiator can go back and forth, being hard or soft when called for, often following the lead of the other person.

You may encounter a variety of styles people take when negotiating. Here are a few of them.

"Intimidators" are very effective people because they often get everything they want. When they're allowed to be intimidating, they'll push you into a corner. Again, the way to counter is to mirror their language. If they're talking in your face, talk right back in their face. A lot of people are afraid of that. When somebody comes on really strongly, they think of that person as powerful. You have to understand that they're just people like you and their style has nothing to do with who they really are. It's just their style and style doesn't resolve anything.

The "noncommittal" character is difficult to get to answer you. To deal with this type of person, present your issue in black and white. Say, "The question I am asking you is, 'Will you give me one third of the expenses in advance? Can you answer that question for me?'" Then, don't let it go. Keep asking for the answer to the question until you get it.

When dealing with "liars" and people who have truly bad memories, keep a pad of paper and keep making notes. You'll have the other person thoroughly convinced that you have a record of everything about the conversation. That helps to improve their memory because they know you have recorded all the details.

If you know a person is an absolute liar, don't do business with them. Eventually, a liar will get you. If, however, you find yourself dealing with a liar, after you make all your notes, read them to the person. Say, "I just want to review this whole agreement with you."

Some people need detail, others do not. You'll make your best agreements with people if you deal with them the way they like to be dealt with. If the buyer is a person who likes a lot of details about how everything is going to happen, what everything costs, then you have to be prepared to give those details. If they don't want to be bothered with details and only care about one thing—how much is this job going to cost?—don't bore them with the details. Get to know your client. What are their expectations in terms of the information they want you to present? If you don't know, assume they want less information. You can always provide more if asked.

People perceive that negotiation is a power process. Granted, power enters into it at times, but it isn't always a determining factor.

There are different types of power.

Inherent power is the power of money or office. If you have two or three million dollars in the bank, you can go out and take any negotiating stance you want. You would not get a lot of deals but you wouldn't care because you have a lot of money. You have a lot of power because you don't need the money.

There is nothing you can do about inherent power. If you've got more money than they have, there's nothing they can do about it. Likewise, if your client has more money than you, there's nothing you can do about it. Ignore it, it doesn't make any difference.

The power of office is something you have to deal with. Photographers often express concern that they are going to have to negotiate with the chief art buyer, the VP of sales or some other "title." The person with title can select whomever they want. But they're talking with you. That's your power. It matches theirs. You can't do anything about it, so don't let the power of office bother you.

Flexible power shifts from job to job and negotiation to negotiation. You never can tell what it's going to be. If the client calls at noon, needs a shot at 4:30 the same afternoon and doesn't know any other photographers in your area, you have the power. However, if a person needs a shot in thirty days, you're one of twenty-five people they have in mind, and it's a picture of a clothespin on a piece of seamless paper, you're not too powerful.

Power also shifts with the amount of time there is to get a job done. Remember, your client has a deadline. Until you get the job, you don't. The power of time is generally on your side. Time will frequently work to your advantage. You know how long it takes for them to select and work with a photographer. If there isn't time to get another photographer, you're obviously in a stronger position to negotiate a good deal.

The power of competition is popular among buyers. They remind you that they can get another photographer to do the job. You have heard it countless times, in many situations. The first thing you have to ask yourself is, "if they want another person to do the job, why did they call me?" They must have selected you for a reason. Chances are, they didn't select you because you're just one of the crowd. You were selected. That is a grant of power. If they wanted the competition, they would be talking to them, not to you.

Photographers can use competition as a tactic, too. If someone calls you to discuss a job for next Thursday, you might reply, "I've got something planned for Thursday, but it's not a done deal. Tell me what it is you're working on. I might be able to hold off." You've told them that they have competition. Don't hesitate to use the power of competition. But choose your words carefully. Instead of saying, "I have another job." Say, "I have something planned." It may be a dentist appointment or a walk in the park, you don't have to say.

The strongest power is ultimately yours. It's the power to say "no." It stops everything. When you say "no," that's the end of it. You always have the power to say "no" when a deal is bad for you.

Jobs are put out on bids to weaken your position through price competition. When facing a bid, ask "How many photographers are bidding this job?" Explain that the bid will require a great deal of analysis, and it could be a waste of your time if they have six other people also bidding. Talk about quality and price. If you discover that price is the main criteria of their bidding process, explain that you definitely need to know who you are bidding against, because if the list includes someone you know is a lot lower in price, you might opt out of the bid.

There are techniques you can use to develop a subtle kind of power. Here are a few:

Woo your clients with extra service. You may ask, "Would you like me to have my assistant pick you up at your apartment on the morning of the shoot?" You're already making the job easier for them. That's salesmanship.

Show strength in your commitment. If they are having trouble deciding whether to hire you, you might say, "I can see that you're worried about this. Maybe you're thinking my price is too high. If I don't deliver what I promised, you are going to look bad. Here's a list of my clients and their phone numbers. I will pay for the phone calls. If you get one person on that list who tells you I don't deliver what I say, when I say, I'll do this job for half the price I just quoted you." You're making a commitment, providing the proof. You're willing to take a risk in order to demonstrate your reliability.

Ultimately, the element of risk comes into play in the power game. Business is a calculated risk. You make decisions based on your ability to take risks. Of course, risk should always be proportional to gain. You have to think about where you want to come out and take the risk accordingly.

In the psychology of negotiation, risk can lead to fear and panic. Here is a scenario: You're feeling good about your business and your work. Suddenly, the phone rings. A client has an assignment for you. Now, everything is different. The pressure is on. You're scared. The client is asking you to do a job, and you know you're going to have to give them a price. What if you're wrong? What if you don't get the job? In just a few minutes, your whole disposition has changed 180 degrees. You've panicked.

Panic comes from fear. There is nothing wrong with being afraid. Everyone experiences it at times. What's important is learning to confront fear. Yes, people do go out of business by saying "yes" to bad deals. However, when somebody offers you a bad deal, you can overcome the fear by understanding that you're not going to go out of business by saying "no." You overcome the fear of saying "no" to bad deals and the fear of taking risks by having enough sales opportunities so that, simply, on the law of averages, you will do enough business to enable you to keep working and keep making a profit.

Some Negotiation Tactics

If the most powerful word in negotiating is "no," the second most powerful word is "yes." Salespeople say that you should never ask a question that can be answered "no." Don't ask if you can have the order. Ask how many pieces they want to order.

Try saying something like this: "In the past jobs we've done for you, we have always done our best to satisfy your clients, and I think we've accomplished that. Everything we do for you is delivered on or before the deadline, and within budget. Obviously, you want us to continue that record. We can do this new job for $5,000 plus expenses. We'll have it wrapped up in two days. Do you want us to shoot on Tuesday or Wednesday?"

First you established some "yes" thinking, then you told them you're doing the job and asked them what day they'd like you to shoot. Don't just ask, "Do I have the assignment or not?" Make the assumption that you have it. Make it hard for the other person to say "no."

Here are some other popular negotiating tactics:

A red herring. This is usually an irrelevant or very minor point that you bargain for up front, in order to have it later when you need it. When negotiating, you often need to have something to concede, or trade, in order to match a concession by the other person. You trade the red herring.

An example of a red herring being used in an assignment negotiation can be illustrated best by this hypothetical scenario.

Your goals in the negotiation include receiving an advance on expenses. The client is not inclined to give advances, and you have learned this from research or from prior experience.

The job calls for casting and hiring two models, whose fees will amount to $1,500 for the day. Normally, you would front the money for the models and pass the expense on to the client in your invoice. The job will have expenses of $4,500 and you would rather not carry that amount.

You set up the red herring in the negotiation by making the point (to the client) that you want them to pay the models directly. They (as expected) do not want to do this. After some discussion you suggest that the matter be put aside to be resolved later. Keep in mind that this example assumes you are not concerned, in fact, about paying those fees and seeking reimbursement. Your goal is simply to get some money up front if you can.

Later, after the rights, fees, and expenses have been agreed upon, you ask for an advance on expenses. Again the client is inclined to say "no" and does.

You don't accept the "no" (graciously) and point to the fact that the direct payment of models has not been resolved. And it ($1,500) combined with other expenses ($3,000) represents $4,500 that you have to finance. Worst of all, the model fees will have to be paid quite promptly—stressing your cash flow while you wait for the client to pay your invoice.

Then you ask why they won't pay the models directly. Let's say they object to the need to set up another vendor record and payment on the job. You in turn—with empathy for the bookkeeping hassle—suggest a solution.

You offer a compromise: You will drop your demand for direct payment of the models, if they give you an advance on expenses. This way, your cash-flow problem is eased and their one vendor need is accommodated. So, each of you has satisfied a need at no added cost to the job, and no added hassle.

You have traded off your red herring for a gold fish!

Limited authority: Frequently imposed on you by the other side, this is a difficult tactic to handle. When the person you are negotiating with is not empowered to make a deal, they take your offer to someone else who refuses it. This forces you to rework the deal, even if it's already at your bottom-line price.

One way to respond is to put yourself in an equally powerful position. Say something like this: "Look, you have limits on what you can do. So do I. I won't sign off on this deal until you get an approval. I reserve the right to ask for changes if you can't get the deal we agree on approved." Now you are negotiating on the same ground.

How do you find out if a person has limited authority? Just ask. "If you and I can reach an agreement on this job today, do you have the authority to sign?" If the answer is no, you can try, "I'd like to have the opportunity to speak with someone who has the power to sign on this offer. Can I speak to that person?" If the answer is still no, respond, "In that case, I reserve the right to withdraw any part of the deal on the table."

The tactic of silence: Being able to remain quiet is a must for the successful negotiator. Listening is an art. You can't listen while you're talking. The person who asks a question and waits for an answer is in control. If you listen to the answer, the opportunity will arise to develop an option. If a person wants a buyout, ask "Why do you want a buyout?" Then wait for the answer. If you don't get the answer, repeat the question.

The tactic of why: Never be afraid to ask "why." Good businesspeople usually respect your interest in their concerns and their reasons. Ask "why." If you understand their problems, you're better able to help them find a solution. You may not find a solution, but at least you show a sincere interest in their problems.

The good-guy, bad-guy tactic: Let's say you send your rep to drive the hardest deal possible, but you also want the job badly. You sit in on all the discussions. Your rep and the buyer reach an impasse, but you know the job meets the bottom line. The rep is pushing to get something, and you say, "Look, I don't normally do this, but we haven't worked a lot with this client, and I really want to show them what we can do, so I'm going to interject here and say we'll do it for their price."

The reverse tactic: Another tactic is to plead "limited authority," saying that you have to consult someone else (such as your partner, business manager, or the photographer if you are acting as an agent) to lower the price but that, if you take it for review, all previous offers are withdrawn. The person with "authority" could either lower the price or insist on something higher than your last offer—it's the buyer's gamble.

Flinching: Giving a visual signal to the other person is a nonverbal way of saying "no." This is a common tactic to let people know that you can't really handle what you are hearing. It can be unnerving to the other party.

The broken record: In this tactic, you keep asking for what you want until you get it. "I really have to have an advance. I know you said I can't have an advance, but I really have to have an advance. You don't want to give me one, but if I don't have an advance it may jeopardize the quality of this job. I must have an advance." They may give you the advance just to shut you up.

Nibbling: Nibbling isn't getting a little bit at a time until you've got the job. It's done after you've made the deal. While negotiating, you may discuss various elements, but the whole deal is wrapped up at one time. You get the job. You agree on price and rights. Then you nibble. You might say, "How about half the expenses in advance on this one?" Why wait until after the original deal is struck? Because if it's a sensitive point, you're better off waiting instead of risking the whole deal over it. You nibble. If they say no, you drop it, but you still have the job.

Funny money: This is reducing something to terms of dollars so your client can understand how feeble an offer is. An editor says, "We want to shoot this job for $400." You say, "Wow, I'm spending a half day to come here to see you, then get back to the studio and make some notes. Then I've got half a day to get equipment prepared and film tested. I'll travel for half a day and shoot for a full day. I'll spend one more day bringing film to the lab, picking it up, and editing it. There will be another half day of administrative time, bookkeeping, invoicing, and phone calls. That's four days of work. You're offering me $400. That's $100 a day. Who can work for $100 a day?"

When you break the money down to understandable units of time, you show the client how the money doesn't fit the time and effort involved. Always be prepared to present facts to back up your position.

Being outrageous: It can be a good tactic on occasion. Here's an example. The client says, "I can get your competitor to do this for that price. Heck, I can get anybody to do it for that price." At that point, pull out a list of competitors, complete with their phone numbers, and say, "I always want to be of service to people who I think are going to be good clients. If you really don't feel I'm the person for this job, here is a list of my competition. I know I'm the best person for this job, but if you don't agree, I can't argue with you. I've just failed to convince you and that's my fault. However, if you want to call my competitors, I've made it easy for you." That's outrageously calling their bluff.

Trial balloon: This is an excellent tactic. Use it to find out something without making a commitment or putting your client on the spot. For example, someone just told you all about a job and you want to get $5,000 for it. Instead of saying it will cost $5,000, you say, "What would you say if I told you this job was going to cost $5,000?" You didn't say it cost $5,000, you said "what if." By making your fee or proposal a "what if" question, you minimize the risk and leave yourself a chance to recover from it. You haven't presented it as a fact, but rather as a trial. Another example of a trial balloon is to say, "How would you feel if I asked you for all the expenses in advance?"

Avoid signs of weakness: People who don't look you in the eye when they talk to you are disturbing. Likewise, when you want to negotiate with a client, look them in the eye and talk to them. It's not a who-blinked-first contest. When you stand up and talk to a person, stand up straight and talk to them. Don't lean up against the wall like you need support and are about to fall over. Look confident. Why? It's psychological. Your image is important. These are signs of strength. Slouching in a chair, leaning over a table, or burying your head in your hands are all signs of weakness.

Don't couch your words: Don't be afraid to say it the way it is, and don't send out confusing signals. For example, if you don't like what they offer, and you have an option, tell them. Say, "No, that's really unacceptable to me, but let me offer this as a possible alternative." If it's unacceptable, it's unacceptable. Don't spend twenty sentences saying no. Just say no and offer your alternative. Also, don't say "yes, but." It's a confusing signal. It doesn't mean yes at all, it means no or maybe.

What do you do when a client refuses to negotiate, when they say take it or leave it? First, don't see it as complicated. It's the simplest situation in business. All options and alternatives have been reduced to two. Take it or leave it, you have to choose. If it really is a take it or leave it offer, does it meet your bottom-line needs? If it does, take it. If it doesn't, leave it.

Should you automatically accept that a deal is take it or leave it just because someone says it is? No, not until you test it. Just as photographers get purchase orders from agencies that have a lot of verbiage on the back which seems to be set in stone yet is negotiable in most cases, the take it or leave it offer is intended to make you think that you're not entitled to object. But if you do object, you might change it.

What you might say is, "I hate to deal with these take it or leave it deals. I think they're fundamentally unfair. Let me ask you a question. Don't you think that the best way two people make a deal is to make one that is fair for them both?" If they say no, they are saying they don't believe in fair dealing, and risk losing their suppliers. Let's assume they say yes. You might respond, "Then I'm really surprised at your take it or leave it deal because, even though I know you think it's fair, you're not giving me the opportunity to explain why it doesn't meet my needs. Allow me to explain why that's so and what it would take to get this within the parameters that allow me to do this job. Then we can finish this meeting knowing we both got a fair deal."

Always try to turn the take it or leave it offer into a negotiation. If you can't open a negotiation, then evaluate the deal based on what you're being offered and what your needs are. In dealing with a firm take it or leave it offer, you have to know your bottom line, the point beyond which you cannot go. Once you know that, the decision is simple.

Dealing with the Assignment Issues

The two substantive issues you'll negotiate most often are usage and fees. The key to being a good negotiator of these is to understand the relationship of the two and why you need what you're asking for. To do that, you must understand the copyright/value relationship and the two great nemeses in photographic usage—work-for-hire and copyright transfers. Many photographers use those terms interchangeably. However, they are not the same.

A work-for-hire is a provision under the Copyright Act which says that if you are the employee of a party, such as a staff newspaper photographer getting a salary, then the copyright to your work belongs to your employer because everything you do is a work-for-hire. That is a federal law. In a work-for-hire situation, the copyright belongs to the buyer or employer from the moment the picture is taken. They are the author, you have no rights of authorship or ownership.

Work-for-hire can exist under limited circumstances for an independent contractor. There are nine categories of work that are eligible for work-for-hire treatment. The ones that affect photographers the most are "collective works" and "derivative works."

If you are an independent contractor, a work-for-hire can exist only if you have signed a written agreement to that effect.

In a copyright transfer, you own the copyright and you transfer that ownership to the buyer. You are selling an intangible asset—the copyright—so you have something to bargain for—the value in that copyright.

There is a provision in the Copyright Law called "recapture," which allows you to regain your copyright thirty-five years after you transfer it. If you signed a work-for-hire agreement, you have no recapture right because you never had the copyright in the first place.

In a copyright transfer, you are bargaining for the value of your copyright. Some photographers sell their copyright because they believe their work has no future value.

However, you don't know what the future value will be. Future value is based on usage—how long and how often they'll use it, or for what other uses it can be licensed.

You could shoot a can of tuna fish and think the photo has no future value. The client says he is just going to use it in an advertising campaign this year, but in a poor economy more and more campaigns are being extended and rerun. Photographers who sell copyrights don't get reuse fees on any of these reruns. Photographers who retain copyright get paid again.

In addition, you can't know how valuable the photograph will be as a stock image in the future. No one can predict what images will have historical value. You may have one of the most recent pictures of a certain subject which, twenty years from now, someone might need. And, certainly, you can't predict reuse by a client.

Most photographs taken on assignment have little future value as stock. In a given stock file, only two or three percent of photographs will ever sell. The problem is, no one knows which two or three percent. If you could figure that out, you'd be very wealthy because you could corner the market by shooting a few dozen pictures a week. Still, future stock sales is another reason to not sell copyright.

Yet another reason is that it creates a precedent and a mindset by the client. Buyers begin to believe that this is the way things are always done. Suppose a client wants you to photograph a clothespin. You agree to sell the copyright to that photograph because you don't see any future value. A month later, the same client calls you because one of their accounts makes the paint for the space shuttle and they need a photograph of the next launch. They've made special arrangements for you, they've even built a tower where you can shoot. Like before, they want to buy the copyright. This time, however, you see the future value of the photograph and refuse to sell it. The client is confused and asks, "Why not? You sold me the copyright just last week."

You have a problem. You said that you sell copyright, now you won't. This is a bit ridiculous. If a photograph has no value, obviously no one would want to buy it anyway. Then, when the photograph does have value, you won't sell it. It's very inconsistent. You should have a standard policy. Don't get in a position where, in the middle of a negotiation, you must explain why you're going to sell copyright on one job and not on another.

Once you do adopt a standard policy of not selling copyright or signing a work-for-hire, you'll need some explanations. Here are a few.

You could say, "I won't sign a work-for-hire because it makes you the author and denies me any recognition. It's as if I don't even exist. In addition, it gives you the copyright for life, and I don't want to do that."

Or you might offer this reasoning: "I'm sure you agree that the most important thing any businessperson must do to stay in business is go out there and sell. Well, I'm in the visual business, and if I want to sell my services, I have to be able to promote myself. The only way I can do that is to show people what I do. If I sell the copyright to my images, I no longer have the right to use any of them. I can't display them. I can't publish them in a source book. I can't even show the work in my portfolio. I wouldn't have been able to show you the work I did to get this assignment. No, selling the copyright is the kiss of death for my business."

If you must negotiate further, at the very least be sure to secure promotional rights to the photograph. If it turns out to be a great shot, you can still use it for promotion and advertising.

Even then, you might persist and ask the client, "Why do you want the copyright?" Remember that a good negotiator uses the answers of the other party to create options to satisfy needs. Here are some possible answers to that question that you might hear from clients, and how you might reply.

To avoid future negotiations: Your client might say, "I don't want to have to negotiate for every use down the line. I'm not sure how I'm going to use this, and I don't want to have to come back to you every time I do and pay another fee."

Your reply might be, "If you want to extend the use of media, you can do it anytime, and all you have to do is pay me X percent of the original fee." (Not the expenses.) By setting the price up front you may disarm the concern over negotiating a price later. The fee is guaranteed.

To protect the corporate image: You may hear something like, "These are corporate executives. One day a photographer shot a picture of our president and the next week I found it in a business magazine article that wasn't complimentary to us. We want the copyright to prevent that from happening."

To protect a proprietary interest: The client might say, "These pictures are of secret processes. We don't want the whole world to see them. Nobody in the world has machinery like ours. This is very confidential information and we need to control it." Or they might say, "The letters XYZ will be on all those buildings you're shooting and we don't want the XYZ logo published without our control."

Proprietary interest and corporate image are tougher items to deal with because there are companies that want to protect certain processes and people. You might give your absolute assurance that none of the photographs they declare are proprietary will ever be used by you. You might leave the proprietary work in their custody and keep only those that are nonproprietary.

Ownership of the transparency is not ownership of the copyright. They are separate under the law. You can own a transparency and not own the copyright. Now (through custody of the original) their interests are met. If they want to use those images and exploit them, as copyright holder you have a right to be paid for that value.

To avoid liability: You may hear, "We want the copyright transfer because we're afraid that we might damage images and be sued. If we own the copyright you've got nothing to sue us for."

You might alleviate the client's concern about liability by saying, "My paperwork can include language that states that payment of the fee in full is considered compensation in full for any damage. I'll cover your liability for that."

For you, this means taking a minimal risk of uncompensated damage, but would you go after the client in that kind of situation? You might have a difficult time getting a high value per transparency in the court, when they paid the expense of creating the work. Remember, you have to prove a slide is worth $1,500 or whatever you claim it is. This way, you've exempted them from what might be a minimal liability in damages.

You shouldn't disregard your client's needs if you want to maintain a relationship.

You've got to protect the client's interest, and you can do it without selling the copyright.

There are companies that have a policy that they must own everything. They are usually unbending on this point. If you choose to sell copyright, make sure you are paid appropriately for it because you'll never have any residual income from it. In short, receive an equivalent value for what you sell.

Chances are, if they want the copyright, they intend to use it often. Be sure to get paid for the value of that extensive usage. No one can insist that you shouldn't sell copyright. But everyone knows that copyright has value, so obtain that value by either holding onto the residual rights or, if you're selling the copyright, by getting paid for that residual value.

Within copyrights there are many individual rights. There are advertising rights, magazine rights, book rights, television rights, geographic and language rights. You can sell specific, exclusive rights, which means the licensee can do anything with the photographs, within the scope of those rights. The exclusive rights for advertising for an image means a client can do anything it wants in advertising. You can grant exclusive rights for a specific number of years. If the client doesn't need editorial rights, because it's not going to publish a magazine, why should it buy them? Buying specific exclusive rights is like buying a limited copyright. The photographer still owns the exclusive rights to the image for other media or for other uses, such as magazines, books, etc., while the client has specific exclusive rights which assure that the photo will never be sold by the photographer for a similar purpose during the term of the client's exclusive rights.

Generally, clients seek to buy more rights than they need, so you should have different prices. You should have the copyright price, the exclusive right price, the unlimited/nonexclusive right price and a limited/nonexclusive right price. If clients insist on the copyright, put that price on the table. If they ask why it's so high, tell them it's because they want to buy the copyright, but that you can get this down to a much lower fee if they want to talk about limits, such as exclusive or limited rights.

Never ask your clients what rights they want. You want to know what rights they need. Instead of using the word "rights," which is a red flag, use the word "usage." You could simply ask, "How do you intend to use these photographs?" If they want to create an ad, ask how long the campaign will be, what media, and geographic area, etc. After you have all the information you need, explain that you will work up your fee on that basis. The clients need to use your photograph. Sell them usage.

If clients tell you they don't understand usage, explain it this way: "You're an advertising agency. When you place a full-page, black-and-white ad in a magazine's July issue, you sign an advertising contract and pay for one-month's space. If you want to run it for a year, you've got to pay more for it. It's the same with photographs. The more you want to use it, the more you must pay." The fact is, they understand usage. They deal with it every day in terms of media space. All you're doing is using the same pricing that their other suppliers use.

Another popular refrain from clients is this: "I paid for this and I own it. I should be able to do anything I want with it." Your answer: "You pay for advertising space too but you still don't get to use it over and over again unless you pay accordingly. Usage is a fair way to charge. Perhaps you're just not used to hearing it in photography. Let me explain why I have to sell according to usage."

Now give them your reasons. If you are shooting a product for a manufacturer, you might try something like this: "You sell widgets. Suppose I bought a widget and took it home and the next day you look in the newspaper and see a story about a man who found a way to clone your widget. He turned it into ten widgets. Would you be upset? Of course, because you were losing business that was rightfully yours."

Continuing, you say, "When I give you a photograph, you don't have to come back to me ever again for that photograph. You can reuse it over and over. If I don't control the use of my images, my volume of sales will be reduced. You don't have to clone a photograph, it's self-cloning. That's why I must charge for usage."

Another client scenario goes like this: "Listen, when I go to the stationery store and buy a box of stationery, I own it." Your reply could be, "Suppose the stationer found out that every time you took a sheet of paper out of that box, another one automatically replaced it. Instead of selling you the box outright, they will lease you the right to use the box since you would never have to buy another one. They would be charging you for usage."

Ultimately, when negotiating copyrights, you have to convince the client that your need doesn't conflict with its interest. If it does, you'd better take a hard look at this deal because if you're hurting your client's interest, eventually you're not going to have a client. Meeting your needs and meeting the needs of your client are not irreconcilable, if both parties are open-minded.

Negotiating Fees for Assignment Photography

There is a point in every negotiation when the issue becomes money. How much will you charge for the work you are being asked to do? It is a simple question, but a difficult one to answer because there are so many factors.

Many photographers are uninformed when it comes to pricing for services. For those who have no experience or training to guide them through the process, refer to chapter 3, "The Art of Pricing and Estimating."

In general, the fee to do an assignment will include these factors:

- The basic fee. This amount accommodates total nonbillable expenses, such as electricity, depreciation, salaries, rent, and other overhead items. It is usually calculated by taking the total of these items and dividing it by the total days of shooting projected for the year. This number, in turn, is multiplied by the total days the assignment will take to shoot.
- The creative fee. This is the amount you charge to shoot the photographs. Some jobs require more skill and equipment than others, so the creative fee varies. It can be calculated per day or per job. Obviously, if you are being asked to shoot a job which is quite simple and could be done by almost anyone, you will not charge as much on this line as when you are called to do a job that requires many years of experience and/or special equipment or facilities.
- The usage fee. This is what you will charge for licensing your clients with the

right to use the photographs they need. Since the value of a photograph to your client is more dependent on your creativity than your overhead, the usage fee can be calculated as a factor of the creative fee. For example, one-time magazine editorial use might be a factor of 0.5, while exclusive print media advertising use might be 3.0, and a transfer of copyright might be a factor of 6.0. These are simply examples, not recommendations. What factors you apply in your business depends on your own and regional industry circumstances.

* Markup. This is a percentage of the total expenses meant to compensate the photographer for the cost of financing the expenses and the cost of securing materials, testing, stocking, etc. Some photographers include it in their expenses. However, this is often a red flag to the buyer. Instead, place it in the fee. It constitutes what might be called a variable overhead fee. Then, the individual components, when added together, present the assignment fee, which you will convey to the client. Remember, too many details simply complicate the negotiation by causing microscopic scrutiny and evaluation.

The next step is to create a range within which you can negotiate the fee. It is a relatively simple task. In the following example, the asking price is the fee you want to get, and the bottom line is the fee you need to meet your established minimums. The difference between those two numbers is the spread or negotiation range.

	ASKING	BOTTOM LINE
Basic expense fee	$500	$500
Creative photo fee	$1,000	$1,000
Usage licensing fee	$500	$300
Expense markup fee	$50	0
Total fee for assignment	$2,050	$1,800

In this example, your negotiating range is $250. The asking price is the amount you want for the job, while the bottom-line price is what you need, or the lowest fee you will agree to.

The fee you would ask the client at the start of the negotiation process is $2,050. If your client accepts it, you have fulfilled a want. There are those who would say that if your client accepts your first offer, then your price was too low. If the price you ask for is not accepted, then you must start negotiating. The key is to remember that any disagreement is the start of a negotiation, not the end of a possible deal.

It's reasonable to assume that a client will balk to some degree at the first price you offer. When that happens, it is important that you hold your ground for a while. If you are prepared to lower a price at the first objection, it is a signal that you are not confident of the true value of the job and your ability to get the price. It is also an invitation to the other person to try bringing the price down. Even though you may have to do that to secure the assignment, it is not something that should be done without discussion.

Assume that you just asked a client for a $5,000 fee for an assignment. The client objects to the price. What's your next step? Generally, it is wise to ask the client what he or she perceives as a reasonable price for that work. You could ask the question this way: "The fact that we don't see eye to eye on this makes me think one of us is missing something. Tell me, what do you think is a fair fee for this job?"

If the answer is far from what you quoted, you have to explore why the difference exists. What are you or the client overlooking or incorrectly pricing in the assignment? Make sure you have a full understanding of the job specs, usage, etc. Take another look at your figures and see if you miscalculated. If you didn't, ask the buyer to explain how he or she came to the quoted figure. Pay attention, find out what he or she is overlooking and point it out.

If there is only a slight difference between the two positions, you might simply concede the difference as a goodwill gesture, assuring the client that you'll absorb the difference to show that you want to work with him or her.

If the difference is simply too much to absorb, try to work through the range to a point between your quote and the client's expectation. This is when salesmanship is essential. Insist that you are worth every penny you quoted, yet find some way to come down a bit. There are different approaches.

If you are ready to give the client some reduction, you can ask for a trade-off. You might ask for the expenses in advance, as it will lessen your cash flow needs and that is worth some reduction in price. You could ask for part of the fee in advance, using the same rationale as the advance. Or, you could ask for some portion of the rights package (usage) to be altered. For example, perhaps the client asked for the right to use an image for three years, even though it didn't know if it would use the image that long. Ask the client to cut the usage to two years and pay the difference if and when it uses the image for the third year.

Whatever reason you offer, be sure it makes sense and has value close to the amount you are giving up. Explain your reason for lowering your price. That will minimize the chance that the client will see you playing a game to get more money. Determining what is appropriate is not always easy. After all, there are two points of view on the matter, yours and your client's. Those two points of view will not always line up close to one another. But if you understand how you arrived at your quote, you can explain it and hopefully get it or come close.

If you are not ready to lower your quote, try appealing to your client's past experience with you. Suggest that the amount you are asking for is in line with your quality and reliability.

Some simple rules

There is no simple formula to follow in negotiating an assignment fee, but there are some simple rules you can follow:

1. Never reduce your price without giving a reason, whether it is a trade-off for similar value, a goodwill gesture or an acknowledged reconsideration of the assignment's demands.
2. Justify your price based on your experience, capability, creativity and so forth. You decided on the creative portion of the fee by examining the talent, equipment, style, and other requirements of the assignment. Use those factors to sell the fee.

3. Mention other assignments of a similar nature, whether done for the same client or a different one. Demonstrate that you received a fee similar to the one quoted for the present job being negotiated. Show a tearsheet of the work.
4. Remind the client that the choice is lower price or quality, and that quality includes getting the job done on time, within the estimated price, and in a creative manner. Remind the client that quality is what you are quoting. It's not a photograph that you are quoting, it is reliability and quality.
5. Be direct and confident. Reassert that the fee you are offering is reasonable, and show concern if the client cannot recognize that fact.

Finally, remember that there is no such thing as the right fee or the fair fee. You will get what you negotiate. If any one person could always identify the perfect fee for every photographic assignment, he or she would be indispensable in the industry. Fee negotiation is a balancing of interests: yours, your client's, and, in the case of an ad agency, its client's.

Still, that balancing is an act of substantial proportion. Your fee has to be relative to the value of the photograph. When advertising clients are spending $2 million for media space, why should they be able to procure the rights to an assigned photograph for $1,000? If they think enough of their product to buy that kind of space to advertise it, they should be ready to spend a reasonable amount of money for the right to use the photograph in that space.

Value is not only relative to the experience, creativity, capability, and reliability that you bring to the job, it is relative to the many other costs they are prepared to incur in their project.

Negotiating Fees for Stock Photography

In stock photography, price negotiating is particularly intense because both buyer and seller have power. Although the buyer decides whether or not to "buy," it is the stock photographer who has something the buyer wants.

The first step in negotiating is gathering information. Here are some questions to ask:

1. Who is the buyer, and what does that tell me about the ability to pay?
2. What is the image, and how unique is it? Are there a hundred similar to it, or thousands? How likely is it that the buyer has an alternative already selected?
3. How will the image be used—in what media, for how long, and at what size? What will the circulation or distribution be?
4. When must the buyer use the image? Is there a deadline?
5. Where will the image be published—in what region or country?
6. Why is this particular image being pursued? What makes the buyer want it? Is it a unique solution for the buyer?
7. How much can the buyer pay, and under what circumstances will he or she pay the limit?

How do you get the answers? Some of these questions may be answered when the buyer requests an image. Others may require more detective work or hypothesizing on the basis of other information. But having the answers is important to your ability to negotiate a fair price.

A common pitfall, to be avoided at all costs, is letting a buyer insist on a price before you have all the information you need to determine a fair price. Prices are based on evaluation of facts, and you cannot properly price your work without all the facts.

In a stock photography sale, the issue is usually the fee for the use of the work. Rights, distribution, and the term of license are usually dictated by the client's predetermined needs. Stock is for a specific application, so generally all that remains to be determined is how much it will cost.

Expectations can play an important role in negotiating stock costs. The other party probably expects to pay more than they are offering; at the same time he or she probably expects that you are asking for more than you will finally accept.

In addition, don't forget the most important point in negotiating a price—you must know your bottom line. What is the minimum fee that you will accept? A good negotiator knows the bottom line and lets the buyer know when he or she has reached it. Make it clear when you are at that point, that you cannot go any lower. Your counterpart must now take it or leave it. Never, absolutely never, go below your bottom line.

Also, if you do change your price, don't do it in a vacuum. Give a reason for the change. Don't present yourself as a person who inflates the price so it can be cut later. That invites buyers to try for more cuts. When you negotiate, you must have a reason for every stance you take.

What reasons might you give for changing your price? It could be that you have just reexamined their specifications and realized that you have some slack. It could be that the finished reproduction offers a promotional benefit, and you are prepared to accept extra tearsheets as additional compensation. Or the client may have been fair with you in the past when the budget allowed and you are prepared to be flexible. No matter what your reason, make sure the other person knows what it is—and that you don't go below your bottom line.

To avoid pointless negotiating, it's a good idea to establish the pricing parameters on the initial contact. It can be a significant time-saver if you do not send images unless the person has a budget that can meet your minimum pricing standards.

When you price a stock photograph, what exactly are you pricing? Are you pricing a service or a commodity? Although a stock photograph bears some resemblance to a commodity, it has an intangible quality in that every stock photograph is the product of a particular vision, different from others, even when they deal with the same subject matter. Stock photographs are not a commodity.

But can they be compared to a service? After all, they have already been produced. Consider, however, that stock photographs are either outtakes from an assignment or the result of a planned effort to create the stock—a kind of self-assignment. In other words, stock photography is the result of a service with one distinct advantage: the photographer has taken the risk out of purchasing a service. In effect the stock shooter, by anticipating need, has provided a service in advance of the request, assuring the buyer a risk-free transaction. No commodity or service does that. Stock photography is unique and it needs its own pricing system—one that takes into account not only the originality of the photograph but also the lack of risk for the buyer.

Factors in Stock Photography Pricing

The first thing stock pricing must do is recover the costs of creating the photographs. Obviously, to do that, you have to identify the costs, and the total amount of those costs. That is somewhat harder than it seems because there are two kinds of costs: fixed costs, which stay the same regardless of volume of production or sales, and variable costs, which move upward as production and sales increase. Rent, insurance, basic telephone charges, and equipment are all fixed costs. Variable costs include film, processing, taxes, and postage. Clearly variable costs have to be estimated on the basis of projected operations. How do you do this?

Consider the potential volume of your sales and the expenses necessary to make and fulfill those sales. Then add the cost of production of new material or a portion of that cost. Your projections can be based on your own experience, the experiences of others, or industry statistics.

Next you will have to project your sales and create a base price. If you have been selling stock for some time you probably have a sales history and can evaluate how many sales you make a year at any given level of sales.

Remember these simple formulas:

Break-even price = All costs ÷ quantity to be sold
Selling price = Break-even price + Profit + Added value

It is important to emphasize that this system is based on a projection of sales and expenses. If your projection is wrong, then your price base and final price are also wrong.

Be sure to evaluate your estimates over time. If they prove to be high or low, whether the change is in sales or expenses or both, you must alter your input accordingly. Readjusting your pricing is important to making profits. In time, experience will make your estimates accurate, but careful review of performance is advised.

Guides and Surveys

There are several guides to pricing stock photography. These are available in book form and also in computer-readable, disc-based programs.

In addition, ASMP conducts and publishes pricing survey results for the reference of its members only.

The guides reflect the opinion of experts in the stock photography field, while the survey results are statistical compilations taken from surveys conduct by ASMP among its members.

These guides and surveys can serve as an excellent way to check your pricing in relation to industry-accepted prices.

Assessing Added Value

Stock photographs can have added value from two sources. First, the photograph is worth more if it has some element of uniqueness, whether from the specialized nature of the subject matter, its limited supply, or if it was unusually expensive to produce.

Another important source of added value comes from the nature of the application: brochure, package design, point of purchase, advertisement, editorial illustration, book cover, promotional kit, television insert, film strip, etc. Also consider the circumstances: size of use, circulation, time limitations, geographic distribution, uniqueness of the image, quality of the image, extraordinary research time, unusually long client-holding period, availability of releases.

It is generally accepted that the more important the use and the greater the prominence of the photograph, the more it will cost the buyer. A national advertising use is priced higher than a regional one, a major news magazine use higher than a text book image. What's at issue here is how important the photograph is to the client. It is logical that the image's importance increases in direct proportion to the cost of that chosen media. But how do you set a value on all this? There is no simple formula. The knowledge comes from experience, market trends, investigation of industry standards, consultation with other photographers and stock agencies, and some seat-of-the pants insight.

In the pricing method, it is your ability to formulate the numbers, assess the added value, and negotiate the price that will determine the ultimate profitability of your stock photography business.

Always remember, if you are in business to produce an income for yourself, then you should be negotiating for a fair, competitive price that assures you an income after you have recovered all the usual expenses that are associated with a stock photography sale.

Pricing an Image

Many photographers price stock photos as if they had just produced the image. For a photograph's leasing price, they first arrive at the base expense by adding all the costs of the photograph's production to their normal overhead requirements and then add a fee for usage, a fee for time and service, and a sum for profit to the base expense. If it sounds as if they were pricing a photograph done for an assignment—you're right, it does.

Any stock photograph has the same cost structure whether it was originally produced as an assignment outtake or especially for stock. A stock photo, like an assignment photo, is a "service" provided to a client. All images are not the same, as each shows a different solution to a client's needs—widgets on the shelf couldn't do this.

Even for the same usage, the fee charged to lease a photograph of a "family" portrayed by five models will be greater than for a photograph of flowers in a field.

When pricing photographs, keep in mind the factors that differentiate one photograph from another and can determine value. Many experienced professionals view their work as falling into five categories:

1. A pleasing, technically excellent photograph of an existing situation that is not directed by a photographer. This includes some editorial shots and many scenics.
2. A pleasing, technically excellent production photograph—of a situation directed by a photographer. This includes setup shots with model-released talent, props, and the like.
3. An exceptional photograph from the first category—for example, an outstanding scenic that would be difficult to reproduce due to extraordinary lighting or weather, or an editorial photograph of a high-tech facility to which access is very difficult to obtain.
4. An exceptional photograph from the second category, such as a complex production photograph with extra talent, trained animals, special location, or helicopter fees.
5. An exceptional photograph of a unique moment or event that would be impossible to re-create.

Consider these five factors in determining whether a premium price is warranted for a particular photograph and in explaining your price to a client.

Who to Ask about Prices

How do you find a basic minimum figure for different categories if you have no experience? How do you make sure prices are up-to-date? Here are several approaches used by experienced photographers:

1. Consult colleagues experienced in stock. Photographers are usually happy to share their knowledge of the business.
2. Consult your stock agency if you have a nonexclusive contract. Your agent can be a helpful source of information.
3. Consult other stock agents strong in marketing. If you don't pester them with too many calls a week, many agents are willing to help with a perplexing price quote, or a base rate.
4. Refer to the guidance in this chapter for analyzing your business costs and figuring out a base price.
5. Keep informed about cost-of-living increases, and business statistics published by the federal government.
6. Consult stock pricing guides.

A Photographer's Perspective on Pricing and Negotiating

To those unfamiliar with the market for stock photography, the pricing of stock photographs can be very confusing. The same picture, for example, may command different prices in different situations. Agreeing with a buyer on a price can be as simple as a ten-second phone call, or it can require several visits to the buyer's office, with review of layouts and consultations with other photographers. If the buyer is a trusted client and the use is standard—a half-page in an established magazine—pricing may be almost automatic. Other times, however, pricing becomes complicated, especially if the photograph itself is a one-of-a-kind image, or if there is a combination of different formats using the same picture.

How do you arrive at a price that satisfies both you and the buyer—the fair market price? It is a step-by-step process that begins by considering the client's budget and the specific use of a photograph. You must also consider any unique merits of the particular photograph and the individual situation of the buyer. Negotiation is the final step that leads to agreement on a price.

A basic principle in pricing is: the larger the total budget of the entire project, the more the buyer should be able and willing to spend for the photograph. Application of this principle has divided the market for stock photographs into three broad categories, each with a developed price range of its own:

- Advertising. This is usually the highest paying use of stock photos because of the large investment required to buy media space, the immediate profits realized, and the revenues the photograph will help create if the advertising is successful.
- Corporate/Industrial. The use of photography in company annual reports, promotional trade shows, public relations, recruitment booklets, and the like, is a less direct form of advertising and promotion than consumer advertising, thus it usually has a more moderate budget.
- Editorial. This use is defined as photographs that run in magazines, books, or on TV for their illustrative or informational value. The budget of an entire project may be large—for example, for an encyclopedia—but a large number of pictures are usually required, so the per-page budget is relatively modest.

In sum, the three main uses for stock photos are advertising (highest paying), corporate/industrial (middle range), and editorial (low range). There are also unusual uses with their own price rationale—for example, place mats or playing cards.

Another area deserving special consideration is the usage termed "advertorial." Advertorials often appear in magazines as special sections or inserts advertising a place or service, most commonly for tourism. In this type of usage, the photographs are used to support the editorial content, but the entire section is advertising and is marked as such in accordance with federal law. Though often editorial in style, the photographs in an advertorial are part of an advertising program, and this should be considered in pricing. An additional concern is copyright notice. Since the magazine's overall copyright notice does not cover advertisements, and since many of these sections are designed to be removed from the magazine itself, photographers may want to stipulate that the copyright credit must appear adjacent to the photograph.

Five Factors in Use

A second basic principle in pricing is: any use that increases the visibility of the photograph increases its value. After the broad use of a stock photograph has been determined, this second principle—"amount of visibility"—comes into play. Any increase in the visibility, by any means (beyond the stated minimum customarily specified for a particular use), further increases the value of the photograph to the buyer and therefore earns a higher fee for the seller. Factors to consider are: physical size, circulation or print run, geographical distribution, additional versions or editions, and extensions of the time the image is used.

1. Size. Throughout the industry, the size of reproduction (such as full page or half-page) is an accepted and realistic method of measuring the photograph's value, just as size is one accepted way for magazines and newspapers to charge for advertising space. This concept carries over to billboards, exhibition prints, posters, and the like. It is important to note, however, that the relationship of size to price is not exactly proportional. If, in a hypothetical example, a full-page editorial or advertising rate is considered to be 100 percent, the fee charged for half-page use might be 70 percent (not 50 percent), and for a quarter-page, which should be the minimum base fee, it might be 65 percent (not 25 percent). The point is that there is a base fee paid for the initial reproduction rights. Size influences the price, but not in direct proportion.

2. Circulation and print run. This is an obvious way to measure how many times the photograph will be reproduced, which in turn is a measure of how many copies of a book or magazine may be sold, or how many potential buyers will be influenced by the photograph in a catalog. The greater the number of reproductions, the more valuable the photo probably is to the buyer, but again, the price scale is not directly proportional. Doubling the print run of a sales brochure from five hundred thousand to a million, for example, might increase the average fee for a full page by 40, not 100, percent.

    In print advertising, it should be noted, the total circulation figure is considered to be the sum of the circulation of each magazine multiplied by the number of insertions. There are directories, such as the *Gebbie Press Directory*, which provide circulation figures of a multitude of publications. In TV advertising, the multiplier is the number of times the commercial is aired.

3. Distribution. The value of a stock photograph can be radically affected by whether the use is worldwide, national, regional, or local. In TV, a commercial on a national network has more visibility than one on a metro New York station, which in turn may have ten times the viewers of a St. Louis station. In the greeting card market, worldwide rights in English, rather than U.S. only, mean many more potential buyers and greater profits.

    In certain industries, such as book publishing, the value of customary and standard distribution rights is fairly well established. But the business practices of some of the more recent users of stock photography are unfamiliar, and the values of distribution rights have either not been established or seem unrelated to past pricing experience. For example, in uses that are very commercial such as posters, packaging, and novelties, the distribution rights can be a primary basis for determining the fee.

4. Versions. If a stock photo is used in more than one published format, it is considered to have added value for the buyer. In book publishing, there might be an additional language edition or a trade paperback following the original hard-

cover version. In another situation, an annual report cover might be used as an institutional ad, or a national consumer ad might be reworked as a point-of-purchase display card. The accepted pricing procedure in these instances, when the extensions of usage are known beforehand, is to price the primary use fully, as if it were the only usage, and then discount each additional use a certain percentage, based on the total package.

5. Time. The length of time a photo is visible becomes a factor when, for example, a photographic billboard is used for six months rather than the usual thirteen-week cycle. There is also an increase in visibility when a wall calendar is designed to display one photograph for the entire year compared with the "twelve-hanger" format with a different photo for each month. Time also has a dollar value when you agree to limit the visibility of the photo—for instance, if you agree to an "exclusive" on a baby food package and do not let the photo appear anywhere else for three years.

When setting your price for a stock photograph there is one simple truth which should be kept in mind, and expressed to the client as a selling point. The truth is that there is no risk to the client in stock photography. Unlike assignment photography, the buyer sees exactly what the finished result will be: no guesswork, no unmet expectations, no reshoots, no delays. This absence of risk through uncertainty should be capitalized on whenever the client is turning to stock after considering the assignment option.

This truth is a weight on the seller's side of the scale. The buyer should balance the scale with a payment for that peace of mind.

A Summary on Negotiating

Negotiating is a dignified and respectable method of reaching agreements. In photography, only part of the value of a photograph can be measured in hard numbers and assigned a dollar figure; negotiating is the only practical method of taking all the factors mentioned above and translating them into a fair market price—one that both buyer and seller are willing to accept.

There are as many styles of negotiating as there are people, but here are some common negotiating principles that apply to everyone in the stock photography business:

1. Accept the process of negotiating as a normal and essential part of a stock photo sale. Become as skilled at negotiating as you are at making photographs.
2. Prepare yourself by studying and understanding the basic principles and market factors that shape stock photo prices. Knowledge is the key to comfortable and businesslike negotiating.
3. Become familiar with the relationships of prices to such variables as size, circulation, and distribution, uniqueness, risk, etc.
4. Learn the inner workings of different segments of the market (advertising, design studios, textbook publishers, etc.) in order to understand their motivations and needs. Find out how buying decisions are made.
5. Remember that in a successful negotiation both buyer and seller are satisfied.

That means accepting that both have the right to back away from a deal "this time." Leave the door open for future business.

6. Be friendly and frank, positive and professional in your discussions.

7. Understand that the buyer sees the value of your photograph only in terms of how it will be used in the immediate project. Don't be insulted if an average price is offered for one of your favorite photos.

8. If a buyer is inexperienced, be willing and able to explain the market factors that affect prices.

9. Ask questions until you are completely satisfied that you know exactly how the photo will be used and precisely what rights are needed.

10. Write down information during discussions to help organize your thoughts. Categorize and save this information—it can be an invaluable reference for similar sales in the future, particularly when dealing with the same client.

11. Try to get an idea of how much negotiating leeway you have. Search for indications of the buyer's budget range. Ask how much they've paid in the past for similar projects.

12. Have a clear picture of the price range paid for such work. If you are unsure when talking with a buyer, excuse yourself, find out, and phone back. This is an acceptable practice.

13. Be cautious about quoting an exact figure when negotiations enter the "money'" stage. Quote your price and encourage a response. The buyer may be willing to pay more than your figure and it's almost impossible to raise a price once you've quoted low.

14. Take time to calculate your bottom line and never go below this figure. If you sell for less than you need, you are jeopardizing your own security. If the buyer can't meet your bottom price, amicably explain why you have to walk away from the sale. This buyer may have a different budget the next time.

15. If you get bogged down in agreeing on a price, don't give in to the urge to split the difference or accept the buyer's last offer. There are other things to try. You might ask for a trade-off, such as tearsheets for promotional mailers. Or you might offer an inducement, such as an additional usage, so the buyer will get added value for your price.

Once the negotiating is done—don't forget the invoicing. Make sure all the rights you have agreed on are clearly specified in your delivery memo and invoice.

___

Negotiating Tips

Investigate
1. Who is the client?
2. What image(s) do they want?
3. When do they need it?
4. Where will the image be used?

5. How
   - will it be used?
   - big will it be displayed?
   - many copies will be made?
   - long will it be used?
   - exclusive are the rights?
6. Finally, how much is the budget?

Evaluate

What does that indicate about their purchasing ability (price range)?
Might this image command a higher price?
Do they have time to shop some more?
Is the audience local, national, or international, and how does that affect price?
How is the price influenced by
   - advertising, brochure, editorial, or other usage?
   - ¼ page, billboard, or other size?
   - circulation, distribution, and press run quantities?
   - one-time, one-month, one-year usage?
   - limitations on other sales?
How much should you ask for in light of the above?

Now negotiate

1. Be aware of these traditional tactics:
   - The red herring: making an item seem important so that you can use it as a trade-off later.
   - The trade-off: giving up or giving more of something in order to get something you seek.
   - Limited authority: going to someone for authorization beyond your limits. This tactic allows you to reopen an almost closed negotiation.
2. Show empathy. Always understand the other person's point of view. Explain that you do, then ask the other person to understand yours. Follow with some candid talk.
3. Use candor. Let the person know you really want to make a deal and you know he or she want to also; you can then move on to a compromise.
4. Don't ignore any position; deal with everything that's offered. Failing to respond indicates either a lack of concern for your counterpart's point of view or a weakness in your position.
5. Disarm with a question. Ask the other party why they are making a certain demand. Make them explain it. Sometimes they can't, and this will show them they can bend a little.
6. Listen carefully. Every answer and statement contains information you need to offer a solution.
7. Develop options. This tactic is the key to successfully concluding negotiations. A good negotiator is option oriented and proposes alternatives until the right combination is found.

Chapter 5

Rights and Value: In Traditional and Electronic Media

Scott Highton

The term "electronic rights" covers an ever-widening collection of licensable rights. As increasing amounts of media content are delivered in electronic forms, the scope of the phrase "all electronic rights" becomes ever-more extensive.

For clarity and comprehension, we will present the following definitions used by ASMP in this chapter.

Media—tangible means for distributing an image. Generally, there are three types of media:

- Print—on paper or other tangible printed material
- Electronic—digital or analog data on optical or magnetic media
- Film—celluloid-based material

Application—a particular vehicle within a given medium (magazine, annual report, encyclopedia)

Product—a capture or presentation means (videotape, paper, CD-ROM, etc.)

For photographers, print and electronic media offer the greatest opportunity for publication. However, these opportunities are quickly diminished if the reproduction rights are not carefully defined, controlled, and priced. Most photographers would not license "all print reproduction rights" to a client unless there was a very high fee. Print rights include magazines, books, encyclopedia, posters, brochures, etc. In keeping with that logic, it is unwise to license "electronic reproduction rights" without limitations.

Electronic rights include many products, such as videotapes, videodiscs, CD-ROMs, on-line presentation, broadcast television, cable television, and more. To grant reproduction rights of images by using only the phrase "electronic rights" is to undermine profit-making potential. While an image in print would normally be used in only one application, an electronic application using that same image can be served up in many different forms. A successful on-line product can easily end up as a CD-ROM or vice versa.

Value of Content

Audiences have come to expect more visual information in electronic media so the demand for images is increasing. The means of determining the value of images in the electronic marketplace is similar to that of the print market. While the media and the markets might be different, the rights and business practices recommended by ASMP for print are also applicable to licensing rights in electronic media. Electronic media should not be considered replacements for print markets, but rather, as new markets for photographs. Therefore, the additional demand for photography in electronic media effectively increases the overall value of photography.

When licensing rights or usage, photographers should be specific about which media they are granting rights for. Although electronic and print markets frequently overlap, they should always be considered distinct and separate for the licensing of rights or usage.

Determination of the value of visual content in both markets depends upon a variety of factors. However, two principles of business never change.

1. Compensation should reflect the value of the image(s).
2. Value is always relative.

The specific factors affecting image value are:

Competition. What level of competition exists? What is the availability of similar images from other sources? If images are unique and exclusive, they should command better fees.

Novelty. Novel (new) images are those which have a new look and have not been seen by the market at large. Freshly produced images are generally more valuable. Innovation by style, technique, and artistry also adds value.

Importance. The intended size, placement, and repeated use of an image in an application adds value. The relative volume of images also indicates importance. If a photograph is the sole image appearing in an application, it is usually more valuable than if it were one of a hundred.

Distribution Volume. Circulation, press run, units pressed, and the number of on-line accesses all influence value. Generally, the greater the distribution, the greater the value.

Application Market. Each application has a market. Consumer, trade, institutional, and corporate are all specific markets. Generally, the larger the market, the greater the value. The exceptions to this are in niche market applications, where great selectivity is exercised. Here, the importance of an image is even greater, since the goal of niche marketing is maximum impact on a small, select group. In short, every hit or contact has high value.

Period of Use. The longer an application is in use, the greater the value.

Risk Factors. A model or property release can provide inadequate protection if it, for instance, does not allow image alterations. Yet, risk to both client and photographer increases in any commercial use of an image, whether the image is altered or not, because the commercial use of an image implies that someone is profiting from its use. A signed model or property release does not eliminate the possibility of a dispute. It lessens the likelihood of one and provides a defense. This is why model or property-released photos command greater fees than unreleased ones.

Assessing value is both a science and an art. One can scientifically determine specific size, placement, number of copies, and similar statistics. Risk can be assessed to some degree based on the use and the terms of releases. However, the level of competition and the novelty of an image are elusive. Assessing these factors is more of an art. It requires that the photographer learn how the particular user values the image. The difficulty lies in the fact that experienced photo buyers (clients) are often reluctant to share this information.

Pricing and Compensation Structures

Electronic media should be regarded as new markets for publication. Pricing for any publication, be it electronic, print, or otherwise, should be based on industry standards of usage, volume, and other accepted practices. Elsewhere in this paper are examples based on the pricing system developed by the Media Photographers' Copyright Agency (MP©A). Regardless of the media, any rights granted should be clearly stated and should reflect equitable compensation for usage.

Photographers should be most wary of entering into speculative arrangements that might result in the loss of control of their copyrights or prevent them from earning any further income from their work, yet allowing others to profit greatly. Also, if photographers accept the risk of a small return in the event of poor sales, they should demand a significantly greater return if sales are good. If photographers share the risks, they should also share the rewards.

Compensation for usage is structured in different ways. Some of these are:

1. Flat fee—the photographer is paid a single, fixed amount for the use of his or her photograph(s). Generally, the broader the license or the more usage extended, the higher the fee will be. If the usage goes beyond the original license, additional fees must be negotiated and paid. The flat fee is often the simplest arrangement for both photographer and buyer.

Example: *An image is licensed for up to ¼ page, one-time, nonexclusive use in a consumer weekly magazine, with a 2,000,000 maximum circulation for a fee of $250. If the final usage is ½ page instead, the license fee might increase to $350 or $400.*

2. Structured tier fee schedule—a schedule of fees agreed upon between the photographer and client. The photographer's fee increases when distribution of the product reaches certain levels, such as the number of on-line accesses, the number of CDs pressed, or the number and size of each broadcast.

Example: *A photograph is reproduced as a cover of a brochure, on a nonexclusive basis, with reprinting rights extended to the client for a one-year period.*

Up to 20,000 copies—fee is $870
20,001 to 50,000 copies—$270 is added
50,001 to 100,000 copies—$150 more is added

In this case, if the buyer prints 20,000 copies or less, the photographer is paid $870. If an additional print run of 35,000 is made (totaling 55,000), the photographer is paid an additional $420. If an additional press run is made after the one-year term of the license, the fee reverts to the starting point.

3. Percentage of sales fee—the photographer receives a percentage or a stipulated fee for every sale. This could be an amount based on the selling price of every disc, publication, or book, or it could be a stipulated fee for every download or access to an application. Frequently, this would be in addition to a base or guaranteed minimum for the usage. In this manner, the photographer can accept the risk of a small return if the product is not successful, yet share in the reward if the product succeeds.

Example: *A photograph is reproduced as an 11 inch × 14 inch framed print for a 12 percent royalty on the wholesale price, before taxes and delivery fees. The wall art might sell in a retail outlet for $50 with the wholesale price at $25. At a 12 percent royalty, the photographer receives $3 per unit sold. The photographer might negotiate a $1,500 minimum guarantee, paid as an advance against the first 500 units sold. An additional royalty of $3.00 per unit sold would be paid to the photographer for every unit after that.*

4. Per unit (produced or sold) fee—the photographer's fee is based upon a fixed payment per unit produced or sold, with units produced being the most popular method.

Example: *A photograph is reproduced as a full-screen image in an on-line editorial application.*

A pricing mechanism is needed which allows for pricing per access to the on-line image. A royalty based upon total number of accesses is in order. Using the chart on page 227, we take a mastering fee of $30 and add it to the distribution fee. If there are 10,000 accesses, the fee is $30 plus $60, equaling $90. If the accesses are 50,000, the fee would be $30 plus $100, totaling $130.

A Sample Pricing System

When it comes time to set the value of images in an actual transaction, all the foregoing information must be applied. To do that, photographers take different approaches, depending upon whether the images licensed are generated on assignment or are selected from an existing library (stock).

Assignment pricing can be complex, and the basis of pricing varies. Advertising, editorial, corporate, and architectural photography each has its own pricing peculiarities. Stock photography licensing, however, is more standardized and can more readily be used to demonstrate pricing systems that take value factors into account.

In an effort to illustrate the use of value factors, and to show a specific licensing method, we have received permission from the Media Photographers' Copyright Agency (MP©A) to publish some of its fee structures and value factors.

The MP©A pricing system is based upon the following criteria:

1. *Mastering fee*—payment for the right to make a master copy, from which all other copies are made. This master could be, among other forms, a printing plate, a digital file in a computer, or a film negative for a motion picture. Regardless of the media or means by which it is captured, the master is the first copy from which all copies to be distributed are made.

2. *Distribution fee*—payment for the total copies made, published, viewed, etc.

3. *Multiples*—factors which are used to adjust the price for value added attributes such as size, novelty, multiple reproductions.

The tables on pages 227–229 are examples of the MP©A basis price list for brochures, educational books, and editorial use. An example of how the lists are used follows each listing.

Other Factors in MP©A Fee Structure

License Duration Default

The default license duration is twelve months after the date of the initial license. The default reproduction size for these is ¼ page.

Multiple Reproductions in Same Application (Print or electronic)

1st time:	Original fee
2nd time:	Additional 75% of original fee
3rd time:	Additional 65% of original fee
4th time:	Additional 50% of original fee

MP©A Category 1: Brochures, Flyers, Promo Cards, etc.

Mastering Fee: $100 per image, plus Per Unit Distribution Fees

VOLUME	X	MULTIPLIER	ADDITIVE DISTRIBUTION = FEE	MASTERING FEE + DISTRIBUTION FEE = LICENSE FEE	QTY. LICENSED
5,000 (min)		.02	100	200	5,000
Next 15,000		.006	+90	290	20,000
Next 30,000		.003	+90	380	50,000
Next 50,000		.001	+50	430	100,000
Next 150,000		.0005	+75	505	250,000
Next 250,000		.0002	+50	555	500,000
Next 500,000		.00015	+75	630	1,000,000

Next 2,000,000	.00008	+160	790	2,000,000
Over 3,000,000	.00004	+40/million	—	

Example:

1. A brochure in a quantity of 50,000:

Mastering Fee	$100
50,000 Distribution Fee	$280 (100 + 90 + 90)
TOTAL LICENSE FEE	$380

MP©A Category 2: Textbooks, Encyclopedias, Trade Books, Picture Books

Mastering Fee: $100 per image, plus Per Unit Distribution Fees

VOLUME	×	MULTIPLIER	=	ADDITIVE DISTRIBUTION FEE	MASTERING FEE + DISTRIBUTION FEE = LICENSE FEE	QTY. LICENSED
10,000 (min)		.005		50	150	10,000
Next 10,000		.004		+40	190	20,000
Next 20,000		.003		+60	250	40,000
Next 20,000		.002		+40	290	60,000
Over 60,000		.001		+10/ten thousand	—	

Example:

1. A textbook in a quantity of 15,000:

Mastering Fee	$100
10,000 Distribution Fee	$50 (min. 10,000 use)
Next 5,000 Distribution Fee*	$20 (.004 × 5,000)
TOTAL LICENSE FEE	$170

* This quantity is a portion of the next 10,000 line which is shaded in the above example. If the quantity had been 17,000, the multiplication would be .004 × 7,000.

MP©A Category 3: Editorial Magazines, Newspapers, Newsletters, etc.

Mastering Fees

TYPE	PER APPLICATION*	MONTHLY	FREQUENCY OF USE WEEKLY	DAILY
Consumer Print		$50 *(*Example 2)*	$30 *(*Example 1)*	$20
Trade Print		$40	$20	$10
Corporate Print		$40		
Institutional Print		$30		
Any Electronic Uses	$30 *(*An application is a CD-ROM, one use on-line, etc.)*			

Circulation Fee (circulation, accesses on-line, units pressed)

VOLUME	×	MULTIPLIER	=	DISTRIBUTION FEE
100		.1		10
1,000		.02		20
5,000		.01		50

10,000	.006	60
25,000	.003	75 *(Example 3)*
50,000	.002	100
100,000	.0012	120
250,000	.00054	135
500,000	.0003	150
1,000,000	.00017	170 *(Examples 1 and 2)*
2,000,000	.00009	180
3,000,000	.00007	210
4,000,000	.000055	220
5,000,000	.000046	230
6,000,000	.00004	240
Over 6,000,000	.00002	Add $20 per million

Licensing Fee = Mastering Fee + Distribution Fee

Examples:
1. A weekly printed consumer magazine with a circulation of 1 million
   Mastering ($30) + Distribution ($170) = Total ¼ page ($200)
2. A monthly printed consumer magazine with a circulation of 1 million
   Mastering ($50) + Distribution ($170) = Total ¼ page ($220)
3. An on-line magazine (or CD-ROM) with 25,000 units pressed (or 25,000 accesses)
   Mastering ($30) + Distribution ($75) = Total 1 screen ($105)

Copyright Title Transfers

Copyright is an intangible asset, and it can be leased or sold. All of the previous examples are based upon the photographer retaining copyright ownership of his or her work and licensing usage. There are, however, cases where photographers are asked to transfer the ownership of copyright. In such cases, determining the complete value of the image(s) and copyright are of primary importance. The photographer should note:
- The buyer is placing great importance on the image, since they want the copyright.
- The image will never produce additional revenue for the photographer and that revenue loss is value which should be compensated.

There are two common arrangements for clients to obtain copyright from photographers.

1. Assignment of copyright ownership—generally, an undesirable arrangement for photographers and other content creators, since it involves a complete transfer of copyright title to the buyer. The creator will lose all control over the use of the work, and will be unable to make any future income from royalties, residual sales, resale, or stock licensing of the material. If the photographer's client sells the images to a stock agency or decides to market the images as stock themselves, the photographer will be put in the impossible position of competing directly with his or her own work.

Generally, the needs of most clients can be satisfied through usage terms and written guarantees by the photographer not to resell the material to competing clients, making a copyright transfer unnecessary. In the rare event that a copyright assignment is deemed by a photographer to be truly necessary, an appropriate fee should be negotiated by the photographer to compensate for future income that he or she will be unable to earn from the material.

Example: *A photographer whose fee for a specific package of limited rights is normally $1,500 per day might have an increased fee for copyright assignment of $6,000 to $10,000 per day.*

2. Work-for-hire—ASMP is opposed to work-for-hire arrangements for all independent contractors. Under a work-for-hire, the photographer not only loses the copyright to the work from the moment he or she creates it, but also loses all rights to authorship. This includes loss of the right to be identified as the author of his or her own work. Additionally, photographers cannot recapture their copyright ownership after thirty-five years, a right they have when they assign it. In any situation where ownership of the copyright is absolutely required by the buyer, photographers should consider arranging an assignment of copyright, at a rate which fairly compensates them for the entire value they are giving up, rather than doing a work-for-hire.

Copyright Protection

Digital technology has made it far easier to copy photographic images. High-quality scanning, image capture, and digital reproduction devices, available at relatively low cost, have resulted in a greater risk of unauthorized copying of copyright protected material. ASMP supports the protection of electronically distributed images through the use of watermarks, encryption, pixel-embedded copyright notices, and other effective protection schemes. These techniques should be used on all sizes of electronic files, since even the smallest files can be easily interpolated on a desktop computer to yield reproduction quality images.

Physically protecting a photograph from unauthorized reproduction is a task separate from copyright protection. The majority of unauthorized reproductions is usually the result of a client's being confused about what usage was licensed by the photographer. Photographers should make sure the client understands that it is illegal to use an image for any purpose or time period other than that permitted by agreement.

Multimedia

Electronic publication, particularly of multimedia titles, represents a merging of two major industries—traditional print publishing and motion picture/television production. Both industries have relied for decades primarily on independent contractors and content providers. For the print industry, this includes writers, photographers, illustrators, and editors, while the film industry also includes actors, producers, directors, musicians, voice-over talent, set designers, crew, and countless others. The two industries, however, have evolved separately in their approach to acquiring content.

The publishing field generally treats content from outside (nonemployee) sources as material which is licensed for specific use. This is how most independent still photographers have structured their businesses, as well. Photography and writing done on assignment for a client are owned by the author and are licensed for limited use to that client.

The film industry, however, is different and far more complex. The simplest documentary film can rarely be done entirely by a single person due to the need for a camera person, audio technician and an interviewer or producer, at minimum. Most productions require even more people, and therefore, are considered collective works. Through necessity, production companies usually hire their contractors, including photographers and cinematographers, under work-for-hire arrangements. Contribution to a collective work and contribution to a motion picture or audiovisual work are both categories enumerated in the Copyright Act as qualifying as work-for-hire.

Multimedia has created a hybrid of these two industries, along with a conflict between them regarding rights. This has resulted in two different models for the acquisition of content for multimedia—a print publishing model and a film model. Although not yet an industry standard, some multimedia producers coming from the print industry generally adopt the print publishing model, and are willing to license specific and limited use or consider royalty payments to photographers and other content providers working on assignment. Producers from the film and television side tend to use the film model, wanting to pay flat fees for assignments and to own all rights to the material.

There are no advantages for photographers under the film/TV model. Content and its ownership are key elements in the expanding electronic marketplace. ASMP urges all photographers to carefully consider the long-term value of copyright before agreeing to transfer its ownership to another party.

Moral Rights

Moral rights, which are different from copyrights, give creators the right to control attribution (credit) and the integrity (alteration) of their work. Moral rights protect the integrity and the paternity of the original work of an artist. They provide a level of sanctity to artists' original creations. Unfortunately, in the United States, there are currently no moral rights attached to images made for publication. Only fine art works, created for exhibition, and of which 200 or fewer copies are made, are eligible to receive moral rights protection.

Generally, moral rights in the U.S. are enforced through contracts governing the license of photographers' work to their clients. Two contractual terms—photo credits and alteration limitations—are generally used to do this.

Photo credits—A key part of the compensation photographers receive for most uses of their work is the photo credit and/or copyright notice. This credit is as justified in electronic media as it is in print. For photographers, the credit lines accompanying published images provide important name and professional recognition. Many photographers require that their fees be tripled when their photos are reproduced without proper credits. It is important to stipulate this up front in written contractual terms, however. Visible copyright notices also serve to remind the viewing audience that the images are protected under copyright law. The ease with which digital files can be copied makes the use of copyright credits important. Placement of credits and copyright notices are an element in any fee negotiation. It doesn't do photographers any good to have their work seen by millions of people if those people can't identify the photographer. Prominent credits and copyright notices make a difference, and further assure the protection of images in the many countries outside the U.S. that have more strict laws governing moral rights.

Alteration—A photographer might wish to allow a client to alter his or her work where alteration is customary—such as in advertising, or may wish to restrict alterations where they are taboo—such as in news reporting. Regardless of whether or not one will allow alteration of one's work, *always insist on indemnification from the client* if the work undergoes any alteration. Keep in mind that alterations include element changes, subtractions, and/or additions. Appropriate contractual language for dealing with credit and alteration can be found in chapter 6, "Formalizing Agreements."

Ethics

While countless new concerns have arisen with the advent of electronic and digital technologies, many of these are identical to those which photographers have experienced for years. The digital tools and electronic delivery systems available today simply provide better abilities and more opportunities, both to photographers and users of photography. These tools also facilitate undetectable alterations to photographic images, which can deceive the viewer.

ASMP is opposed to any alteration of the content of a news photograph. ASMP is also opposed to the undisclosed manipulation of the content of photographs presented as fact in editorial and documentary coverage, or in any other forum where photographs imply truth and fact. We urge all photographers and publishers to exercise caution when considering the alteration of photographic content.

Conclusion

A whole new realm of usage rights has been brought upon photographers with the advancement of digital and electronic technology. No longer are the mass distribution and reproduction of photographic images limited to print publications. Electronic media are already dwarfing the scope and distribution capabilities of traditional print. Photographers have the responsibility as visual communicators, content providers, and copyright owners to understand electronic technologies in order to serve their clients' changing needs. We must understand these new markets before we can adequately and fairly license our work for use in them.

Talk with your clients. Talk with each other. Learn together. It's a new world of opportunity for everyone.

Chapter 6

Formalizing Agreements

Richard Weisgrau

Every business day, photographers have a need to communicate transactional information to their prospects and clients. It might be the information in an estimate, the agreement expressed in a confirmation, or the verification of a delivery of photographs. Regardless of the nature of the communication, a record of your communications is important, especially when they set the terms, conditions, price, and license to use your work.

There are two types of communication: oral and written. Many of our communications are oral. No one could take the time in business to write everything down. However, some things are important enough to require a written record. Certainly any communication defining the fees for, and licensing of, your work should be in writing.

Photographers need a written record of their dealing with services, licenses, compensation, delivery, and value. Estimates, confirmations, invoices, delivery agreements, and copyright licenses should be simple and straightforward and embody the terms under which you conduct your business.

These agreements are often expressed through the use of forms, an easy means of communication, which require less time than other written means. However, some photographers prefer to use friendlier formats like letters, while others turn to more formally drawn contracts. Regardless of which you choose, the important point is to use, and to keep a copy of, some form of written communication when you carry out your transactional dealings.

Timely communication is very important. You should begin to communicate the transactional details of an assignment, whether proposed or awarded, immediately after your first contact with the prospective client. Too many photographers rely on their invoice to set the terms of their agreements. The danger of expressing your terms on the invoice is that it arrives after the work is done. If it contains any surprises in its content, which were not discussed prior to the work being done, it will be contestable, and could be considered an attempt to impose a contract after the fact. In such a case, some or all of the invoice's terms would not be binding on the client.

Keep in mind that you always want to present your terms, fees, etc. before the work is started. If a client has full access to your terms and other details prior to the work being started, and allows you to start and complete the work, it will be difficult for the client to protest. When a client is fully informed and proceeds with the work, it implies that a contract was in force, and that the conduct of the client (in allowing the work to proceed) amounts to a consent to your previously presented stipulations, terms, conditions, fees, etc.

A contract is formed between parties when certain conditions exist. There must be an offer, an acceptance, and consideration. An estimate is an offer to perform work with certain stipulations. An acceptance could be a purchase order matching the estimate, a letter awarding you the work, a client-signed confirmation, or an oral OK on the telephone. It is this oral acceptance which can present a problem, if denied later. This is where consent by conduct, allowing you to do the work, can be a factor. Remember, unless your stipulations were in the client's hands before the consent by conduct, you might not be able to enforce your stipulations. Do your paperwork in a timely fashion.

You should be aware that having the correct forms and releases is no guarantee that you will not be involved in a legal dispute. The purpose of correct paperwork is to avoid misunderstandings, to lessen the possibility of legal disputes, and to protect you and strengthen your position if they do eventuate.

Letter Agreements

Form letters, easily prepared and stored in your computer, are a softer way to present your paperwork. They have the advantage of appearing more personal and less aggressive than forms. The same stipulations made on form agreements can be made in form letters. However, one should exercise care not to cushion the language of the letter to the degree that the enforceability of the document comes into question. To avoid this, a transactional form letter should be specific and to the point, and not use any camouflage, or ambiguous wording. Hidden terms and ambiguity are frowned on by arbitrators and judges alike, not to mention everyday businesspeople who want to be up front about the details of their deals.

While we had considered including a sample letter agreement in this publication we ultimately decided not to do so. Any letter agreement which would be continually paraphrased would soon begin to take on the look and feel of a form agreement. We suggest that those photographers who wish to use letters to frame their agreements do so in their own style, then have the end result reviewed by their attorney. Additionally, in an age of computer and facsimile delivery of documentation and faceless transactions, it appears that the efficiency of a form is more acceptable than ever.

Forms

For many years, photographers have relied on forms to present their estimates, confirmations, invoices, delivery agreements, and other business communications. Forms have the benefit of being quick and simple to complete. Generally, they have a disadvantage however. They are seemingly set in stone, carry inapplicable terms and conditions, and often call for more information than one needs to present to the client. However, with the advent of the computer, it is possible to create form agreements which have only those elements which we need to convey for the specific work.

Let's take a look at some of the various forms which a photographer might use in his or her business and what purpose they serve.

The Estimate

An estimate is used to communicate the projected cost of the work to a prospective client. Additionally, it should embody other important details. These are a description of the work to be done, the media usage allowed for the stated fee, and terms and conditions which govern the transaction, performance, payment, etc.

The estimate should be sent to a client prior to starting any work. Even in those cases where an estimate is provided on the telephone, you should alert your client to the fact that you are sending a written estimate confirming the telephone estimate. Send the estimate by whatever means that will assure timely delivery, in time for your client to review it before the work starts, and you should have proof of delivery. A fax machine or fax modem is an indispensable device for this purpose.

The Confirmation

After your estimate is received, negotiated, and approved, including when it is accepted orally over the telephone, you should confirm the final details of the transaction. This might be done by having the client sign a copy of the estimate and return a copy to you. Or, it can be done by sending a separate confirmation to the client which embodies the details of the transaction. It might be the same form as your estimate but with a different heading, or it might be a letter referring to the estimate and stating that the work will proceed under the details as embodied therein, and with a copy attached.

Again, the confirmation should be sent to the client prior to the start of the work, if it is to have maximum force in any dispute which might arise. Work which is properly estimated and confirmed prior to the start of work is the least likely to be contested later. The properly executed confirmation, more than any other document, is an "ounce of prevention."

The Invoice

Everyone wants to get paid, and the invoice is the classic means of presenting your request for payment for services rendered. Invoices usually end up in accounts receivable departments of companies, and therefore are not in files pertaining to assignments. This is another reason why the invoice is not the best place to present your terms and conditions, and licensing of rights. There is no point in having them reside only in the accounting department's folders. You need these terms in the project work folder in the office of the assigning party.

Still, you should restate any stipulations on your estimate or confirmation on the invoice, or include a copy of the prior document. This emphasizes the details, and reinforces your position.

The following is a checklist of items which should be included on assignment, portfolio, and stock delivery memos.

Assignment Delivery Memo
Heading: Date, Job #, P.O. #, A.D., Client, etc.
Description of contents enclosed: Number, format, color or B&W, prints or transparencies
Terms and conditions of use: (same language as Estimate, Assignment Agreement/Confirmation)
Requirements (Suggested language):
Return unselected film by (date)
Return published film by (date)
If contents are proofs
For review only
Make selection based on composition and expression
Final image will be full frame unless specific crop or proportion is indicated
Notes:
Please review the attached schedule of images
Count will be considered accurate and quality deemed satisfactory for reproduction if exceptions have not been reported within 24 hrs
Your acceptance of this delivery constitutes your acceptance of all terms whether signed by you or not
Acceptance signature and date:

Portfolio Delivery Memo
Headings
Description of contents enclosed
$ Value of contents and case
Requirements (Suggested language):
For review only
No reproduction rights granted
Images may/may not be copied for file reference only
Portfolio to be returned by (date)
Notes:
Acceptance signature and date:

Stock Delivery Memo
Headings

Terms and conditions of use (either for review or specific license)

Description of images: Quantity, original, duplicate, format, ID number, value

Total: Count, $ value

Notes:

Acceptance signature and date:

The Delivery Memo

Never deliver your photography without a proof of delivery, and a memo presenting the terms of that delivery. Your work, whether assignment or stock photography, has value. That value should be protected for both your clients' and your interest. The delivery memo is similar in effect to a contract for a rental. It confirms that a prospective client has received something of value, and asserts the obligations of the recipient to return it or pay for it. What could be simpler and more reasonable?

When you ship assignment work, you should include an assignment delivery memo. It is like a packing slip, detailing the contents of the shipment, and the information needed for the client to match the shipment of work to its specific project. When you ship stock photography, the delivery memo serves to quantify and value the work, and the terms under which it is delivered to and may be retained by the recipient.

A properly executed stock photography delivery memo is not guaranteed to have the force of a contract. Some courts have held that the delivery memo, when preceded by a telephone conversation in which terms and conditions of delivery could have been discussed, is a contract after the fact. Indeed, many a recipient is astonished to find out that the transparencies which they have received are worth a small fortune.

The enforceability of a stock photography delivery memo is not guaranteed. Specific facts of a given situation will determine if the document has a binding effect on the recipient. Nonetheless, one should never fail to send a delivery memo. It is better than sending nothing at all.

The Predelivery Confirmation

Some stock photographers, in an effort to protect their work, have begun to use a predelivery confirmation. This form presents the stipulations which must be agreed to before you will send the work. Generally, it is faxed to the prospect, who must sign and return it before the photographer releases the shipment of photographs for delivery. When signed by a duly authorized party, it should have a binding effect. When your work has recognized value, it would seem quite advisable to use one of these forms.

The Form's Face

It is generally accepted that the face of a form has more weight than the reverse side, as does large print over small print. It is important, therefore, to have certain information on the face of the form. This information includes the job description, grant of media usage, price (fees and expenses), and payment terms and conditions. Remember that the estimate and confirmation are the most important paperwork you can have to protect your interest, and this information should be clearly stated thereon.

One very good element to employ on your paperwork is a condition precedent regarding payment. A condition precedent is a stipulation which conditions the sale in such a way as to have a binding effect if the purchaser accepts your proposal.

Here is an example:

On the front of the estimate, confirmation, and invoice, near the statement of price, your paperwork might carry this legend:

Media Usage RIGHTS GRANTED, as defined herein, are granted conditionally upon receipt of full payment of price indicated herein. Failure to make payment voids any media usage granted, and constitutes copyright infringement.

Licensing Considerations

When writing a license or defining use, you should be as specific as possible. Various licensing considerations are presented below to assist you.

Copyright Rights—(your authority to license rights)

Copyright owners have the right to control the following uses of their works:

1. Reproduction—making copies by any means
2. Derivation—making new work(s) based upon yours
3. Distribution—publication of your work (distribution to the public)
4. Performance—showing your work (by mechanical means)
5. Public Display—exhibition of your work

Examples of Copyright Rights:

Reproduction	Derivation	Distribution	Performance
Display	Photocopying	Art reference	Electronic
Slide show	Exhibit	Scanning	Art rendering
Print	Compositing		

Types of Media and Application:

Print	Electronic	Film	Posters
Television	Motion picture	Brochures	Videotape
Film strip	Billboards	Laser disk	Audiovisual show
Bound pages	CD-ROM	Slide show	Books*
CD-Interactive	Magazines*	Books*	Product packaging
Magazines*			

*Note: Books and magazines could be print (bound pages), electronic (CD-ROM or CD-Interactive) or via electronic bulletin board services.

What factors should a license include:

1. Copyright rights involved
2. Media use

3. Specific application
4. Geographic limits
5. Quantity limits (press run/circulation)
6. Time limits on rights
7. Size and placement of work

For a checklist of additional considerations, see next page.

An example: Images to be reproduced and distributed in print version of *Hooplah Magazine*, one time only, between January and March, 1997. Circulation not to exceed 1,000,000 copies in North America only. Images to be used inside magazine and up to ¼ of a page per image.

Checklist of considerations for licensing use of images
I. Grant of Rights
    1. term
        a. period of years
        b. life of product
        c. copyright life of product
    2. extension
        a. versions
        b. additional pressings
        c. revisions
    3. exclusivity
        a. nonexclusive
        b. limited exclusivity
        c. full exclusivity
    4. territory
        a. limited
        b. unlimited
    5. restrictions
        a. mechanical (to press disks)
        b. on screen only
        c. print with the product
        d. advertising/promotion of product
        e. public display
        f. broadcast
        g. derivative
        h. alteration
        i. file storage size per image
        j. transmission
        k. printout from disk or screen
II. Define Application
    1. type (disk, on-line, cable T.V., etc.)
    2. title(s)

3. quantity

4. labeling

5. encryption

6. protection of images

III. Compensation

1. flat fee

2. fee stepped to quantity

3. advance plus royalty

4. advance against royalty

5. royalty

IV. Conditions *(Note: suggested terms and conditions as outlined on pages 7 through 11 generally apply)*

1. warrantees

2. obligations

3. remedies

4. status of provider digital files

V. Miscellaneous

1. designation of agent

2. settling disputes

3. audit rights

4. definitions

Specifying Usage

The following are examples of common usage situations for which you would construct a license to grant rights. Always keep in mind, however, that each situation is unique. In book usage, for example, such factors as chapter openers, frontispiece, hard- or softcover, and book club editions could be part of a license.

A license of rights for such uses as audiovisual, wall murals, postcards, posters, greeting cards, and art decor should specify the limitations on size, number, time, location, and any other factor relating to the particular use to avoid questions or disputes that might otherwise arise later.

New uses for photography arise daily, but the following samples should help you in constructing licenses for your own business. Do it well so that both the seller's and the buyer's rights are understood.

Advertising Rights Granted

One-time, nonexclusive usage by (client) as (¼-, ½-, full-page, or spread) image for (consumer or trade) ad, limited to (number) insertions for (national or regional) circulation in (color or B&W), as (define media and application types) for (number of months, years, or unlimited). Subject photograph is of (description) and is copyrighted by (photographer). All rights are reserved except those noted on this invoice.

Annual Report or Brochure Rights Granted

One-time, nonexclusive usage by (client) in (title of annual report or brochure), limited to a print run of (number) as (cover or inside), used no larger than (page, spread, or wraparound) in (color or B&W). Subject photograph is of (description) and is copyrighted by (photographer). All rights are reserved except those noted on this invoice.

Magazine Rights Granted

One-time, nonexclusive (e.g., English, French) language rights for editorial usage in (name of magazine), with a printed circulation of (number), for (month or edition and year) for distribution in (country or region), to be published only as (cover or inside, portion of page, number of pages). Subject photograph is of (description) and is copyrighted by (photographer). No rights granted for advertising or promotion of cover or inside pages. All rights are reserved except those noted on this invoice.

(Note: Define whether the media is print, electronic, or both.)

Terms and Conditions

Another important part of your form agreements, after the specific details of the work, price, and rights, will be the terms and conditions which you use to govern the transaction. There are many possible combinations of these elements, depending upon the nature of the work. This text has been prepared so that you can customize your terms and conditions depending upon your own needs in general or specifically. That is, you can use this information to customize standard forms or to construct forms made to order for each use.

Conditions on the Front Side of Your Assignment Form

The front of your form agreements should contain the most important conditions you are imposing as a part of your offer to perform work or acceptance of work. We have listed seven conditions which we see as extremely important.

These seven conditions are prominently placed to avoid any claim that the client did not see or was not aware of them. The conditions operate as follows:

1. Allows a variance in estimated expenses.
2. Makes the transfer of usage rights conditional upon payment in full.
3. Makes the use specified the only use allowed, and requires written additions.
4. Sets payment terms, and imposes a rebilling fee for unpaid invoices. (Some might prefer to charge interest for unpaid invoices.)
5. Requires that advance payments be received before you begin assignment.
6. Refers the client to the other terms and conditions on the reverse side. (See below.)
7. Forms an agreement by the client's conduct if you are allowed to do the work.

Many ASMP members have asked ASMP to develop a set of terms and conditions which are "softer and more client friendly." After much consideration, we decided not to do this. ASMP's responsibility is to provide the best protection, in its judgment, for you and your business. Softer, friendlier terms are generally weaker terms. While the individual photographer may choose to take this path, we thought it inappropriate to lead the way. Straightforward, factual, and fair terms are nothing to shy away from.

Signed or Unsigned

There are two approaches taken with these forms. On one we provided a sample of language to be used if you are going to get your paperwork signed. We recommend that you get signed paperwork, as it is the most enforceable.

However, we understand that some clients will refuse to sign anything. We have attempted to construct the acceptance language on the bottom of the forms to be as enforceable as possible whether signed or not. Still, a signature is best if you can get it.

Terms and Conditions on the Reverse Side of Your Forms

The terms and conditions on the reverse side of the forms serve very useful business and legal purposes. You should understand these terms, when to apply them, and what options are available. The following section is intended to provide the photographer with a better insight into the protective language used on the reverse side of the forms, and when to apply it.

The best way to prepare your forms is to customize them to your specific policies and for the specific job. To do this, you should have a firm understanding of what each term establishes by its presence, and when each applies. This is not a place for guess-work. If you are not sure, get competent advice. If still in doubt as to whether a term applies, it is better to include it than to exclude it. Printed here are the terms and conditions which are normally found on the reverse side of a form. These specific terms are meant to be used with the specific terms and conditions which appear on the front of the form. These terms are discussed in the preceding section.

Term #1

Question: Are you supplying images in some form? If yes, use term #1.

[1] "Images" means all viewable renditions furnished by Photographer hereunder, whether captured or stored in photographic, magnetic, optical, or any other medium whatsoever.

This term defines "images" in a manner to include all visuals furnished by you regardless of medium. The word "images" appears throughout the terms and conditions, and use of this definition is critically important to protect your interest.

Term #2

Question: Do you intend to own the processed film, prints, etc., and the copyright to the work? If yes, then use term #2.

[2] All Images and rights therein, including copyright, remain the sole and exclusive property of Photographer. Unless otherwise provided herein, any grant of rights is limited to one (1) year from the date hereof and to the territory of the United States.

This term establishes that you retain ownership to: 1) the tangible images—prints, disks, transparencies, etc., and 2) the copyright to the images.

The term also sets defaults on the use of the images, if you do not specify other limits in the usage specifications, to: 1) a maximum of one year, and 2) to the U.S. only.

Term #3
Question: Do you want to hold your client responsible to return your images in good condition, and in a reasonable period of time? If yes, then use term #3.

[3] Client assumes insurer's liability (a) to indemnify Photographer for loss, damage, or misuse of any Images, and (b) to return all Images prepaid and fully insured, safe and undamaged, by bonded messenger, air freight, or registered mail, within thirty (30) days after the first use thereof as provided herein, but in all events (whether published or unpublished) within thirty (30) days after the date of final licensed use. Client assumes full liability for its principals, employees, agents, affiliates, successors, and assigns (including, without limitation, independent contractors, messengers, and freelance researchers) for any loss, damage, delay in returning, or misuse of the Images.

This term places responsibility on the client for:
1. Protecting your interest for any loss, damage, or misuse of the images.
2. Returning the images by specified means.
3. Returning the images by specified deadlines.
4. For any losses, misuse, etc. by any party receiving the images from the client.

Term #4
Question: Do you want to set a default for the value of your work? If yes, then use term #4. However, be sure to attach the required schedule(s) if they apply.

[4] Reimbursement by Client for loss or damage of each original photographic transparency or film negative shall be in the amount of One Thousand Five Hundred Dollars ($1,500), or such other amount set forth next to said item on the attached schedule. Reimbursement by Client for loss or damage of each other item shall be in the amount set forth next to said item on the attached schedule. Photographer and Client agree that said amount represents the fair and reasonable value of each item, and that Photographer would not sell all rights to such item for less than said amount. Client understands that each original photographic transparency and film negative is unique and does not have an exact duplicate, and may be impossible to replace or re-create.

This term sets the traditional $1,500 value per item for your original photographic images, unless you specify otherwise on a separate list. The value of non-original items are to be specified on an attached schedule.

Note: If you are routinely supplying dupes, scans on disk, or tape, etc., you should include the value of such items in the clause. Keep in mind that any declared value must be reasonable and provable if it is to be accepted by a court.

Term #5
Question: Are you requesting a copyright credit line with your images? If yes, then use term #5 and be sure to specify the placement.

[5] Photographer shall receive credit for Images as specified on the face hereof unless no placement is specified.

This term requires that a credit line be given as stated on the front of the form and in the place specified. No credit is required if no placement is specified.

Note: If you are doing work in applications where credit lines are not normally given, you can leave the placement blank or remove the term from your form. Copyright credit is not required to retain your copyright, but is desired and has specific advantages if used.

Term #6

Question: Does the work you are doing require alteration of the image you supply to the client? If yes, use option #6C. If no, use option #6A or 6B.

[6] Option A: Client will not make or permit any alterations, including but not limited to additions, subtractions, or adaptations, in respect of the Images, alone or with any other material.

[6] Option B: Client may not make or permit any alterations, including but not limited to additions, subtractions, or adaptations, in respect of the Images, alone or with any other material, except that cropping, and alterations of contrast, brightness, and color balance, consistent with reproduction needs may be made.

Terms 6A or B should be inserted when you will not allow the client to alter the image in any way.

[6] Option C: Client may make or permit any alterations, including but not limited to additions, subtractions, or adaptations, in respect of the Images, alone or with any other material, subject to the provisions as stated in [7] below.

Term 6C permits the client to make alterations, but makes them responsible for any consequences to those alterations, in accord with term [7].

Note: Some applications for images, like advertising, require that images be altered. It would seem necessary to give the client permission to make such alterations provided that you are protected from any consequences of the alteration.

Term #7

Question: No question here at all. Use this term on all your paperwork. It's the safest way.

[7] Client will indemnify and defend Photographer against all claims, liability, damages, costs, and expenses, including reasonable legal fees and expenses, arising out of any use of any Images for which no release was furnished by Photographer, or any Images which are altered by Client. Unless furnished, no release exists. Photographer's liability for all claims shall not exceed in any event the total amount paid under this invoice.

This protects you if the images are used in an application requiring a release, and you have not supplied same, and for images altered by the client. It also establishes that there is no release unless you have supplied it.

Note: Some releases protect better than others. If you want to transfer the responsibility for assessing the force of the release to the client, you might consider adding this optional clause to the term's language:

Copies of any available model release are attached hereto. Determining the suitability of same for any application is the sole responsibility of the client.

If you add this language, you must attach copies of the actual release(s) for the work.

Term #8

Question: Is your client supplying props or other items for the shoot? If yes, use term #8.

[8] Client assumes full risk of loss or damage to or arising from materials furnished by client hereunder and warrants that said materials are adequately insured against such loss, damage, or liability. Client shall indemnify Photographer against all claims, liability, damages, and expenses incurred by Photographer in connection with any claim arising out of use of said material hereunder.

This term is intended to transfer responsibility for any client supplied materials, props, etc. on the assignment. The principle is meant to transfer the bailee responsibility you have for another's property while it is in your care. It is not a substitute for insurance, but an added safeguard to protect your interest.

Term #9

Question: No question here. Use this term on all your paperwork for maximum protection.

[9] Client may not assign or transfer this agreement or any rights granted hereunder. This agreement binds and inures to the benefit of Photographer, Client, Client's principals, employees, agents, and affiliates, and their respective heirs, legal representatives, successors, and assigns. Client and its principals, employees, agents, and affiliates are jointly and severally liable for the performance of all payments and other obligations hereunder. No amendment or waiver of any terms is binding unless set forth in writing and signed by the parties. However, the invoice may reflect, and Client is bound by, oral authorizations for fees or expenses which could not be confirmed in writing because of insufficient time. This agreement incorporates by reference Article 2 of the Uniform Commercial Code, and the Copyright Act of 1976, as amended.

This term prevents the client from assigning responsibility for the agreement to another party. It also limits changes to the agreement to be made in writing, unless they are made by the client during the assignment. Finally, it calls for the application of certain laws to the agreement, as a means of reinforcing the agreement's strength.

Term #10

Question: Is arbitration or court your preferred alternative for dispute resolution? If you want arbitration, use option #10A. If court, use option #10B or, if you wish to keep your options open, use #10C.

[10] Option A: Except as provided in (11) below, any dispute regarding this agreement shall be arbitrated in [PHOTOGRAPHER'S CITY AND STATE] under rules of the American Arbitration Association and the laws of [STATE OF ARBITRATION]. Judgment on the arbitration award may be entered in any court having jurisdiction. Any dispute involving

$_____ [LIMIT OF LOCAL SMALL CLAIMS COURT] or less may be submitted without arbitration to any court having jurisdiction thereof. Client shall pay all arbitration and court costs, Photographer's reasonable legal fees, and expenses, and legal interest on any award or judgment, in the event of any award or judgment in favor of Photographer.*

This optional language forces disputes to arbitration in the state which you place in the term. It allows you to take any claim within the limits of small claims court to that court without arbitration. It also places the responsibility for legal fees, court costs, etc. on the client should you win your case.

[10] Option B: Except as provided in [11] below, any dispute regarding this agreement shall be adjudicated in [PHOTOGRAPHER'S CITY AND STATE] under the laws of [STATE]. Client shall pay all court costs, Photographer's reasonable legal fees, and expenses, and legal interest on any award or judgment, in the event of any award or judgment in favor of Photographer.

This optional language forces any dispute to the courts of the state which you place in the term. As in Option A, it makes the client responsible for all legal fees, expenses, etc. if you prevail.

[10] Option C: Except as provided in (11) below, any dispute regarding this agreement shall be, at Photographer's sole discretion, either (1) arbitrated in (use 10A language), or (2) adjudicated in (use 10B language).

Note: You should confer with a your legal advisor to determine if arbitration is a suitable avenue for dispute resolution in your jurisdiction. Arbitration is not necessarily the best avenue for dispute resolution, although it can be. Legal action through the courts is generally more expensive than arbitration.

Both options make the federal courts the forum for copyright infringement cases under term #11.

The language intended to compel the payment of legal fees and costs is not a guarantee that the arbitrators or judge will award them. While the language attempts to make it a contractual commitment, it is not the final determiner.

Term #11

Question: No question here, use this on all your paperwork. It is the law.

[11] Client hereby expressly consents to the jurisdiction of the Federal courts with respect to claims by Photographer under the Copyright Act of 1976, as amended.

This clause makes the federal courts the forum for a copyright infringement case. This is in keeping with the federal copyright law itself, which defines the federal courts as the courts of proper jurisdiction for such action.

Term #12

Question: Do you pay freelance and staff overtime? If yes, consider using term #12.

[12] In the event a shoot extends beyond eight (8) consecutive hours, Photographer may charge for such excess time of assistants and freelance staff at the rate of one-and-one-half their hourly rates.

This term sets eight consecutive hours as a standard day, and reserves the right for you to charge overtime fees for your staff and assistants.

Term #13

Question: Do you want to be paid for a reshoot demanded by a client? If yes, use term #13.

[13] Reshoots: Client will be charged 100 percent fee and expenses for any reshoot required by Client. For any reshoot required because of an act of God or the fault of a third party, Photographer will charge no additional fee, and Client will pay all expenses. If Photographer charges for special contingency insurance and is paid in full for the shoot, Client will not be charged for any expenses covered by insurance. A list of exclusions from such insurance will be provided on request.

The charges for a reshoot are established in this term. If the reshoot is required by the client, it sets 100 percent of the original fee and expenses as the payment. It requires expenses only when a reshoot is required because of the act of a third party or an act of God. It also allows that no expenses covered by insurance will be charged to the client if it has paid a fee for the coverage.

Note: This clause does not absolve you from having to reshoot at your own expense if your negligence is the cause of a reshoot.

You should consider deleting the statements about insurance if you do not make such contingency insurance available to your clients.

Term #14

Question: Do you want to establish a cancellation policy? If yes, use term #14.

[14] Cancellations and postponements: Client is responsible for payment of all expenses incurred up to the time of cancellation, plus 50 percent of Photographer's fee. If notice of cancellation is given less than two (2) business days before the shoot date, Client will be charged 100 percent fee. Weather postponements: Unless otherwise agreed, Client will be charged 100 percent fee if postponement is due to weather conditions on location and 50 percent fee if postponement occurs before departure to location.

This term sets up a cancellation policy and speaks clearly for itself.

Note: You might want to consider the use and language of this term in light of your own policy before you accept this specific language as a default.

Releases and Permissions

Model Release Forms

Model releases are important to avoid lawsuits. This "release" is a document that says that the person being photographed has given consent to the use of the image.

The purpose of the release is to protect the photographer against an invasion-of-privacy lawsuit. Generally, these actions arise when an image is used without authorization for purposes of "trade or advertising." In addition, a release may protect the photographer against a libel suit. Libel suits generally allege that the person in the image has been subjected to some form of embarrassment, loss of status, etc., by virtue of the image's publication. The risks in these areas are extremely serious. Legal actions, when instituted, often involve claims of many hundreds of thousands of dollars.

Another difficult area involves images reproduced in exhibitions, books, and the like. Most legal opinion holds that the use of such images is as protected as that of any subject pertaining to current events, politics, etc. (The commercial sale of individual fine art photographs may not enjoy such protection.) There is, however, some opinion indicating that the First Amendment was primarily intended to protect social, political, economic, and similar commentary, and that the further one gets from that, the greater the need for a release.

Libel

On the question of libel, as distinguished from the right of privacy, a different legal question is posed. The primary issue is not whether the nature of the usage was protected, but instead whether the person in the image was depicted in a truthful and non-defamatory manner.

In portraying public figures, the courts will allow more leeway about inaccurate associations, provided that the publication is not both (a) substantially false and (b) published as knowingly false or in reckless disregard of the truth.

In some of the gray areas, the type of medium used may also be important. For example, courts sometimes recognize that there is only a short time for checking information available to newspaper publishers, while a longer lead time is available to book or magazine publishers.

The gray area between protected "news or editorial" uses and unprotected "advertising or trade purposes" can be confusing. In many jurisdictions, a magazine or book cover is as protected as the contents, even though the cover is used, in effect, to "sell" the publication. But if that same image is used to advertise any other product aside from the publication itself, then that additional use will be considered an unprotected advertising purpose.

Other interesting contrasts abound. In one case, a manufacturer's purely instructional manual was held to be an unprotected promotional publication (despite its being, at least in large part, substantially for educational purposes). On the other hand, editorial "service" material (e.g., fashion items) in regular news media have been held protected in some cases.

Sample Release Forms

Included here are various model release forms, including an adult model release, a minor model release, a property release, a simplified release, and a pocket model release.

Adult Model Release

This is an all-encompassing release, and the one generally recommended. It covers a wide range of areas, including a waiver by the subject to inspect or approve any finished image, the right of the photographers and their assigns to alter or distort the image, and a complete "hold harmless" clause if there is a liability from any use of the image whatsoever.

Simplified Model Release

This form is one that many professional photographers use. It does not afford the overall protection of the general release, but if the use of the image is to be a rather restricted one, it may be easier to obtain a signature on this form than on the longer one. However, note the wording: ". . . if the use is to be a rather restricted one . . ." In other words, get the longer release signed if possible.

Minor Model Release

The minor release has substantially the same language as the adult release, except that it provides for the signature of a parent or guardian of the minor, required by virtually all states. Of course, you or your attorney should check the statutes in your state on what age constitutes a minor. Also, be warned that parents may not have the legal authority to guarantee that their release will be completely binding. In a legal action over the release, a court could hold that the parents did not have the authority to bind the minor. While this is unlikely to happen in the case of paid professional models, it cannot be ruled out, especially where nonprofessional models are involved.

Pocket Model Release

The pocket model release affords reasonable protection with a minimum of words. Use the longer release forms whenever possible, however.

Assignment Model Release

Even in situations where someone is photographed for a very specific assignment and client, a release is needed. This minimal release simply gives acknowledgment that the model allowed the photo to be taken. This release gives no rights for other uses to the photographer or the client than those specified on the face of the form. Frequently, it is the only type of release that a professional model will sign.

Property Release

A property release, signed by the owner or agency for the owner, may be required for places that are photographed. Some photographers also use this release for pets, automobiles, works of art, and similar property. Courts have recognized that the owner has a commercially valuable right in exploiting the depictions of his or her property. When the property can be clearly identified from the image by the owner, it is important to have a property release. As with model releases, property releases are required when the images are used for trade or advertising purposes. As with model releases, it is always smart to protect yourself from a variety of claims by obtaining a signed property release wherever you are shooting. Another potential concern is if a property changes hands. Depending on the terms of the sale and other factors, the original property release might not be valid. It is advisable to ascertain the current ownership of a property if a photograph is going to be published, particularly if the intended use is in advertising.

Indemnification Agreement

There are times in one's work when a party you contract with has to take a risk. It might be a model being asked to sit on the edge of a roof of a tall building, or being asked to pose with a lion. In each of these situations, the photographer is at special risk. If the lion, trained as it might be, gets spooked and bites the model, or a gust of wind causes the model to lose balance and fall off the roof, you might be held liable for the damages.

Obviously, the best way to deal with risk is to insure for it. However, it is prudent to secure an indemnification agreement from those parties who might be at risk, while rendering services to you, on your shoot. We have included a sample indemnification agreement in our grouping of sample forms. This, like all agreements, will be influenced by state law and court decisions. Having this form reviewed by your attorney for its effectiveness under your state laws is a good idea.

Keep in mind that you are responsible for injury to your employees, and you cannot be indemnified by them under law. You are supposed to carry worker's compensation insurance for this purpose. It would not be uncommon for an injured freelance assistant or model to claim that he or she was your employee if he or she signed such an indemnification agreement. If the authorities found him or her to be an employee, you would be liable, in spite of the agreement. Here is one case where an independent contractor's agreement is in order.

Independent Contractors Agreement

All too often, ASMP sees photographers caught up in cases where their freelance assistants, and often models, claim to have been employees. They do this when they run out of work and seek unemployment benefits, or when they are injured on a job and not covered by insurance.

The problem is that government agencies seem to go out of their way when reviewing the cases to make the claimant an employee. We expect it is because they don't like to deny citizens claims when there is someone there to pay for it. You, the photographer, could be held responsible if you do not have the proper insurance, or have not treated the claimant's payments as wages.

We also see problems where state and federal tax examiners hold freelance assistants, models, and other service providers to be employees of photographers, and then tax and penalize the photographers for failure to withhold the proper taxes. This is good for the government treasury and bad for the photographers, and you can't insure against it.

While there is no guaranteed way to protect yourself from this danger, we suggest that you have independent contractors execute an agreement acknowledging their status with you. A sample form is included in the packet of sample forms. Again, a legal review is recommended, as state laws will have a major bearing on the effectiveness of such an agreement.

We have added a condition precedent to the agreement which is intended to fend off the cases of the kind we have described above. Still, there are no guarantees in business.

The Terms and Conditions and other language on the front and back of forms and other sections of this chapter are available in ASCII format on Macintosh and MS-DOS disks. As the disks will be in ASCII, users will have to format their own forms and insert the terms and conditions as required. There will be a nominal fee for the disk. Please note, the disk can be used only in conjunction with the information in this book. For information about this, please get in touch with ASMP National at (609) 799-8300.

Adult Release

In consideration of my engagement as a model, and for other good and valuable consideration herein acknowledged as received, I hereby grant to _____ ("Photographer"), his/her heirs, legal representatives, and assigns, those for whom Photographer is acting, and those acting with his/her authority, and permission, the irrevocable and unrestricted right and permission to take, copyright in his/her own name or otherwise, and use, reuse, publish, and republish photographic portraits or pictures of me or in which I may be included, in whole or in part, or composite or distorted in character or form, without restriction as to changes or alterations, in conjunction with my own or a fictitious name, or reproductions thereof in color or otherwise, made through any medium at his/her studios or elsewhere, and in any and all media now or hereafter known for illustration, promotion, art, editorial, advertising, trade, or any other purpose whatsoever. I also consent to the use of any published matter in conjunction therewith.

I hereby waive any right that I may have to inspect or approve the finished product or products and the advertising copy or other matter that may be used in connection therewith or the use to which it may be applied.

I hereby release, discharge, and agree to save harmless Photographer, his/her heirs, legal representatives, and assigns, and all persons acting under his/her permission or authority or those for whom he/she is acting, from any liability by virtue of any blurring, distortion, alteration, optical illusion, or use in composite form, whether intentional or otherwise, that may occur or be produced in the taking of said picture or in any subsequent processing thereof, as well as any publication thereof, including without limitation any claims for libel or invasion of privacy.

I hereby warrant that I am of full age and have the right to contract in my own name. I have read the above authorization, release, and agreement, prior to its execution, and I am fully familiar with the contents thereof. This release shall be binding upon me and my heirs, legal representatives, and assigns.

_____   _____
DATE   NAME

_____   _____
WITNESS   ADDRESS

Simplified Adult Release

For valuable consideration received, I hereby grant to _____ ("Photographer") the absolute and irrevocable right and unrestricted permission in respect of photographic portraits or pictures that he/she had taken of me or in which I may be included with others, to copyright the same, in his/her own name or otherwise; to use re-use, publish, and republish the same in whole or in part, individually or in any and all media now or hereafter known, and for any purpose whatsoever, for illustration, promotion, art, editorial, advertising, and trade, or any other purpose whatsoever without restriction as to alteration; and to use my name in connection therewith if he/she so chooses.

I hereby release and discharge Photographer from any and all claims and demands arising out of or in connection with the use of the photographs, including without limitation any and all claims for libel or invasion of privacy.

This authorization and release shall also inure to the benefit of the heirs, legal representatives, licensees, and assigns of Photographer, as well as the person(s) for whom he/she took the photographs.

I am of full age and have the right to contract in my own name. I have read the foregoing and fully understand the contents thereof. This release shall be binding upon me and my heirs, legal representatives, and assigns.

_____
DATE

_____
WITNESS

_____
NAME

_____
ADDRESS

Minor Release

In consideration of the engagement as a model of the minor named below, and for other good and valuable consideration herein acknowledged as received, upon the terms hereinafter stated, I hereby grant to_____ ("Photographer"), his/her legal representatives and assigns, those for whom Photographer is acting, and those acting with his/her authority and permission, the absolute right and permission to take, copyright and use, reuse, publish, and republish photographic portraits or pictures of the minor or in which the minor may be included, in whole or in part, or composite or distorted in character or form, without restriction as to changes or alterations from time to time, in conjunction with the minor's own or a fictitious name, or reproductions thereof in color or otherwise, made through any medium at his/her studios or elsewhere, and in any and all media now or hereafter known, for art, advertising, trade, or any other purpose whatsoever. I also consent to the use of any published matter in conjunction therewith.

I hereby waive any right that I or the minor my have to inspect or approve the finished product or products or the advertising copy or printed matter that may be used in connection therewith or the use to which it may be applied.

I hereby release, discharge, and agree to save harmless and defend Photographer, his/her legal representatives or assigns, and all persons acting under his/her permission or authority or those for whom he/she is acting, from any liability by virtue of any blurring, distortion, alteration, optical illusion, or use in composite form, whether intentional or otherwise, that may occur or be produced in the taking of said picture or in any subsequent processing thereof, as well as any publication thereof, including without limitation any claims for libel or invasion of privacy.

I hereby warrant that I am of full age and have every right to contract for the minor in the above regard. I state further that I have read the above authorization, release, and agreement, prior to its execution, and that I am fully familiar with the contents thereof. This release shall be binding upon the minor and me, and our respective heirs, legal representatives, and assigns.

_____	_____
DATE	FATHER/MOTHER/GUARDIAN
_____	_____
MINOR'S NAME	ADDRESS
_____	_____
MINOR'S ADDRESS	WITNESS

Pocket Release

For valuable consideration received, I hereby grant to _____ ("Photographer") and his/her legal representatives and assigns, the irrevocable and unrestricted right to use and publish photographs of me, or in which I may be included, for editorial, trade, advertising, and any other purpose and in any manner and medium; to alter the same without restriction; and to copyright the same. I hereby release Photographer and his/her legal representatives and assigns from all claims and liability relating to said photographs.

_____
NAME (PRINT)

_____
SIGNATURE

_____
STREET ADDRESS

_____
IF MINOR, SIGNATURE OF PARENT/GUARDIAN

_____
DATE

_____
PHONE

_____
CITY/STATE/ZIP

_____
WITNESS

Property Release

motion picture film footage

For good and valuable consideration herein acknowledged as received, the undersigned, be-ing the legal owner of, or having the right to permit the taking and use of photographs of, certain property designated as_____ , does grant to _____ ("Photographer"), his/her heirs, legal representatives, agents, and assigns the full rights to take and use such photographs and copyright same, in advertising, trade, or for any purpose. *Contingent upon the conditions set forth.*

The undersigned also consents to the use of any printed matter in conjunction therewith.

The undersigned hereby waives any right that he/she/it may have to inspect or approve the finished product or products, or the advertising copy or published matter that may be used in connection therewith, or the use to which it may be applied.

The undersigned hereby releases, discharges, and agrees to save harmless and defend Pho-tographer, his/her heirs, legal representatives, and assigns, and all persons acting under his/her permission or authority, or those for whom he/she is acting, from any liability by virtue of any blurring, distortion, alteration, optical illusion, or use in composite form, whether intentional or otherwise, that may occur or be produced in the taking of said picture or in any subsequent processing thereof, as well as any publication thereof, even though it may subject the under-signed, his/her heirs, representatives, successors, and assigns, to ridicule, scandal, reproach, scorn, and indignity.

The undersigned hereby warrants that he/she is of full age and has every right to contract in his/her own name in the above regard. The undersigned states further that he/she has read the above authorization, release, and agreement, prior to its execution, and that he/she is fully familiar with the contents thereof. If the undersigned is signing as an agent or employee of a firm or corporation, the undersigned warrants that he/she is fully authorized to do so. This release shall be binding upon the undersigned and his/her/its heirs, legal representatives, successors, and assigns.

_____   _____
DATE   NAME

_____   _____
WITNESS   ADDRESS

Indemnification Agreement

(MODEL) hereby agrees to protect, defend, indemnify, and hold harmless (PHOTOGRAPHER) from and against any and all claims, losses, liabilities, settlements, expenses, and damages, including legal fees and costs (all referred to collectively as "Claims"), which (PHOTOGRAPHER) may suffer or to which (he/she/it) may be subjected for any reason, even if attributable to negligence on the part of (PHOTOGRAPHER) or any other entity, arising out of or related to any act, omission or occurrence in connection with the creation, production, or use of any image, or the performance of any service relating to this Agreement or its subject matter. This provision shall apply to Claims of every sort and nature, whether based on tort, strict liability, personal injury, property damage, contract, defamation, privacy rights, publicity rights, copyrights, or otherwise. (MODEL's) obligations under this provision shall survive the performance, termination, or cancellation of this Agreement.

_____		_____
DATE		NAME
_____		_____
WITNESS		ADDRESS

Independent Contractor Agreement

AGREEMENT entered into as of the _____ day of _____, 19____, between _____ located at _____ (hereinafter referred to as the "Photographer") and _____, located at _____ (hereinafter referred to as the "Contractor").

The Parties hereto agree as follows:

1. Services to be Rendered. The Contractor agrees to perform the following services for the Photographer.

_____

_____

_____

2. Schedule. The Contractor shall complete the services pursuant to the following schedule:

_____

_____

_____

3. Fee and Expenses. The Contractor shall be paid as follows:
The Photographer shall reimburse the Contractor only for the listed expenses.

_____

4. Payment. Payment shall be made as follows:_____

5. Condition precedent to Agreement. Contractor does not consider himself/herself eligible for nor has any intention to, and will not, apply for unemployment or workmen's compensation benefits in a claim against the Photographer.

6. Relationship of Parties. Both parties agree that the Contractor is an independent contractor. This Agreement is not an employment agreement, nor does it constitute a joint venture or partnership between the Photographer and Contractor. Nothing contained herein shall be construed to be inconsistent with this independent contractor relationship.

7. Proprietary Rights. The proprietary rights in any work produced in conjunction with this Agreement shall be vested solely and exclusively in the Photographer.

8. Miscellany. This Agreement constitutes the entire agreement between the parties. Its terms can be modified only by an instrument in writing signed by both parties, except that oral authorizations of additional fees and expenses shall be permitted if necessary to speed the progress of work. This Agreement shall be binding on the parties, their heirs, successors, assigns, and personal representatives. A waiver of a breach of any of the provisions of this Agreement shall not be construed as a continuing waiver of other breaches of the same or other provisions hereof. This Agreement shall be governed by the laws of the State of _____.

IN WITNESS WHEREOF, the parties hereto have signed this as of the date first set forth above.

_____   _____
PHOTOGRAPHER   CONTRACTOR

Straight Shooter Studio, Inc.

123 Anystreet, Hometown, ZX 12345 • Telephone: 123-555-1212 • Fax: 123-555-2121

Estimate

THIS ESTIMATE IS VALID FOR NINETY DAYS FROM THIS DATE OF ISSUE:_____ REFERENCE #_____

Client:

Assignment Description:

Usage Specifications:

Estimated Price: FEES _____ EXPENSES _____ TOTAL _____

Note: For details of fee structure and expenses, refer to attached schedule.

Advance Payments: FEES _____ EXPENSES _____ TOTAL _____

Conditions of Transaction:

1. The copyright to all images created or supplied pursuant to this agreement remain the sole and exclusive property of the photographer. There is no assignment of copyright, agreement to do work for hire, or intention of joint copyright expressed or implied hereunder. The client is licensed the above usage specifications in accord with the conditions stated herein. Proper copyright notice, which reads: © 19_____ Straight Shooter, must be displayed with the following placement:_____ . Notice is not required if placement is not specified. Omission of required notice results in loss to the licensor and will be billed at triple the invoiced fee.

2. All expense estimates are subject to normal trade variance of 10 percent.

3. Usage specifications above convert to copyright license only upon receipt of full payment.

4. Usage beyond that defined above requires additional written license from the licensor.

5. Invoices are payable on receipt. Unpaid invoices are subject to a rebilling fee of _____.

6. Advance payments must be received at least 24 hours prior to assignment commencement.

7. The sale is subject to all terms and conditions on the reverse side hereof.

8. If client orders the performance of any services required to complete the above described assignment, it constitutes an acceptance by conduct of this estimate in its entirety, whether signed by you or not.

_____   _____
SUBMITTED BY   DATE

_____   _____
ACCEPTED BY   DATE

Straight Shooter Studio, Inc.

123 Anystreet, Hometown, ZX 12345 • Telephone: 123-555-1212 • Fax: 123-555-2121

Assignment Confirmation

Date assignment to begin: _____ Reference # _____ Date of Confirmation _____

Client:

Assignment Description:

Usage Specifications:

Estimated Price: FEES _____ EXPENSES _____ TOTAL _____

Note: For details of fee structure and expenses, refer to attached schedule.

Advance Payments: FEES _____ EXPENSES _____ TOTAL _____

Conditions of Transaction:

1. The copyright to all images created or supplied pursuant to this agreement remain the sole and exclusive property of the photographer. There is no assignment of copyright, agreement to do work for hire, or intention of joint copyright expressed or implied hereunder. The client is licensed the above usage specifications in accord with the conditions stated herein. Proper copyright notice, which reads: © 19_____ Straight Shooter, must be displayed with the following placement:_____ . Notice is not required if placement is not specified. Omission of required notice results in loss to the licensor and will be billed at triple the invoiced fee.

2. All expense estimates are subject to normal trade variance of 10 percent.

3. Usage specifications above convert to copyright license only upon receipt of full payment.

4. Usage beyond that defined above requires additional written license from the licensor.

5. Invoices are payable on receipt. Unpaid invoices are subject to a rebilling fee of _____.

6. Advance payments must be received at least 24 hours prior to assignment commencement.

7. The sale is subject to all terms and conditions on the reverse side hereof.

8. If client orders the performance of any services required to complete the above described assignment, it constitutes an acceptance by conduct of the original estimate in its entirety.

This confirms the details of the assignment which you have awarded to Straight Shooter Studio, Inc. Thank you for selecting us to fulfill this important need.

Straight Shooter Studio, Inc.

123 Anystreet, Hometown, ZX 12345 • Telephone: 123-555-1212 • Fax: 123-555-2121

Invoice

Date of Invoice:_____ Reference #_____ Your P.O.# and Date_____

Client:

Assignment Description:

Usage Specifications:

Price:

FEES _____	TOTAL PRICE _____
EXPENSES _____	LESS ADVANCES _____
SALES TAX _____	BALANCE DUE _____
	PLEASE REMIT $ _____

Conditions of Transaction:

1. The copyright to all images created or supplied pursuant to this agreement remain the sole and exclusive property of the photographer. There is no assignment of copyright, agreement to do work for hire, or intention of joint copyright expressed or implied hereunder. The client is licensed the above usage specifications in accord with the conditions stated herein. Proper copyright notice, which reads: © 19_____ Straight Shooter, must be displayed with the following placement:_____ . Notice is not required if placement is not specified. Omission of required notice results in loss to the licensor and will be billed at triple the invoiced fee.

2. All expense estimates are subject to normal trade variance of 10 percent.

3. Usage specifications above convert to copyright license only upon receipt of full payment.

4. Usage beyond that defined above requires additional written license from the licensor.

5. Invoices are payable on receipt. Unpaid invoices are subject to a rebilling fee of _____.

6. The sale is subject to all terms and conditions on the reverse side hereof.

7. If client orders the performance of any services required to complete the above described assignment, it constitutes an acceptance by conduct of the original estimate in its entirety.

_____
PROVIDER E.I.N. OR S.S.#

_____
WORK DELIVERED VIA

_____
DATE WORK DELIVERED

_____
WORK DELIVERED TO

Terms and conditions for reverse side of Assignment Estimate, Confirmation, Invoice.

[1] "Image(s)" means all viewable renditions furnished by Photographer hereunder, whether captured or stored in photographic, magnetic, optical, or any other medium whatsoever.

[2] All Images and rights therein, including copyright, remain the sole and exclusive property of Photographer. Unless otherwise provided herein, any grant of rights is limited to one (1) year from the date hereof and to the territory of the United States.

[3] Client assumes insurer's liability (a) to indemnify Photographer for loss, damage, or misuse of any Images, and (b) to return all Images prepaid and fully insured, safe and undamaged, by bonded messenger, airfreight, or registered mail, within thirty (30) days after the first use thereof as provided herein, but in all events (whether published or unpublished) within thirty (30) days after the date of final licensed use. Client assumes full liability for its principals, employees, agents, affiliates, successors, and assigns (including without limitation independent contractors, messengers, and freelance researchers) for any loss, damage, delay in returning, or misuse of the Images.

[4] Reimbursement by Client for loss or damage of each original photographic transparency or film negative shall be in the amount of One Thousand Five Hundred Dollars ($1,500), or such other amount set forth next to said item on the attached schedule. Reimbursement by Client for loss or damage of each other item shall be in the amount set forth next to said item on the attached schedule. Photographer and Client agree that said amount represents the fair and reasonable value of each item, and that Photographer would not sell all rights to such item for less than said amount. Client understands that each original photographic transparency and film negative is unique and does not have an exact duplicate, and may be impossible to replace or re-create.

[5] Photographer shall receive credit for Images as specified on the face hereof unless no placement is specified.

OPTION: [6A] Client will not make or permit any alterations, including but not limited to additions, subtractions, or adaptations in respect of the Images, alone or with any other material. OR

[6B] Client may not make or permit any alterations, including but not limited to additions, subtractions, or adaptations in respect of the Images, alone or with any other material, except that cropping, and alterations of contrast, brightness, and color balance, consistent with reproduction needs may be made. OR

[6C] Client may make or permit any alterations, including but not limited to additions, subtractions, or adaptations in respect of the Images, alone or with any other material, subject to the provisions as stated in [7] below.

[7] Client will indemnify and defend Photographer against all claims, liability, damages, costs, and expenses, including reasonable legal fees and expenses, arising out of any use of any Images for which no release was furnished by Photographer, or any Images which are altered by Client. Unless furnished, no release exists. Photographer's liability for all claims shall not exceed in any event the total amount paid under this invoice.

[8] Client assumes full risk of loss or damage to or arising from materials furnished by client hereunder and warrants that said materials are adequately insured against such loss, damage, or liability. Client shall indemnify Photographer against all claims, liability, damages, and expenses incurred by Photographer in connection with any claim arising out of use of said material hereunder.

[9] Client may not assign or transfer this agreement or any rights granted hereunder. This agreement binds and inures to the benefit of Photographer, Client, Client's principals, employees, agents, and affiliates, and their respective heirs, legal representatives, successors, and assigns. Client and its principals, employees, agents, and affiliates are jointly and severally liable for the performance of all payments and other obligations hereunder. No amendment or waiver of any terms is binding unless set forth in writing and signed by the parties. However, the invoice may reflect, and Client is bound by, oral authorizations for fees or expenses which could not be confirmed in writing because of insufficient time. This agreement incorporates by reference Article 2 of the Uniform Commercial Code, and the Copyright Act of 1976, as amended.

OPTION: [10A] Except as provided in (11) below, any dispute regarding this agreement shall be arbitrated in [PHOTOGRAPHER'S CITY AND STATE] under rules of the American Arbitration Association and the laws of [STATE OF ARBITRATION]. Judgment on the arbitration award may be entered in any court having jurisdiction. Any dispute involving $_____ [LIMIT OF LOCAL SMALL CLAIMS COURT] or less may be submitted without arbitration to any court having jurisdiction thereof. Client shall pay all arbitration and court costs, Photographer's reasonable legal fees, and expenses, and legal interest on any award or judgment in the event of any award or judgment in favor of Photographer. OR

[10B] Except as provided in [11] below, any dispute regarding this agreement shall be adjudicated in [PHOTOGRAPHER'S CITY AND STATE] under the laws of [STATE]. Client shall pay all court costs, Photographer's reasonable legal fees, and expenses, and legal interest on any award or judgment in the event of any award or judgment in favor of Photographer. OR

[10C] Except as provided in (11) below, any dispute regarding this agreement shall be, at Photographer's sole discretion, either (1) arbitrated in (use 10A language), or (2) adjudicated in (use 10B language).

[11] Client hereby expressly consents to the jurisdiction of the Federal courts with respect to claims by Photographer under the Copyright Act of 1976, as amended.

[12] In the event a shoot extends beyond eight (8) consecutive hours, Photographer may charge for such excess time of assistants and freelance staff at the rate of one-and-one-half their hourly rates.

[13] Reshoots: Client will be charged 100 percent fee and expenses for any reshoot required by Client. For any reshoot required because of an act of God or the fault of a third party, Photographer will charge no additional fee, and Client will pay all expenses. If Photographer charges for special contingency insurance and is paid in full for the shoot, Client will not be charged for any expenses covered by insurance. A list of exclusions from such insurance will be provided on request.

[14] Cancellations and postponements: Client is responsible for payment of all expenses incurred up to the time of cancellation, plus 50 percent of Photographer's fee. If notice of cancellation is given less than two (2) business days before the shoot date, Client will be charged 100 percent fee. Weather postponements: Unless otherwise agreed, Client will be charged 100 percent fee if postponement is due to weather conditions on location and 50 percent fee if postponement occurs before departure to location.

Schedule of Fees and Expenses

CLIENT_____ DATE_____ REFERENCE #_____

Photography	_____	_____	$ _____
Preproduction	_____	_____	$ _____
Travel	_____	_____	$ _____
Weather delays	_____	_____	$ _____
Other	_____	_____	$ _____
Casting	Fee	_____	
	Film	_____	
	Casting from files	_____	
	_____	_____	$ _____
Crew	Assistants	_____	
	Home economist	_____	
	Production coordinator	_____	
	Stylists: hair	_____	
	props	_____	
	wardrobe	_____	
	Trainer/animals	_____	
	Welfare/teacher	_____	
	_____	_____	$ _____
Film and	Editing	_____	
Lab charges	Polaroid	_____	
	Prints	_____	
	Roll film	_____	
	Sheet film	_____	
	_____	_____	$ _____
Insurance	Liability	_____	
	Photo Pac	_____	
	Riders/binders	_____	
	_____	_____	$ _____
Location:	Scout	_____	
	Film	_____	
	Research	_____	
	Location Fee	_____	
	Permits	_____	
	Travel	_____	
	_____	_____	$ _____
Messenger/	Messenger	_____	
Shipping	Out-of-town	_____	
	Trucking	_____	
	_____	_____	$ _____

Props	Purchase	_____	
	Rental	_____	
	Food	_____	
	_____	_____	$ _____
Rental	Camera	_____	
	Grip truck	_____	
	Lenses	_____	
	Lighting	_____	
	Special Effects	_____	
	Special Equipment	_____	
	_____	_____	$ _____
Sets	Carpenter/painter	_____	
	Hardware/lumber	_____	
	Paint/wallpaper	_____	
	Set design/research	_____	
	Backgrounds/backdrops	_____	
	Studio materials	_____	
	Surfaces	_____	
	_____	_____	$ _____
Studio	Build days	_____	
	Shoot days	_____	
	Overtime	_____	
	Strike Set	_____	
	_____	_____	$ _____
Travel	Airfares	_____	
	Excess baggage	_____	
	Cabs	_____	
	Car rental/mileage	_____	
	Truck/car rental	_____	
	Motor home/dressing room	_____	
	Parking tolls/gas	_____	
	_____	_____	
	Lodging, per diems (est.)	_____	
	Hotel	_____	
	Meals	_____	
	_____	_____	$ _____
Wardrobe	Costume design	_____	
	Seamstress	_____	
	Purchase	_____	
	Rental	_____	
	Special makeup/wigs	_____	
	_____	_____	$ _____

Miscellaneous	Gratuities	_____			
	Long-distance phone	_____			
	Nonprofessional talent	_____			
	Working meals	_____			
	_____	_____		$ _____	

Model details		NUMBER	HOURS	TOTAL TIME
	Adults	_____	_____	_____
	Children	_____	_____	_____
	Extras	_____	_____	_____

Get it in writing!

Photographers need a written record of their dealing with services, licenses, compensation, delivery, and value. Estimates, confirmations, invoices, delivery agreements, and copyright licenses should be simple and straightforward, and embody the terms under which you conduct your business.

Straight Shooter Studio, Inc.

123 Anystreet, Hometown, ZX 12345 • Telephone: 123-555-1212 • Fax: 123-555-2121

Predelivery Confirmation Facsimile

RETURN VIA FAX TO: 111-111-1111

To: _____   Fax No: _____

_____   Transmission Date: _____

_____   Transmission Time: _____

Thank you for requesting a submission of stock imaging of the following subject(s):

_____

We will prepare and release our submission for your consideration upon receipt of a signed copy of this confirmation of certain terms and conditions precedent to delivery. Your review and acknowledgment will help to avoid misunderstandings.

Should you require an explanation of any of these terms and conditions, please call us at the above phone number. After reviewing, please sign the form in the space provided below and fax the signed copy to the return fax number listed above.

[1] "Image(s)" means all viewable renditions furnished by Photographer hereunder, whether captured or stored in photographic, magnetic, optical, or any other medium whatsoever.

[2] After 14 days, the following holding fees are charged until return: Five Dollars ($5.00) per week per color transparency and One Dollar ($1.00) per week per print.

[3] Submission is for examination only. Images may not be reproduced, copied, projected, or used in any way without (a) express written permission on Photographer's invoice stating the rights granted and the terms thereof and (b) full payment of said invoice. The reasonable and stipulated fee for any other use shall be three times Photographer's normal fee for such usage.

[4] Reimbursement by Client for loss or damage of each original photographic transparency or film negative shall be in the amount of One Thousand Five Hundred Dollars ($1,500), or such other amount set forth next to said item on the attached schedule. Reimbursement by Client for loss or damage of each other item shall be in the amount set forth next to said item on the attached schedule. Photographer and Client agree that said amount represents the fair and reasonable value of each item, and that Photographer would not sell all rights to such item for less than said amount. Client understands that each original photographic transparency and film negative is unique and does not have an exact duplicate, and may be impossible to replace or re-create.

[5] Additional terms and conditions regarding the use, return, and responsibilities of the parties accompany the images when delivered.

I have reviewed the above terms and conditions and acknowledge my acceptance of them with the understanding that my responsibility for the shipment will begin at the time they are received by me or my company. I also acknowledge that I am authorized to make such a commitment for my company.

_____   _____   _____
SIGNED   TITLE   DATE

Straight Shooter Studio, Inc.

123 Anystreet, Hometown, ZX 12345 • Telephone: 123-555-1212 • Fax: 123-555-2121

Assignment Photography Delivery Memo

Date assignment to begin: _____ Reference # _____ Date of Confirmation _____

Client:

Assignment Description:

Usage Specifications:

Estimated Price: FEES _____ EXPENSES _____ TOTAL _____

Note: For details of fee structure and expenses, refer to attached schedule.

Advance Payments: FEES _____ EXPENSES _____ TOTAL _____

Conditions of Transaction:

1. The copyright to all images created or supplied pursuant to this agreement remain the sole and exclusive property of the photographer. There is no assignment of copyright, agreement to do work for hire, or intention of joint copyright expressed or implied hereunder. The client is licensed the above usage specifications in accord with the conditions stated herein. Proper copyright notice, which reads: © 19____ Straight Shooter, must be displayed with the following placement:_____ . Notice is not required if placement is not specified. Omission of required notice results in loss to the licensor and will be billed at triple the invoiced fee.

2. Usage specifications above convert to copyright license only upon receipt of full payment.

3. Usage beyond that defined above requires additional written license from the licensor.

4. The sale is subject to all terms and conditions on the reverse side hereof.

5. If client orders the performance of any services required to complete the above described assignment, it constitutes an acceptance by conduct of the original estimate in its entirety.

Please review the attached schedule of images. Count shall be considered accurate and quality deemed satisfactory for reproduction if said copy is not immediately received by return mail with all exceptions duly noted. Your acceptance of this delivery constitutes your acceptance of all terms and conditions on both sides of this memo, whether signed by you or not.

_____   _____
ACKNOWLEDGED AND ACCEPTED   DATE

Terms and Conditions for Assignment Photography Delivery Memo

[1] "Image(s)" means all viewable renditions furnished by Photographer hereunder, whether captured or stored in photographic, magnetic, optical or any other medium, whatsoever.

[2] All Images and rights therein, including copyright, remain the sole and exclusive property of Photographer. The license to use the delivered Images are not conveyed by this document.

[3] Client assumes insurer's liability (a) to indemnify Photographer for loss, damage, or misuse of any Images, and (b) to return all Images prepaid and fully insured, safe and undamaged, by bonded messenger, airfreight, or registered mail, within thirty (30) days after the first use thereof as provided herein, but in all events (whether published or unpublished) within thirty (30) days after the date of final licensed use. Client assumes full liability for its principals, employees, agents, affiliates, successors, and assigns (including without limitation independent contractors, messengers, and freelance researchers) for any loss, damage, delay in returning, or misuse of the Images.

[4] Reimbursement by Client for loss or damage of each original photographic transparency or film negative shall be in the amount of One Thousand Five Hundred Dollars ($1,500), or such other amount set forth next to said item on the attached schedule. Reimbursement by Client for loss or damage of each other item shall be in the amount set forth next to said item on the attached schedule. Photographer and Client agree that said amount represents the fair and reasonable value of each item, and that Photographer would not sell all rights to such item for less than said amount. Client understands that each original photographic transparency and film negative is unique and does not have an exact duplicate, and may be impossible to replace or re-create.

[5] Photographer shall receive credit for Images as specified on the face hereof unless no placement is specified.

OPTION: [6A] Client will not make or permit any alterations, including but not limited to additions, subtractions, or adaptations in respect of the Images, alone or with any other material. OR

[6B] Client may not make or permit any alterations, including but not limited to additions, subtractions, or adaptations in respect of the Images, alone or with any other material, except that cropping, and alterations of contrast, brightness, and color balance, consistent with reproduction needs may be made. OR

[6C] Client may make or permit any alterations, including but not limited to additions, subtractions, or adaptations in respect of the Images, alone or with any other material, subject to the provisions as stated in [7] below.

[7] Client will indemnify and defend Photographer against all claims, liability, damages, costs, and expenses, including reasonable legal fees and expenses, arising out of any use of any Images for which no release was furnished by Photographer, or any Images which are altered by Client. Unless furnished, no release exists. Photographer's liability for all claims shall not exceed in any event the total amount paid under this invoice.

[8] Client assumes full risk of loss or damage to or arising from materials furnished by client hereunder and warrants that said materials are adequately insured against such loss, damage, or liability. Client shall indemnify Photographer against all claims, liability, damages, and expenses incurred by Photographer in connection with any claim arising out of use of said material hereunder.

[9] Client may not assign or transfer this agreement or any rights granted hereunder. This agreement binds and inures to the benefit of Photographer, Client, Client's principals, employees, agents, and affiliates, and their respective heirs, legal representatives, successors, and assigns. Client and its principals, employees, agents, and affiliates are jointly and severally liable for the performance of all payments and other obligations hereunder. No amendment or waiver of any terms is binding unless set forth in writing and signed by the parties. However, the invoice may reflect, and Client is bound by, oral authorizations for fees or expenses which could not be confirmed in writing because of insufficient time. This agreement incorporates by reference Article 2 of the Uniform Commercial Code, and the Copyright Act of 1976, as amended.

OPTION: [10A] Except as provided in (11) below, any dispute regarding this agreement shall be arbitrated in [PHOTOGRAPHER'S CITY AND STATE] under rules of the American Arbitration Association and the laws of [STATE OF ARBITRATION]. Judgment on the arbitration award may be entered in any court having jurisdiction. Any dispute involving $____[LIMIT OF LOCAL SMALL CLAIMS COURT] or less may be submitted without arbitration to any court having jurisdiction thereof. Client shall pay all arbitration and court costs, Photographer's reasonable legal fees, and expenses, and legal interest on any award or judgment in the event of any award or judgment in favor of Photographer. OR

[10B] Except as provided in [11] below, any dispute regarding this agreement shall be adjudicated in [PHOTOGRAPHER'S CITY AND STATE] under the laws of [STATE]. Client shall pay all court costs, Photographer's reasonable legal fees, and expenses, and legal interest on any award or judgment in the event of any award or judgment in favor of Photographer. OR

[10C] Except as provided in (11) below, any dispute regarding this agreement shall be, at Photographer's sole discretion, either (1) arbitrated in (use 10A language), or (2) adjudicated in (use 10B language).

[11] Client hereby expressly consents to the jurisdiction of the Federal courts with respect to claims by Photographer under the Copyright Act of 1976, as amended.

Straight Shooter Studio, Inc.

123 Anystreet, Hometown, ZX 12345 • Telephone: 123-555-1212 • Fax: 123-555-2121

Stock Photography Delivery Memo

Date shipped:_____ Reference #_____ Your P.O.# and Date_____

Client:

Description of Images:

QTY.	ORIG.(O) DUPL.(D)	FORMAT	PHOTOGRAPH SUBJECT/ID NO.	VALUE (IF OTHER THAN $1,500/ITEM) IN EVENT OF LOSS/DAMAGE

Total Count: _____

Title in the copyright to all images created or supplied pursuant to this agreement will remain the sole and exclusive property of the photographer. There is no assignment of copyright title, agreement to do work for hire, or intention of joint copyright expressed or implied hereunder. The client is licensed only by subsequent written license on an invoice. Proper copyright notice, which reads: © 19_____ Straight Shooter, must be displayed with the following placement: _____. Notice is not required if placement is not specified. Omission of required notice results in loss to the licenser and will be billed at triple the invoiced fee.

Check count and acknowledge receipt by signing and returning one copy. Count shall be considered accurate and quality deemed satisfactory for reproduction if said copy is not immediately received by return mail with all exceptions duly noted. Photographs must be returned by registered mail, air courier, or other bonded messenger which provides proof of return.

SUBJECT TO ALL TERMS AND CONDITIONS ABOVE AND ON REVERSE SIDE

_____   _____
ACKNOWLEDGED AND ACCEPTED   DATE

Your acceptance of this delivery constitutes your acceptance of all terms and conditions on both sides of this memo, whether signed by you or not.

Terms and Conditions for Stock Photography Delivery Memo

[1] "Image(s)" means all viewable renditions furnished by Photographer hereunder, whether captured or stored in photographic, magnetic, optical, or any other medium whatsoever.

[2] Submission is for examination only. Images may not be reproduced, copied, projected, or used in any way without (a) express written permission on Photographer's invoice stating the rights granted and the terms thereof and (b) payment of said invoice. The reasonable and stipulated fee for any other use shall be three times Photographer's normal fee for such usage.

[3] All Images and rights therein, including copyright, remain the sole and exclusive property of Photographer. Unless otherwise provided herein, any grant of rights is limited to one (1) year from the date hereof and to the territory of the United States.

[4] Client assumes insurer's liability (a) to indemnify Photographer for loss, damage, or misuse of any Images, and (b) to return all Images prepaid and fully insured, safe and undamaged, by bonded messenger, airfreight, or registered mail, within thirty (30) days after the first use thereof as provided herein, but in all events (whether published or unpublished) within thirty (30) days after the date of final licensed use. Client assumes full liability for its principals, employees, agents, affiliates, successors, and assigns (including without limitation independent contractors, messengers, and freelance researchers) for any loss, damage, delay in returning, or misuse of the Images.

[5] After 14 days, the following holding fees are charged until return: Five Dollars ($5.00) per week per color transparency and One Dollar ($1.00) per week per print.

[6] Reimbursement by Client for loss or damage of each original photographic transparency or film negative shall be in the amount of One Thousand Five Hundred Dollars ($1,500), or such other amount set forth next to said item on the attached schedule and/or on the face hereof. Reimbursement by Client for loss or damage of each other item shall be in the amount set forth next to said item on the attached schedule and/or on the face hereof. Photographer and Client agree that said amount represents the fair and reasonable value of each item, and that Photographer would not sell all rights to such item for less than said amount. Client understands that each original photographic transparency and film negative is unique and does not have an exact duplicate, and may be impossible to replace or re-create.

[7] Photographer shall receive credit for Images as specified on the face hereof unless no placement is specified.

OPTION: [8A] Client will not make or permit any alterations, including but not limited to additions, subtractions, or adaptations in respect of the Images, alone or with any other material. OR

[8B] Client may not make or permit any alterations, including but not limited to additions, subtractions, or adaptations in respect of the Images, alone or with any other material, except that cropping, and alterations of contrast, brightness, and color balance, consistent with reproduction needs may be made. OR

[8C] Client may make or permit any alterations, including but not limited to additions, subtractions, or adaptations in respect of the Images, alone or with any other material, subject to the provisions as stated in [9] below.

[9] Client will indemnify and defend Photographer against all claims, liability, damages, costs, and expenses, including reasonable legal fees and expenses, arising out of any use of any Images for which no release was furnished by Photographer, or any Images which are altered by Client. Unless furnished, no release exists. Photographer's liability for all claims shall not exceed in any event the total amount paid under this invoice.

[10] Client may not assign or transfer this agreement or any rights granted hereunder. This agreement binds and inures to the benefit of Photographer, Client, Client's principals, employees, agents, and affiliates, and their respective heirs, legal representatives, successors, and assigns. Client and its principals, employees, agents, and affiliates are jointly and severally liable for the performance of all payments and other obligations hereunder. No amendment or waiver of any terms is binding unless set forth in writing and signed by the parties. However, the invoice may reflect, and Client is bound by, oral authorizations for fees or expenses which could not be confirmed in writing because of insufficient time of shooting. This agreement incorporates by reference Article 2 of the Uniform Commercial Code, and the Copyright Act of 1976, as amended.

OPTION: [11A] Except as provided in (12) below, any dispute regarding this agreement shall be arbitrated in [PHOTOGRAPHER'S CITY AND STATE] under rules of the American Arbitration Association and the laws of [STATE OF ARBITRATION]. Judgment on the arbitration award may be entered in any court having jurisdiction. Any dispute involving $_____[LIMIT OF LOCAL SMALL CLAIMS COURT] or less may be submitted without arbitration to any court having jurisdiction thereof. Client shall pay all arbitration and court costs, Photographer's reasonable legal fees, and expenses, and legal interest on any award or judgment in the event of any award or judgment in favor of Photographer. OR

[11B] Except as provided in [12] below, any dispute regarding this agreement shall be adjudicated in [PHOTOGRAPHER'S CITY AND STATE] under the laws of [STATE]. Client shall pay all court costs, Photographer's reasonable legal fees, and expenses, and legal interest on any award or judgment in the event of any award or judgment in favor of Photographer. OR

[11C] Except as provided in (12) below, any dispute regarding this agreement shall be, at Photographer's sole discretion, either (1) arbitrated in (use 11A language), or (2) adjudicated in (use 11B language).

[12] Client hereby expressly consents to the jurisdiction of the Federal courts with respect to claims by Photographer under the Copyright Act of 1976, as amended.

Straight Shooter Studio, Inc.

123 Anystreet, Hometown, ZX 12345 • Telephone: 123-555-1212 • Fax: 123-555-2121

Stock Photography Invoice

Date of invoice:_____ Reference #_____ Your P.O.# and Date_____

Client:

Description of Images:

Usage Specifications:

Price: USE FEES _____   TOTAL PRICE _____

                         RESEARCH FEE _____   SALES TAX _____

                         HOLDING FEES _____   TOTAL _____

                         SHIPPING _____

                         OTHER _____

                                             PLEASE REMIT $ _____

Conditions of Transaction:

1. The copyright to all images created or supplied pursuant to this agreement remain the sole and exclusive property of the photographer. There is no assignment of copyright, agreement to do work for hire, or intention of joint copyright expressed or implied hereunder. The client is licensed the above usage specifications in accord with the conditions stated herein. Proper copyright notice, which reads: © 19_____ Straight Shooter, must be displayed with the following placement:_____ . Notice is not required if placement is not specified. Omission of required notice results in loss to the licensor and will be billed at triple the invoiced fee.

2. Usage specifications above convert to copyright license only upon receipt of full payment.

3. Usage beyond that defined above requires additional written license from the licensor.

4. Invoices are payable on receipt. Unpaid invoices are subject to a rebilling fee of _____.

5. The sale is subject to all terms and conditions on the reverse side hereof.

6. Use of any image described above constitutes acceptance of all terms and conditions expressed, whether on the face or reverse of this invoice.

Terms and Conditions for Stock Photography Invoice

[1] "Image(s)" means all viewable renditions furnished by Photographer hereunder, whether captured or stored in photographic, magnetic, optical, or any other medium whatsoever.

[2] All Images and rights therein, including copyright, remain the sole and exclusive property of Photographer. Unless otherwise provided herein, any grant of rights is limited to one (1) year from the date hereof to the the the territory of the United States.

[3] Client assumes insurer's liability (a) to indemnify Photographer for loss, damage, or misuse of any Images, and (b) to return all Images prepaid and fully insured, safe and undamaged, by bonded messenger, airfreight, or registered mail, within thirty (30) days after the first use thereof as provided herein, but in all events (whether published or unpublished) within thirty (30) days after the date of final licensed use. Client assumes full liability for its principals, employees, agents, affiliates, successors, and assigns (including without limitation independent contractors, messengers, and freelance researchers) for any loss, damage, delay in returning, or misuse of the Images.

[4] Reimbursement by Client for loss or damage of each original photographic transparency or film negative shall be in the amount of One Thousand Five Hundred Dollars ($1,500), or such other amount set forth next to said item on the attached schedule. Reimbursement by Client for loss or damage of each other item shall be in the amount set forth next to said item on the attached schedule. Photographer and Client agree that said amount represents the fair and reasonable value of each item, and that Photographer would not sell all rights to such item for less than said amount. Client understands that each original photographic transparency and film negative is unique and does not have an exact duplicate, and may be impossible to replace or re-create.

[5] Photographer shall receive credit for Images as specified on the face hereof, unless no placement is specified.

OPTION: [6A] Client will not make or permit any alterations, including but not limited to additions, subtractions, or adaptations in respect of the Images, alone or with any other material. OR

[6B] Client may not make or permit any alterations, including but not limited to additions, subtractions, or adaptations in respect of the Images, alone or with any other material, except that cropping, and alterations of contrast, brightness, and color balance, consistent with reproduction needs may be made. OR

[6C] Client may make or permit any alterations, including but not limited to additions, subtractions, or adaptations in respect of the Images, alone or with any other material, subject to the provisions as stated in [7] below.

[7] Client will indemnify and defend Photographer against all claims, liability, damages, costs, and expenses, including reasonable legal fees and expenses, arising out of any use of any Images for which no release was furnished by Photographer, or any Images which are altered by Client. Unless furnished, no release exists. Photographer's liability for all claims shall not exceed in any event the total amount paid under this invoice.

[8] Client may not assign or transfer this agreement or any rights granted hereunder. This agreement binds and inures to the benefit of Photographer, Client, Client's principals, employees, agents, and affiliates, and their respective heirs, legal representatives, successors, and assigns. Client and its principals, employees, agents, and affiliates are jointly and severally liable for the performance of all payments and other obligations hereunder. No amendment or waiver of any terms is binding unless set forth in writing and signed by the parties. However, the invoice may reflect, and Client is bound by, oral authorizations for fees or expenses which could not be confirmed in writing because of insufficient time of shooting. This agreement incorporates by reference Article 2 of the Uniform Commercial Code, and the Copyright Act of 1976, as amended.

OPTION: [9A] Except as provided in (10) below, any dispute regarding this agreement shall be arbitrated in [PHOTOGRAPHER'S CITY AND STATE] under rules of the American Arbitration Association and the laws of [STATE OF ARBITRATION]. Judgment on the arbitration award may be entered in any court having jurisdiction. Any dispute involving $____[LIMIT OF LOCAL SMALL CLAIMS COURT] or less may be submitted without arbitration to any court having jurisdiction thereof. Client shall pay all arbitration and court costs, Photographer's reasonable legal fees, and expenses, and legal interest on any award or judgment in the event of any award or judgment in favor of Photographer. OR

[9B] Except as provided in [10] below, any dispute regarding this agreement shall be adjudicated in [PHOTOGRAPHER'S CITY AND STATE] under the laws of [STATE]. Client shall pay all court costs, Photographer's reasonable legal fees, and expenses, and legal interest on any award or judgment in the event of any award or judgment in favor of Photographer. OR

[9C] Except as provided in (10) below, any dispute regarding this agreement shall be, at Photographer's sole discretion, either (1) arbitrated in (use 9A language), or (2) adjudicated in (use 9B language).

[10] Client hereby expressly consents to the jurisdiction of the Federal courts with respect to claims by Photographer under the Copyright Act of 1976, as amended.

Chapter 7

Copyright

Richard Weisgrau

Copyrights are intangible assets which usually have monetary value. The Copyright Act of 1976 made clear that photographers are the copyright owners of their images, except when those images were made as an employee, or when the photographer has conveyed the copyright to another party in a written and signed agreement.

Copyright is a legal right to control the copying, reproduction, distribution, derivative use, and public display of your photographs, and to sue for the unauthorized use (infringement) of your work.

Copyright is earned the moment you fix your photographic expression in a tangible form; that is, when you create the latent image on film. Registration with the Copyright Office or placement of a copyright notice on the image is not required, although it is advised.

Although most images are copyrightable, some are not. To be copyrightable, images must be original. Originality is essential to copyright. If you exactly copy a photograph, the copy cannot be copyrighted, since it has no originality. (In fact if the first photograph is copyrighted, you would need the original photographer's permission to copy it.)

Making a substantially similar copy of someone else's copyrighted image without authorization constitutes copyright infringement. It is usually necessary to show that the alleged infringer had access to the original work—but the images may be so closely identical that no explanation other than copying is possible.

Ideas, themes, and concepts are not copyrightable. Only the original expression of those ideas, themes, and concepts in some tangible form, like a photograph, can be copyrighted. You might have an idea for a great photograph, but you get no copyright until you make the actual photograph. An art director might have a great concept, but that concept cannot be copyrighted. Having an idea or concept does not entitle one to a share of the copyright of the photograph. The copyright belongs to the one(s) who author the tangible expression of the concept or idea.

Copyright Notice

ASMP recommends that all photographs carry a copyright notice, even though it is no longer required by law. The lack of notice could provide an infringer with a defense of "innocent infringement." This defense could seriously limit the recovery of damages in an infringement claim.

Copyright notice is a way of saying: "This is my work—if you want to use it, ask me." This stance reinforces the value of your work and alerts everyone that you are prepared to protect that value.

There are three ways to display a copyright notice:
- © 1997, Pat Photographer
- Copyright 1997, Pat Photographer
- Copr. 1997, Pat Photographer

Although all three are acceptable, it is generally thought that © 1997, Pat Photographer is the most widely recognized internationally.

A word of caution is called for on the subject of notice. Some persons when typing or word processing and some computer programs use a "c" in parentheses (c) as a substitute for a ©. To the best of our knowledge, this form of notice has never been rejected by a court, but there is no guarantee that a court would uphold a (c) as proper notice. The law calls for a © or the word "Copyright" or "Copr."

Copyright Registration

A copyright owner can register the copyrighted work with the Copyright Office in Washington, D.C. There are excellent reasons for registering your copyrights. The cost of prosecuting a copyright infringement case can be very high, particularly when an alleged infringer can afford a rigorous defense. Outspending the copyright owner is a tactic that is often used to break a photographer's determination to enforce his or her rights. Most infringers know that photographers have limited resources and will not be able to spend all that is necessary to prosecute a well-fought case. They are also aware of the fact that without timely registration an award of attorney's fees will be out of reach, further limiting the potential resources of the photographer, since most lawyers will not take such a case on a contingency fee basis. On the other hand, infringers are much more likely to settle out of court when confronted with the probability that they will likely have to pay your legal fees, as well as theirs, on top of an award of statutory damages.

Statutory damages are limited by law to a maximum of $100,000 per infringement. Many people construe this to mean that infringements often receive awards near this amount. In fact, that is not the case. A survey of recent cases shows that awards for statutory damages are made after evaluating certain factors, including willfulness, extent of unauthorized use, and the commercial value of the unauthorized use(s). An award could be for $500, $5,000, or $50,000, or any other amount, at the discretion of the court. Still, since the attorney's fees are also covered, any award will exceed the monetary cost of prosecution.

The copyright law treats published and unpublished photographs differently, in relation to registration as a prerequisite for infringement remedies.

The law prohibits awards for statutory damages or attorney's fees for any infringement of copyright: (a) Of an unpublished work, occurring before the date of its registration, or (b) After the first publication of a work and before the effective date of its registration, unless such registration is made within three months after the first publication of the work.

Under copyright law, the word published means: The distribution of copies of a work to the public by sale, other transfer of ownership, by rental, lease, or lending. Offering to distribute copies to people or businesses for purposes of further distribution, public performance, or public display constitutes publication. Therefore, when you send images to your stock agencies, which will do further distribution (submission and licensing), you have legally published your work. A public performance or display, in and of itself, does not constitute publication. Exhibiting your photographs in public does not constitute publication, unless you exhibit them through another party, such as a gallery, which offers them for sale (for further distribution).

A simple restatement of the law is that you can't collect attorney's fees and statutory damages unless you have registered an unpublished work before the infringement, or unless you registered a published work within three months after its first publication. Note: For published work, the law does not speak about three months after any publications, but rather three months after its first publication.

You can register a published work at any time following three months after first publication, but that registration will only preserve remedies of attorney's fees and statutory damages for infringements that occur after the registration.

The law is written with a three-month allowance after first publication to allow you time to learn of the publication, obtain copies, and file the registration.

The following two examples will help clarify the application of the law.

Example 1: You shoot a brochure cover and the brochure with the image cover is published for the first time on July 1. You register the image on September 30. Later, you discover that the image was infringed on August 31. Since you registered within three months of first publication, you may seek an award of attorneys' fees and statutory damages even though the infringing began a month before the date of registration.

Example 2: You shoot a brochure cover and the brochure with the cover image is published for the first time on July 1. You register the image on December 1. Later you discover that the image was infringed on August 31 and January 15. You are not fully protected for the August 31 infringement, since you failed to register within three months after first publication. You are fully protected for the January 15 infringement since it happened after registration.

At ASMP, we find that few unpublished works are infringed, and that most infringements are of published works, and, as such, they occur six months, a year, or even longer after a photo's first publication. Obviously, this leads one to the conclusion that to be well protected you have to register either immediately after publication or before it.

In summary, it is important to remember that although the copyright law of the United States does not require a photographer to register his or her works to own the copyright to them, timely registration will serve the photographer's interests if the registered work is infringed by providing eligibility for attorney's fees and statutory damages. Your opponent's knowledge that these remedies are available to you will often enable you to negotiate a settlement without filing suit, or within a reasonable period of time after filing suit. Registration should be made before or immediately after publication.

How to Register

Registration is simply the process of filing copies of photographs accompanied by an accurate and complete registration form with the U.S. Copyright Office, and receiving a certificate of registration to show that such a deposit has been made. Any copyrightable work can be registered, a motion picture, a book, a painting, a CD-ROM, a slide show, and, yes, photographs. But, just as the copyright law treats published and unpublished works differently, so do the regulations which govern registration. We'll examine these differences further on.

There is a $20 fee for registering a copyrighted work. Obviously, the greater number of photographs included in one registration, the less expensive the registration costs per image. If you consider that on a given day a photographer can produce hundreds of separately copyrightable images, clearly registration could cost thousands of dollars unless done in some bulk fashion.

Registration can be made of single images or of groups of images. The single image registration is much the same for published and unpublished work. A photographer completes Copyright Registration Form VA, adds two copies of a published work or one copy of an unpublished work, and the $20 filing fee. This is sent to the Copyright Office in Washington, D.C. **(See Copyright Office information and how to register your copyright at the end of this chapter.)**

When registering a group of photographs things become more complicated. There are options for photographers, again the options are divided by published or unpublished. And, the relative ease of the process is influenced by whether the work has been published or not.

Published photographs will be accepted by the Copyright Office for registration in groups under these narrow conditions, only:

1. Each photograph in the group was first published as a contribution to a collective work within a twelve-month period. (A collective work is a magazine, periodical, etc.)
2. The author is an individual photographer, not an employer or other party for whom the photograph was made as a work for hire.

3. If published prior to May 1, 1989, each photograph as first published contained a separate copyright notice which names the applicant as the copyright owner.

4. Copies of the collective work(s) in which the group of photographs appeared must be filed with the registration (this is called the deposit).

As you can see, only a few published images meet these criteria. One could readily draw the conclusion that group registration of published photographs is not very feasible as a safeguard system to protect one's rights.

Still, there is a bright light of opportunity in the remaining option—the group registration of unpublished images. This opportunity lies in the regulations governing such registration, which are much broader than those for published works.

Group registration of unpublished works are allowed under the following conditions:

1. All the photographs must be by the same photographer.

2. They cannot have been published (as defined previously herein).

3. Copies of the photographs must be in an acceptable form of deposit (which we will define).

4. Each collection must be given an identifying title (any name will do, e.g., Photographs of Pat Photographer 1997).

5. The entire copyrightable subject matter of each photograph has to be visible (full frame).

That's it. There are no other restrictions. A photographer can register thousands of unpublished images in a single application and for a single $20 fee. There is no time limit—the unpublished photographs could have been taken yesterday or over the last twenty years. These rules are very liberal when compared to the regulations for published works.

To make a bulk registration of unpublished images a photographer must submit a completed Form VA with the $20 fee. Also required is one copy of a deposit containing all the images to be registered. The deposit can be in any one of the several forms described below:

1. A group of individual transparencies in protective plastic pages.

2. A group of contact sheets (color or black & white).

3. A group of positive contact sheets made from slides ganged together, as when placed in protective plastic pages.

4. A group of color laser copier reproductions of slides, ganged together as in #3 above.

5. And finally, after discussions with ASMP, the Copyright Office has officially approved a videotape on VHS format containing as many images as the tape can hold while preserving the visibility of each image for a least two seconds per image. This means a 120-minute tape could hold thirty images per minute for a total of 3,600 images per tape. Again, the full frame of the original must be visible. Note: Each tape requires its own Form VA and $20 registration fee.

With this officially approved deposit form, photographers now have a simple, affordable, easily managed system to register their unpublished images.

Note: A sample of Form VA is included at the end of this chapter.

Preparing for Registration

Before establishing a system for registering your unpublished photographs, certain analysis is in order. First, one must recognize that most of a photographer's work is unpublished, and, at some point, all work is unpublished. Now, the simple fact is that any infringement is likely to be of a published work. So by registering all unpublished work, you will be protecting any photograph which is to be published later.

Second, one must recognize that many times, particularly in stock work, the photographer doesn't know which images have been published for months after that publication. When you add to that fact the difficulty of group registration of published work, it seems clear that the easiest, least expensive, and most timely choice is to register your unpublished work.

If you decide to register your unpublished work, you will have to consider that unpublished work is divided into four categories:

1. Inventory of images on hand, but not considered viable for eventual publication (rejects).
2. Inventory of images on hand that is part of your stock file and is likely to be sent to your stock agency. (Remember—the sending of work to your stock agency constitutes publication, as offering your work to a party for further distribution.) You should apply for registration before you send your submission to your stock agency.
3. Assignment photographs which will be, as outtakes, sent into inventory.
4. Assignment photographs which will be sent to the client for possible use.

While you might reasonably decide not to register images that fit into category 1, above, categories 2, 3, and 4 seem important to register.

There are no serious logistical problems for dealing with category 2 and 3 images. Regardless of the way that you create the deposit, you have time to get the work done. However, category 4 images, those waiting to go to a client for a job, present a greater problem because the time available for creating the deposit is limited.

For the most part, if shooting black and white or color negative film, a color contact sheet can be made to serve as the deposit for registration. But when you have photographed with transparency film, the task of making the deposit is harder to plan.

Although a color contact sheet or a color laser copy of a group of transparencies is an acceptable form of deposit, the equipment to produce these is not readily available; the cost of these methods on a per image basis is high as only twenty 35mm slides can fit one sheet, and less when larger formats are used.

Clearly, a videotape deposit offers some distinct advantages. Not only does it reduce the cost per image registered with the ability to put up to 3,000 images onto a tape, which can cost as little as $5, but it also can be done by any photographer who owns either a video camera and recorder or a camcorder. There are various devices readily available to those who want to build dedicated systems to record their work. They range from self-contained copy devices, such as Tamron's Fotovix, to inexpensive attachments for a slide projector, such as the Vivitar Slide Duplicator. Many photography and video magazines contain ads for such devices.

The final consideration is to reduce the time it takes to create this registration deposit to avoid delays in delivering the edited photographs to your client. This process can be kept to a minimum by using the video option for a deposit.

Obviously, assignment photographs will have to be edited, and if the video registration deposit can be made immediately after processing, there will be little loss of time.

If the video recording is to be done after the edit, it is important to remember that those images to be sent to your client should be put on tape first, then sent on their way to the client. After that, the remainder of the images can be added. The final act is completing Form VA and sending the tape off to the Copyright Office.

Duplicates and Similars

Many photographers create in-camera duplicates of photographs which they take. Inasmuch as these photographs are identical to one another, only one of them needs to be registered to protect the group of duplicates.

However, similars, those photos which are like but not identical to another image, should be registered as unique images. While one could academically debate the extent of similarity and therefore the need to register some similars, it makes no sense to risk a loss of copyright protection when one considers the economy of bulk registration.

We strongly suggest that similars be registered with your bulk application.

Registering Your Copyright and Obtaining Forms

See information at the end of this chapter for complete information on registering your copyright with the U.S. Copyright Office.

Licensing the Right to Use Your Photographs

As the copyright owner, you have to license someone to use your image before they can legally do so. A license is simply a permission to use the photograph within the licensed parameters.

An exclusive license must be in writing. A nonexclusive license does not have to be granted in writing—although ASMP strongly urges all photographers to grant licenses in written form. This avoids subsequent disagreements about the terms of the license. In the absence of a written license, the photographer and client are in an awkward position. If a dispute over usage arises, differing recollections of rights granted can only be resolved by negotiation or legal action. Legal action is certainly costly and to be avoided if possible. Negotiation, while suitable to resolve disagreements, is best done before use begins, not after the fact. Negotiate the license, then confirm the usage rights in a written copyright license.

Under the copyright law, an "exclusive" grant of rights means a transfer of all or part of copyright. Avoid these words, unless you intend to transfer some copyright ownership to the client.

If a client insists, or you wish to offer exclusive rights, consider limiting the rights as you would limit any other grant of rights. That is, you should properly grant the exclusive rights for a certain time period, a certain geographic area, and a certain media, such as advertising, books, etc. By applying limitations to the exclusive license you are narrowing the transfer of copyright. By setting a time period you are assuring the expiration of the transfer.

The rights which you license should be based upon the outcome of the negotiations that you have conducted with your client. Generally, you will grant rights to meet the particular uses for which the client wants the work. The fee will usually increase as rights granted increase.

Buyouts and All Rights

"Buyout" and "all rights" are confusing terms and are thought by some to mean a transfer of copyright. However, these terms have inconsistent trade definitions, depending upon personal understanding, and, consequently, are not reliable in licensing terminology.

We urge you not to use such terms in licensing clients the rights to your photographs. It is better to clearly state whether or not the copyright is being transferred.

An "all rights" agreement without a transfer of copyright is a permission to a client to use your image as desired, while the copyright remains with you. This gives the client the widest range of rights for the time allowed in the license without a transfer of copyright ownership.

Transfer of Copyright

You can transfer copyright ownership to another party. Copyright, like any asset, can be bought and sold. The only requirement in the law is that a transfer of copyright ownership be in writing and signed by the copyright owner. Photographers should exercise care in signing client purchase orders. ASMP has seen many examples of purchase orders which have a copyright transfer included in the terms and conditions. Signing such a purchase order would result in the loss of your copyright.

There is no law that says you have to transfer copyright to a client. Remember, even though the client might be the originator of the concept or idea, this does not entitle them to the copyright of the photograph which you, the photographer, originate.

Work-for-Hire

Work-for-hire is another way the client can become the copyright owner. The difference between work-for-hire and a copyright transfer is rather simple. In the case of a copyright transfer, you own the copyright until you transfer it. In a work-for-hire situation, you never own the copyright. It is owned by the client from the moment the work is created, and the client is by law the author of the photograph. The photographer is denied authorship and is treated as a tool of the client.

Work-for-hire exists automatically in the case of an employee taking photographs for the employer. As provided in the copyright law, no agreements are required.

An independent contractor ("freelancer") can do work-for-hire only in certain circumstances. First, the work must be commissioned—that is specifically ordered by someone, and if it is commissioned, it can be work-for-hire only if the photograph comes within one of the nine specific categories enumerated in the Copyright Act as qualifying for work-for-hire:

- Contribution to a collective work
- Contribution to a motion picture or audiovisual work
- Translation
- Supplementary work
- Compilation
- Instructional text
- Test
- Answer material for a test
- Atlas

The category most frequently involving photographers is a contribution to a collective work such as a magazine or other periodical.

The work-for-hire agreement must be signed by the photographer and by the commissioning party. The agreement must be executed before the work commences.

Work-for-Hire and Copyright Differences

Although many see work-for-hire and copyright transfer as the same thing, they are not.

Under the law, if you transfer the copyright you can get it back after thirty-five years. This "recapture" provision of the law was designed to allow photographers the eventual control over their body of work. Also, when negotiating a copyright transfer, you have the ownership and can bargain for the price of the copyright.

In a work-for-hire situation, you never have the copyright. You have no recapture right at any time. You are simply selling your services for a fee. That fee should reflect the present and the future value of the copyright. If you created a work-for-hire and later want the copyright to the work, the only way you can get it is to negotiate with the copyright owner to transfer it to you.

Finally, work-for-hire status will by law apply to all photographs taken on the assignment, not just to those used by the client. A transfer of copyright can be customized and apply to all the photographs or some portion thereof, such as only those used by the client.

Fair Use

The copyright law allows someone to copy your work without penalty in certain cases. This is called "fair use." In order to qualify for "fair use," the photograph would usually have to be copied for educational, classroom, news reporting, or other educational or public-interest purposes. Fair use is always subject to interpretation. There is no simple rule to apply to determine when an unauthorized use is "fair use." Each case has specific facts that must be examined before such a determination can be made. This is one reason why it is important to consult with a knowledgeable copyright attorney before jumping to conclusions about infringement.

Copyright and Collections

In recent years, the trend has been to invoice the client with terms stating that the grant of rights to use the photograph is not in force until the invoice is paid in full. It should be understood that under this provision nonpayment may be both a breach of the client's contractual obligation and infringement of the copyright. This can create a legal question about the best way to enforce your rights—a question best answered by competent legal counsel.

It is important to understand that such terms conditioning rights grants by payment must generally have been presented to the client as a condition preceding the sale. In other words, when such a condition is presented only after the work is done, it is less likely to be enforceable.

Definitions from The Copyright Act of 1976

"Audiovisual works" are works that consist of a series of related images which are intrinsically intended to be shown by the use of machines or devices such as projectors, viewers, or electronic equipment, together with accompanying sounds, if any, regardless of the nature of the material objects, such as films or tapes, in which the works are embodied.

A "collective work" is a work, such as a periodical issue, anthology, or encyclopedia, in which a number of contributions, constituting separate and independent works in themselves, are assembled into a collective whole. A contribution to a collective work can itself be copyrightable.

A "compilation" is a work formed by the collection and assembling of preexisting materials or of data that are selected, coordinated, or arranged in such a way that the resulting work as a whole constitutes an original work of authorship. The term "compilation" includes collective works.

A "derivative work" is a work based upon one or more preexisting works, such as a translation, musical arrangement, dramatization, fictionalization, motion picture version, sound recording, art reproduction, abridgment, condensation, or any other form in which the underlying work may be recast, transformed, or adapted. A work consisting of editorial revisions, annotations, elaborations, or other modifications which, as a whole, represent an original work of authorship, is a "derivative work."

A "joint work" is a work prepared by two or more authors with the intention that their contributions be merged into inseparable or interdependent parts of a unitary whole. Each joint copyright owner can grant nonexclusive licenses to third parties subject to a duty to account to the other joint owners for their share and profits.

"Motion pictures" are audiovisual works consisting of a series of related images which, when shown in succession, impart an impression of motion, together with accompanying sounds, if any.

A "transfer of copyright ownership" is an assignment, mortgage, exclusive license, or any other convenience, alienation or hypothecation of a copyright or of any of the exclusive rights comprised in a copyright, whether or not it is limited in time or place of effect, but not including a nonexclusive license.

Registering Your Copyright and Obtaining Forms

Registration is handled through the: Register of Copyrights, Library of Congress, Washington, D.C. 20559; phone: (202) 707-2000.

A twenty-four-hour hotline for obtaining registration forms is: (202) 707-9100.

A sample of Form VA, the basic form for registering all works in the visual arts, is included at the end of this chapter. In addition to photographs as such, this form should also be used for registering the following items when they are primarily or exclusively photographic in nature: books, advertising materials, and most single contributions to periodicals. When these items consist primarily of text, they should be registered in class TX.

If first publication occurs in a separately copyrighted work, such as a magazine, you can still register the copyright in class VA as a contribution to a collective work, thus securing the advantages of statutory damages and legal fees in an infringement case. This procedure is safer than relying upon the registration of the collective work itself.

FORM VA
For a Work of the Visual Arts
UNITED STATES COPYRIGHT OFFICE

REGISTRATION NUMBER

_____

VA   VAU

EFFECTIVE DATE OF REGISTRATION

_____

Month   Day   Year

DO NOT WRITE ABOVE THIS LINE. IF YOU NEED MORE SPACE, USE A SEPARATE CONTINUATION SHEET.

1

TITLE OF THIS WORK ▼   NATURE OF THIS WORK ▼ See instructions

PREVIOUS OR ALTERNATIVE TITLES ▼

PUBLICATION AS A CONTRIBUTION If this work was published as a contribution to a periodical, serial, or collection, give information about the collective work in which the contribution appeared.   **Title of Collective Work ▼**

If published in a periodical or serial give: Volume ▼   Number ▼   Issue Date ▼   On Pages ▼

2 a

NAME OF AUTHOR ▼   DATES OF BIRTH AND DEATH
                                                       Year Born ▼   Year Died ▼

Was this contribution to the work a   AUTHOR'S NATIONALITY OR DOMICILE   WAS THIS AUTHOR'S CONTRIBUTION TO
"work made for hire"?   Name of Country   THE WORK   If the answer to either
☐ Yes   OR { Citizen of ▶_____   Anonymous?   ☐ Yes ☐ No   of these questions is
☐ No   Domiciled in▶_____   Pseudonymous? ☐ Yes ☐ No   "Yes," see detailed
                                                                                                             instructions.

NOTE

Under the law, the "author" of a "work made for hire" is generally the employer, not the employee (see instructions). For any part of this work that was "made for hire" check "Yes" in the space provided, give the employer (or other person for whom the work was prepared) as "Author" of that part, and leave the space for dates of birth and death blank.

NATURE OF AUTHORSHIP Check appropriate box(es). **See instructions**
☐ 3-Dimensional sculpture   ☐ Map   ☐ Technical drawing
☐ 2-Dimensional artwork   ☐ Photograph   ☐ Text
☐ Reproduction of work of art ☐ Jewelry design ☐ Architectural work
☐ Design on sheetlike material

b

NAME OF AUTHOR ▼   DATES OF BIRTH AND DEATH
                                                       Year Born ▼   Year Died ▼

Was this contribution to the work a   AUTHOR'S NATIONALITY OR DOMICILE   WAS THIS AUTHOR'S CONTRIBUTION TO
"work made for hire"?   Name of Country   THE WORK   If the answer to either
☐ Yes   OR { Citizen of ▶_____   Anonymous?   ☐ Yes ☐ No   of these questions is
☐ No   Domiciled in▶_____   Pseudonymous? ☐ Yes ☐ No   "Yes," see detailed
                                                                                                             instructions.

NATURE OF AUTHORSHIP Check appropriate box(es). **See instructions**
☐ 3-Dimensional sculpture   ☐ Map   ☐ Technical drawing
☐ 2-Dimensional artwork   ☐ Photograph   ☐ Text
☐ Reproduction of work of art ☐ Jewelry design ☐ Architectural work
☐ Design on sheetlike material

3 a

YEAR IN WHICH CREATION OF THIS   b DATE AND NATION OF FIRST PUBLICATION OF THIS PARTICULAR WORK
WORK WAS COMPLETED This information   Complete this information Month ▶ _____ Day▶ _____ Year▶ _____
                    must be given   ONLY if this work
                  ◀ Year in all cases.   has been published.   ◀ Nation

4

COPYRIGHT CLAIMANT(S) Name and address must be given even if the claimant is the same as   APPLICATION RECEIVED
the author given in space 2. ▼   _____
                                                                                             ONE DEPOSIT RECEIVED
See instructions   _____
before completing   TWO DEPOSITS RECEIVED
this space.   _____
TRANSFER If the claimant(s) named here in space 4 is (are) different from the author(s) named in   FUNDS RECEIVED
space 2, give a brief statement of how the claimant(s) obtained ownership of the copyright. ▼

DO NOT WRITE HERE / OFFICE USE ONLY

MORE ON BACK ▶ • Complete all applicable spaces (numbers 5-9) on the reverse side of this page.   DO NOT WRITE HERE
                • See detailed instructions.   • Sign the form at line 8.   Page 1 of _____ pages

EXAMINED BY		FORM VA
CHECKED BY		
☐	CORRESPONDENCE Yes	FOR COPYRIGHT OFFICE USE ONLY

DO NOT WRITE ABOVE THIS LINE. IF YOU NEED MORE SPACE, USE A SEPARATE CONTINUATION SHEET.

PREVIOUS REGISTRATION Has registration for this work, or for an earlier version of this work, already been made in the Copyright Office?

☐ Yes ☐ No If your answer is "Yes," why is another registration being sought? (Check appropriate box) ▼

a. ☐ This is the first published edition of a work previously registered in unpublished form.

b. ☐ This is the first application submitted by this author as copyright claimant.

c. ☐ This is a changed version of the work, as shown by space 6 on this application.

If your answer is "Yes," give: **Previous Registration Number** ▼   **Year of Registration** ▼

5

DERIVATIVE WORK OR COMPILATION Complete both space 6a and 6b for a derivative work; complete only 6b for a compilation.

a. Preexisting Material Identify any preexisting work or works that this work is based on or incorporates. ▼

b. Material Added to This Work Give a brief, general statement of the material that has been added to this work and in which copyright is claimed. ▼

6

See instructions
before completing
this space.

DEPOSIT ACCOUNT If the registration fee is to be charged to a Deposit Account established in the Copyright Office, give name and number of Account.

Name ▼   **Account Number** ▼

7

CORRESPONDENCE Give name and address to which correspondence about this application should be sent.   Name/Address/Apt/City/State/ZIP ▼

Area Code and Telephone Number ▶

Be sure to
give your
daytime phone
◀ number

CERTIFICATION* I, the undersigned, hereby certify that I am the

check only one ▼

☐ author

☐ other copyright claimant

☐ owner of exclusive right(s)

☐ authorized agent of _____

Name of author or other copyright claimant, or owner of exclusive right(s) ▲

of the work identified in this application and that the statements made
by me in this application are correct to the best of my knowledge.

Typed or printed name and date ▼ If this application gives a date of publication in space 3, do not sign and submit it before that date.

Date ▶

☞ Handwritten signature (X) ▼

8

**Mail
certificate
to:**

**Certificate
will be
mailed in
window
envelope**

Name ▼

Number/Street/Apt ▼

City/State/ZIP ▼

9

YOU MUST:
• Complete all necessary spaces
• Sign your application in space 8

SEND ALL 3 ELEMENTS
IN THE SAME PACKAGE:
1. Application form
2. Nonrefundable $20 filing fee
   in check or money order
   payable to *Register of Copyrights*
3. Deposit material

MAIL TO:
Register of Copyrights
Library of Congress
Washington, D.C. 20559-6000

*17 U.S.C. § 506(e): Any person who knowingly makes a false representation of a material fact in the application for copyright registration provided for by section 409, or in any written statement filed in connection with the application, shall be fined not more than $2,500.

March 1995—300,000   ♻ PRINTED ON RECYCLED PAPER   ☆U.S. GOVERNMENT PRINTING OFFICE: 1995-387-237/41

285

Filling Out Application Form VA

Detach and read these instructions before completing this form.
Make sure all applicable spaces have been filled in before you return this form.

BASIC INFORMATION

When to Use This Form: Use Form VA for copyright registration of published or unpublished works of the visual arts. This category consists of "pictorial, graphic, or sculptural works," including two-dimensional and three-dimensional works of fine, graphic, and applied art, photographs, prints and art reproductions, maps, globes, charts, technical drawings, diagrams, and models.

What Does Copyright Protect? Copyright in a work of the visual arts protects those pictorial, graphic, or sculptural elements that, either alone or in combination, represent an "original work of authorship." The statute declares: "In no case does copyright protection for an original work of authorship extend to any idea, procedure, process, system, method of operation, concept, principle, or discovery, regardless of the form in which it is described, explained, illustrated, or embodied in such work."

Works of Artistic Craftsmanship and Designs: "Works of artistic craftsmanship" are registrable on Form VA, but the statute makes clear that protection extends to "their form" and not to "their mechanical or utilitarian aspects." The "design of a useful article" is considered copyrightable "only if, and only to the extent that, such design incorporates pictorial, graphic, or sculptural features that can be identified separately from, and are capable of existing independently of, the utilitarian aspects of the article."

Labels and Advertisements: Works prepared for use in connection with the sale or advertisement of goods and services are registrable if they contain "original work of authorship." Use Form VA if the copyrightable material in the work you are registering is mainly pictorial or graphic; use Form TX if it consists mainly of text. **NOTE:** Words and short phrases such as names, titles, and slogans cannot be protected by copyright, and the same is true of standard symbols, emblems, and other commonly used graphic designs that are in the public domain. When used commercially, material of that sort can sometimes be protected under state laws of unfair competition or under the Federal trademark laws. For information about trademark registration, write to the Commissioner of Patents and Trademarks, Washington, D.C. 20231.

Architectural Works: Copyright protection extends to the design of buildings created for the use of human beings. Architectural works created on or after December 1, 1990, or that on December 1, 1990, were unconstructed and embodied only in unpublished plans or drawings are eligible. Request Circular 41 for more information.

Deposit to Accompany Application: An application for copyright registration must be accompanied by a deposit consisting of copies representing the entire work for which registration is to be made.

Unpublished Work: Deposit one complete copy.

Published Work: Deposit two complete copies of the best edition.

Work First Published Outside the United States: Deposit one complete copy of the first foreign edition.

Contribution to a Collective Work: Deposit one complete copy of the best edition of the collective work.

The Copyright Notice: For works first published on or after March 1, 1989, the law provides that a copyright notice in a specified form "may be placed on all publicly distributed copies from which the work can be visually perceived." Use of the copyright notice is the responsibility of the copyright owner and does not require advance permission from the Copyright Office. The required form of the notice for copies generally consists of three elements: (1) the symbol "©", or the word "Copyright," or the abbreviation "Copr."; (2) the year of first publication; and (3) the name of the owner of copyright. For example: "© 1995 Jane Cole." The notice is to be affixed to the copies "in such manner and location as to give reasonable notice of the claim of copyright." Works first published prior to March 1, 1989, **must** carry the notice or risk loss of copyright protection.

For information about notice requirements for works published before March 1, 1989, or other copyright information, write: Information Section, LM-401, Copyright Office, Library of Congress, Washington, D.C. 20559-6000.

LINE-BY-LINE INSTRUCTIONS
Please type or print using black ink.

1 SPACE 1: Title

Title of This Work: Every work submitted for copyright registration must be given a title to identify that particular work. If the copies of the work bear a title (or an identifying phrase that could serve as a title), transcribe that wording *completely* and *exactly* on the application. Indexing of the registration and future identification of the work will depend on the information you give here. For an architectural work that has been constructed, add the date of construction after the title; if unconstructed at this time, add "not yet constructed."

Previous or Alternative Titles: Complete this space if there are any additional titles for the work under which someone searching for the registration might be likely to look, or under which a document pertaining to the work might be recorded.

Publication as a Contribution: If the work being registered is a contribution to a periodical, serial, or collection, give the title of the contribution in the "Title of This Work" space. Then, in the line headed "Publication as a Contribution," give information about the collective work in which the contribution appeared.

Nature of This Work: Briefly describe the general nature or character of the pictorial, graphic, or sculptural work being registered for copyright. Examples: "Oil Painting"; "Charcoal Drawing"; "Etching"; "Sculpture"; "Map"; "Photograph"; "Scale Model"; "Lithographic Print"; "Jewelry Design"; "Fabric Design."

2 SPACE 2: Author(s)

General Instruction: After reading these instructions, decide who are the "authors" of this work for copyright purposes. Then, unless the work is a "collective work," give the requested information about every "author" who contributed any appreciable amount of copyrightable matter to this version of the work. If you need further space, request Continuation Sheets. In the case of a collective work, such as a catalog of paintings or collection of cartoons by various authors, give information about the author of the collective work as a whole.

Name of Author: The fullest form of the author's name should be given. Unless the work was "made for hire," the individual who actually created the work is its "author." In the case of a work made for hire, the statute provides that "the employer or other person for whom the work was prepared is considered the author."

What is a "Work Made for Hire"? A "work made for hire" is defined as: (1) "a work prepared by an employee within the scope of his or her employment"; or (2) "a work specially ordered or commissioned for use as a contribution to a collective work, as a part of a motion picture or other audiovisual work, as a translation, as a supplementary work, as a compilation, as an instructional text, as a test, as answer material for a test, or as an atlas, if the parties expressly agree in a written instrument signed by them that the work shall be considered a work made for hire." If you have checked "Yes" to indicate that the work was "made for hire," you must give the full legal name of the employer (or other person for whom the work was prepared). You may also include the name of the employee along with the name of the employer (for example: "Elster Publishing Co., employer for hire of John Ferguson").

"Anonymous" or "Pseudonymous" Work: An author's contribution to a work is "anonymous" if that author is not identified on the copies or phonorecords of the work. An author's contribution to a work is "pseudonymous" if that author is identified on the copies or phonorecords under a fictitious name. If the work is "anonymous" you may: (1) leave the line blank; or (2) state "anonymous" on the line; or (3) reveal the author's identity. If the work is "pseudonymous" you may: (1) leave the line blank; or (2) give the pseudonym and identify it as such (for example: "Huntley Haverstock, pseudonym"); or (3) reveal the author's name, making clear which is the real name and which is the pseudonym (for example: "Henry Leek, whose pseudonym is Priam Farrel"). However, the citizenship or domicile of the author **must** be given in all cases.

Dates of Birth and Death: If the author is dead, the statute requires that the year of death be included in the application unless the work is anonymous or pseudonymous. The author's birth date is optional but is useful as a form of identification. Leave this space blank if the author's contribution was a "work made for hire."

Author's Nationality or Domicile: Give the country of which the author is a citizen or the country in which the author is domiciled. Nationality or domicile **must** be given in all cases.

Nature of Authorship: Catagories of pictorial, graphic, and sculptural authorship are listed below. Check the box(es) that best describe(s) each author's contribution to the work.

3-Dimensional sculptures: fine art sculptures, toys, dolls, scale models, and sculptural designs applied to useful articles.

2-Dimensional artwork: watercolor and oil paintings; pen and ink drawings; logo illustrations; greeting cards; collages; stencils; patterns; computer graphics; graphics appearing in screen displays; artwork appearing on posters, calendars, games, commercial prints and labels, and packaging, as well as 2-dimensional artwork applied to useful articles.

Reproductions of works of art: reproductions of preexisting artwork made by, for example, lithography, photoengraving, or etching.

Maps: cartographic representations of an area such as state and county maps, atlases, marine charts, relief maps, and globes.

Photographs: pictorial photographic prints and slides and holograms.

Jewelry designs: 3-dimensional designs applied to rings, pendants, earrings, necklaces, and the like.

Designs on sheetlike materials: designs reproduced on textiles, lace, and other fabrics; wallpaper; carpeting; floor tile; wrapping paper; and clothing.

Technical drawings: diagrams illustrating scientific or technical information in linear form such as architectural blueprints or mechanical drawings.

Text: textual material that accompanies pictorial, graphic, or sculptural works such as comic strips, greeting cards, games rules, commercial prints or labels, and maps.

Architectural works: designs of buildings, including the overall form as well as the arrangement and composition of spaces and elements of the design. NOTE: Any registration for the underlying architectural plans must be applied for on a separate Form VA, checking the box "Technical drawing."

3 SPACE 3: Creation and Publication

General Instructions: Do not confuse "creation" with "publication." Every application for copyright registration must state "the year in which creation of the work was completed." Give the date and nation of first publication only if the work has been published.

Creation: Under the statute, a work is "created" when it is fixed in a copy or phonorecord for the first time. Where a work has been prepared over a period of time, the part of the work existing in fixed form on a particular date constitutes the created work on that date. The date you give here should be the year in which the author completed the particular version for which registration is now being sought, even if other versions exist or if further changes or additions are planned.

Publication: The statute defines "publication" as "the distribution of copies or phonorecords of a work to the public by sale or other transfer of ownership, or by rental, lease, or lending"; a work is also "published" if there has been an "offering to distribute copies or phonorecords to a group of persons for purposes of further distribution, public performance, or public display." Give the full date (month, day, year) when, and the country where, publication first occurred. If first publication took place simultaneously in the United States and other countries, it is sufficient to state "U.S.A."

4 SPACE 4: Claimant(s)

Name(s) and Address(es) of Copyright Claimant(s): Give the name(s) and address(es) of the copyright claimant(s) in this work even if the claimant is the same as the author. Copyright in a work belongs initially to the author of the work (including, in the case of a work made for hire, the employer or other person for whom the work was prepared). The copyright claimant is either the author of the work or a person or organization to whom the copyright initially belonging to the author has been transferred.

Transfer: The statute provides that, if the copyright claimant is not the author, the application for registration must contain "a brief statement of how the claimant obtained ownership of the copyright." If any copyright claimant named in space 4 is not an author named in space 2, give a brief statement explaining how the claimant(s) obtained ownership of the copyright. Examples: "By written contract"; "Transfer of all rights by author"; "Assignment"; "By will." Do not attach transfer documents or other attachments or riders.

5 SPACE 5: Previous Registration

General Instructions: The questions in space 5 are intended to find out whether an earlier registration has been made for this work and, if so, whether there is any basis for a new registration. As a rule, only one basic copyright registration can be made for the same version of a particular work.

Same Version: If this version is substantially the same as the work covered by a previous registration, a second registration is not generally possible unless: (1) the work has been registered in unpublished form and a second registration is now being sought to cover this first published edition; or (2) someone other than the author is identified as a copyright claimant in the earlier registration, and the author is now seeking registration in his or her own name. If either of these two exceptions apply, check the appropriate box and give the earlier registration number and date. Otherwise, do not submit Form VA; instead, write the Copyright Office for information about supplementary registration or recordation of transfers of copyright ownership.

Changed Version: If the work has been changed and you are now seeking registration to cover the additions or revisions, check the last box in space 5, give the earlier registration number and date, and complete both parts of space 6 in accordance with the instruction below.

Previous Registration Number and Date: If more than one previous registration has been made for the work, give the number and date of the latest registration.

6 SPACE 6: Derivative Work or Compilation

General Instructions: Complete space 6 if this work is a "changed version," "compilation," or "derivative work," and if it incorporates one or more earlier works that have already been published or registered for copyright, or that have fallen into the public domain. A "compilation" is defined as "a work formed by the collection and assembling of preexisting materials or of data that are selected, coordinated, or arranged in such a way that the resulting work as a whole constitutes an original work of authorship." A "derivative work" is " a work based on one or more preexisting works." Examples of derivative works include reproductions of works of art, sculptures based on drawings, lithographs based on paintings, maps based on previously published sources, or any other form in which a work may be recast, transformed, or adapted." Derivative works also include works "consisting of editorial revisions, annotations, or other modifications" if these changes, as a whole, represent an original work of authorship.

Preexisting Material (space 6a): Complete this space **and** space 6b for derivative works. In this space identify the preexisting work that has been recast, transformed, or adapted. Examples of preexisting material might be "Grunewald Altarpiece" or "19th century quilt design." Do not complete this space for compilations.

Material Added to This Work (space 6b): Give a brief, general statement of the **additional** new material covered by the copyright claim for which this registration is sought. In the case of a derivative work, identify this new material. Examples: "Adaptation of design and additional artistic work"; "Reproduction of painting by photolithography"; "Additional cartographic material"; "Compilation of photographs." If the work is a compilation, give a brief, general statement describing both the material that has been compiled and the compilation itself. Example: "Compilation of 19th century political cartoons."

7,8,9 SPACE 7,8,9: Fee, Correspondence, Certification, Return Address

Deposit Account: If you maintain a Deposit Account in the Copyright Office, identify it in space 7. Otherwise leave the space blank and send the fee of $20 with your application and deposit.

Correspondence (space 7): This space should contain the name, address, area code, and telephone number of the person to be consulted if correspondence about this application becomes necessary.

Certification (space 8): The application cannot be accepted unless it bears the date and the **handwritten signature** of the author or other copyright claimant, or of the owner of exclusive right(s), or of the duly authorized agent of the author, claimant, or owner of exclusive right(s).

Address for Return of Certificate (space 9): The address box must be completed legibly since the certificate will be returned in a window envelope.

Chapter 8

Electronic Technology

Allen Rabinowitz, Roger Ressmeyer, and Richard Weisgrau

I f you're not using a computer in your business, whether for correspondence, accounting, tracking sales, invoicing, or mailing lists, you're probably not as efficient as you could be.

The digital revolution has had, and will continue to have, a major impact on commercial photography as both a creative and business tool. From creating unique imagery to keeping the books straight, the computer has become indispensable to many photographers. This chapter will deal with the essentials of buying and maintaining a digital workstation, how the computer can help in a number of business applications, and the ramifications of the digital revolution on stock and copyright.

Regardless of your standard of computer literacy, be prepared to take full responsibility for the research which is absolutely essential to the final selection of hardware and software programs. Also, don't underestimate the time and commitment required to learn and master software, whether business or imaging. And if you delve into computer imaging, don't think that technology is a replacement for talent. The computer is simply a useful tool to make you more efficient and better at what you do.

Before going any further, digest this advice:

- Write down your needs and try to match them with software.
- Make sure the software you buy is returnable after a trial period if it doesn't meet expectations. If demonstration software is available, get it first.
- Don't expect computer salespeople to make your decisions for you. If you were buying a new car, you would read reviews on performance and seek the advice of friends and associates—computerization demands at least this degree of commitment to research.

- Subscribe to some leading computer magazines even if only for six months. You won't need to understand all of the articles, but it will provide an excellent overview of available technologies and trends applicable to our industry.
- Don't be afraid to ask questions of associates or acquaintances who use computers in similar creative businesses. Provided you don't abuse the privilege, most professionals who are well-versed in computers will quickly share hardware and software experiences.
- Most computer questions and problems can be resolved from within user groups which can be either casual or structured organizations of compatible individuals. Try to find one in your community and join. Membership fees are usually quite low.
- Seek out a competent computer consultant who understands your software and your goals. Use the consultant on an hourly basis to help set up your business and creative systems.
- You will get greater satisfaction from your computer if you become "keyboard literate"—in other words, learn to touch type. There are plenty of programs available to help you learn. It will be one of the best investments you will ever make.

Some Basics

First, two important—if simplistic—definitions. The computer system is made up of "hardware" and "software." The hardware is the physical equipment—the central processing unit, keyboard, monitor, and such peripherals as scanner, printer and/or other input and output devices as well as floppy disk drives and storage media containing the software. More ethereal than material, the software (also called "the program") is actually the magnetized data contained on disks which tells the computer how to operate and what to do when a command is entered. Think of the hardware as the camera and the software as the light acting on film.

While the variation between how assorted models of cameras operate is negligible—any two 35 mm cameras will make images with the same film—there is a world of difference between computer brands. For example, a software program designed to run on an Apple Macintosh system will not necessarily work on an MS-DOS–based personal computer (PC). This, however, may be a nonissue in the not-too-distant future when the next generation of computers appears on the market. These computers will be able to run any program designed for a multitude of operating systems.

With whatever software is used, be aware of the power and memory requirements necessary to run it on your system. A personal computer uses two different types of data storage or memory, either hard disk or random access memory (RAM). The more memory available, the more powerful the computer. RAM contains information the computer uses to run the system. Think of it as short-term memory contained on a chip, as well as the working space or temporary storage area for the program being run or on the screen. When you turn off the computer, information in RAM is erased.

The measurement unit for memory is the "byte," which is the amount of space needed to store a single character—whether it's a number, letter, or code. The amount of data storage is usually given in either kilobytes (KB), which equals 1,024 bytes, or mega-bytes (MB),which is over one million bytes. The memory requirements for software will be listed for hard disk and RAM.

Business

Like other businesspeople, photographers have discovered the computer to be an essential and invaluable tool for everything from keeping books in order to compiling lists for self-promotional mailings.

Most photographers initially become involved with computers as a means of better organizing and managing business functions. The computer helps you view your business in ways you never would have imagined before. Information which might have taken hours to find and figure out with paper, pencil, and an adding machine can now be discovered within minutes by virtue of the right software and a few keystrokes. Such factors as profitability or materials purchase comparisons from year to year, or quarter to quarter, become more easily attainable.

Not only can you know more about internal business workings, but you can also keep detailed histories on clients with a digital biographical file—listing information ranging from past dealings to which soft drink they like to drink on a shoot—which can be brought up on your computer screen within seconds. In a business based on personal bonds, having that information quickly at hand can go a long way to cementing relationships.

After becoming somewhat proficient with operating a computer, you might venture into exploring its creative side. You might be curious about creating digital imagery or manipulating existing photography, and, with the help of some basic software, possibly interested in expanding your business into this area. However, after a certain point, a decision must be made about obtaining a second computer. While some photographers frown on running both business and imaging applications on the same computer, there are systems with multitasking capabilities to facilitate the same system being used for both business and imaging. Keep in mind that creative applications require huge amounts of memory and unless your system has the speed and memory to switch from one program to another with little delay it might be preferable, if you can afford it, to have one computer dedicated to imaging and one to business.

The decision to expand computer capability, or to acquire a second system, like the initial decision to acquire a computer, should be primarily a financial one. If your time is better spent on the creative end of computing, then an office manager or other assistant can be productive on the business side. Although it is to your benefit to have a good working knowledge of business applications, it's advantageous to spend the time productively creating unique images. When acquiring a second computer, consider, for example, a "notebook" or portable model which offers the option of having computing ability at hand when on location or in a client's office. However, be aware that using a notebook computer is not the best way to run your entire business. Also, the hard drive capacity is more limited, as is memory expansion, and generally the laptops are slower than desktops. While the portables are very useful if you travel a lot and want computing capability on the road, a more modest desktop, which will cost less, is usually a better choice for business applications.

Determine the kind of software which will best serve your business needs and proceed from there. Before purchasing software, research the various business programs available. Ask friends and colleagues, particularly those who are also owners of photography businesses, about the software they use. The best testimonial any product can have is favorable reviews from users. Software manuals, in general, are not easy to follow. And while it's logical to invest time trying to make sense of a manual to get the most from your software once you've bought it, a better source of information—before you buy a program—is often a third-party book or magazine articles. A bookstore or library will have these books which usually provide accurate, down-to-earth information. You'll save a lot of money if you read a book before deciding if you want the program.

Determine your needs and goals before buying software. Expandability is one of the important factors you need to look for in a software package. When purchasing a program, it's wise to consider business goals a year or two down the road rather than where they stand today.

Choose programs which tie various components of your business together, because business flows through the day, and you are constantly navigating in and out of various aspects of that current. Being able to have immediate access and the ability to change hats instantly is a time-saver. Ask such questions as:

- Is the software designed to grow with the user's business?
- Does the software have multiuser options if employees are added?

Like most industries, photography has vertical market software written specifically for it. Though general business programs are adequate for a number of a photographer's needs, software specifically created for photo studio management will allow you to get right to the root of what it takes to keep your business on track. Unlike generic programs which offer such features as billing, receivables tracking, materials reports, and basic accounting functions, these programs contain features specific to the photo business, such as managing a stock photo library, estimating, tracking studio inventory, client data, mailing lists, and labels.

When buying software, find out about what kind of support will be available. Varying degrees are offered, ranging from none to unlimited free support. Some vendors offer a limited amount of free support with purchase and then charge for additional time, while others charge from the first question. If this is an important criteria, then the degree of support offered should be weighed into any purchase.

Some photographers may be tempted to write programs which relate to their specific needs. Although an experienced programmer might be able to take an off-the-shelf database program and customize it for a specific purpose, for most people, it's a time-consuming, difficult process. You might have to invest hundreds of hours on a project that might have an overall negative impact on your photography.

Under no circumstances should you copy software for use by anyone but yourself. As concerned as photographers are about copyright infringement, they should recognize and respect the copyright of the software's creator. No matter how basic the program might be, it's covered by the same intellectual property laws which protect your work.

When choosing hardware, remember what you are looking for is speed, memory, and capability, not necessarily a name brand. Many of the components in clones are identical to those in name-brand computers. But the manufacturer's track record is important, and time should be spent researching a system. Ask around, talk with colleagues.

Although state-of-the-art may be better for quality creative work, for most business applications, an older model might suffice. Many can run up-to-date software and the programs which were current when the computer was new.

A fact of life you'll have to face—probably at the most inconvenient time—is that something will fail. Like film, disks can have physical flaws, and every hard disk degrades over a period of time. In fact, every hard disk is rated for an MTBF (mean time between failures) factor. Rather than lose everything in a crash, take steps to protect data. Backups should be done on a regular basis—a good rule of thumb is to do a backup anytime you've done something you don't feel like doing again. Some photographers express a dislike of backup programs, stating that they discourage people from actually going through the process of making backups. The old system of backing up using floppy disks is still possible but it's antiquated and slow by comparison with the cartridges and digital audio tape (DAT) backup systems which are inexpensive and efficient. Keep in mind that a DAT, which can store huge volumes of information, is slow to access and is not intended for working with files.

It's important to maintain your paper files. Even the biggest proponents of the technology feel that vital documents such as contracts, invoices, and estimates should be outputted as hard copy. Not only will the client's accounting department want to keep such documents on paper, but it's also necessary for tax purposes.

Communications

Using a modem, which is simply a device which connects your computer via telephone to other computers, provides the opportunity to communicate with colleagues and clients almost instantly. A modem also provides access from your computer to electronic bulletin boards and information services. The speed with which a modem operates is its baud rate, typically 300, 1200, 2400, or 9600 and faster. A baud rate of 1200 or 2400 will suffice for sending and receiving most text files. However, if you intend accessing the World Wide Web, you will need a much faster modem.

Many computers have internal modems as standard features and numerous models of external modems and communications software are available. As with other computer equipment, the best advice you can get on modems and communications software will be from others who use them. This is where a computer user group can be an invaluable source of information.

Electronic bulletin boards and forums via networks such as CompuServe and Internet provide the facility to gather and exchange information via your computer.

One of the most useful communications tools is the fax machine which can, in a few seconds, transmit or receive letters, forms, layouts, and composites. Fax/modem software which allows you to send and receive fax messages from your computer is also handy. Faxes via modem are of high quality, and if you want to capitalize on this quality, use a laser printer to print messages. However, it's not recommended that your fax/modem be the primary business fax machine. If it were, your computer would have to be on all the time, tying up your resources and also subjecting the computer to potential problems such as lightning strikes. The ideal situation is to have a separate fax for the office, preferably on a dedicated phone line, and also have the capability to send faxes from your computer. And, if you have a portable notebook computer with an internal modem, you can have fax capability and access to electronic mail on the road with just a connection to a phone line.

Stock and Keywording

Computers have both simplified and complicated the task of organizing a collection of photographs.

There is no disputing that computers have simplified labeling slides, and numerous programs to perform that task are available. Also available, and often integrated into powerful studio management programs, is software for preparing delivery forms, invoices, and tracking and pricing stock photos. And there are programs which will generate bar code information for even more sophisticated tracking of stock images. Labeling slides is a basic essential. Computerizing other facets of managing your stock library is more complex, and, as with other aspects of computers in your business, you have to consider the advantages and disadvantages of computerized and manual systems.

Technology has made it possible to deliver images via such electronic media as compact disks or on-line networks to a greater number of prospective clients. It's also become a trickier proposition to make sure the client gets the exact picture needed. At a time when stock photography is becoming an art director's growing choice for photo illustration, photographers need to be ahead of the pack in giving that client the easiest path toward making a selection. More than just the arranging of images, computerization of the cataloging process has forced stock shooters to reconsider not only how they organize their files, but also what they shoot and how they describe it.

Since a number of top stock agencies have committed large chunks of inventory to CD-ROM, getting images on these discs has become competitive. In this new environment, the photographer who is attuned to such factors as having the kinds of images being sought and giving them the proper identifiers is more likely to get noticed. Unfortunately, too many have overemphasized the importance of the technology delivering the imagery and have underemphasized the property itself. Before loading the first piece of information about an image onto whatever medium, it's up to you to make a mature, disciplined analysis of the material being delivered.

When dealing in the digital environment, give careful consideration to the type of photos submitted to a stock agency. Given the cost of scanning images onto disks or files for on-line networks, cleaning up the scan and coming up with the right keywords, use discretion before getting too deep into the digital process.

The computer can be a useful tool for everyday organizational purposes. If a particular shoot produces a number of images you believe are worth saving, yet not of the quality to submit for stock usage, put some effort into using the computer for labeling the images and indexing them into some broad, general categories so they can be found easily if a need for them arises. Realize, however, that the vast majority of these images will probably never be used.

Once the photos are selected, they need to be distinguished by the choice of identifiers called "keywords." In searching through electronic media, the client enters a few select words which produce a directory of possible images to fill that requirement. For your own cataloging purposes, you need only a few choice terms to help find an image. But, in the marketplace, the right keywords can make the difference between a successful image and one which just takes up space on a disk. If the digital universe contains over one million possible images, the person doing the search will narrow that process down very tightly or else be overwhelmed with responses. The photographer who wins out is the one who gives the criteria essential to winnowing the search down to very specific types of responses.

Though stock agencies are primarily responsible for assigning keywords to images, you should put pressure on your agency to gain input into the process, or, at the very least, get to view the keywords and proofread them to make sure nothing has been left out which you feel is significant before they're placed on the CD-ROM. Once on there, they can't be changed. The art and science of choosing the right keywords is ever evolving. The trick is to choose words which convey the essence of the photo in a way that a client will quickly connect to his or her concept. Ideally, the keyword is more to sell a photo than describe it. You can verbally portray a photo in ways which have no value for selling that image and will only clutter up search procedures. When two people are talking visually, the continuity of language is very important if they don't have the same image in front of them. If the photo is of a Caribbean island, for example, the keywords should be geared toward a client's needs rather than the photographer's intent. You might choose such keywords as "Jamaica," or "beach," or "palm trees." But, the same photo also conveys such ideas as "leisure," "vacation," or "the good life."

Give a client a sufficient number of options. No matter what words you believe best match the image, they may not be the words the art director would use to call up the same image. Make sure that the keywords include both singular and plurals as well as all the words that have the same meaning.

It's important to be a part of this keywording process in order to recognize the type of photos needed to succeed in the new world of stock. By thinking about the keywords which will help sell the image, you can better anticipate and prepare for future shoots in terms of concepts. By getting involved with the keywording process, you become more aware, and therefore, more productive.

Creativity

Most photographers who have seen examples of what can be accomplished with the aid of digital technology are curious to see its impact on their work. They see the digital future and are eager to explore it; viewing the computer as neither a threat nor a creative miracle, but rather as a tool which enhances photography.

Though a useful instrument, computers may not be for every photographer. Determine why you want to get involved before purchasing the first piece of equipment or software. If the answer is to do the kind of work which will help you grow as an artist and attract new business, or to accomplish goals not attainable via traditional photographic means, you've taken the first step on the road to the digital future. A popular misconception is that the only kind of work which can be done on the computer is avant-garde, surrealistic photography. It's indeed easier to generate imagery, or adapt and manipulate existing images and accomplish unusual things that you otherwise might not have been able to do. More than anything, however, digital technology allows you to do what you already do, better. Just because you have the use of this new tool doesn't mean you should throw out your sensibilities. The three basic creative applications for which photographers acquire computer equipment are retouching, image enhancement, and image manipulation—primarily cutting and pasting elements of a photo or the combination of two or more images. Before making the investment of time and money, determine whether you want to do this kind of work or if you should farm it out.

Especially with cutting-and-pasting or image combination, it might benefit both the photographer and client to send such work to traditional prepress operators. However, be aware that whoever does the work might have claim on the copyright for the final image, as a derivative created by them. This can be controlled by proper purchasing paperwork in which you reserve the rights to all works derived from your work. But, you should still have a working knowledge of what can be accomplished with sophisticated prepress systems and software so you can plan shoots accordingly and produce photos which can be easily manipulated for the client's use.

For the number of things most people want to retouch, doing it yourself is probably not cost effective. As the cost of computers goes down, this becomes more economically viable. But, if you can offer this service in-studio as part of the overall photo project, this ability will make you more valuable to clients. Many photographers do not do their own darkroom work because it is more cost effective to contract it to labs. This may be true for digital image processing too.

Having decided to explore this digital route, the next step is gaining the knowledge to begin working. In addition to getting information from books and magazines on the subject, take classes on computers and specific software applications and seek out photographers working in the area. Talk to art directors and designers to get their input on what works best for the kind of work they like or want to do.

Trade shows, where most of the leading manufacturers exhibit, are another good source of information. You can inspect the equipment, talk with the representatives, and take the time to explore both hardware and software. Since the reps will push the system's strengths and not talk about weaknesses, ask pointed questions and carefully weigh all information afterward. The reps will gladly ply you with all manner of sales literature, which you can take home to compare specifications. The more knowledge acquired before making a purchase, the better prepared you'll be to choose the right equipment and software for your purposes.

Getting Started in Digital Imagery

After ascertaining goals in acquiring computer technology, research the specific system needed to create digital imagery.

One of the first choices is: which platform will serve as the workstation. There is continuing debate about which system is best for digital imaging, and while Apple Macintosh emerged as the system of choice for most designers and art directors, advancements are leveling the playing field between systems. In addition, become familiar with such items as scanners and output devices. These peripherals might influence your choice of platform.

A basic question is which comes first, the hardware or the software? Determine which software will best serve your creative purposes and then select a platform which can run it.

The pace of change in software design is rapid and today's standard may be tomorrow's discount bin remainder. Adobe's Photoshop™, which seems to be the leader in photo design and production software, can be used on both Macintosh and IBM-compatible platforms.

Remember that a large amount of RAM is necessary to have the full image available on the screen for processing without having to go into the hard disk and as mentioned previously, when power to the computer is terminated, RAM is erased.

Photoshop™, for example, recommends 8 MB of RAM on Macintosh, and 8 or more MB of RAM on IBM-type systems. How much power is needed to compete successfully in the arena of digital imagery? Since the programs needed require large amounts of memory, it's a good rule of thumb to have at least three times the size of your working file in RAM. Thus an 18 MB file would require 54 MB of RAM. Of course, you could install 100 MB of RAM, but that might be more than you need. The "three times files size" RAM allows you to have more immediate memory available which allows access to the whole image—or a large portion of it.

You can become familiar with computers and software before purchasing by leasing a computer or renting time on a system. If you have a special relationship with a lab or a retoucher, they might provide you the opportunity to become familiar with the technology.

The choice of a system, however, should be based on more than what's the latest—or "coolest"—thing, and instead depend on such factors as finances, the kind of business being done, and your capabilities. The trick is to not overbuy, but rather, buy the things which will produce revenue.

Above all, you must work through a fairly complex business decision which weighs in those previously mentioned factors along with a serious estimate of what effects this investment will have on your bottom line. Realize that the money outlay is continual, and because of the changes in technology and additions which come on the market, investment in a computer is never really finalized. Although photographers—like other creative types—are not always the best people for this kind of assessment, you have to leave the creative mode and assume a businessperson's frame of mind. In order for the computer to successfully help you grow your business, you must consider the financial aspects of this purchase.

Acquiring a System

Armed with reams of information culled from newspaper and magazine articles, notes taken during discussions with colleagues and clients, pamphlets and brochures from trade shows, and a wealth of instructional books, you're ready to acquire a system. But, where is the best place to get the hardware and software necessary for entering the digital imaging arena? Chances are, the local computer retailer will not have the special equipment you need. A better bet is to find a representative for a company which specializes in prepress workstations, or contact companies which specialize in supplying color separators and/or service bureaus with their hardware. The vendor's track record for support is a key determinant in choosing where to buy. The dealer should be reputable and capable of helping with inevitable problems.

Some companies will lease equipment on a short-term or month-to-month basis. That's a good way to get used to working on a computer and be up to speed when it comes time to purchase a system. Because of the way technology advances, the chances are the rented system will be outdated by the time you're ready to buy.

When people purchase a sound system for their home, they usually take a tape or compact disc they're familiar with to the retailer to hear how it sounds on a number of systems and components. The same approach needs to be taken when testing computer systems.

Take an image or two to a digital service bureau, and have them scan them onto a file or a Photo CD. In addition to having something to test on the system, you can also get a practical demonstration of the steps necessary to open and work on a file. Although the scan or CD will cost some money, it's far cheaper to pay for it and the output, than discover a large sum has been spent on the wrong computer. The salesperson probably will try to substitute the canned demonstration of the system's capabilities, but insist upon a demonstration using your file as well. After the disk is loaded onto the computer, ask the salesperson to demonstrate four or five real-life applications you are interested in accomplishing. After the presentation, ask if the system is capable of outputting the result to the type of digital file format or media you would use.

Though used to purchasing photo gear, photographers need to gain a different perspective on costs when dealing in digital equipment. While there isn't a large gap in cost between the cheapest and most expensive cameras and accessories, you'll find a wide disparity in computer prices. Generally, the equipment you want most and best suits your needs is out of your price range.

Before purchasing any piece of equipment, calculate whether acquiring this new tool will:

- Pay for the hardware and software in a reasonable time. Because computer equipment becomes outdated quickly, two years is suggested by some practitioners.
- Pay for the time it will take to learn the computer.
- Pay for the additional time spent on each job.
- Make a profit on top of all that in exchange for the risk.

Like every other business decision, getting involved with new technology is a matter of balancing profit to risk.

Whether or not to match up software with clients is another question to decide. If your goal is to produce finished art, then good equipment needs to be acquired. If the application is to communicate with clients and provide an on-site service where art directors can inspect work in progress, the system need not be top of the line.

A point to remember is this: one only needs a basic computer system with some sort of external storage medium, such as a removable magnetic or hard drive, so that scans and prints can be done by a service bureau. It's when the photographer adds imaging peripherals to the basic system, such as scanner, film recorder, and dye sublimation printer, that it gets very expensive and complicated. Also, the photographer may opt not to do the imaging work but once familiar with the technology can direct others.

Though the computer is an expensive investment, it's also an investment that may need to be repeated in a short time. Because of the pace of change with technology (there are usually upgrades in software about every six months), figure that a system will be out of date within two years. In fact, just at the very second you're finally feeling comfortable with your system, a company has just put the finishing touches on a new bigger, better, faster, and cheaper piece of equipment or software which has made your computer nearly obsolete.

Computers can be upgraded, and additional memory can be added; be resigned to purchasing a new state-of-the-art system to stay competitive. When working out the financial details on purchasing a computer, keep this information in mind. After all, it doesn't make much sense to take out a long-term loan for a system which will be obsolete and put you at a competitive disadvantage before the last coupon is torn from the loan book.

Digital Cameras

In addition to powering equipment for image manipulation, computer chips are also becoming an integral part of image capturing. Many of today's cameras rely on computer circuitry to control and guide essential operations, but in some cameras, the chip has become the recording medium for images. Increasingly, innovations such as still video and digital cameras are used in areas such as news gathering and catalog work.

Digital cameras, which have become a useful tool for catalog photography, convert images to data just as conventional photographs are scanned to make separations, but there is no film, no processing, and no scanner. If your business involves making a large number of images which don't need to run very large—and you have the money to invest—digital photography may be worth exploring. Digital cameras involve more than just photography, and the client can bypass a separator and other prepress steps if the system is used on a job—and this should be figured into a photographer's fee. Also, while the image quality from digital cameras generally does not equal film's, the images that some of the more expensive digital cameras and backs are capable of producing, and at reasonably large magnifications, are equal to film. Weigh carefully the economics of investing in this equipment.

If image quality is not a major consideration, digital cameras provide several advantages. Not only do you have a nonchemical (and pollution-free) way of creating an image, but additionally, a saving in time between capturing the image and having it in someone's hands.

However, be aware of the limitations in using digital cameras for certain kinds of work. For example, few alternatives exist for cameras which have swings and tilts. If you specialize in fashion, realize some systems cannot use electronic flash. At present, digital systems for commercial photography are best suited to large catalog studios or as an added in-house capability of businesses that provide a complete service from concept to prepress.

Invariably, technology has a way of meeting demand, and in the future digital photography could come to equal—and perhaps surpass—the quality of silver-based film.

The Learning Curve

After researching, exploring and finally, purchasing a digital workstation, you're ready to start producing—or are you? Just like getting started in anything else, there's a tremendous amount of knowledge to be assimilated, and hours of practice, before you're ready to market this new service. All this education, however, needs to take place while you're still earning a living. Even mastering simple retouching, for instance, might require three nights per week of trial and error for three or four months before you became proficient enough to do it for a client's job. To gain sufficient proficiency in one of the imaging programs, however, might require a much larger investment of time.

For someone doing a significant amount of billing and whose time is valuable, it may pay to go through a training seminar even before purchasing a computer. In addition, instructional videos are available for some Macintosh programs. However, a caveat is in order: As with anything associated with computers, research these training videos. It's best to ask other photographers if such material has been truly helpful. It's been noted that some videos have passed along wrong information. Though photographers are usually the kind of active people who may not spend much time reading, studying the software manuals or reading other authoritative material should be at the top of your "things to do" list. They might not be the most exciting reads, but these publications contain material you would never discover alone. There are other factors which go into the learning curve. For example, you'll learn that the picture on a computer's monitor can differ from the image on film as much as a Polaroid can.

Using the Computer as a Tool

Once you and your computer system are up and running, the next step is turning it into an income generator. Initially, your rate structure should be reassessed to justify the cost of the equipment and factor in this new expertise. Computer work needs to be priced differently from traditional jobs. Because the digital marketplace is already highly competitive, realize that just because a state-of-the-art piece of equipment has been added, clients will not necessarily beat a path to the studio door.

Not only will a promotional effort be needed to inform existing and potential clients about this new capability, but you need to get these clients to think of you as both an image creator and an image manipulator. Along with the additional billable services you offer clients, the way jobs are estimated and billed need to be reviewed. Determine how many new jobs per month can be done with the new equipment and how your time will be divided. One fallacy to overcome is that the computer will facilitate more jobs in less time. In fact, you'll probably spend more time on each job because of the fiddling with little details which were never considered prior to acquiring a computer.

Time should be spent thinking about how much more can be earned on jobs that were previously unobtainable. A reasonable estimate should be determined of how much time can be billed on the workstation each week without overbooking and overloading yourself. Though clients are usually glad to see the addition of new capabilities in a photographer's studio, they often don't like paying for it. However, if the same service is being provided by an outside vendor, the client would think nothing of approving it on an expense sheet. It's up to you to explain how this new addition helps produce a more cost-efficient or higher quality job for the client. An important selling point is that the client's image manipulation needs can now be handled in the studio, saving time and the hassle of going to outside vendors.

In order to determine a reasonable price, find out what suppliers in the market are charging for such services and adjust accordingly. This should be reflected in your price, but under two different schedules—one for photographic work and the other for postproduction. If clients are used to paying just for the photograph, it may be necessary to spell out on the bill the time used for postproduction. This can be listed as "system work" or "system time." Since clients are used to paying for this service under these terms, listing it as a usual-to-them expense helps get it through with a minimum of red flags.

Maintenance, Storage, and Backup

While technical mishaps are inevitable, there are steps you can take to ensure that all is not lost in case of something as major as a system crash. Proper maintenance begins with the purchase of the computer and ascertaining service and support.

One preventive maintenance method is to use utilities to defragment the hard disk on a regular basis. This moves all the data from each file onto contiguous sections of the disk so that the access head does not have to travel far, which speeds the process up. A hard drive crashing in the middle of the job is a major problem and buying a new hard disk is a probability. However, all might not be lost as there are utilities which can retrieve data. So, if this misfortune befalls you, don't toss the computer away. Seek help from a consultant or a local user group and, depending on the type of crash, you might be able to retrieve your data.

To prepare for those disasters, it's to your benefit to back up files often. To be safe, you may choose to have only the file being worked on that day on the hard drive. Once the job is complete, a backup of the finished file, with all the pertinent steps in between, can be made. Some photographers believe that if the original photo is kept, it isn't vital to have backup files of the steps needed to get to the image, since the original film is the best backup.

Since floppy disks don't hold enough information for a complete file, the data should be stored on an archival device, such as optical recorders or 8 mm stream tape. This tape resembles an eight-track tape, and can hold 150 MB of information, which should be enough for the file and some interim steps. Other archival materials include digital audiotape (DAT), which resembles an audiotape but collects digital information rather than analog sounds. This is a reliable backup system.

Another option for quick access is an optical disk. This device—which looks like a compact disk—records information as light and can hold up to four or five jobs in progress. A number of photographers use a removable magnetic or hard drive to store information and transport it to output. SyQuest and Bernoulli are two drives commonly used to transfer information.

Once a standard is agreed upon by manufacturers, compact disks will probably be the storage and backup medium of choice. Compact disks on which information can be "written" (i.e., recorded) are currently available, but until standardization, an investment in the technology is chancy. If your compact disk writer or playback is not the one chosen, it means purchasing a whole new recorder and spending time copying all files.

Some photographers feel that the lab or service bureau which does their output is the best place to store their files, so a copy can be obtained simply by calling. However, most service bureaus charge a fee for both the storage and the media used.

Outputting and Service Bureaus

Once the work is completed on the digital image, you may need something tangible for the client. This is accomplished by a number of output devices, such as dye-sublimation printers or laser- or ink-jet printers.

If a high-quality, high-resolution transparency is needed, an output device can be quite expensive, with film recorders often costing in the six-figure range. The solution is to take a file to a service bureau, just as you would take film in for processing.

In addition to graphics arts service bureaus, many photo labs have added digital equipment and are now positioning themselves as full-service bureaus for all forms of image processing. If you are satisfied with the quality of service the lab has provided for film, it might be best to stick with this lab for digital imaging too. Probably, the lab's technicians will know your preferences and tastes. If a level of comfort and trust has been established between you and the lab, there's no reason to look elsewhere if that lab can also accommodate your digital processing needs.

Selecting a place for digital image processing is much like choosing a lab. Ask other photographers and clients who they use and inquire about the kind of equipment and its capabilities. Communication is another important factor in choosing a service bureau. Because some service bureau operators are more computer- than image-oriented, they may not understand your instructions and needs. Photographers must realize that since computer operators have different backgrounds and reference points, bridges allowing smooth communication need to be built. You need to feel that the people handling your files are both capable and sensitive to the unique needs of a particular image. The ideal person is someone capable of speaking both the language of computers and that of photography.

A file of the image should be brought in and, after processing, carefully inspected to make sure it's satisfactory. It might be useful to have a print of the image handy for comparison. During the processing phase, ask questions of the technician to ascertain his or her talents and knowledge. While looking over the technician's shoulder, be aware of certain things and ask the technician:

- Is the workstation calibrated?
- Is the monitor accurate in terms of color balance?

If you're satisfied with a service bureau make sure your equipment is calibrated to theirs. A good service bureau will help regular customers with this process. When told that the file is being used to acquaint the photographer with their capability, some service bureaus might offer a discounted rate for the processing, or may even do it at no charge.

When to Upgrade

Just when you're really comfortable with the computer and using it to its optimum, the realization will come that there are shortcomings because it's not fast enough or it doesn't have sufficient memory. Or, there's new software or a new effect worth trying, but due to the limitations of the system, it can't be attempted on existing equipment. Perhaps the computer is not capable of producing work quickly enough to satisfy the standards that clients have come to expect. Because of that, you are losing jobs to those with more state-of-the-art equipment. At that point, the obvious solution is a new computer.

As with the initial purchase, this is a decision which must be carefully weighed, with assessments of both the financial and creative ramifications. A key factor should be whether any upgrade will increase business or revenue capabilities. If you believe a more powerful computer will provide better service for clients, then the choice is easy.

Some photographers buy their initial system with the idea that it will need to be upgraded within a short time. Of course, there are software upgrades, and new periph-erals become available. You should keep abreast of all these developments by word of mouth, reading publications, and visiting retailers and trade shows.

Once a new system is up and running, what should be done with the old one? The odds are it's more out of date than useless. It can be transformed into a dedicated function such as printing labels or for E-mail, be used for personal work or as the "kid's computer," or donated to any number of educational or charitable institutions where it can still serve a useful purpose.

New Markets

Electronic technology has opened new markets for photographers and some are already capitalizing on these opportunities. For instance, the CD-ROM market is taking off, and photographers are using this medium for stock catalogs and self-promotion. A downside is that CD-ROMs have also become an outlet for clip art disks, and ASMP has urged photographers not to license their work to these disks which give users virtually unlimited usage with small returns per image to the photographers.

However, the CD-ROM technology has created another avenue for photographers producing books who can now consider CD-ROM spin-offs. One of the first and most successful ventures into this area was by Rick Smolan whose book *From Alice to Ocean* has become a popular CD-ROM.

CD-ROMs also can be used for self-promotion, but that potential depends on whether your clients have a CD-ROM drive to view your work. Another possibility for self-promotion and other marketing is having a smaller number of photographs put on a floppy disk which can be accessed on a computer.

One of the advantages of having your images on a floppy disk as distinct from a CD-ROM is that many buyers, and probably most designers, have computers on their desks capable of accessing floppy disks. Fewer have CD-ROM drives. However, this situation will change as more photo buyers acquire CD-ROM drives.

Other potential markets are on-line, interactive education programs and entertainment games, and a huge demand for photographs in this area is predicted.

Some photographers who have mastered desktop publishing software, such as Quark Xpress™ or PageMaker™, and are using Photoshop™ or similar programs to import photographs, have also produced their own printed promotional materials.

The new technologies also make it possible for photographers to broaden their range of service, either independently or in alliance with others, such as designers. Photographers who are strong in design can offer expanded services by becoming conversant in all facets of prepress production. Others could consider forming an alliance with a designer to become a production shop.

If you do expand your capabilities and are able to provide a broader range of prepress services, bear in mind the added value you give your client—charge accordingly. You must be able to profit from your investment in new equipment and your skills.

Copyright

Though the computer may be considered a great creative tool, its use in photography has opened a Pandora's box in terms of copyright. Like all innovations in communications and media, from the phonograph to radio to television to satellites, the digital revolution has advanced the frontier of copyright law. It should be remembered that when the first U.S. copyright law was written in 1790, the birth of photography was almost a half-century away. Currently, lawmakers are examining and drafting legislation which will update the copyright laws to deal with digital technologies.

What can a photographer do to protect against copyright infringement? The new environment means not only additional opportunities for image creation, but also additional openings for unscrupulous individuals to take advantage and usurp reproduction rights of images. The climate calls for both a good working knowledge of digital imaging and increased vigilance on the part of photographers.

The ability to manipulate and combine images complicates the question of what constitutes copyright infringement. Infringement is a use of a copyrighted work without the copyright holder's permission.

An act of copyright infringement is judged by:

- Proof of access by the alleged infringer to the image in question is shown to exist. (If there is a great similarity between the two images, access might be assumed.)
- Concluding that an ordinary observer would believe one image is indeed copied from another.
- How much of the total work is used.
- Whether the use results in commercial harm.

Joint copyright is another issue brought to the forefront by the digital revolution. When two or more images are combined, all creators possess a copyright to the new work (see "Definitions from the Copyright Act of 1976" in the chapter 7). Each has an unrestricted right to use the image, but all copyright holders must share any proceeds equally.

The widespread use of CD-ROM catalogs also opens up potential problems in many photographers' minds. Their feelings center on the idea that an electronic copy of an image might yield something of the same quality as the original photo. The growth of on-line networks also fuel their fears.

The CD-ROM catalog is not the only technology that is open to abuse. An original image from a magazine, brochure, stock catalogue, or other source can be scanned into a computer and digitally altered without the copyright holder knowing this was done.

Some see a danger in the practice of magazines storing the scans they make of photos. There are no guarantees that the photo will not be reused, or perhaps manipulated without the photographer's authorization and without additional payment.

Given the potential for abuse, how can you best protect your copyrights in this new digital world? Some suggestions include the placement of an electronic watermark in the form of a copyright symbol on all images incorporated on CD-ROM catalog or on-line networks. Others recommend encryption, a scrambling of the digital content which requires special keys to decode. (See "Image Protection Standards for the Digital Era" at the end of this chapter.)

However, don't overlook protection provided by traditional means. Always write language into such documents as contracts, estimate forms, and delivery memos clearly defining allowable usages for a particular image, with precise wording on the length of time the image may be used and the specific way the client can use it, as well as a statement clearly declaring the image may not be manipulated and/or altered electronically without the copyright holder's express written permission.

All paperwork that passes to the client should stipulate that if the photo is scanned, those scans will be either destroyed or erased. Because of the expense involved, don't expect the user to mail back an electronic file with the scans of the images.

While any documents should contain this information, an invoice may not be the best place to define the client's photo usage rights. Copyright stipulations on the invoice could easily be considered contracts after the fact, meaning you would have a difficult time enforcing the agreement. In addition, most invoices are sent to the client's accounts receivable department. The people responsible for the image's use and welfare may never get to see the invoice. Copyright stipulations should be sent to the client before the work is done or the sale is made. This makes those stipulations a condition of the sale and much more enforceable.

Before signing any contracts submitted by a client, inspect them carefully to discover what they might say about electronic reproduction rights. This language might be buried in a section of the contract for other nondigital uses. Before submitting any images to a stock agency for a CD-ROM or an on-line network, ask the agency a number of questions about the project, such as:

- Does the agency intend to register the copyright for all images being used?
- How large will the digital file containing photo information be?
- Will the image file on the disk produce a high-resolution, high-quality image?

If the agency does not provide this information, look elsewhere.

The most important thing photographers can do to protect their copyrights is step up their vigilance, which in today's electronic technology era, is more important than ever before. When you have dealings with a client, track the possible venues where the client might use his or her image. Get on any mailing lists the client might have. Also endeavor to acquire any brochures or other printed material the client may produce as well as the company's annual report.

Although the chance for unauthorized use is greater in the digital environment, photographers need to balance this against a rapidly expanding market for such imagery which will provide more opportunities. Although problems exist in regard to copyright, they're primarily extensions of what has existed before. Realize the electronic realm is simply another medium that has its own problems.

The best way to retain copyrights in the light of new technology is to be more precise in the language of communications with clients and continue the practices you've used in the past to safeguard your rights. No matter what the future may hold in the way of newer and more amazing technologies, paying attention to the basics of good business will still be the key to staying on top of the copyright situation.

Image Protection Standards for the Digital Era

Roger H. Ressmeyer

The guidelines presented here first appeared in an image security report prepared by photographer Roger Ressmeyer for the MP©A board and have since been endorsed by ASMP, the Time Inc. Picture Collection, and the Electric Picture Round Table. Mr. Ressmeyer is now a Senior Editor at Corbis Corporation, and many of these guidelines have been adopted by Corbis. However, the recommendations presented here reflect Mr. Ressmeyer's personal views and not those of Corbis Corporation.

This report focuses on the challenge of protecting images in the much more vulnerable environment of cyberspace. Whatever protection the photographer uses today must remain effective for ten, twenty, or one hundred years, since a digitally stored image might last for centuries after the original negative or transparency has faded into oblivion.

Modern technology evolves so rapidly that encryption, watermarking, and other high-tech protections are likely to be defeated almost as soon as they are applied. As a bottom line, we strongly recommend a low-tech approach that can't be defeated by present or future technology: *Before release to a client or into any environment (such as the Internet) where copying is possible, each and every image must have a copyright credit embedded (bitmapped) into it, in pixel form as part of the image itself.*

Keep in mind that from both the freelance photographer's and the photographer agent's point of view, it is imperative that image ownership be protected at all times. When selecting a digital photo agency or when having your images scanned, ensure that the organization understands this basic requirement: To protect the image, a clearly legible statement of authorship (credit) and also of copyright ownership (legal notification) must be attached to the image before any distribution, and preferably from the moment of scanning.

Since there are already hundreds of image file formats as well as format conversion and batch-processing programs like HiJaak™ and DeBabelizer™, whatever convention you use for copyright and credit notification must work any way the image is viewed or stored now or in the future. We cannot assume that any single image format will become the standard in the future, and we cannot assume that images scanned and originally stored in one format will be viewed and used in that same format. Therefore, we recommend our "low-tech" solution.

Don't be confused by technicians and art directors who have different ideas—your credit must be stored in the image bitmap itself for full protection. Information can also be stored in "alpha channels," "headers," or in attached databases. However, information stored these other ways can too easily be stripped away and discarded without notice when the image is opened by conversion programs. Face it, in thirty years a researcher will be happy enough just to get the image open, and will not be concerned about hidden data stored in some obsolete format. Try opening word processing documents from just a dozen years ago, and you will understand the implications of obsolete formats.

We also recommend that this bitmapped credit should not lie on top of the image, where it would destroy otherwise usable picture area. We recommend treating it like an artist's signature line beneath the image, but still within the bitmapped file. Using the language of Photoshop™, the "canvas size" of the image needs to be increased, leaving a black bar at the bottom with reversed, white type for the copyright notice. The black bar with reversed type makes it clear that the credit data are an integral part of the image area. With common run-length compression schemes, this plan will increase disk storage space by no more than 2 percent per image.

To make the copyright credit legible, the height of this bar depends on the file size. Since ASMP supports adjacent, readable credit lines, we recommend the following sizes:

- Thumbnails (192 × 128 pixels) and preview images (384 × 256 pixels): Bar 12 pixels high, type 10 pixels high.
- Screen Resolution (640 × 480 pixels) and Comps (1280 × 1024 pixels): Bar 36 pixels high, type 30 pixels high.
- Print Resolution (3072 × 2048 pixels) and Full 35mm Resolution (6144 × 4096): Bar 72 pixels high, type 60 pixels high.

Of course, any bitmapped credit can be cropped out by the user. But as long as the photographer or image provider always includes the credit and copyright notice within the image, the legal burden of copyright protection is placed more squarely on the user who receives that image.

When adding a text-based credit line in Photoshop™ or other image processing program, the © symbol is easy to insert: option-G makes a © when using the Macintosh; CRTL-ALT-C does the same thing in Word for Windows. Most computers also have "character map" or "key caps" routines for copying symbols such as © and inserting them into written documents.

We also recommend that inclusion of one other type of data in the image bitmap—an image serial number to identify the picture and to enable access to unique image information regarding restrictions, model releases, and captions. Without this number, the scanned image could become unusable, since publishing without knowledge about image restrictions and model releases puts both the photographer and the user at legal risk. (This is not the case when all images are model released and free of all restrictions. Unfortunately that is not the nature of most picture collections.)

Imagine how much easier it is to "misfile" photos in the digital age! When an image has been selected by an art director, it will most likely be converted into another format for use in a layout or multimedia product, breaking the connection to the original file. Everyone benefits from a bitmapped serial number when positive identification is required.

Encryption and watermarking also provide valuable safeguards, but they are especially vulnerable as technology evolves. Encryption schemes can and will be broken, and must never be relied upon as the only form of protection. Always include a copyright credit in addition to encryption and watermarking.

Nor does low-resolution distribution protect images. Some image publishers will say, "But your image is safe if we only release a low-resolution copy." This logic is absolutely false. No matter how small the file size, no image is safe without some form of protection. Pixels can be "interpolated" or electronically multiplied, doubling or quadrupling the size of any image. While interpolation will only get better as new software is developed, even today's technology is impressive. In 1994, I used Photoshop™ to interpolate several ½ MB "thumbnail" files. By juggling the sequence of interpolations, I created finished images that were over 72 MB in size. No interpolation artifacts were visible. Therefore, we must conclude that low resolution does not guarantee image protection. It will only get worse in the future, and today's small images will already be out there.

We recommend using encryption and/or watermarking for all images that are screen resolution (640 × 480 pixels) or larger, so the client is forced to register for permission (and pay a fee) before they receive clean copies of higher-resolution images.

Also, at the lower resolutions which are typically used as "thumbnails" and "previews" during picture searches, (192 × 128 and 384 × 256 pixels), we suggest watermarking a large copyright symbol directly into the image, on top of the picture. (Using a program such as Photoshop™, this is accomplished in RGB mode by first changing the foreground color to 128 value for red, green, and blue. Select the text tool and type in a (C) that is at least 100 pixels high. While the text selection is floating, center it in the picture and change the opacity value to 50 percent.) On the screen, such a watermark is barely visible, but when the image is copied, color separated, printed, film recorded, enhanced, or transmitted, the copyright sign remains with the file and the symbol often becomes more visible.

The following six examples illustrate various typical resolutions of digitized images, and how the copyright notice, credit and serial number can be bitmapped onto the image.

Please note: Antialiasing is a software interpolation process which makes fonts appear smoother. It eliminates the "stair stepping" of pixels by blurring out the corners of individual letters. We do not recommend anti-aliasing for bitmapped credits, since the small letters will become too blurry to read comfortably when they are antialiased.

Example 1: THUMBNAIL IMAGE 192 × 128 pixels. A 12-pixel-high black bar has been added to the bottom of the picture, making the final image size 192 × 140 pixels. The copyright notice is the smallest size that is legible: 10-pixels-high, Univers Plain, all capital letters, not antialiased. The floating "watermark" copyright symbol is 120 pixels high, mid-gray in color, and 50% opaque to reveal the underlying image. Such a watermark is strongly recommended for "thumbnail" and "Comp" images, which will be widely exposed to theft due to usage in digital on-line catalogues for image selections.

ROGER RESSMEYER – ©1994 CORBIS   RR009823

Example 2: PREVIEW IMAGE 384 × 256 pixels. A 12-pixel-high black bar has been added to the bottom of the picture, making the final image size 384 × 268 pixels. (The bar and type are identical to the one in the thumbnail, example one. Extra space in this image size allows the agency credit and image number.) The copyright notice is the smallest size that is legible: 10-pixels high, Univers Plain, all capital letters, not antialiased. The floating copyright sign is 240-pixels high, mid-gray in color, and 50 percent opaque to reveal the underlying image.

ROGER RESSMEYER — ©1994 CORBIS RR015372

Example 3: SCREEN-RESOLUTION IMAGE 640 × 480 pixels. A 36-pixel-high black bar has been added to the bottom of the picture, making the final image size 640 × 516 pixels. The copyright notice size is based on screen legibility for this and the next largest image size: 30-pixels high, Univers Plain, all capital letters, not antialiased.

ROGER RESSMEYER — ©1994 CORBIS   s/n RR009823

Example 4: COMP IMAGE 1280 × 1024 pixels. A 36-pixel-high black bar has been added to the bottom of the picture, making the final image size 1280 × 1060 pixels. The copyright notice size is based on screen legibility for this and the next smallest image size: 30-pixels high, Univers Plain, call capital letters, not antialiased.

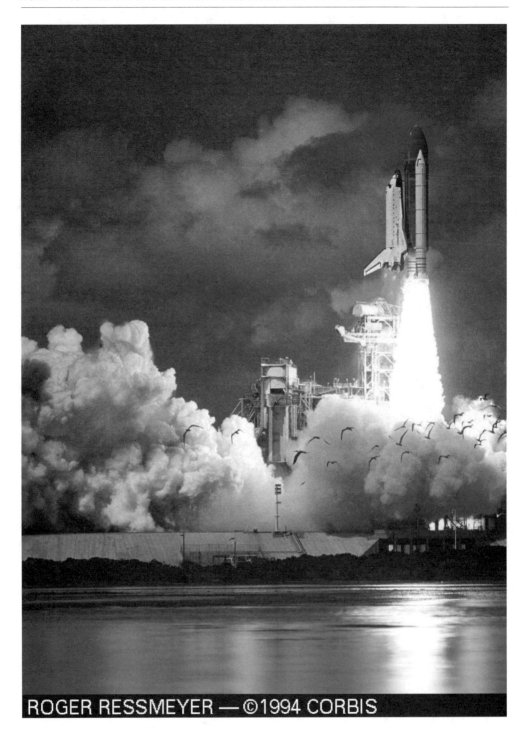

ROGER RESSMEYER — ©1994 CORBIS

Example 5: PRINT RESOLUTION IMAGE (3072 x 2048 pixels, about 18 MB) IMAGE HAS BEEN CROPPED FROM RIGHT TO FIT PAGE. A 72-pixel-high black bar has been added to the bottom of the picture, making the final image size 3072 x 2120 pixels. The copyright notice size is based on screen legibility for this and the next larger image size: 60-pixels high, Univers Plain, all capital letters, not antialiased.

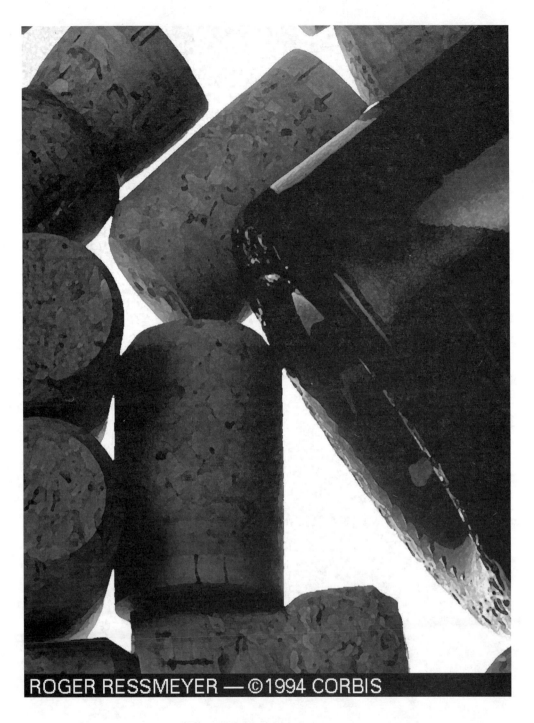

ROGER RESSMEYER — ©1994 CORBIS

Example 6: FULL 35MM RESOLUTION (6144 × 4096 pixels, about 72 MB) ¹/₂ OF IMAGE HAS BEEN CROPPED FROM TOP, ³/₄ FROM RIGHT TO FIT PAGE. A 72-pixel-high black bar has been added to the bottom of the picture, making the final image size 6144 × 4168 pixels. This image size is used for larger reproductions and large format details, because it maintains all the details of an original 35mm transparency. Copyright notice size: 60-pixels high, Univers Plain, all capital letters, not antialiased.

Chapter 9

Business and Marketing Strategies

Bruce Blank (creating a business plan); Ira Mark Gostin (fifteen tips for success); Maria Piscopo (marketing yourself, the joys of telemarketing, publicity to help sell photography, finding the names of potential clients); Mark Tucker (independent contractor or employee); Richard Weisgrau (getting work, the art of selling)

Creating a Business Plan

A word of advice before you start reading this section on developing a business plan: every business, regardless of size, should have a written operations document. You might think that just because you're a one- or two-person business there's no need for a plan. Right? Wrong! The principles of a business plan apply to any size business. The complexity and magnitude might differ, but the purpose is the same.

An analogy is planning a trip. How are you going to get there if you don't know where you're going? Taking the time to chart your course before you start—right now—is very important.

The time invested in preparing a solid, well-thought-out business plan will make running a photography business (or any business for that matter) considerably easier. It is also necessary if success is to be a reality rather than a pipe dream. Unfortunately, entrepreneurs are "doers" rather than proposal writers by nature. They would much rather be in the trenches than the command center. Also, much of what is floating around their heads will be difficult to put on paper and articulate to others. Many of these business concepts have become second nature (like knowing that you should overexpose ¼ stop when you need a little more shadow detail). Photographers may even have a more difficult time considering their creative nature: right- versus left-brained (creative versus analytical). One advantage is the fact that your entire career has been spent solving problems. So let's solve a few problems.

Why?

One of the most useful aspects of a well-thought-out business plan is the fact that it will allow you to make mistakes on paper instead of in real life. You will use it to develop ideas about how the business will be run, what your management philosophy will be, where the money will come from and, importantly, where it will go. It will be your chance to examine this new entity from all perspectives: marketing, operations, finance, etc. It will be a model which will allow you to do some cerebral testing prior to risking time and limited financial resources.

Another aspect of a business plan, which too often gets forgotten a few months after the actual start-up, is the fact that this tool will give you something to measure the actual success and performance of your business over time. For example, the financial projections can be used as a foundation for an operating budget that is more than an educated guess. Just as budgets will need to be adjusted as time passes, the plan should also be used to evaluate operations, philosophy, and management on an ongoing basis.

Don't waste your time drafting a business plan and allowing it to collect dust. Use it. Annually (perhaps during the week between Christmas and New Year) you should spend time reflecting, remembering, and dreaming. Take this week (business will be slow anyway) to reread the last published plan and rewrite it using all the experience you've gained in the last twelve months. Then use it again.

During the next year, periodically pull the plan out to see how you're doing—what is working, what's not working, where the money is coming from, what you can do to keep more of it, etc. Don't keep this plan a secret! Let others read it and welcome their input. Two heads are better than one! Undoubtedly, someone else will see something you've missed. And another completely different perspective could save your neck. The plan is an ongoing project and an important tool to chart not only a start-up, but also the continued existence of "the studio."

Historically, business plans have been used to raise money. This is what most people think of when they hear the words "business plan." If you are seeking funding, your plan will have to excite investors, convey a genuine sense of optimism, and be accurate. You'll need to walk a fine line between content and tone, risks must be addressed (but not dwelled upon), numbers must be realistic, and the presentation has to be professional and easy to comprehend. The tone should be businesslike; use graphics, clear type, and a professional-looking binder. Spelling and grammar must be impeccable, always keep in mind who is going to read it (bankers, venture capitalists, etc.) so be wary of being too "schmaltzy." Realism will be more important than hype. The plan has to create a bridge between "Madison Avenue and Wall Street," so be wary.

Since a business plan will be changed and reviewed, do it on a word processor (or have it done by someone else and keep the disk). Keep your copy in a three-ring binder with room for additions and handwritten notes. (The copies for bankers, etc., can be made to look "pretty"—yours is the working model.) Make sure that each copy is clearly dated and you know which is the most recent—you don't want to give your banker a copy with two-year-old financials. Also, keep a log with names of those who received copies, what version they received, and when they received it. There will be people who you will want to keep current, so knowing who has which copy of the plan will make that easier to manage. There will be others who may need to see your business plan occasionally (i.e., leasing companies and important creditors such as labs for large projects, equipment, and material suppliers).

Considering that planning of this type is probably more important to small companies than larger companies (a smaller company is less likely to survive a disaster than a larger company with more resources), an accurate up-to-date business plan is essential. It will help to maintain consistency in management and operations as time passes and is probably the first chance a start-up has to do serious strategic planning.

How?

Keep in mind outside professionals will be able to take your ideas, plans, and concepts and mold them into a polished plan. It is important to get help and seek professional advice once the basic plan is outlined. Let's face it, no one knows what's on your mind better than you. You have to start the process, but help can be obtained from your accountant and attorney. You do need one or both. They can give you ideas where to start, what information to include, how to calculate financial projections, and will probably ask many questions—which should generate more ideas. Once the plan is started and is on paper, they will see aspects you missed, be able to make suggestions, and help create the finished piece.

In the plan, answer the questions raised by those who read the drafts. Your job is to anticipate and educate—not everyone knows exactly what a photographer does. If questions cannot be answered immediately, make sure this is admitted in the plan. This shows that you are aware and it isn't something that has been overlooked. You will not write a business plan over a four-day weekend—be prepared for it to take weeks, even months. And remember, it's never completely finished! Before you start writing consider these things:

- What will the business actually do? It may sound like a stupid question, but remember Aunt Martha thinks that photographers only shoot brides and babies. She hasn't a clue where the ads in the magazines come from; and remember there are a lot of Aunt Marthas out there.
- Who will steer this ship and what makes that person the right person for the job? This is a good time to look inward and do some serious evaluating of your own psyche and motives.
- If you want to get rich, are you really willing to work twenty-hour days and weekends?
- What makes you so much better than the rest of the photographers already out there?
- What makes your services special?
- Can you solve problems?
- Are you the only one in the area who knows how to use the latest lighting gadget?
- What other experiences can you bring to the business?
- How will you market what you do, and who's out there waiting to buy?
- What does your book look like?
- Is there a big enough client base to support your expectations?

- Where are the clients, and how do you plan to reach them?
- Will you advertise in sourcebooks?
- Will you use mailers?
- Can you rely on established contacts?
- Can you really afford to do this?
- Do you have the resources available or will you need funding?
- How much do you need to make after you've invested in equipment and promotional materials?
- What is the revenue potential (be realistic!) vs. the day-to-day costs?
- How many billable days a month do you think you will have? And what will you do when your expectations are not met?
- What are other start-up costs (besides rent, electric, telephone, insurance, office supplies, furniture, leasehold improvements, advertising, equipment, equipment repairs, materials used for promo shots (remember, clients are typically billed for materials used for assignments), employee expenses, professional fees (accountant, lawyer, etc.), taxes, business licenses, and permits?

What?

The following are the basic components of a real business plan. You should elaborate as much as possible. Remember, the more complete the plan is, the better prepared you will be.

I. Executive summary *(This is not a mere outline of what's in the pages to follow. It should be about two to four pages and emphasize the key elements in the plan, and show the company's "reason for being.")*
   A. The purpose of the plan
      1. Revenue procurement
      2. Detail an operational plan for controlling the business
      3. Test financial feasibility of a business concept
   B. Define the company
      1. Define what the company will do
      2. Explain what needs the company will satisfy
   C. Market analysis
      1. Define the target market
         a. Geographic
         b. Demographic
         c. Size
      2. Evaluate competition
   D. Marketing and sales activities
      1. Marketing plans and strengths
      2. Sales strategies
      3. Keys for overcoming competition
   E. Company organization and personnel
      1. Important managers and owners

2. Important operational personnel
3. Utilization of outsourced personnel

F. Financial information
1. Source and use of funds
2. Historical information (if available)
3. Explanation of how financials were prepared (Note: the executive summary is typically followed by a Table of Contents)

II. Company description

(This is just an overview since much will be explained in detail elsewhere.)

A. Nature of the business
1. What needs exist
2. How the company will satisfy these needs

B. The company's strengths
1. Ability to better serve market needs
2. Service efficiencies
3. Personnel
4. Geographic/demographic strengths

III. Market analysis

(This section should demonstrate your knowledge of the industry and your particular market.)

A. Industry description and outlook
1. Describe the photo industry
2. Define the size of the industry
   a. Historically
   b. Presently
   c. In the future (five and ten years)
3. Industry characteristics and trends
   a. Historical, present, future

B. Target markets
1. Narrow market to a manageable size
   a. Define characteristics of the market
   b. What are the markets needs, and how are those needs being met now?
   c. Define purchasers and decision makers
   d. Define seasonal and cyclical trends
2. Primary market size
   a. Number of potential customers
   b. Yearly spending for services your company will offer
   c. Growth potential for defined market
3. Current market penetration
   a. Existing similar businesses vs. potential client base
4. Methods for identifying specific members of target market
   a. Directories

      b. Business publications

      c. Business networking

    5. Methods to be used to reach identified members of target market

      a. Source books

      b. Direct mail

      c. Portfolio presentations

      d. Past contacts

    6. Important trends and anticipated changes within your primary target market

    7. Potential secondary markets

      a. Define potential

      b. Explore future needs

  C. Marketing test results

    1. Number of potential customers contacted

    2. Information supplied to potential customers

    3. Potential customer reactions

  D. Competition

    1. Identify by product/service and market segment

      a. Existing competition

      b. Potential competition (how long will you have an edge?)

      c. Direct vs. indirect competition

    2. Competitive advantage

      a. Customer needs

      b. Track record and reputation

      c. Market share

      d. Revenue resources

      e. Support staff

      f. Facilities

    3. Weaknesses (disadvantages)

      a. Customer needs

      b. Track record and reputation

      c. Market share

      d. Revenue resources

      e. Support staff

      f. Facilities

    4. How important is your target market to your competition?

    5. What could prohibit your competition

      a. Finances and cost of start-up

      b. Time

      c. Facilities and support staff

      d. Customer loyalty

IV. Products and services

  (Do not try to make this section an operations manual for the business. Excess detail will have a negative impact on readers. Detail is appropriate for your copy.)

A. Detailed service description (users' standpoint)
  1. Specific benefits of your service
  2. Your ability to meet needs
  3. What advantages do you present over competition
B. Copyrights and trade secrets
  1. Existing copyrights with marketability
  2. Anticipated copyrights
  3. Aspects of your service that could be considered trade secrets
  4. Existing agreements with employees/clients
C. Research and development and continued education
  1. Activities in process
  2. Future activities
  3. Anticipated result of R&D
    a. New products and services
    b. Improvements on current products and services
    c. Complimentary products and services
  4. R&D of others in the industry
    a. Technological advances
    b. Industry trends

V. Marketing and sales activities
  (*Here you will need to include both general and specific information The objective will be to prove that your marketing efforts will bring sales that are capable of supporting your projections in the financial section that will follow.*)
  A. Marketing Strategy (overall)
    1. Market penetration objectives
      a. Large market share vs. competitors
      b. Elevated profitability
    2. Growth plans and strategy
      a. Increased sales over time
          i. Reputation
         ii. Increased client base
        iii. Additional services to meet needs
    3. Increased distribution potential
    a. Additional sales staff (rep)
    b. Additional markets
    4. Marketing communication
      a. Promotional activities
          i. Mailers
         ii. Sourcebook pages
        iii. Other
      b. Public relations
      c. Personal selling
          i. Portfolio presentations

        ii. Reputation and word-of-mouth

B. Sales strategy

  1. Sales force

    a. Internal

    b. Independent sales staff

    c. Size of sales force

    d. Compensation

  2. Seeking new leads

    a. Identifying prospects

    b. Qualifying prospects

    c. Prioritizing prospects

  3. Sales activities

    a. Number of sales calls per period

    b. Average number of sales per call

    c. Dollar amounts of average sale

VI. Operations

(Here again, too much detail is fine for internal copies of the plan, but try to keep details to a minimum for external copies. Only you need know who's supposed to lick stamps!)

A. Management procedures

B. Production procedures

C. Production capacities

D. Competitive advantages

  1. Facilities and equipment

  2. Staff experience

  3. Availability of outside resources

E. Suppliers

VII. Management and ownership

(The skills and talents of owners and managers are key elements in the equation. If the plan is being used to raise funding, remember that, to investors, people are as, if not more, important than ideas.)

A. Legal structure

  1. Sole proprietorship

  2. Partnership

  3. Corporation

B. Owners, partners, directors

  1. Names

  2. Positions

  3. Involvement

  4. Expertise

C. Key people in the business equation

  1. Name and position

    2. Responsibility and authority

    3. Previous experience and education

    4. Unique skills and talents

  D. Planned additions to management team

    1. Advisors and paid professionals

    2. Additional key staff

VIII. Organization

  (The objective is to define who will do what and where responsibilities will be placed.)

  A. Descriptions of positions

    1. Primary duties

    2. Authority

    3. Compensation

  B. Anticipated human resource requirements

IX. Funds required and the use of these funds

  A. Current funding requirement

    1. Amount

    2. Timing

  B. Funding requirements—the next five years

    1. Amounts

    2. Timing

  C. Use of funds available

    1. Capital expenditures

    2. Working capital

      a. The rule of thumb is six-months' working capital

  D. Impact of new capital on company's financial position (if seeking funding)

  E. Long-range financial strategies

X. Financial data

  (This section contains financial representation of the information presented in all the other sections. Various information can be included, if appropriate.)

  A. Historical information (previous three years)

    1. Income statement

    2. Balance sheet

    3. Statement of changes in financial position

    4. CPA involvement in the above

      a. Audit

      b. Review

      c. Compilation

  B. Future financial projections (five years)

    1. Next year (by month or quarter)

      a. Income statement

      b. Balance sheet

     c. Cash flow statement

     d. Capital expenditure budget

  2. Final four years (by quarter or year)

     a. Income statement

     b. Balance sheet

     c. Cash flow statement

     d. Capital expenditure budget

  3. Type of prospective financial data

     a. Forecast (owner's best estimate)

     b. Projection ("what if" scenarios)

  4. CPA involvement

     a. Audit

     b. Review

     c. Compilation

  5. Analysis/explanations of financial data

XI. Exhibits and Appendices

(Any additional detailed or confidential information that will add credibility to the plan. You may want to keep these separate and include them on an "as needed" basis.)

  A. Résumés of key people

  B. Professional references

  C. Samples of work (photographs)

  D. Market studies for the proposed area

  E. Important published information

  F. Significant contracts

    1. Leases

    2. Partnership and ownership agreements

    3. Insurance contracts

    4. Miscellaneous

A comprehensive business plan is a huge undertaking, but so is owning and managing a photography business. The preceding outline is a guide to be adapted to your situation. Before you start writing anything, enlist the help of an accountant experienced in creating business plans. He or she can guide you and help customize this outline to suit your needs. There may also be help available through the business school at a local college or university. Explore that possibility. Also, many larger, nationwide accounting firms have "new business services" departments. One resource is the Ernst & Young Entrepreneurial Services Group. Ernst & Young is one of the largest accounting firms in the country with over 100 offices nationwide. Much of the information in this section came from its Entrepreneurial Services Group, which assists potential new business owners in planning their start-up.

With the proliferation of computers, many software packages have been written to aid in the formation of a business plan. One of these packages might help get you started. A software package should not replace a qualified accountant or attorney. Since the computer industry is ever changing, research software at a local computer outlet. There are publications which list software packages, and these lists are updated regularly. Your local computer store will probably have one of these books and can help you find the right package.

Don't discount the local library and bookstores. Although not as "high tech" as using a computer to write your business plan, there are many books on this subject (and probably much less expensive than software).

Creating your business plan will be a tremendous amount of work, but the result could prove invaluable. Use the plan—now and for the future.

Marketing Yourself

Unfortunately, most promotion is done on a sporadic basis (or worse, when sales are already down!) and without the supporting efforts that could make those advertising dollars spent more effectively. Who is your target market? How do you know anyone has seen your ad or direct mail?

Today, you don't have the luxury of being just a photographer. Today, you own a photography business. All successful businesses have a written marketing plan. So, today's the day to (finally) write your plan or update the one you have written.

Cost-effective and successful promotion of your photography requires a marketing plan for three basic areas. These are advertising, public relations, and personal selling. It is important to understand how closely they can work together and how poorly they work alone. Imagine an umbrella in three sections: advertising, public relations, and personal selling. This umbrella is your overall marketing strategy. One-third or even two-thirds of an umbrella will not work for you as well as the whole umbrella.

Advertising is a nonpersonal form of marketing because it is designed to reach large groups of people simultaneously without your personal time and attention. When you can't pinpoint your buyers, buying a display ad in a creative sourcebook makes sense.

The best reason to advertise is that it is more efficient to reach all your potential clients at once than to call them one at a time. If you have a unique style to tell the world about, it's more efficient to expose thousands of people to the style so they can contact you when they have a project for that style. It's difficult (if not impossible) to call art directors and ask, "What are your needs for stylistic images?" Your display ad allows thousands of clients to see the work and identify themselves as potential clients.

The reason a photography client is looking at photographers' ads is because he or she is looking for something he or she doesn't already have. Your design objective for the ad is to give clients a strong and distinct impression and to ask people to respond to the ad. Be sure to build in the umbrella factor. For example, if people respond to your ad, add them to your mailing list. Make your advertising work with your direct mail and selling, not independent of them!

Direct mail is another form of advertising popular with photographers and buyers. If you can clearly identify your client base—perhaps your style is more unusual—then direct mail is a better investment. Please don't be dissuaded from direct mail because some clients tell you they throw mailers away. If 90 percent of your clients toss out your piece, you should be ecstatic! That means 10 percent have responded, about three times higher than the average response. But direct mail is becoming more and more sophisticated. Strong design and powerful copy are necessary, not optional.

Four important factors will determine the success of your direct mail.

1. The mailing list must be current with the name of the client or buyer for the firm you wish to work with. The firm is not the client—the true client is the art director, marketing director, or person who chooses the photographer. Someone has to keep this list up-to-date. This could be the time to hire a marketing assistant.

2. The mailing list must be composed of people who buy your kind of photography. If you can't clearly identify potential clients by what they buy, such as food or fashion photography, then you'll find it difficult to be as successful with direct mail. Display ads might be a better buy and to tie your advertising into your direct mail, try to get a mailing list from the publications you advertise in.

3. A response mechanism (such as an 800 phone number or reply card) is essential. It's impossible to call everyone you mail to; so have people call you!

4. Regular mailings are important to build the exposure you need to reach the people you want to work with. One-shot mailings do not work as well as regular mailings planned around your other efforts such as ads and press releases. Don't forget about the visual impression you must make! A buyer will need to see your logo, company name, and any other visual message you want to communicate six to sixteen times before they recognize who you are and what you do. Plan your advertising and direct mail; work the plan!

Getting Work

"What is the best way to get work?" That is probably a question photographers ask themselves, and others, more often than any other. There is a complex, though simply stated, answer to that question—you get work by selling. You sell your talent, services, experience, and capability. It's not enough to be a good photographer. The people who get work are those who sell themselves to the client.

Essentially a photography business consists of these steps:
- Prospecting—finding the potential buyers
- Selling—converting each prospect to a client
- Photographing—performing the service
- Financing—being compensated for the service

As most successful photographers will confirm, it is the first two steps that take the most time and effort, and require the greatest efficiency. If you spend most of your time tending to the last two steps, it is like the tail wagging the dog. One thing is certain, without sales there is no business, and without prospects, there are no sales.

Prospecting is locating the individual, qualified buyer. Finding the names of agencies and firms is not prospecting, but it is the first step. After you have the names of the companies, you have to get the names of the individuals who hire photographers. If doesn't matter if you buy that list, find it in a book, or get it by calling all the listings in the Yellow Pages. The only important factor is that the list be current.

Having targeted your prospective clients you have to get their attention, then make appointments and sell to them.

These efforts are helped by promotion. Promotion, often confused with selling, is a complementary process. Most photographers create visual promotional pieces, then mail them to prospects, some buy advertising in marketing directories, some do both.

For the average photographer, a direct-mail promotion is probably the best way to maximize the promotional dollar. You get individual space, and can direct the promotion to a specific person known to you. (Advertising books are effective, but your competition is in the same book, and the publisher picks the people to whom it is sent.)

Numerous promotional pieces are produced each year. Art directors are inundated with them, so if yours is to work, you have to make it stand out. It has to be worth a second look, or it will be trashed. If you make it worth a third look, it might even end up on the art director's wall.

To sell someone, you have to speak with him or her, and in some markets (e.g., advertising agencies, audiovisual, film, and video firms, and some galleries), it is preferably done face-to-face. So you should have a strategy to get an appointment.

The best way to get an appointment is to ask. One way is to write, another is to call. A telephone call is frequently accepted, especially if you are known to the person you are calling. Hopefully, the promotional piece you sent will be remembered and your name along with it. Still, you can reinforce the promo piece by writing a simple letter and telling the person that you intend to call in a couple of days to set up an appointment.

The Art of Selling

Writing a letter in advance of calling does not necessarily get your call accepted, but it does get your name in front of the prospect, and each time you do that you are a bit closer to being remembered. Persistence pays off if you don't become a pest. Take a break between contacts. Sooner or later you will succeed. Then, if you present your case just right, you will get an appointment.

When you get an appointment, you will begin with the selling process. The art of selling can be broken down into two parts: presentation and closing. You have to do both to have a consistently effective sales program.

The presentation is when you get a chance to show your "wares" to the prospect. If you have done your homework, your portfolio will contain shots that are representative of the type the agency commissions. Keep the portfolio manageable. The prospect has limited time and wants to see the best you have, not everything you have. If you have tearsheets of published work, show them, but only if they are good. Poor samples hurt you, even if they are a result of poor use of good photographs. You'll probably get ten to fifteen minutes, so limit the quantity to something that can be looked at in half that time. Too large a stack will prompt the viewer to hurry through the images, which is likely to undervalue the work.

Don't talk about the specific photographs. They have to speak for themselves. Tell clients about yourself, your background, the type of assignments you have worked on, or your clients. Make them like you. It is easier to buy from someone you like. Ask questions about them: people like you when you take an interest in them. Most of all, ask them to try you on some small job so you can have a chance to prove yourself.

During the closing portion of your sales presentation, always ask for work. That is what you are there for, and that is what you should ask for. Many photographers don't do this. They rationalize the failure to specifically ask for work with an excuse that the obvious reason for the visit was to get work. In selling, the one thing that should never go unsaid is that you want the person in front of you—the prospect—to contract for your services. If you want work, ask for it.

Finally, when someone has taken the time to see you and your work, he or she deserves a thank you. Not just a "thanks" when you're leaving the door, but a letter expressing it in a sincere and warm way, which is also a way of reinforcing the recognition of your name in his or her mind. Remember, every time your name comes before that person in a meaningful way, he or she is a little closer to remembering it.

You have to develop strategies for following up with art directors and buyers that will not create resentment on their part. They have busy schedules coupled with tight deadlines. Wasting their time is surely going to get a negative reaction. The best way to avoid being perceived as a nuisance is to ask yourself if there is a good reason to make contact. Do you have something new to show? If so, you have reason to call. Generating new samples through your own test shooting is a good way to produce a constant flow of images that an art director has not yet seen. But the photos have to show something new, not just in subject, but in technique or treatment. If what you show does not introduce some new element, you run the risk of being perceived as boring. Developing a variety of material for your portfolio is important. It allows you to keep coming back with something new. It keeps them interested, and if it is original or creative enough, it might even convince them that you are one of those bright new talents.

None of this comes easily. There are a lot of would-be photographers out there. What separates the "would be's" from the "will be's" is the commitment to do not only what is required to survive, but also what is required to excel. You have to shoot for excellence if you are to stand out and be noticed. Therein lies the key: excellent marketing, sales, photography, and business practices will make potential clients want to work with you.

The Joys of Telemarketing

Telemarketing scripts are vital to the success of your phone calls to arrange portfolio appointments. You may have the greatest advertising and direct-mail campaign, but you still have to talk to clients.

These calls can't be impromptu. Why? Because today's market requires you to make better use of your time and get more information about what clients want so you have the best chance to get jobs. If you are happy with the amount of business and work you are getting, stop reading here. If it is not broken, don't fix it. This is for photographers who want to get more out of precious time on the phone. Telemarketing scripts are not "canned" presentations. They are a technique to improve the effectiveness of your personal and telephone presentations. The technique is simply to write the anticipated conversation as you would like it to evolve. Be sure to plan for all contingencies. No matter what a client's response, you must have prepared your reply. Not only will this technique help you get more out of every call, but you will approach the entire chore with more motivation and inspiration. You may even like it, but this is not required for effective telemarketing. All that is necessary is that you pick up the phone and do it.

Steps for Script Writing

1. First, find out what the client does, then make the phone call. Talk food photography to food clients, corporate photography to corporate clients.
2. Open with a brief and specific introduction of your services. First get people's attention, then tell them what you want.
3. Come up with something interesting. After all, you are most likely trying to replace another photographer. Why should they switch?
4. Anticipate objections and questions about your services and have very concise answers available. Never hang up the phone without achieving some specific objective. Get an appointment or a piece of information. Successfully accomplishing your objective keeps you motivated to continue telemarketing.
5. Always use sentences beginning with "How, who, what, when, where, and why" to facilitate the information gathering, reduce the time you spend on the phone, and reduce the dead-ends that come with a "no"!

Don't expect these new techniques to feel comfortable initially. Anything not practiced usually is quite uncomfortable. You will feel like you are "pushing" yourself. What you are actually doing is "pulling" out the information needed to get the work. Besides, if being comfortable was important, you wouldn't have become a photographer. Now, you need to be a business owner. Let's look at some typical scripts of situations most common to photographers.

Getting an Appointment

"Hello, I am a food photographer and my name is _____. I am interested in the XYZ restaurants account and would like to show my portfolio to you this week. When would be a good time to come by?"

The key word here is "when." It gives you more options to continue a conversation than if you had asked, "May I come and show my portfolio?" The easy answer to that question is "no" and doesn't give the client time to seriously consider your request (and his or her needs).

Showing the Portfolio

Ask these open-ended questions to get information, confirm the information, and verify agreements you have reached such as:

- How often do you use a new photographer?
- What other photography needs do you have?
- When will you be looking at bids on that job?
- Who else in the office buys this kind of photography?

Follow-up

- When would be a good time to check back on that job?
- How do you feel about a follow-up call in three weeks?
- What will you look for in the bids on that job?
- Who will have final approval on the photographer?

Scripts do not have to be elaborate, but they do have to be written with all possible responses (yours and the photo buyer's) indicated. It is simply a matter of thinking through what you want to communicate and what you want to learn from the other person. You will find your communications and presentations not only easier, but more effective. If you have ever completed any phone call and thought afterward, "Why didn't I think of that?" or "Why didn't I mention that?" then scripting your responses is the answer.

Publicity to Help Sell Photography

Public relations is an excellent but underappreciated form of promotion for photographers. In a tight economy, being known and having credibility can give you an important edge. First, let's dispel a myth. You don't get publicity just because you're a good photographer. You get it because you ASK to be considered for it!

For example, an image in *Communications Arts* magazine may prompt someone on your mailing list to finally call you. Or your name in the local paper may get someone (even who is in a meeting) to come to the phone when you call. Publicity can be the final key to a successful marketing plan.

The most common tool of public relations is the press release. The press release is a standardized form of communicating some newsworthy item to the editors of publications. Be sure to check (today!) that your media list is up-to-date with the editor's names of your client's publications (trade publications), local newspaper and your local ASMP chapter newsletter (if you are an ASMP member). Client publications seem an obvious choice. In addition, everyone reads the local paper and because the goal of public relations is repeated exposure of your name and firm, some of this more general exposure could influence a buyer.

If you are an ASMP member and are not sending your press releases to your chapter newsletter—why not? That one additional mailing could lead to an important job referral. Everyone should know what you do as a photographer so they can tell his or her friends. If you're not sending in regular releases, please don't complain about the lack of chapter benefits. ASMP works when YOU do.

Here are some examples of newsworthy items that could generate a press release to any media, client, community, or peer:

1. You relocate or open your studio.
2. You add personnel to your staff.
3. You celebrate the anniversary of your firm.
4. You finish a big, important job or work with a name client.
5. You win an award for your photography.
6. You expand with additional services for clients.
7. You participate in a community service project.
8. You are elected to a chapter board of directors.

Finally, you can publicize, build name recognition, and help clients get to know you by joining their professional associations. Membership in these client or industry groups offer the following benefits to photographers:

1. Personal nonselling contact at meeting with potential clients.
2. Advertising (very expensive) in their newsletter.
3. Free listings in their membership directory.
4. Publication of press releases in their newsletter.
5. Opportunities to participate in community service projects.

Even though this networking can take the form of personal contacts, it is important to remember you are NOT SELLING ANYTHING. You are simply increasing the number of contacts with your target market, their awareness of your services, and your chances of getting work. Some other areas to look at for additional publicity are entering award competitions, writing articles, and giving seminars. Most of these will generate additional press releases as well as provide their own public relations benefits.

Finding the Names of Potential Clients

Tracking down names of potential clients is easy when you know where to look.

Target marketing involves narrowing down to a manageable size the vast world of potential clients and then pinpointing (by name) the actual "targets" in that market. Don't let a fear of being locked into one type of design or illustration keep you from targeting a market. When you begin to feel locked in, you can always explore another market. By the same token, it doesn't matter how many different kinds of work you do; prospective clients perceive only what you can do for them. Successful target marketing is simply matching one of your many skills and portfolios to a client's needs.

The first step in target marketing is to define a specific market. You can do this by deciding who you want to work for or what you want to do. If you are an illustrator, for example, a logical choice for whom to work might be an advertising agency because it buys for many different kinds of clients. Every ad agency has a roster of clients for which it buys illustration services, and its objective is to find the right artist for the job.

That will be someone who has experience with the type of product and/or service the client has given the agency to promote. For example, an agency with food clients will be looking for an illustrator with food illustration experience.

Another way to define a market is to categorize your work by subject or type of work you do. The simplest way to categorize your illustration work is to break it down into two categories: product or people illustration. Product illustration has many areas (markets) to explore, such as computers, electronics, food, fashion—to name a few. People illustration is needed by service industries such as banking, real estate, insurance, medical, educational, and financial institutions.

Once you identify some markets that interest you, you will need to pinpoint the names of firms, ad agencies, or corporations in those markets. Some places to find names include:

1. The local library. The library has many resources, including the librarian. You can ask where to find the names of, say, insurance firms in your area. No matter what you are seeking as a client leads list, the library should have it and someone to help you find it.

2. Trade and market directories. They list names, addresses, and phone numbers of firms. Some are cross-referenced by type of product or service offered or by a geographic reference. For example, if you want the names of advertisers, *The Standard Directory of Advertisers* and *The Standard Directory of Advertising Agencies* are comprehensive sources for agencies located across the country. *The Adweek Directory of Advertising Agencies* covers five regions of the U.S. in five volumes, listing the top 50 ad agencies in the nation and 200 to 550 agencies billing $1 million per year, depending on the region. The membership roster of the American Marketing Association also includes addresses of ad firms. Be sure to check the new on-line directories, keyworded by industry.

   Other fields have their own directories. The graphic and industrial design edition of *The Design Firm Directory* contains a state-by-state listing of over 1,500 design firms and their major clients. General market directories like *Artist's Market* and *Photographer's Market* are updated annually and list markets alphabetically. Check your library reference section for these and other trade directories.

3. The daily newspaper. Look in the business section for new products, services, and mergers, and you will find clients who need design and illustration for new promotional material. Don't overlook weekly business newspapers. They often profile new businesses in the community as well as general lists of top firms in different industries.

4. Trade shows. A great place to gather leads as well as to view a firm's current brochures and other literature that use design and illustration.

5. Trade or business publications. A magazine article on the top publicly held firms, for instance, is an excellent source for annual report clients. Some magazines concentrate on a particular market—such as medicine—and offer information on prospective clients as well as trade shows, mergers, etc.

With a little digging you can come up with sources of leads that aren't published, but well worth your time pursuing. Chambers of commerce, local business organizations, and local chapters of trade associations all may be able to supply you with client information.

People prefer to work with people they know, and one of the best ways to find and meet potential clients is to participate in an organization. Most groups have special "associate" memberships available, and the cost is minimal compared to the potential gains. Often, the membership directory you receive upon joining may be helpful for learning names. If you can go to regular meetings, you can meet and get to know people who could become potential clients or contacts. Contacts such as other designers or illustrators may refer clients they can't accommodate when they have too much work, when they don't have your particular expertise, or when they simply don't do the kind of work needed. One of the best ways to sell your work is to establish relationships with potential clients, and joining an organization is a good way to begin building those relationships. You should not "sell" at this stage, however, but you can gather leads. Furthermore, since you aren't selling, it is a fairly relaxed and nonthreatening situation for you to be in.

After you have the name of a firm, you will need to identify the person who would be your actual client. The important thing to remember is that the company is not your client, per se, an individual buyer is. In any given company, there may be many clients for your services, and you would be wise to contact each one. Never assume because you are working with one client in a company that potential clients in other departments or divisions will know who you are and what you can do for them.

With most companies you can tell the buyer by his or her job title. In ad agencies, it is the creative director, art director, or art buyer. In corporations, it is the marketing manager, sales manager, product manager, or corporate communications manager. Don't overlook firms with their own in-house advertising departments.

A simple phone call can identify the name of your potential client. Once you have a name, you have a target, and then you can begin to sell.

Fifteen Tips for Success

Planning is the key to success in today's rapidly changing business environment. If you think you don't need a plan for your photography business, please read this! Success = Planning + Business Strategy + Photographic Talent! And if you are an established professional photographer, emerging professional, or delving into market expansion, the following are important and relevant tips to keep your business on the right track:

1. Structure. First and foremost, you are no longer someone with a camera. You must consider yourself a small business proprietor. With the current downsizing and restructuring of resources taking place in corporate America, operating as a small business is mandatory to be competitive and guarantee survival.

2. Associate. You must associate with people who do what you do. Strength in numbers is an old saying, but highly applicable in this context. Whether you join a trade association, attend meetings, or join an on-line organization, it is imperative that you associate with others in your specialty. Until we, the photographic

industry, stop looking at each other as the enemy, and start looking at each other as colleagues, true success will be far away. Joining is not enough—you must participate. You can only get out of any association what you put into it.

3. Ask. Don't be afraid to ask for help. Most newspapers have a business section and many have small business sections. Your local chamber of commerce may also have resources that you can use whether you are a member or not. Keep an eye out for companies that produce small business workshops and seminars, and call the local number for the Small Business Administration for numbers of other resources. Build your own resource network to assist you.

4. Time management. One of the drawbacks of not having a structured, traditional job, is the loss of the structure itself. Do not let self-employment translate into taking it easy. Being self-employed means working long hours. Some type of time and day planner is critical. Whether it is a notebook calendar system like the Day Runner, or a computer or electronic organizer system, you must have a way of planning and tracking your time. If you are not sure how to set up your time management system, check with some of your various resources or your office supply representative. Network with your peers, see what works for people you respect.

5. Personal time. This is definitely easier said than done. However, burn-out can cause your photography to suffer as well as the image that you project. No matter how rough things are, or how stressed or tired you may be, you have to project yourself as energetic and ready to take on the world. Allow yourself some time to relax, exercise, get fresh air, and, in general, just wind down a little and recharge. Schedule this time as you would an appointment so you are sure to do it!

6. Learn the laws. Learn what it takes to be in business in your community. Do you need a business license? Business phone line? City business license? Your resource network will be able to help answer these questions. Give everyone that you come in contact with your business card!

7. Use professionals. Evaluate your strong and weak points. If you are not good at bookkeeping and accounting, hire someone. Capitalize on your personal strengths. If you can't write a press release to save yourself, hire someone, or find a small agency that you could trade-out photography against publicity work. Trade-outs in this area work well, but make sure you are consistent with the value of your photography. Don't ever give it away!

8. Plan your business strategies. When planning a vacation you would never just jump in the car and drive off. You would at least get a map, decide where you want to go, and then pick your route. In business, many photographers print business cards, and the next thing you know, they're in business. It's crucial to sit down and figure out a plan. The plan is very simple in that it contains goals, and the strategy to accomplish those goals. Within the business plan itself, there should be a marketing plan. The business plan also contains financial information, deadlines, and overall strategies as to working the business. The business plan should give an outsider a concise and accurate look as to what you want to do, how you are going to do it, what your marketing strategies are, who you

want to sell to, and your overall goals for success. There are numerous places to find assistance with the business plan, including books as well as seminars, computer programs, workshops and professional marketing consultants.

9. Marketing—the plan. For most photographers, this is the critical document. The marketing plan is what separates the "guys with cameras" from the successful business owners. If you are a photographer who shoots location and products in the studio, those are two different goals, and in most cases would have two completely different strategies. The marketing plan should have each goal listed separately. Following the goals should be the specific strategies, what your business's message will be, the marketing tools that you will use to convey that message to your target market, a conclusion, and then a schedule of implementation. The main key to a successful marketing plan is not to just write it and put it on a shelf. It is a document that needs to be reviewed regularly, updated regularly, and revised as necessary.

10. Know your market. To whom do you want to sell your photographic services? Are you going to market yourself nationally, regionally, locally? By carefully charting out your target market(s), you will insure that your marketing dollars are not wasted. For instance, if you want to photograph small products in your studio, do not waste money on direct mail by sending your cards to art directors from ad agencies that specialize in marketing children's clothing.

11. Budget marketing time and money. The best plans in the world are worthless if an adequate budget is not allocated, as well as the necessary time to implement the strategies outlined in the marketing plan. A realistic budget should be set after a complete review of all aspects of the marketing plan. Once a budget is set, it should be carefully implemented to initiate the entire campaign. You will need to create and support an advertising or marketing campaign. Time needs to be allocated as well. Make sure that you stay on your marketing schedule by allocating a few hours per week to ensure that work keeps coming in.

12. Promote yourself. Once you've got your business established, your business plan written, your marketing plan outlined, your schedule set, and your money allocated, it's time to promote yourself. Don't use the shotgun approach. As anyone who has purchased advertising will attest, you can't just buy an ad and wait for the phone to ring. Does your answering machine or voice mail say what you do? Do your business cards? Do people who know you understand exactly what kind of photography you do? Be gospel about it, make those around you excited about what you do!

13. Be image consistent. All your printed materials should be consistent in looks and in the message. Make sure that the typefaces and graphics convey the proper image. You want your name and promotional message to be recognized immediately when your materials hit a prospective client's desk. Hire a designer, get a consultation from an image specialist. All of these things will help associate your name to what you do.

14. Follow through. Make sure that you follow through on commitments. If you tell a prospective client that you will be at their office at 2:00 P.M., be there a few

minutes early! If you receive a job lead from someone, send them a thank-you note, whether you get the job or not.

15. Appreciate and accept the value of your services. Finally, do not underestimate what you provide to the client. If you see yourself as "just a photographer," they will as well. However, what will they see if you present yourself as the president of a company which provides imaging and consulting?

It doesn't take as much work as this may sound. Spend a few hours every Monday working on marketing. Check your white board for the month's marketing deadline, and schedule time to complete the needed tasks. If you work the marketing as a campaign, it all falls into place. Then, you are no longer cold-calling prospective clients, just reintroducing yourself. Now, get out there and promote!

Avoiding Potential Pitfalls

There's enough to worry about in trying to make a living from professional photography without having your life complicated by legal or tax problems. Accordingly, if you have any doubt about any accounting or tax matter, seek professional advice. You are urged to read the information about Professional Services in chapter 11. We at ASMP deal with a variety of problems encountered by photographers. Many of these could have been avoided by simply getting everything in writing. But two major areas of concern, and ones which are very confusing, are: sales tax and the independent contractor or employee dilemma. Photographers must be aware of these matters. Another potential problem is overextending credit and trying to pay off too much debt. The following items might help you avoid these problem areas.

Don't Carry Too Much Debt

Many businesses make the mistake of trying to carry too much debt reasoning that any debt is simply an added operating cost. Overlooked is the fact that repaying debt eats into your profit. The more money you owe, the more you will have to earn, often just to maintain your financial status quo.

As an example, a studio owner might add another $1,500 a month to overhead by borrowing to buy new expensive equipment and rationalize the added burden by claiming another day's billing will take care of it. Actually, the studio will have to generate $1,500 extra profit each month, something very different from simply billing an extra $1,500, to meet that extra debt. If your net profit is 33 percent, you will need to bill an additional $4,500 to pay a $1,500 loan payment.

An experienced studio owner who has seen how too much debt can cripple a business offers this advice:

- Be aware that operating expenses and repaying debt are not the same thing.
- Average your business's revenues over at least three or four months, preferably a year, to determine how much debt you can safely carry. Don't base the carrying capability of business debt on one good month of revenues.
- If you find you're overextended, rather than trying to get bigger to pay down the

debt, go the other way and cut down on expenses. Invariably there will be costs that can be cut.

- Before incurring more debt, carefully weigh up your financial situation to determine if your business will really benefit as a result. How long will it take to recover the costs of the equipment you are financing? Ask yourself: Is this extra debt really worth it?
- Above all, keep reminding yourself that extra debt comes out of your profit.

Sales Tax

If there is a subject both complex and complicated, it's the state-run sales taxes. There are differences from state to state on how much and under what circumstances sales tax should be charged. Overall, state sales tax laws are very confusing, but it is an area which potentially holds a large liability for the photographer. Many photographers can tell horror stories of being confronted with large tax bills for not collecting sales tax—in their own state or in others they've done business in. Usually it was a misunderstanding of the state's tax codes, not an attempt to avoid paying taxes, which led to their predicament.

Here are some basic steps you can take:

- Ask an accountant with which authority you should register your business, and get your sales tax registration number.
- Obtain that authority's guidelines on sales tax. Clarify any matter you're unsure about.
- Generally, charge sales tax on the full amount of an invoice.
- If resale exemptions apply, make sure you get a copy of the client's resale certificate.
- If you are doing business in other states, or have a rep in another state, get professional advice on your sales tax liability.
- If you have any doubts about sales tax matters, seek professional advice immediately. That way you will be taking steps to avoid any surprise and probably costly, tax bills.

Is Your Assistant an Independent Contractor or an Employee?

This is a dilemma that continues to confront small businesses. Historically, commercial photographers have regarded freelance assistants as independent contractors. At the end of the year, if the assistant has earned more than a certain amount (at writing, $600) the photographer sends the assistant a 1099 Form. From that point, the assistant takes care of paying taxes.

But the issue is clouded, and photographers are advised to treat this matter carefully. There have been attempts to have the relevant laws changed, and this could happen. After all, it is not just photographers who are affected.

The laws concerning independent contractor or employee vary from state to state, but the following twenty common-law factors might help photographers determine their assistants' status. If any one of these suggests an employer/employee relationship, you probably should treat the situation as such. It is also suggested that you refer to the Independent Contractors' Agreement information and form in chapter 6, "Formalizing Agreements."

1. Instructions. Has the employer retained the right to require the worker to comply with instructions regarding when, where, and how the work is to be performed?
2. Training. Has the right to provide training with regard to methods of performing work been retained by the employer?
3. Integration. After determining the scope and function of the employer's business, see if the services of the worker are merged into it.
4. Services rendered personally. Does the employer require the worker to perform the work personally; or does the worker have the right to hire a substitute without consulting the employer?
5. Hiring, supervising, and paying assistants. Hiring, supervising, and paying wages of assistants usually shows control over all individuals on a job.
6. Continuing relationship. Usually indicates an employer/employee relationship, even though the arrangement contemplates that the services are part-time, to be performed at frequently recurring but irregular intervals, e.g., employee being on call, or whenever work is available.
7. Set hours of work. When employer establishes set hours of work, this indicates control—prevents worker from being "master of his own time," which is a right of an independent contractor.
8. Full-time required. Restricts worker from doing other work. On the other hand, independent contractors are free to work when and for whom they choose. However, "full-time" does not necessarily mean an eight-hour day, five days a week—may vary with intent of the parties and nature of work.
9. Doing work on employer premises. Implies control by employer; is physically within employer's direction and supervision. However, there is control when an employer has the right to direct a person to travel a designated route, or work at specified places at certain times.
10. Order or sequence set. Employer has control if he or she retains the right to set patterns of work for employees.
11. Oral or written reports. Indicates control—worker is compelled to account for actions.
12. Method of payment. Payment by the hour, week, or month usually indicates an employer/employee relationship—while payment by the job or on a straight commission might mean the worker may be an independent contractor.
13. Payment of business or travel expenses. If employer pays worker's expenses, the worker is usually an employee; employer retains right to control worker's activities in order to control expenses.
14. Furnishing tools and materials. If employer furnishes tools and materials, this indicates an employer/employee relationship. Employer can control the tools the worker uses and, to some extent, in what order. There are numerous exceptions, however, e.g., carpenters, auto mechanics, and barbers who often furnish their own tools.

15. Significant investment. Investment by the worker in facilities used to perform work for another may tend to establish worker as an independent contractor. Lack of investment, however, may indicate dependence of worker on employer, and that an employer/employee relationship exists.

16. Working for more than one firm. Generally is evidence of an independent contractor status. However, it is possible for a person to work for a number of firms and be an employee of one or all of them.

17. Making services available to general public. Individuals who make services available to general public are usually independent contractors. Some tests are: (a) do they have an office or place of business; (b) do they hire; (c) are they listed in business section and/or Yellow Pages; (d) do they advertise in newspapers, trade journals, radio, etc.; and (e) do they run their own business, or act in managerial capacity for another firm?

18. Right to discharge. Strongly indicates employer/employee relationship. Control is implicit in the power to discharge. An independent contractor normally cannot be fired except for failure to produce results, per his or her contract.

19. Right (of worker) to terminate. An employee generally has right to resign at any time without incurring any liability; an independent contractor agrees to complete a specific job, and is responsible for its satisfactory completion or incurs legal liability for failure to complete.

20. Realization of profit or loss. Persons who can realize a profit or loss as a result of their services are generally independent contractors; and persons who cannot are generally employees.

Maria Piscopo is an art/photo representative and consultant based in Southern California. She is the author of the *Photographer's Guide to Marketing & Self-Promotion,* 2nd Edition, published by Allworth Press. For information on her videos, seminars, and upcoming conference dates, visit her Web site, http://e-folio.com/piscopo.

Chapter 10

Book Publishing

Bill Hurter and Amy Stone

A t some time most photographers contemplate publishing a book and many have, successfully. It can be both prestigious and lucrative. While new electronic technology has opened up other potential markets, the traditional business principles of book publishing hold true. There are several approaches to get started.

Proposing the Idea

1. The photographer can originate an idea that he or she proposes to illustrate and/ or write.
2. A photographer and writer can propose a book project jointly, working as a team. How the income and expenses are divided is a matter of individual negotiation between the parties.
3. A writer or publisher can request a photographer to illustrate all or part of a book. In these cases, the photographer should receive a separate contract, advance, and royalties from those of the author.
4. A photographer can be assigned to shoot the pictures for a book. A flat fee is the most usual mode of payment, although royalties (which are potentially more lucrative) can often be negotiated.
5. A photographer can license his or her own photographs directly to the author or publisher, or through a stock agency that represents his or her photography.

Elements of the Book Proposal

Editors are looking for material that is fresh, creative, and professional. Editors are also looking for individual reliability, i.e., someone who won't drive them crazy. The quickest way to get rejected is to submit inappropriate material. Know the publishing house and the type of books they normally publish, and submit material accordingly.

In order to have a book published, the photographer must come up with a salable idea, which requires a knowledge of both the subject and the market. Always query the publisher first. Write one or more publishers a detailed description of the kind of book you want to do, the number of pictures you feel it would require, and any other details which would help them decide if they want to see an outline which you should offer. Include a title and a list of your previous publishing experience.

Ethically, you may send simultaneous queries to various publishers. You are merely asking if they are interested in your project, you are not promising them anything. It is advisable to say something like, "I am currently querying five publishers to expedite my efforts." If your idea is salable, you'll get a request to see sample photographs and an outline. Note: If a publisher requests a submission that includes photographs, you should make clear in your cover letter that: (i) the images are provided solely for the purpose of the publisher's consideration of the photographer's book proposal; (ii) ownership of the images, and of the copyright in them, remains with the photographer; and (iii) the publisher is obliged to return the images within a certain period of time. If original transparencies are submitted, the photographer should assign a reasonable value to them in the event they are damaged or lost. It is preferable to send duplicates initially and originals if later required. Ideally, these requirements would be set forth in a short, simple agreement that you and the publisher would both sign. If that is not possible, then the photographer should either include a signature line on the cover letter for the publisher to acknowledge its agreement to the terms, or at least state specifically in the letter that failure to object to the terms constitutes acceptance of them. Bear in mind that if the publisher does not agree in writing to be bound by the terms of your submission, it may be difficult to enforce those terms against the publisher in the event of a dispute.

After an initial positive reaction from the publisher, the idea should be presented in the form of a proposal, which should consist of a cover letter, visuals, sample text, a table of contents (i.e., an outline), and a partial dummy, if possible and practical. The latter is possibly the most important element of the "serious" proposal, because it shows the publisher the visual and aesthetic concept of the book. A dummy is a handmade "skeleton" of your book, with sample (typeset) copy and photocopied photos laid out on sample pages. The biggest asset of a dummy is that it guarantees that you and your publisher are both talking about the same book.

There are differing points of view on the value of a dummy. David R. Godine, a major publisher of photo books in the Boston area, for instance, wholeheartedly believes in the dummy. He prefers that a photographer outline each image, size and cropping, to produce a "tight dummy, done to size, with every image laid out as the photographer would want it to appear." The more complete the dummy is, according to

Godine, the fewer communication problems will occur throughout the publishing process. Although he appreciates the ways other publishers put together a book, Godine prefers to call on the artistic instincts of great photographers. "I have found that the better the photographer, the more they like the challenge of putting together a series of sequenced spreads, which is what a book really is. They like it because it gives them that much more control, and if they are real artists, the book almost always comes out better as a result of their effort."

Although your dummy may be complete, a publisher may reserve the right to alter, edit, or otherwise redesign your material in almost any fashion desired, depending on the terms of the contract. The elements of the contract are discussed elsewhere, but you should think carefully about whether granting the publisher complete authority to alter or redesign your work is something you can live with later in the editing process. You may feel more comfortable carving out some limitations on the publisher's authority in this regard, or at least insisting that you be consulted before your material is altered or redesigned.

Lou Jacobs, Jr., a photographer who has vast experience in photo-book publishing, on the other hand, reasons that a dummy is unnecessary and impractical. He maintains that most publishers prefer to devise their own layouts. He says, "In the majority of cases I know, dummies were not followed, and the work could have been avoided." Further, he maintains that "No worthwhile publisher should fail to visualize a book if your pictures are excellent and the theme is salable."

Jacobs suggests making a partial dummy, like twelve pages, to show the publisher/ editor the kind of presentation you have in mind. At the same time, one could submit twenty to forty slides or prints as samples of your work on the specific theme, perhaps in some sort of order, with caption data. Keep in mind that some books, such as a large-format, coffee-table photo book, might require a dummy while others might not.

A salable idea must be one that is original and that does not compete with too many existing titles. Study the book market, and in particular, the niche you wish to fill; i.e., children's books, coffee-table photo books, how-to photography books, etc. Books in Print, available as a library reference, lists annually published books by subject, author, and title. Use it to decide if your proposal idea is unique.

A comprehensive listing of publishers and their subject categories can be found in Literary Market Place, a library reference, as well as *Writer's Market* and *Photographer's Market*. The latter will be most worthwhile to those photographers interested in selling existing photographs to publishers.

Elements of the Book Contract

The following section includes a series of headings with which you should be familiar. They are the essence of your book contract, but in layman's terms.

The value of an attorney or agent who specializes in publishing contracts cannot be overemphasized when evaluating the publisher's complex list of rights, terms, and conditions. It is better to know what you are agreeing to before you sign a contract than to be informed of it later. Since the income from a book may be small—a few thousand dollars—make an arrangement up front with an attorney for a modest fee for a few hours of advice. It is most unwise to sign any book contract without first consulting a knowledgeable expert to advise you specifically on what you are agreeing to, and what your rights and obligations are under the contract. The meaning of a few simple words ("shall" is very different from "may") often has a significant impact on your rights and obligations.

Publication Rights

There are many types of rights that can be negotiated as part of your book contract. One basic principle to remember is that by granting limited publication rights to the publisher, you are not conveying your copyright. Publication rights are simply one aspect of your copyright. Think of publication rights as a license to the publisher to utilize one part of your copyright—which you still own. Here are a few of the many types of publishing rights you may encounter:

- All rights. Publisher receives all rights to your materials. In effect, this is a transfer of your copyright, and unless specified otherwise you retain no rights at all in your material. Not only is this excessive and unnecessary in most cases, a broad grant of "all rights" will prevent you from using the images in the book for other purposes. This can be avoided by limiting the grant of rights by references to some benchmark, i.e., the right to publish and sell your material in books only (or in one book specifically), or for a certain period of time, or within a specified geographic area.
- Worldwide publication rights. These rights are similar to all rights because you grant the publisher unlimited use of your materials worldwide. If these rights are granted, they should be limited in some way, such as in certain media (e.g., books only), or for a limited duration.
- U.S. publication rights. A territorial right to market your materials within the boundaries of the United States.
- First North American publication rights. Another territorial right, but only the initial (i.e., first) right to market your materials.
- Foreign publication rights. Another territorial right; it too should be limited to books only or specified for a time period.
- Serial publication rights. This is the right to excerpt or otherwise serialize your work in magazines or other publications. This is often done as a promotional effort to publicize the book.
- Reprint publication rights. I.e., when a book is reprinted. The standard allocation of profits from reprint rights is 50-50, half for the publisher, half for the author.
- Paperback publication rights. Another form of reprint rights; i.e., a second publication of the book in paperback form.

You should understand what each term means in order to best determine which rights you want to grant the publisher. For instance, a publisher may wish to purchase worldwide publication rights to your material for a specified period of time. This condition not only takes your images out of circulation for the specified time period, but it may mean that the images could be packaged and sold to a foreign publisher without your receiving additional income.

Most times, the publisher demands exclusive publication rights and all subsidiary rights, such as reprint (second, third, and any subsequent editions) rights, serial rights, syndication, advertising, and publicity rights. These rights are usually deemed necessary by the publisher to effectively promote the sale of the book, and to guarantee its perpetuity. The definition of these rights can vary from contract to contract. As you negotiate your contract, bear in mind that virtually everything is negotiable. Also remember that different types of rights each have a unique monetary value to you and the publisher. For instance, syndication of all or part of your book might have great value to both parties because of the tremendous publicity syndication would generate for the book.

Be particularly wary of an all-rights provision. This, in effect, transfers all rights to your material and to other works derived from your material, to be used in any form deemed appropriate by the publisher. You may not wish, for example, to see your original portrait of the President of the United States, done as part of a book on fine portraiture, used on T-shirts or posters. Not only might that be aesthetically objectionable, but it might also be financially punitive.

Publishers now routinely include clauses covering electronic media rights. These rights might cover such uses as educational software or CD-ROM books, in which you follow along with the images and narration on a TV or computer. Alternatively, electronic media rights may include the right to reproduce or transmit in digital form some or all of the photographs in a book on a computer network. Rick Smolan, publisher of the first CD picture book, *Alice to Ocean* (an Apple CD and a Kodak Photo CD are packaged with every book), believes that CDs are the wave of the future in publishing. At this time, electronic rights, and particularly Photo CD licensing, don't add much financially to the value of the book contract; there are currently too few players and too many formats out there to make it lucrative. However, as the medium gains acceptance, you may see books published exclusively for the TV screen for viewing on an Apple Macintosh computer or in CD-ROM products or other digitally based computer media. These rights potentially have high future value which you must consider before signing. At the very least, insist upon some form of compensation (e.g., a royalty) for granting the publisher any sort of electronic media rights, rather than letting those potentially valuable rights go for "free."

In order to protect yourself from unauthorized use of your images that may come in the form of an unspecified right, you should insist on a clause in your contract guaranteeing that all unspecified rights that you have not specifically granted to the publisher in writing are reserved by you.

Delivery and Return of Materials

When the original images leave your hands and are sent to the publisher, you must be guaranteed that the images will remain safe and be treated carefully for the duration of their stay with the publisher. Always send original images by a traceable form of mail delivery, such as registered or certified mail, or by a reputable overnight delivery firm, such as Federal Express or Airborne. It's always a good idea to insure your images when mailing them.

Each image should have an individual file number by which you can list, track, caption, and otherwise retain order. If you do not use a numbered filing system for your images, devise one for your book projects. Black-and-white and color prints need separate numbers also.

Once the images are received, the publisher should be required to agree in writing to take responsibility for them. The publisher should insure the pictures against loss or damage while they are in the publisher's possession. This time frame includes all stages of production. Be certain that your images are protected by specifying such responsibility in your book contract. You should ask that original transparencies and negatives be insured for some mutually agreed upon value. Also, specify a value for reproduction-grade duplicates, if used in the book. All images should be insured for both loss and damage. Some of your original images may be worth much more than others. Determine if there are any provisions for such highly valuable originals. Again, be sure such items are clearly understood by both parties, and are included in your book contract.

The point at which your images are to be returned to you must be determined. A more-or-less standard time frame for the return of your materials is thirty days after publication. Make sure that the photographs will be returned in a safe and insured manner.

Copyright

Copyright is extremely important. The book should be copyrighted in the photographer's name, not in the publisher's. If the book is a joint effort between you and a writer, the book can easily be copyrighted in both names simply by denoting the text as copyrighted by the author, photos are copyrighted by you.

When using other people's pictures that you license or that are given to you to use, the contract should stipulate that such photographs will be listed as copyrighted in the name(s) of the photographer. If you are using the photographs of others, it is important to have a written understanding with the owner of the copyright in those images as to the scope and terms of the publication rights granted (i.e., for what publications, appropriate credit, royalties, return and liability for slides, etc.).

Approval

Many first-time authors and photographers do not make a provision for design approval and end up being extremely dissatisfied with the book in its final form. Can you negotiate any right of approval? Certainly. At a minimum, you can request and be given the periodic right of inspection, while the book is in the design and production phases. Don't be disappointed later: ask for the right of approval or inspection up front, and spell it out in the contract! But keep in mind that approval and inspection are different.

If you had submitted a dummy as part of your original book proposal, and it was accepted, at least in concept, then you have the grounds for periodic inspection and approval rights. Detailed discussions in advance of the design and production phases can eliminate many potential problems.

The other side of this coin is that many publishers expect the average photographer to "stick to f-stops," and while input on design may be useful to both sides, it may not be any more than conversation. Still, one can ask or insist depending upon your convictions on the matter. If you negotiate for the rights of approval and/or inspection, make sure that those rights are clearly spelled out in your book contract.

Warranties

Warranties are a type of disclaimer that both the photographer gives to the publisher and the publisher gives to the photographer. The photographer warrants that, to the best of his or her knowledge, he or she has the rights to publish the photographs as required by the contract, and that the photographer has the right to enter into a legal contract with the publisher. Remember that this warranty extends not only to your photographs but also to those of others that may be included in the book under your authorization. Further, the photographer/author warrants that the words to his or her manuscript are his or her own, and that there has been no plagiarism.

The publisher, in turn, must guarantee that the photographer will not be liable for any legal actions arising from information inserted into the book without the photographer's approval. Warranties should be spelled out clearly in your book contract.

Advances

An advance is money paid up front to the photographer/author to ensure the successful completion of the book. Advances are usually charged against royalties that the book will eventually earn.

Some publishers may agree to pay expenses separately from an advance (so that the expenses do not have to be earned via royalties, as does an advance); others may increase the size of the advance to make a project more feasible, but require all moneys to be earned by the author via royalties. If you anticipate high expenses in producing the photos for your book, it is advisable to ask for a nonreturnable allowance for expenses. Usually, however, publishers expect photographers to pay their own expenses as part of the cost of production.

Normally, the advance is paid in either two or three portions: on signing the contract, on delivery (and subsequent acceptance) of the content, and on publication of the book. It is preferable, however, to be paid upon signing and acceptance. "Acceptance" means when all photographs and/or writing has been corrected or revised in accordance with the editors' wishes. This may take four to six months from the date of the delivery of manuscript and photos. To be paid on publication is not advisable, as the actual publication date may be as much as a year after you have submitted the book and it has been revised and accepted.

The amounts of advances vary widely. They vary with the sales potential and type of book, the publisher, and your status as a published photographer/author. Advances can be meager, $2,000 to $4,000, or they may be extravagant, in the $20,000 to $40,000 range. Advances are usually negotiable. Remember, if you are being paid an advance against royalties, the bigger the advance, the longer it will be before you see your first royalty check. However, get the largest advance you can, because you may not see any more money if the book doesn't sell well, and the contract should provide that no portion of the advance must be returned even if royalties do not reach the level of the advance.

An advance can be thought of as an investment by the publisher. Without an advance, you are out all of the money required to produce the book. If the book is then rejected, you will be further frustrated. When the publisher advances you funds, the company is making an investment in and a commitment to the product, and as such is sharing some of the publishing risk.

Royalties

Royalties are a percentage of sales that go to the author/photographer. Often, royalties are figured against the retail price of the book, but more often, they are determined on a wholesale or net rate. As an author, the latter arrangement is not necessarily desirable, unless great sales volume is anticipated. However, most publishers seem to be paying on the net price of the book, and since so many people want books published, it's an economy publishers find easy to enforce.

Royalties work on a sliding scale. For example, if you are both the photographer and the writer, you may receive 10 percent of the proceeds on the first 10,000 books sold, 12½ percent for the next 10,000, and 15 percent for anything over 20,000 copies. Additional royalties might include paperback editions (7½ percent), foreign sales (5 percent) direct response sales (5 percent), book club sales (7½ percent), and so on. These are only examples, since the actual figures vary with the type of book and publisher. Of course, like almost everything else in your book contract, royalties are negotiable, and the more prestige you bring to the book by your status as an author or photographer, the better your bargaining power. If you combine efforts with a writer, you should negotiate for a fair share of the royalties.

Royalties on soft-cover books tend to be lower than hardcover editions. Publishers say their profit margin is lower. Royalty percentages vary greatly on the paperback edition of a hardcover book. If a book using photographs is published in hard-cover only, the publisher will usually try to retain softcover rights for itself. In the case of how-to photography books, hard- and softcover versions may be published simultaneously. Occasionally a hardcover publisher of a picture book may offer softcover rights to another publisher, and traditionally, the publisher and the photographer share 50-50 in the proceeds from the sale of such paperback rights. In some cases, the photographer's percentage may increase with higher sales.

Royalties and sales statements are usually mailed at the same time to authors; usually twice a year.

Fees

It is generally not beneficial to the photographer to accept a flat rate on a book project unless you are being contracted to supply only a portion of the photographs. If, for instance, you accepted a flat fee for a book, and it was a runaway bestseller, you would be giving away thousands or even hundreds of thousands of dollars in income.

If you are assigned to photograph a portion of the book or its cover, you should be charging a fair rate plus expenses. If you are assigned to shoot a small number of photographs for the book, you may want to negotiate a flat fee that covers your rate, plus expenses. If you are assigned to shoot a large portion of the photos for the book—20 to 25 percent—you should try to get an advance plus a royalty, based on a percentage of the royalty of the main supplier of photographs.

Photographer's Free Copies

As part of your contract, you should be guaranteed a number of free copies of your book. Ten copies is standard, but you may find that if you can use the book for self-promotion, many more copies (50 or 100) would be beneficial. Usually, the publisher will offer you additional copies at a substantial discount, usually 40 percent. You can also try to make the additional copies a condition of your contract, keeping in mind that you may have to bend on other issues in order to get what you want. Some photographers arrange to buy hundreds or even thousands of copies of the book so that they may sell them independently. In these cases, the discount may be even greater.

Publishers will often make arrangements to give you a discount on books used for promotion. Sometimes, the publisher will charge you as little as 20 percent of the cover price for books sent to reviewers and other possible sources of promotion.

Collaborating with Writers

Because most talented photographers are not, at the same time, talented writers, it is often opportune to team up with a good writer to execute a book project. In fact, the collaboration can be much more than just a division of labor. Ideally, the pair should provide input, assistance, and research into the tasks of the other, making the collaboration a true joint venture.

Generally, if both parties contribute roughly 50 percent of the work, then all financial gains—advances and royalties—should be split 50-50. Expenses, on the other hand, usually amount to more for the photographer than for the writer, and some provision to relieve that inequity should be provided for in the contract.

It is advisable for the writer and the photographer to have separate contracts with the publisher. In fact, before a contract agreement is entered into, it is important for the team to have their own written agreement. This agreement would cover such things as copyright ownership, costs, advances and royalties, and credit, a very important point. In the mind of the public, the name which appears first on the book is usually the name associated with authorship. There are countless ways in which credit can be devised so that the names appear more or less equally, but remember that the name that comes first usually sticks in the public eye.

If the pair is using a literary agent or attorney, it should be decided whose interests that person primarily represents. If the photographer agrees that the writer's literary agent should handle all negotiations, then the photographer should be certain that his or her interests are represented fairly. The ideal is an agent or attorney contracted by both to represent both equally in the negotiations. In some circumstances, however, the photographer may wish to have his or her own agent or attorney to insure that his or her interests are not compromised by joint representation of both photographer and writer.

Discontinuance

Your contract should include a publication date that is binding to both parties. Extensions by either party are usually a necessary part of the process and are not all that unusual. However, the contract itself should protect you against a publisher that goes bankrupt, or after having accepted and approved all of the materials for your book, fails to publish it. In the sample contract that follows, paragraph 6 covers the failure to publish, and provides that in such cases, all rights to all materials revert back to the photographer immediately upon written notification. Furthermore, if a book goes "out of print" in an untimely manner, before you have had a chance to reap a reasonable amount of royalties, you should be able to acquire the plates, photomechanical film, or computer disks used to produce the book at scrap rates, and/or excess copies at unit cost.

Self-Publishing

Publishing your own photography book is an area of great potential risk. But the rewards for a successfully self-published book are equally great, since there are no middlemen: you are, at the same time, author, photographer, publisher, typesetter, designer, layout artist, printer, binder, and, perhaps worst of all, distributor of your own book.

Self-publishing offers you, the artist, complete control over the finished product. When you submit your book to a publisher, you are to some degree, at the publisher's mercy as to what the book will contain, how it will look, how it is marketed, and how it will inevitably sell. The control of self-publishing is complete, but you are also vulnerable: one or more bad decisions could result in disaster.

If you are not skilled at design, enlist the help of a graphic designer. It will be money well spent. You can spend anywhere from $2,000 to $10,000 on the design and layout alone, but it may make all the difference when it comes to potential sales. The best way to find a good graphic artist is by word of mouth. Talk to someone who has worked on a similar type of project with the graphic artist. Find out what kinds of problems were encountered and how they were solved.

Rick Smolan, *Day in the Life* founder and now president of Against All Odds Productions, says that the key ingredient in the sale of any photo book is how good the pictures look. Smolan is essentially a self-publisher and book packager, and as such, critically oversees the printing and design process even to the point where he spends time on press in Japan, where his books are printed, making sure that the printed photos are as dynamic and rich as the originals. Smolan also believes the key to the success of any photo book is how well it is designed. He normally works with a designer from the inception of the project, and usually pays him or her approximately five times the going rate for book design, in order to guarantee the quality he is after.

Before you self-publish your own book, you need to acquire the following: ISBN number (International Standard Book Number), EAN and UPC bar codes (if the book is going to be sold in chain bookstores), LCC number (Library of Congress number— if you want your book sold to libraries), and CIP (provides you with standardized classifying information that is printed on the copyright page). You would also want your book listed in R.R. Bowker's *Forthcoming Books in Print* and *Books in Print*, two volumes which give wholesalers access to the latest titles. Information on these items can be obtained from:

- ISBN Information: R.R. Bowker ISBN Agency, 121 Chanlon Rd, New Providence, NJ 07974; phone: (908) 665-6770.
- Machine Readable Guidelines for the U.S. Book Industry obtainable, free, from: GGX Associates, 11 Middle Neck Rd., Great Neck, NY 11021; phone: (516) 487-6370; fax: (516) 487-6449. GGX can also provide bar-code information.
- Library of Congress Number and information on Cataloging in Publication Program from: Cataloging and Publication Division, Library of Congress, Washington, D.C. 20540; phone: (202) 707-6372.
- Registration for R.R. Bowker's twice-yearly *Forthcoming Books in Print*: Advance Book Information, R.R. Bowker, P.O. Box 31, New Providence, NJ 07974; phone: (908) 665-6749

Another excellent source for information on self-publishing is *Photographer's Publishing Handbook* by Harold Davis, published by Images Press.

Distribution is by far the most difficult aspect of self-publishing. There are three basic ways to distribute self-published books: (1) wholesalers, (2) distributors, and (3) self-distribution, which can be nothing more sophisticated than packing up your car with as many copies of your book as you carry, and visiting every bookstore and library within driving distance. Even then, you are selling the books on consignment, meaning that you don't get paid until the books are sold. Wholesalers fill orders for libraries and the trade. They don't do any marketing or promotion, and they won't warehouse copies of the book for you. Basically, all a wholesaler will do is fill orders, and take a small percentage for their efforts. Bonafide book distributors, on the other hand, may help in the sale and promotion of a book, and will sometimes work with small publishers in producing a more marketable product. It is also possible to work with a combination of wholesalers and distributors, as well as independent sales reps, who carry select titles for various publishers. Another possibility is to sell the book via mail order. This requires an advertising budget, lots of time, and patience.

A slightly different approach to self-publishing is to work with a book packager. You sell the idea to a publisher who then commits to purchasing a set number of copies. The publisher then distributes the books through its normal distribution channels. The advantages are that you still retain the creative freedom of self-publishing—you write, photograph, design, and supervise the production of the book—but you do not then have the headaches of distribution. You get an advance on signing and get the rest of the money when the book copies are delivered to the publisher.

One such success story is Frank Van Riper, who self-published *Faces of the Eastern Shore*, a popular coffee-table picture book about Maryland's eastern shore. Van Riper, a former journalist and author, was committed to self-publish the project, but because of his knowledge of the book publishing field, decided not even to pursue an advance with a publisher. All he wanted was the assurance of a good distribution network. He chose Thomasson-Grant, of Charlottesville, Virginia, who said it would be happy to include the title on its fall list and be the distributor. With that potential problem removed, he arranged for printing in Tokyo. Nothing happened with this book that Van Riper did not want to happen. He chose the best for every phase of production—Pat Marshall Design in Washington, D.C., designed the book, Dai Nippon of Tokyo printed it. Both designer and author wanted to be on press, but it was totally impractical and they had to rely on press proofs, which, according to Van Riper, presented some surmountable problems the first time around. Van Riper learned as he went, describing the printing problems in photographer's terms, and the printer was patient. Everyone involved in the process wanted the book to be the best it could be, and ultimately it was just that.

Since the distributor had very little to do with the book, other than its distribution, Van Riper became the sole source of promotion and publicity. He arranged for TV coverage, gallery-opening publicity, excerpts, and reviews. He wrote all the press releases, and sent them to all sizes of publications and newspapers. He sent out dozens of free copies and made countless phone calls. The promotion of the book was an endless task, but one that Van Riper believes is the most important ingredient in the successful marketing of a self-published book. Some advice Van Riper offers to others interested in self-publishing: secure distribution, work with a small publisher who will be more likely to get behind your title if it believes in it, promote the daylights out of it. "No one will flog a book better than you, if it's your book."

Agents and Attorneys

Book contracts can be incredibly complex, and it's not inconceivable that you could sign something you don't understand. Ask any published author/photographer if they understood everything in their first book contract. The answer will undoubtedly be that the author would do it again differently.

Although it is not necessary, it is nonetheless advisable for photographers to have a negotiating representative, either an attorney or a literary agent. Choosing the agent or attorney is important. That person should be knowledgeable in the area of contract law, and specifically, book publishing, where it pertains to photography. How does one find such a person? One suggestion is that if you are represented by a stock agency, seek its advice. Picture agency personnel usually know of an experienced and knowledgeable agent or attorney.

Literary agents usually work on a commission basis, usually 15 percent, but, again, they may save you that much, or enhance the value of the contract by more than that amount, so it is usually a worthwhile investment. The downside to literary agents is that they often don't know enough about picture books to be helpful. Stock agents, on the other hand, may be more knowledgeable. A stock agent may not charge for some useful advice, since a book will promote the photographer's reputation, which can increase stock sales.

The greatest advantage of an independent negotiator is that the agent/attorney is dispassionate about the negotiation. Their job is merely to get you the best deal and protect your rights. But that person will not become emotionally involved in the negotiations, as you would. For further information on literary agents, picture agents, and attorneys, see *Guide to Literary Agents & Art/Photo Reps*, published by Writer's Digest's books.

Photographer's Book Agreement

The following agreement is hypothetical. It is unlikely that your book contract will look exactly like this, but it is important that you understand the terms outlined here, before you move on to sign an actual book contract. Many of the items you see here might not be included in your book contract, but perhaps they should be. You should at least be aware of their existence. This document represents the ideal, so don't treat it as gospel, but rather, use it as an exercise for the safe navigation through your first successful book-contract signing.

Agreement made this _____ day of _____ ,19 _____ , by and between

_____

corporation (hereinafter referred to as "the Publisher") and_____

_____ , (hereinafter referred to as "the Photographer").

WITNESSETH:

1. Grant of Rights

The Photographer hereby grants to the Publisher, and the Publisher hereby accepts, a limited license to reproduce, publish, and vend a hardcover (softcover) edition of a book, tentatively entitled _____ (hereinafter referred to as "said Book"), containing certain photographs by the Photographer (hereinafter referred to as "said Photographs") upon the following terms and conditions:

2. Delivery of Photographs

On or before _____ 19 _____ , the Photographer shall submit to the Publisher _____ photographs (_____ black-and-white, _____ color transparency, _____ color prints). The Publisher shall then have _____ month (s) from the receipt of said Photographs within which to select the photographs to be used in said Book. Those photographs not selected will be returned immediately to the Photographer, together with the notice of those photographs selected. A list of such photographs to be used shall then be incorporated into this agreement by reference thereto. All photographs not selected shall be excluded from the scope of this agreement, and the Photographer shall have the right to utilize such photographs in any manner whatsoever, without restriction.

All photographs so selected by the Publisher for use in said Book will be returned to the Photographer no later than sixty (60) days after the successful completion of the manufacturing (printing and binding) phase of publication. Successful completion of the manufacturing phase will be by_____, 19 _____ . Said Book is to be published and distributed no later than _____ , 19 _____ , with a minimum of _____ copies so published and distributed.

The Publisher shall not acquire any right, title, or interest in or to said Photographs, and shall not make, authorize, or permit any use of said Photographs other than as specified herein. Without limiting the generality of the foregoing, said Photographs may not be used in any way, including, without limitation, projection, layouts, sketches, and Photostats, except under the terms specified herein.

3. Use of and Return of Photographs

The Publisher shall be responsible for the safe handling and return of all photographs to the Photographer and shall indemnify the Photographer against any loss or damage to such photographs (including those not selected for use in said Book) in transit or while in the possession of the Publisher, its agents, employees, messengers, printers, or assigns.

The monetary sum for loss or damage of an original transparency or original black-and-white or color negative (hereinafter referred to as said original Photograph) shall be determined by the value of each individual photograph. The Publisher and the Photographer agree that the fair and reasonable value of each lost or damaged said original Photograph shall be One Thousand Five Hundred Dollars ($1,500) per photograph. The Publisher shall be liable for all acts of its agents, employees, messengers, printers, or assigns for all loss, damage, or misuse of the materials submitted by the Photographer hereunder. Any such payment shall not, however, be construed to be transfer to the Publisher of any right, title, or interest in or to said materials so lost or damaged.

4. Subsidiary Rights

The following subsidiary rights are agreed to and may be licensed by the party indicated. The proceeds will be divided as specified herein.

SUBSIDIARY RIGHT	LICENSEE	PROCEEDS
(i.e.) foreign	Publisher	7.5%/91.5%*
(i.e.) book club	Publisher	5%/95%
(i.e.) serial newspaper	Photographer	60%/40%
(i.e.) serial newspaper	Publisher	40%/60%

(*Note: In this hypothetical example, the Photographer's portion of the proceeds is listed first.)

If the division of proceeds for any subsidiary right changes after the sale of _____ copies of said Book, indicate which right and the secondary division of proceeds here: _____

_____

Any subsidiary right not set forth in this paragraph is retained by the Photographer.

5. License and Territory

The license granted to the Publisher hereunder is solely for the Publisher's hardcover (softcover) edition of said Book. The license granted hereunder is for one-time, nonexclusive, reproduction use of said photographs in English-language printings in the following countries.

_____

6. Publication

The Publisher agrees to publish said Book within _____ months of the delivery of the approved photographs (and manuscript). Any failure to so publish said Book shall give the Photographer the right to terminate this agreement ninety (90) days after giving written notice to the Publisher of the failure to make timely publication. In the event of such a termination, the Photographer shall have no obligation to return any moneys already received from the Publisher.

7. Approval and Inspection

The Publisher shall publish and distribute said Book at its own expense, in the style and manner and at the price which it shall deem best suited to its sale. Before publication, said Book shall be submitted in its entirety to the Photographer, including, without limitation, the text, its title, its photographs, and the contents of its covers. The Photographer will have the right to correct, modify, and otherwise change any element of said Book without limitation.

8. Advance

The Publisher shall pay to the Photographer, or his/her duly authorized representative specified in writing by the Photographer, upon execution of this agreement, the following nonreturnable advance, which shall be charged against the Photographer's royalties set forth in paragraph 9 (nine) hereof: $_____ . One-half of the agreed upon royalties shall be paid upon execution of this contract by both parties. The remainder shall be paid upon delivery and acceptance of manuscript and photographs.

9. Royalties

The Publisher shall pay to the Photographer the following percentages of the Publisher's U.S. suggested retail list price:

- Ten percent (10%) on the first 10,000 copies sold;
- Twelve and One-Half percent (12½%) on the next 10,000 copies sold;
- Fifteen percent (15%) on all copies sold in excess of the aforesaid 20,000 copies.

It is understood that the suggested retail list price shall be deemed to be not less than $_____ for the purpose of computing the royalties to be paid hereunder.

10. Copyright

Said Book shall be published with due notice of copyright in the name of the Photographer and shall be duly registered by the Publisher in the Copyright Office of the United States of America. Without limiting the foregoing, all copyrights under the Berne Convention, the Universal Copyright Convention, and the Buenos Aires Treaty will be secured; it being specifically agreed that in no event shall said Book be published without a copyright of the photographs in the name of the Photographer. The Publisher shall take all steps necessary, without cost to the Photographer, to effect such copyrights, including any renewal copyrights, if applicable.

11. Photographer's Free Copies

The Publisher agrees to furnish the Photographer with twenty (20) copies of said Book as published, free of any cost or charge to the Photographer whatsoever, for the Photographer's own use. If the Photographer requires copies in addition to the above, the Publisher agrees to furnish such additional copies to the Photographer at a discount of forty percent (40%) from the retail selling price or at the Publisher's actual publishing cost for same, whichever is less.

12. Credit

The Photographer shall receive credit on the dust jacket, cover, title page, and interior of said Book, as well as in advertising under the control of the Publisher, all in size, type, and prominence not less than that afforded any other person or party appearing thereon, and all subject to the Photographer's final and absolute approval. It is a material part of this agreement that no books or other matter be issued without the Photographer's credit as approved by him or her.

13. Accounting

Payment of accrued royalties, accompanied by detailed statements of all sales, licenses, accrued royalties, and deductions, will be made to the Photographer semi-annually, within thirty (30) days after June 30 and December 31 in each calendar year. The Publisher shall keep books of accounts containing true and accurate records of all transactions in its place of primary business, involving the subject matter of this agreement and of all sums of money received and disbursed in connection therewith. The Photographer or his/her duly authorized representative shall have the right at any time and without limitation to check, inspect, and audit the Publisher's books, records, and accounts in order to verify or clarify any and all such statements, accountings, and payments. The expense of such examination shall be borne by the Photographer unless errors of accounting equal or exceed five percent (5%) of the total sums paid or payable to the Photographer shall be found to his/her disadvantage, in which case the expense of such examination shall be borne by the Publisher.

Anything in this paragraph to the contrary notwithstanding, any sum of One Thousand Dollars ($1,000) or more which may become due to the Photographer (after the Publisher shall have recouped its advance hereunder, and not including regular royalty payments) shall be paid by the Publisher to the Photographer within thirty (30) days after the Publisher receives such payments, accompanied by a copy of the statement of account provided by such licensee to the Publisher.

14. Notices

All notices which either party may desire to or be required to send to the other shall be sent by prepaid registered mail and addressed to the parties as follows:

Publisher: _____

Photographer: _____

15. Discontinuance

If, after the initial printing and distribution of said Book, the Publisher decides to discontinue any further publication of said Book, it shall give immediate notice of such determination to the Photographer, and the Photographer shall have the option of purchasing from the Publisher the photomechanical plates and/or film, and/or computer disks for said Book at scrap rates. If the Photographer shall not take over the said plates (and film), engravings, illustrations, and/or copies of said Book and pay for same within ninety (90) days, then the Publisher shall destroy the items not taken and shall furnish the Photographer with an affidavit of destruction thereof. In any event, the Publisher's obligation for payments hereunder to the Photographer shall nevertheless continue.

For the purposes of this agreement, said Book shall be deemed "in print" only when copies are available and offered for sale in the U.S. through normal retail channels and listed in the catalog issued to the trade by the Publisher. Said Book shall not be deemed "in print" by virtue of the reproduction of copies by reprographic processes or if it is available by any medium or means other than the hardcover (softcover) edition referred to above.

If the Publisher fails to keep said Book in print, the Photographer may at any time thereafter serve a request on the Publisher that said Book be placed in print. Within sixty (60) days from receipt of such request, the Publisher shall notify the Photographer, in writing, whether it intends to comply with said request. If the Publisher fails to give such notice, or, having done so, fails to place said Book in print within six (6) months after receipt of said request by the Photographer, then, in any event, this agreement shall automatically terminate and all rights granted to the Publisher shall thereupon automatically revert to the Photographer.

16. Warranties and Indemnities

The Photographer warrants that it owns the copyright in and to the photographs provided to the Publisher under paragraph 2 hereof. Photographer makes no other warranty, express or implied, under this Agreement. Photographer agrees to indemnify and hold harmless the Publisher against any and all claims, losses, costs, damages, or expenses, including reasonable attorneys' fees, arising from or related to the defense against a claim that said Photographs infringe or otherwise violate the rights of any other party. The Publisher warrants that none of the material that it contributes to the Book will infringe or otherwise violate the rights of any other party. The Publisher agrees to indemnify and hold harmless the Photographer and his/her representations, agents, successors, and assigns against any and all claims, losses, costs, damages, or expenses, including reasonable attorneys' fees, arising from or related to the publication of the Book, except to the extent that such claim, loss, cost, damage, or expense arises from or relates to the photographs themselves.

17. Infringements

If there is an infringement by a third party of any rights granted to the Publisher hereunder, the Photographer and the Publisher shall have the right to participate jointly in an action for such infringement. If both parties participate, they shall share the expenses of the action equally and shall recoup such expenses from any sums recovered in the action. The balance of the proceeds shall be equally divided between the two parties. Each party will notify the other of infringements coming to its attention. If the Photographer declines to participate in such action, the Publisher may proceed and will bear all costs and expenses which shall be recouped from any damages recovered from the infringement, and the balance of such damages shall be divided equally between the parties. Nothing in this paragraph shall be construed as an obligation on the part of the Photographer or Publisher to take action against an infringer of all or part of the Book.

18. Arbitration

Any controversy or claim arising out of or relating to this agreement or the breach thereof shall be settled by arbitration in _____ (state), in accordance with the rules of the American Arbitration Association, and judgment upon the award rendered by the Arbitrator(s) may be entered in any court having jurisdiction thereof.

19. Independence of Parties

Nothing contained in this agreement shall be deemed to constitute the Publisher and the Photographer as partners, joint venturers, or fiduciaries, or to give the Publisher a property interest, whether of a legal or an equitable nature, in any of the Photographer's assets.

20. Waivers

A waiver by either party of any of the terms and conditions of this agreement shall not be deemed or construed to be a waiver of such terms or conditions for the future, or any subsequent breach thereof. All remedies, rights, undertakings, obligations, and agreements contained in this agreement shall be cumulative, and none of them shall be in limitation of any other remedy, right, undertaking, obligation, or agreement of either party.

21. Reservation of Rights

All rights not specifically granted herein to the Publisher are reserved by the Photographer and without any limitations whatsoever, regardless of the extent to which same are competitive with the Publisher or the license granted hereunder. This includes, without limitation, the exercise by the Photographer of all copyright rights in the photographs, such as reproduction, distribution and publication of individual photographs.

22. Defaults and Terminations

This agreement shall immediately terminate in the event of the Publisher's bankruptcy, insolvency, or assignment of assets for the benefit of creditors. In the event of termination of this agreement, the Publisher shall grant and convey all rights in said Book back to the Photographer.

Time is of the essence in the performance by the Publisher of its obligations hereunder. If the Publisher fails to pay promptly under the royalties hereunder, or if the Publisher fails to conform or comply with any other terms or conditions hereunder, the Photographer shall have the right, either personally or by his duly authorized representative, to advise the Publisher of such default; and if fourteen (14) days elapse after the sending of such notice without the default having been rectified, this license shall thereupon terminate without affecting the Photographer's rights to compensation or damages in connection with any claims or causes of action the Photographer may have.

The Photographer shall also have the right to terminate this agreement as provided in paragraph 6 (six) and paragraph 15 (fifteen) of this agreement.

23. Successors and Assigns

This agreement and all its terms and conditions, and all rights herein, shall insure to the benefit of, and shall be binding upon, the parties hereto and their respective legal representatives, successors, and assigns.

24. Miscellaneous

The titles of the paragraphs of this agreement are for convenience only and shall not in any way affect the interpretation of any paragraph of this agreement, or the agreement itself.

25. Governing Law

This agreement and all matters or issues collateral thereof shall be interpreted under, and governed by the laws of the State of _____ .

26. Promotion

The Photographer consents to the use of his or her name, and picture for promotion and advertising of said Book. The use of the Photographer's name and photograph should be consistent with the Photographer's reputation.

27. Changes and Modifications

This agreement constitutes the entire agreement between the parties hereto and cannot be changed or terminated orally; and no changes, amendments, or assignments thereof shall be binding except in writing signed by both parties.

This agreement is not binding on the Photographer unless and until a copy thereof actually signed by both the Photographer and the Publisher is delivered to the Photographer and payment of the advance is made.

IN WITNESS WHEREOF, the parties hereto have executed this agreement as of the day and year first above written.

PUBLISHER

By: _____

Title: _____

PHOTOGRAPHER

_____

Chapter 11

Professional Services

Allen Rabinowitz

Just as a photographer relies on the help of such people as assistants, camera and lab technicians, propmakers, and stylists to guarantee that their images are on the money, the advice and expertise provided by accountants, attorneys, and other professionals help ensure the business side of photography is also in focus. Whether for a particular problem or a long-term relationship, such professional service providers can make an important difference in the financial health and security of a business.

Choosing the right professional service provider for a particular need is a crucial decision which should be made with care. This chapter will outline the factors which should go into such a decision as well as some personal actions which can help control the cost of these services.

Attorney

Whether it's for help in writing or reviewing a contract, or representation in resolving a dispute, photographers are dependent upon the advice and assistance of an attorney. Although a photographer might be a skilled negotiator, there will be times when an attorney's training is invaluable. In dispute resolution, the general rule is if a business problem exists, the best possible result can be achieved with the assistance of a knowledgeable, effective attorney. The attorney can advise about the parameters of the law, what might represent a reasonable settlement and how to use leverage in terms of legal position to extract a higher settlement. If your attempt to arrive at a businesslike solution to the problem fails, and legal action is required, you are less likely to have prejudiced your case, and your attorney can better handle it having been in on it from the start.

Identifying the specific legal situation for which an attorney's talents and knowledge are most needed is the first step in choosing one. If, for example, there is a constant series of problems relating to copyright infringement, someone with that particular expertise should be sought. Just as an art director wouldn't consider a tabletop specialist to shoot fashion photos, neither would a photographer hire a tax attorney to handle a problem involving copyright.

Most people, however, prefer to have an attorney who is knowledgeable about them, is familiar with how their business is conducted, and, most importantly, is someone whom they can go to with a variety of legal problems. The most important criteria are: feeling comfortable with the attorney, trust in their expertise and judgment, and a feeling of confidence that if the problem lies outside the attorney's area of expertise, referrals to attorneys with that special knowledge and experience can be provided.

Whether the attorney is a sole practitioner, with a small firm or part of a large, multifaceted firm should not make a difference. Be aware, however, you're not hiring a firm, but rather an individual attorney. The support that the attorney has within the firm may in some instances be a consideration, such as in the context of complex litigation or a transaction requiring tax, pension, and corporate law expertise. But in most situations, the individual attorney's own professional qualifications and expertise should be the controlling consideration. ASMP can refer a member's attorney to specialists for consultations and advice.

Word of mouth is usually a good first step in finding an appropriate attorney. Inquiring among friends and colleagues, as well as reps and clients, can often lead to an attorney with a good understanding of the workings of the photo business. Another good method is to ask attorneys in the community to recommend an attorney with the desired specialized knowledge. If more needs to be discovered about a potential attorney, the legal directories published by Martindale-Hubbell are a good source. Found in most libraries, these directories list such information about attorneys as where they went to school, associations and professional societies they belong to, and articles they've published. The directories grade attorneys on the basis of technical skills and ethics. Seek attorneys rated A–V, i.e., an "A" in technical skills and a "V" for very high ethics.

At a preliminary get-acquainted meeting, the attorney should be asked certain questions. Whether the meeting is to hire that attorney on a one-time basis for a specific case or to establish a long-term relationship, it's important to clarify such terms as:

- The scope of the work.
- The hourly rate as well as the rates of the other attorneys who may be involved and lend assistance.
- The billing cycle for service, whether it is monthly, quarterly, or whatever suits both parties.
- What costs and disbursements the client will be responsible for, and the need for them to be itemized on the bill.
- Requiring that the bills be specific to the tasks performed, the amount of time spent on each task, the specific attorney or legal assistant performing each task, and the hourly rate associated with each segment of work.

Defining who is responsible for expenses becomes especially critical during litigation. Since costs can be substantial during the course of a litigation, whether the photographer will be responsible for them as they're incurred (and billed on an agreed-upon basis), or the attorney will be advancing these costs to be paid out of any settlement or judgment, needs to be ironed out in advance.

If the attorney is working on a contingency basis, where the fees are paid out of a final judgment or settlement, this needs to be clarified in advance and set forth in writing so there's no ambiguity or uncertainty later. Though attorneys usually receive one-third of the settlement or judgment in contingency agreements, this percentage can vary depending on the case and the risk being taken.

After the initial meeting, a retainer agreement spelling out the terms of the relationship should be drawn up. If an attorney refuses to do so, it's advisable to go elsewhere. It should be understood from the beginning of the relationship that the attorney will be billing for any time spent handling legal affairs. This means that even the shortest phone conversation will be reflected in the bill. If you are working on a tight budget, that should be made clear to the attorney, and authorize a limited number of hours to be spent on the case. You can also request to be periodically informed about the amount of time being spent on the case and a weekly accounting. In some cases, you might consider placing a cap on the upper limit of expenditures on the case.

Undertaking litigation can be an expensive proposition with a substantial investment in legal fees. Litigation is extremely time consuming, especially if the photographer is the defendant in a case. In the context of litigation, request the attorney to prepare a projected litigation budget, and monitor how closely it is followed.

There are, however, alternatives to going to court. First, determine if the situation or dollar amount in question warrants the investment in attorney's fees.

In disputes with a low dollar value, small claims courts are a viable option. Many states will put a dollar-amount ceiling on such proceedings, so the photographer must check with the individual state about that amount. For a minimal filing fee, it's possible to get a quick hearing on the dispute, usually within a matter of weeks rather than months. Although attorneys are not required for such hearings, if the photographer is incorporated, the particular state law might require representation by legal counsel. Remember, however, that small claims courts have no jurisdiction in matters of federal law such as copyright.

In certain disputes, consideration should be paid to arbitration or mediation. In arbitration, both parties present their side of the dispute, and the arbitrator makes a decision on how it should be resolved. In some situations, that decision is binding and final, and, in others, the arbitrator's decision is preliminary and can be challenged in court.

In mediation, by contrast, an outside party helps the parties negotiate a solution to the problem, but does not make any independent determinations as to what the solution should be. The mediator's role is that of a facilitator, not a decisionmaker.

In both cases, a person who is knowledgeable about the law, though not necessarily an attorney or judge, will perform the services of a mediator or arbitrator. Usually, these routes are taken when both sides have reached an impasse in their discussions, but choose to have an independent party either resolve or assist them in resolving the issue without having to go to the expense and trouble of court proceedings. Arbitration might be specified in a contract as a method of resolving any dispute under that contract. Organizations such as the American Arbitration Association have established procedures and can make people available to arbitrate disputes. Mediation too can be a remedy provided for in a contract. But, before agreeing to binding arbitration in a contract, consult with the attorney about the pros and cons of doing so.

Including a binding arbitration provision in a contract may serve the photographer's interests in some situations. But in others, such as copyright infringement, a binding arbitration provision will remove access to the courts where more effective remedies may be available.

Whether attorneys should be present at a mediation is up to the disputing parties. If both sides believe they can reach agreement better without their attorneys, they can be excluded. At an arbitration, both sides are generally represented by counsel.

When should one method be chosen over another? If a good relationship existed with the party in dispute, mediation might be preferable. A good faith approach to the situation is required from both parties, and they must genuinely desire to reach an amenable resolution.

In arbitration, the situation has usually reached a point where the parties cannot amicably resolve their dispute and require an outside party to make a decision. Be aware, however, that many arbitrators tend to reach a middle ground where both sides receive something from the decision. If a victory where the winner gets all is desired, then litigation should be pursued.

Along with being unbiased, the arbitrator needs to be someone mutually acceptable to the parties. Though not necessarily an attorney, the arbitrator should be someone with training in dispute resolution who has an understanding of what the applicable legal precedents are in order to arrive at an equitable solution. It may make sense to choose someone who does not possess detailed knowledge of the photo business as that person will not have preconceived ideas about who might be in the right and can reach a decision based on the merits of the case.

Estate Planning

Estate planning is not a topic which comes frequently or easily to people's minds. Although many photographers put a lot of time, thought, and energy into growing their businesses, few devote much consideration to what will become of those businesses after they pass away. Failure to do adequate estate planning during your lifetime could mean a wealth of problems for heirs rather than financial security you'd prefer as a legacy.

Like other owners of small businesses, photographers' estates usually consist of more than just property, cash, and securities. Along with equipment, a stock photography library, and possibly a studio, the business itself is an asset, along with the good name and goodwill garnered through the years. In order to have survivors benefit, care must be taken to prepare the proper documentation.

Probate laws vary from state to state, but some basic things should be followed.

Prime among them is drafting a will and/or trusts which contain detailed language about the disposition of the estate. Where the estate consists includes a closely held business, these documents give the executors, personal representatives, or trustees the power to deal effectively with the property.

Failure to put in detailed language enabling the executor or trustee to make such changes in the structure of the business, such as buying and selling assets, could possibly handcuff the estate. In most states, the executor might have to get the court's permission to perform such duties as the continuation of the business, the sale of assets, or making other changes. The first step to ensuring a trouble-free estate is enlisting the aid of an attorney who is competent and experienced in the area. Along with referrals from friends, colleagues, and clients, the Martindale-Hubbell directories, which list attorneys along with their educational background and specialties, are an important source. Look for experience in estate planning, estate administration, probate, trusts, and estates. Additionally, see that the attorney's firm contains other attorneys with expertise in copyright or intellectual property law. As in all cases, an attorney (and firm) rated "A" in technical skills and "V" for very high ethics is one to seriously consider.

At a preliminary meeting to discuss the relationship, inquire about how the attorney charges for his/her services. Without being asked, the attorney may not volunteer this information or make it clear at the first meeting. Paying for planning services is one area where people truly get what they pay for. When it's done right, you and your family are better off, even if these services cost more than you think they should. In the past, attorneys wrote wills as loss leaders, hoping to make bigger fees administrating the estate. They would charge for estate administration based on the worth of the estate rather than on the basis of the work performed. The approach today is moving toward billing on the basis of time spent for both planning and administration. Though you may feel you're paying too much up front, your spouse and children, however, will usually pay considerably less.

At a preliminary meeting with the attorney, the following details should be spelled out:

- How fees will be calculated, including whether payment will be on the basis of time spent on the planning and administration of the estate.
- Which attorney at the firm will be working the file and what his/her hourly rates are, you should not have to pay a partner's fee if a junior associate, for instance, is assigned to your estate.
- If billing is to be on a time basis, then a ceiling might be imposed on the fees. More likely, the law firm will present an estimated informal range of fees that similar services have cost for others. Realize that such figures might not necessarily apply in every case.

Although there are a number of books and software programs which claim to allow you to write your own will without an attorney's assistance, using them is not in your best interests. Like the client who owns a state-of-the-art camera and doesn't use a photographer for a job, the shooter who writes his or her own will is letting an amateur take the place of a professional, with a similar outcome in quality. These programs and books are designed for universal usage, meaning there's little chance they can work well for any one particular application. The photographer who writes his or her own will runs the risk of creating problems which will cause heirs to pay more to straighten them out than the upfront cost of legal advice would have been.

Dealing with trust and estate documents is an exercise in using precise and proper language. By writing one's own will, the door is open for having the words misinterpreted by someone else reading the document or using words in conflicting ways so they won't be interpreted and applied in the manner the writer had in mind. Additionally, your sense of what a word means may be quite different from what courts have traditionally held it to mean.

One of the major bequests a photographer makes to heirs are the copyrights to a career's worth of images. Under current copyright law, these rights are good for fifty years beyond the photographer's life in most cases. If you've taken the proper steps to protect these copyrights, there should be no problem with the transfer to heirs or beneficiaries. However, if you've been negligent, your heirs will only inherit the problems. Internal organization is the key to a successful transfer. As the surviving spouse or executor will have to go into your office and make sense of what's been left behind, you can help the cause by leaving a blueprint which helps everyone. If the images are organized and filed, and copyright records placed on a computer database, life will be easier and more financially productive for the estate and its beneficiaries. Will and trust documents should make provisions for professional management of these images and their rights. Having some kind of agent in place, or at least arranged for in the will or trust, will maximize revenue for heirs. Choosing an executor (sometimes called a personal representative) is one of the most important decisions in estate planning. Along with trustees, such overseers of an estate are collectively referred to as fiduciaries and are held to the highest standard of behavior imposed by law with a mandate to act in the best interests of the estate and/or its beneficiaries. They cannot act in their own interest and may be barred from acting in the face of any possible conflicts of interest.

If such potential conflicts of interest exist— if, for example, another photographer may be named as executor—the documents will have to deal with how that will be handled. If, for instance, a surviving partner/executor wants to buy out the other's interest in the business from the estate, the terms and rules for that need to be spelled out.

A prime candidate for a fiduciary position is someone you trust and who might also be familiar with the photo business. It's not uncommon, however, to have two executors, one being a close family member such as a spouse or child and the other someone who brings expertise to the table. A professional executor, such as a bank or trust company, might be chosen to manage the estate. In selecting such a fiduciary, choose one experienced in handling estates holding small or closely held businesses. The executor's term of responsibility usually lasts one to three years, after which the responsibility for handling assets, if they haven't all gone to the ultimate beneficiaries, usually goes to trustees.

When setting up the documents, it's important to give the estate's management as much flexibility as possible and specify those powers fiduciaries should have. If you have specific ideas on how photos should be used, these instructions need to be written into the documents. However, this should be done in a way which neither handcuffs nor restricts the management of these images since it can't be predicted how future developments might affect the images or their best use.

This is done by putting into the document language referred to as "precatory," meaning it expresses an intention or wish, but is not legally binding or enforceable. Alternatively, these intentions can be left out of the will, but communicated in the form of a letter of guidance to whomever will handle the stock. Some photographers may choose to leave their stock library in the form of a charitable bequest to a university, museum, or other nonprofit organization. When this is done, the recipient should handle the images as it would a cash bequest and work with the photographer and his or her attorney ahead of time to make sure it gets the gift in a way it wants.

It's wise to periodically review the will or trust documents, especially if there's been a significant change, such as an altering of the tax laws, a difference in the family situation (such as marriage, divorce, or the birth of a child), a revision of the copyright laws, or modification of the structure of the business. As the will or trust is altered to reflect these new realities, you should also review any other relevant financial documents to see how these might impact the estate plan.

Accountant

Often the difference between a photographer's success or failure is not aesthetic taste or visual talents, but rather how they conduct his or her business. To best deal with the myriad of rules involved in state, local, and federal tax laws, the expertise of a certified public accountant is a necessity. The choice of an accountant who is also a well-versed business advisor can mean the difference between a prosperous studio and one where the photographer spends more time dealing with taxes than creating quality images.

The best place to start the search for an accountant is with colleagues or business associates. Word of mouth is usually a good indicator whether an accountant has done a good job in helping another shooter get his or her financial house in order. In addition, stylists, proppers, designers, and other self-employed craftspeople might be able to suggest possible accountants.

When choosing an accountant, be particularly concerned that candidates for the job have industry experience, particularly in the sales tax area. Since these complicated laws vary from state to state, most accountants are not familiar with the sales tax implications relative to photographers and the rendering of photographic services.

If the accountant doesn't possess photo industry experience, however, inquire if he or she has a background in art or art-related fields. The candidate should be familiar with some of the terminology and, at the least, have service businesses as clients. If that accountant has only dealt with such businesses as doctors, manufacturers, or nonprofit organizations, look elsewhere.

When interviewing a potential accountant, ask if he or she is aware of markup procedures, billing procedures, and studio systems and controls. Ask if the accountant has knowledge in:

- State sales tax and payment procedures.
- Payment procedures to freelancers or employees and the distinction between independent contractors and employees. The IRS provides guidelines for contractors/employees, but your accountant should be aware of state interpretations too.
- Terminology and knowledge of the component parts that go into a job such as props, wardrobe, and stylists.

The accountant should also be asked about how he or she bills and what other services will be rendered along with the customary service of preparing an annual tax return. Chief among these services should be tax planning and the preparation of an annual financial statement.

The annual financial statement, generally done on an accrual basis as opposed to the cash basis for the tax return, is a critical tool in tracking business. Not only can it be used in obtaining loans to help the studio grow, but additionally to compare the studio's financial performance against industry models.

A successful annual financial statement will show or track:

- Growth in revenue.
- If expenses are increasing or decreasing as a function of revenue.
- If too much is being spent in a particular area.
- If the company is building net worth and the capability to expand.
- How much income was truly earned on an annual basis.

The financial statement doesn't need to be a tight, formal document, but it should be written down, scrutinized, and analyzed from year to year. This statement can also help you and the accountant prepare a reasonable budget which enables the studio to grow.

In general, the accountant should be called upon for tax and financial information and advice, but not such activities as payroll. If there are two or more employees, that task may be best handled by an outside payroll service. These companies produce payroll checks, do quarterly payroll tax returns, prepare W-2 forms, and take care of deposits with the appropriate regulatory agencies.

Also be wary in using readily available software as an aid in these matters. Though general accounting software may be helpful in such areas as general ledger and accounts payable, it is not strong in the billing/estimating area that's so crucial to your business. Conversely, software geared toward billing and estimating will not provide needed strength in more generalized accounting areas.

Tax planning is another key service provided by an accountant. Rather than a flurried activity that occurs at the beginning of April, the successful photographer/accountant team will have the tax situation well in hand in advance of deadlines.

A knowledgeable accountant will schedule a planning meeting with you about nine months into a year where you'll discuss what needs to be done before year's end to reduce any huge tax burden. In addition to this meeting, you should meet with your accountant at the end of the year to prepare the tax return and annual financial statement and budget for the subsequent year. Additionally, any time a major financial decision needs to be made, meet with your accountant, or at least discuss it over the phone.

You can help the accountant and save on billing by keeping accurate records and preparing relevant information. Summarize monthly cash receipts by category, listing how much was collected in photo fees vs. the job expenses billed out and sales tax. At the end of the year, prepare a list of open accounts receivable and open accounts payable.

Having the appropriate paperwork in order can help both you and your accountant. Make a concerted effort to organize such documents as:

- All disbursements—all paid invoices should be on file.
- All payments to independent freelancers.
- Petty cash files—all items over $25 need to be documented.

In the case of independent freelancers, be especially wary. There are times when a part-time worker, such as an assistant, might be considered an employee rather than an independent contractor. Instead of just issuing a 1099 form at the end of the year (if the person was paid more than $600), you may need to take out withholding and contribute payroll taxes for that individual.

A general rule of thumb is that if you control the destiny of an individual (tell them when to come in, when to leave, provide tools of the trade, and give direction during the day) that person is an employee and not a freelancer. Since there are penalties when someone deemed an employee is treated as a freelancer, consult with your tax advisor on dealing with that situation.

Sales tax, as mentioned earlier, often provides photographers with their biggest tax headaches. In order to better deal with the situation, keep the following general rules in mind:

- Although sales tax rules vary from state to state, most of the time, sales tax is imposed on the full amount of a billing, not just the photo fee or expenses.
- If a client tells you that he's or she's not supposed to pay sales tax, obtain either a resale certificate and/or an exemption certificate from the client.
- Generally, out-of-state services are nontaxable if billed and rendered out of state. (If, for example, a New York photographer does a job in California for a company in that state, the photographer does not have to charge New York sales tax; but, the company might have to pay a California use tax.)
- Labor, facility, and equipment costs are generally nontaxable. Job expenses such as wardrobe, sets, and film are generally exempt if bought for resale. You must present a certificate to the vendor stating the material will be sold or will be part of a job billed to a client.

It is up to you to have the correct sales tax information. If doing a job out of town, consult your accountant on the sales tax rules which apply in that locale. Getting audited by the Internal Revenue Service is a situation that people dread. If such a notice comes, the first thing you should do is not panic. The second is to call your accountant and prepare for the audit. Generally, the IRS notice will pertain to a particular area, such as expenses. It's rare for the IRS to question an entire return. Focus on the area in question and pull out all documentation and review the return. Although you might be able to personally deal with the IRS in some matters, you might feel more comfortable with your accountant on hand. The key to a successful audit is doing the necessary homework and not walking into it unprepared.

You should be accompanied to the audit by a professional who is authorized to represent taxpayers before the IRS. Tax attorneys and CPAs are automatically entitled to provide such representation, while other tax preparers, unless they've received special designation, cannot. If the situation becomes serious or if a significant amount of money is involved, seek an attorney who specializes in tax law. An accountant is not allowed to represent a client in tax court.

If you and your accountant have worked together to produce a sensible business plan and manner of tackling any tax problems, these audits will not be the "encounters from hell" that photographers experience in their worst nightmares.

Insurance

Unfortunately for insurance purposes, most of what goes into the job description "photographer" touches upon almost every exclusion in every existing business insurance policy. Whether shooting from helicopters or on boats, going out of the country or even out of state, the things photographers do in the course of a working day put them in a problematic area for acquiring the basic insurance coverage their businesses need.

Finding a source of insurance is a hard task. Step one is discovering an insurance broker who can handle all needs, but, because of the way the insurance industry is structured, brokers and/or agents either fall in the life and health area, or in the category of property and casualty. Since a broker who deals in disability, for example, may not know much about health or professional coverage, find specialists in the different insurance categories to arrange for coverage.

Like most buyers of insurance, photographers don't know what they're buying until there's a loss; and if they haven't properly prepared, by then it's too late. A self-employed person should carry the following coverages at a minimum:
- Health
- Disability
- Nonowned and hired auto liability
- Workers' compensation (if there are employees)
- General Liability (especially if not incorporated)

Although it's a wise thing to carry, life insurance is not necessarily mandatory. While most photographers will take out insurance on their cameras, few stop to consider the importance of having coverage in the previous five areas. If $20,000 in equipment is lost, for example, at least you're aware of what's gone. But, those other areas contain the potential for catastrophic loss. If something should go wrong and there's not adequate insurance protection, the resulting claims might wipe you out financially. Disability insurance is an area which presents difficulty. Insurance companies would prefer not issuing a disability policy to self-employed individuals because it's difficult for the company to tell if that person will work again since many self-employed people work out of their homes.

Therefore, many self-employed people receive poor definitions of the meaning of "disabled." Where an insurance company might offer a doctor or attorney a disability policy which pays for the entire benefit period (usually up to age 65) regardless if that individual can teach or do something else, photographers would probably receive a policy which might only offer benefits for two years if they could not perform within their occupation, and thereafter if they could not get any gainful employment.

In addition, since disability is based on age and occupation, you may end up paying more per $100 of coverage than a same-age attorney or doctor because insurance companies have determined that a photographer has much more of a chance of becoming disabled.

What can be done in this and other instances? The best bet is to find an agent who has an understanding of the photo business. Such a person can then attempt to find a company which will write a disability policy that takes your career situation into consideration.

Workers' compensation is another area where special notice should be taken. Although you may think hiring freelancers, such as assistants, frees you from needing to purchase workers' compensation coverage, in fact, the definition of what constitutes an employee is solely up to an individual state's workers' compensation board.

In some cases, a person hired for just one day may be defined as an employee. If a freelancer were to get injured in the course of an assignment where he or she was told by you what time to report to work, what to do on the job, and you supplied all the materials necessary to do the job, the workers' compensation board may rule the person is an employee. If you do not have sufficient coverage, the results could be financially disastrous.

There are several factors by which you can feel reasonably comfortable a freelancer will not be defined as an employee:

- If the person is incorporated, and performs the service for parties other than you.
- If he or she provides a certificate of insurance to show he or she has their own workers' compensation insurance.

Workers' compensation is paid based on payroll, and all employees must be covered by such insurance. You can be more aggressive in your posture by stating that not all of the people whom you work alongside are employees and therefore can pay the premium based on a lower payroll. However, if the workers' compensation board rules that a person is an employee, all premiums must be paid retroactively.

Also be aware that your workers' compensation policy will not cover people hired in some states and foreign countries. If hiring people in Ohio, Nevada, North Dakota, Washington, West Virginia, or Wyoming, contact that state's insurance commission or Workers' compensation board for information on obtaining coverage.

Health insurance is another area where the self-employed usually have great difficulty obtaining appropriate coverage. When exploring health insurance programs, inquire how long the carrier has been in business. Try to go with an established company which surely will be there if medical problems arise. If the company goes under and you are left uninsured, it could turn into a financial disaster.

Consider a high deductible and either unlimited coverage or a $2 million lifetime maximum. A limited policy with a low deductible is another option to investigate. In general, people tend to get better value for their dollar with a high deductible which makes the coverage more catastrophic.

There are several pitfalls to be avoided when getting health insurance. Make sure any policy is noncancelable in case the carrier decides to drop its health coverage program. (Note: A noncancelable policy isn't guaranteed to be noncancelable. The carrier might opt to cancel all such policies in a state, but more likely, the insurance companies might sell all such policies to another carrier.) Also, in a number of self-insured programs, the company retains the right to exclude coverage if it finds claims are running too high in any particular area. Stay away from such a policy.

If health insurance benefits are extended to employees, realize the obligation you're taking upon yourself. If the program is not administered properly, problems might lead to expensive lawsuits. Rather than offer health insurance, consider giving employees a lump sum of money to acquire their own health insurance.

Photographers (and, in reality, most others) have difficulty understanding commercial general liability insurance coverage. It protects your legal liability against lawsuits for bodily injury or property damage that occur within the United States or Canada to other people or other people's property, but does not cover any of your property. It also excludes other people's property in your care, custody, or control (you should have bailee coverage for this exposure).

Other important exclusions in this coverage include:
- People eligible for disability benefits under a state statute.
- People considered to be employees covered under workers' compensation.
- Anything having to do with an automobile, aircraft, or watercraft.
- Claims resulting from improper models releases, invasion of privacy, infringement of copyright or trademark, infringement of patent, libel, or slander.
- Anything having to do with pollution.
- Any international act.
- Discrimination or sexual harassment.
- Claims by someone other than an employee to recover damages paid to or sought from a former or existing employee.

In order to have sufficient coverage in the event of claims made in excluded areas, you can purchase policies which can provide the necessary protection. These policies include:
- Fire damage legal liability for your space as an endorsement to the policy.
- Bailee, which protects you for property damage to other people's property in your care, custody, or control including property being moved or photographed. There are exclusions for scratching, chipping, marring, and breakage to antiques, jewelry, furs, and silverware (but riders can be obtained).
- Rental equipment coverage.
- Props coverage—which will cover props, wardrobe, and a limited amount of third-party property damage.

Since general liability excludes any benefits paid by workers' compensation, you may benefit by purchasing a workers' compensation policy before general liability. You may incorporate to give some protection from general liability claims, but you can't protect personal assets against failure to have workers' compensation.

Nonowned and hired auto insurance, while it excludes your own vehicle, is also important coverage to have. This will cover you for vehicular accidents caused by others in your employ driving their own cars or for accidents caused by rental cars under their control. The insurance does not cover physical damage to the car being driven, but rather bodily injury or property damage to other people's property.

In addition to coverage required for most businesses, investigate policies relating to situations specific to photography. These would include lab and stock insurance. Though most lab policies will give back unexposed film, you can obtain negative coverage which protects negatives from fire, theft, and water damage. Policies can also be written which protect you in the case of faulty film stock, errors, and camera malfunction. These policies will cover the expenses involved in recreating the image; but not if someone else paid them. Insuring a stock library also presents a problem. Although $1,500 is usually given as the value of an image, if you tried insuring every photo in your stock library at that amount, the premium for coverage would be enormous. Although people might insure their homes for large sums, few choose to do that for their stock. There are several ways to determine a fair value for a stock library for insurance purposes:

- Figure out the sales value of the entire collection, divide by number of images and come up with a price per image.
- Determine the value of time and expense it would take to recreate the library and divide by number of images and come up with a value per image.
- Hire a qualified photograph appraiser to assess the value. Experts recognized by the courts could serve this purpose.

Though figuring out insurance policies is often a time-consuming and confusing task, making the effort to obtain the best possible coverage will help you in the event of any major problems.

Bibliography

This Bibliography was edited by Don Luce and Jean Miller and compiled by Bruce Cline, Don Luce, Neil Sapienza, and Garie Waltzer of the ASMP National Education Committee, and James Cook. All listings were current and all publications in print at time of publication. The authors regret any inadvertent omissions or errors.

Books and Articles

Advertising Photographers of America. *National Member's Handbook*. Los Angeles, Calif.: APA, 1993.

Allen, Kathleen. *Launching New Ventures*. Dover, N.H.: Upstart Publishing Co., Inc., 1995.

American Society of Media Photographers. *The ASMP Business Bible*. Princeton Junction, N.J.: ASMP, 1994.

American Society of Media Photographers. *Assignment Photography*. New York: ASMP, 1991.

American Society of Media Photographers. "On Buying Photography." New York: ASMP, 1992. *Pamphlet*.

American Society of Media Photographers. *Commissioning Architectural Photography, A buyer's guide for working with architectural photographers*. Princeton Junction, N.J.: ASMP, 1996.

American Society of Media Photographers. *White paper on copyright registration*, Princeton Junction, N.J.: ASMP, 1993.

Amphoto Editors. "Model Release Forms for Photographers." New York: Amphoto, 1981.

Anthony, Joseph. *Kiplinger's Working for Yourself.* Washington, D.C.: Kiplinger's Books, 1993.

ASMP Prosurance. "Insurance Material Package for Photographers." Call Taylor & Taylor at (800) 922-1184.

Attard, Janet. *The Home Office and Small Business Answer Book.* New York: Henry Holt & Co., 1993.

Bacon, Mark S. *Do-It-Yourself Direct Marketing.* New York: John Wiley & Sons, 1994.

Bangs, David H., Jr. *Cash Flow Control Guide: Methods to Understand and Control Small Business's Number One Problem.* Dover, N.H.: Upstart Publishing Co., Inc., 1989.

Baty, Gordon B. *Entrepreneurship for the Nineties.* Englewood Cliffs, N.J.: Prentice Hall, 1990.

Boursier, Helen. *Marketing Madness: Power Marketing for Portrait—Wedding Photographers.* Soulsbyville, Calif.: Studio Press, 1992.

Brackman, Henrietta. *The Perfect Portfolio.* New York: Amphoto, 1984.

Busch, Richard. "Be a Photographer's Assistant." *Popular Photography*, February 1976, pp. 94–99, 131–134. A surprisingly good article, worth looking for.

Castle, Paul. *Promoting Portraits.* Soulsbyville, Calif.: Studio Press, 1988.

Chapman, Elwood N. *Human Relations in Small Business.* Menlo Park, Calif.: Crisp Publishing, 1994.

Chapnick, Howard. *Truth Needs No Ally: Inside Photojournalism.* Colombia, Mo.: University of Missouri Press, 1994.

Copyright Office, Library of Congress. Copyright Basics (*Circular #1*). Washington, D.C.: U.S. Government Printing Office, 1992. Free pamphlet. Call (202) 707-9100 and request information kit #115—General Visual Arts.

Cornish, Clive G. Basic *Accounting for Small Business Success.* Bellingham, Wash.: Self-Counsel Press Inc., 1992.

Crawford, Tad. *Business and Legal Forms for Photographers.* New York: Allworth Press, 1991.

Crawford, Tad. *Legal Guide for the Visual Artist.* 3rd ed. New York: Allworth Press, 1995.

Davidson, Robert L., III. *The Small Business Incorporation Kit.* New York: John Wiley & Sons, 1993.

Day, John. *Small Business in Tough Times.* San Diego, Calif.: Pfeiffer and Co., 1993.

Dicks, J. W., Esq. *The Small Business Legal Kit.* Holbrook, Mass.: Adams Publishing, 1995.

DuBoff, Leonard. *The Art Business Encyclopedia.* New York: Allworth Press, 1994.

DuBoff, Leonard. *The Law (in Plain English) for Photographers.* New York: Allworth Press, 1995.

Eastman Kodak Co. *Conservation of Photographs.* Rochester, N.Y.: Saunders PhotoGraphic, Inc., 1985. Kodak Publication #F-40.

Emily, Carol. *Capital for Women.* Old Tappan, N.J.: Macmillan Publishing Co., 1996.

Evans, Art. *Careers in Photography*. Redondo Beach, Calif.: Photo Data Research, 1992.

Evans, Art. *Photo Business Careers*. Redondo Beach, Calif.: Photo Data Research, 1992.

Farace, Joe. *The Digital Imaging Dictionary*. New York: Allworth Press, 1996.

Farace, Joe. *The Photographer's Guide to the Internet*. New York: Allworth Press, 1997.

Fear, Dan. *Creating a Successful Career in Photography*: The Professional Artist. Seattle, Wash.: Silver Image Gallery, Inc., 1992.

Fisher, Roger. *Getting to Yes: Negotiating Agreement Without Giving In*. 2nd ed. Boston, Mass.: Houghton Mifflin, 1991.

Fishman, Stephen. *Hiring Independent Contractors: A Legal Guide for Employers*. Berkeley, Calif.: Nolo Press, 1996.

Foxman, Loretta. *Resumes That Work*. New York: Wiley Press, 1993.

Freeman, Michael. *The Photographer's Studio Manual*. New York: Amphoto, 1991.

Friedman, Joyce S. *Complete Guide to Being an Independent Contractor*. Dover, N.H.: Upstart Publishing Co., Inc., 1994.

Fry, Fred L. and Charles R. Stoner. *Strategic Planning for the New & Small Business*. Dover, N.H.: Upstart Publishing Co., Inc., 1995.

Gambaccini, Peter. *Getting to the Top in Photography*. New York: Amphoto, 1984.

Grant, Daniel. *The Business of Being an Artist*. 2nd ed. New York: Allworth Press, 1996.

Graphic Artist's Guild. *Handbook: Pricing and Ethical Guidelines*. 8th ed. New York: GAG, 1994.

Haas, Ken. *The Location Photographer's Handbook*. New York: Van Nostrand Reinhold, 1990.

Heron, Michal. *How to Shoot Stock Photos That Sell*, rev. ed., New York: Allworth Press, 1996.

Heron, Michal. *Stock Photo Forms*. New York: Allworth Press, 1991.

Heron, Michal, and David MacTavish. *Pricing Photography: The Complete Guide to Assignment & Stock Prices*, rev. ed. New York: Allworth Press, 1997.

Highton, Scott. *Rights and Value in Traditional and Electronic Media*. Princeton Junction, N.J.: ASMP, 1996.

Hollenbeck, Cliff. *Big Bucks, Selling Your Photography*. Amherst, N.Y.: Amherst Media, Inc., 1992.

Horenstein, Henry. *The Photographer's Source*. New York: Simon & Schuster, 1989.

Ito, Dee. *Careers in the Visual Arts: A Guide to Jobs, Money, Opportunities & an Artistic Life*. New York: Watson-Guptill Publications, Inc., 1993.

Jacobs, Lou, Jr. *Selling Photographs: Determining Your Rates and Understanding Your Rights*. New York: Amphoto, 1988.

Jacobs, Lou, Jr. *Selling Stock Photography: How to Market Your Photographs for Maximum Profit*. New York: Amphoto, 1992.

Jones, J. F. *A Business Guide for the Professional Home-Based Photographer*. Edmond, Okla.: Drakestone Publishing Co., 1989.

Kelley, Victor. *How to Get Into the Business of Photography*. Palm Springs, Calif.: ETC Publications, 1981.

Kieffer, John. *The Photographer's Assistant*. New York: Allworth Press, 1992.

Kravitz, Wallace R. *Bookkeeping the Easy Way*. 2nd ed. Hauppauge, N.Y.: Barron's Educational Series Inc., 1990.

Leland, Caryn. *Licensing Art and Design*. New York: Allworth Press, 1990.

Lilley, Edward R. *The Business of Studio Photography*. New York: Allworth Press, 1997.

Lister, Kate. *Finding Money: the Small Business Guide to Financing*, rev. ed. New York: John Wiley & Sons, 1995.

Lonier, Terri. *Working Solo Sourcebook: Essential Resources for Independent Entrepreneurs*. New Paltz, N.Y.: Portico Press, 1995.

Lonier, Terri. *Working Solo: The Real Guide to Freedom & Financial Success with Your Own Business*. New Paltz, N.Y.: Portico Press, 1994.

Marino, T J., and Donald A. Sheff. *Freelance Photographer's Handbook*. Old Tappan, N.J.: Macmillan Publishing Co., 1980.

McCarthy, Susan. *Nature and Wildlife Photography*. New York: Allworth Press, 1994.

McCarthy, Susan. *Travel Photography*. New York: Allworth Press, 1992.

McKeever, Mike. *How to Write a Business Plan*. 4th ed. Berkeley, Calif.: Nolo Press, 1992.

Merriam-Webster Editors. *Merriam-Webster's Guide to Business Correspondence*. Springfield, Mass.: Merriam-Webster, Inc., 1988.

Metzdorf, Martha. *The Ultimate Portfolio*. Cincinnati, Ohio: North Light Books, 1991.

Milano, Carol. Hers: *The Wise Woman's Guide to Starting a Business on $2,000 or Less*. New York: Allworth Press, 1991.

O'Donnell, Jeff. *Insurance Smart*. New York: John Wiley & Sons, 1991.

O'Hara, Patrick D. *How to Computerize Your Small Business*. New York: John Wiley & Sons, 1993.

Persky, Robert S. and Susan P. Levy. *The Photographer's Guide to Getting and Having a Successful Exhibition*. New York, N.Y.: Consultant Press Ltd., 1987.

Persky, R. S., ed. *The Photographic Art Market: Auction Prices 1993*. New York: Consultant Press Ltd., 1994.

Photographic Grant Sources. Kingston, N.Y.: Embee Press, 1986.

Pickerell, James. *Negotiating Stock Photo Prices 1995—Sellers Guide*. 3rd ed. Rockville, Md.: Stock Connection, 1995.

Pinson, Linda and Jerry Jinnett. *Keeping the Books*. 3rd ed. Dover, N.H.: Upstart Publishing Co., Inc., 1996.

Pinson, Linda and Jerry Jinnett. *The Woman Entrepreneur*. Dover, N.H.: Upstart Publishing Co., Inc., 1993.

Piscopo, Maria. *The Photographer's Guide to Marketing and Self-Promotion*. 2nd ed. New York: Allworth Press, 1995.

Ragan, Robert C. *Step-By-Step: The Complete Handbook for Small Business*. New York: Sterling Publishing Co., 1992.

Remer, Michael, and Richard Weisgrau. "ASMP Copyright Guide for Photographers." New York: ASMP, 1991. *Pamphlet*.

Remer, Michael D., Esq. *Valuation of Lost or Damaged Transparencies*. New York: ASMP, 1992.

Robertson, Cliff. *The McGraw-Hill Small Business Tax Advisor*. New York: McGraw-Hill, Inc., 1992.

Rose, Lance. *NetLaw: Your Rights in the Online World*. Berkeley, Calif.: Osborne/McGraw-Hill, 1995.

Rosen, Frederick W. *Professional Photographer's Business Guide*. New York: Amphoto, 1985.

Rotkin, Charles E. *Professional Photographer's Survival Guide*. Cincinnati: Writer's Digest Books, 1992.

Rough Notes staff, editors. *Business Owners Policy Guide*. Carmel, Ind.: Rough Notes Co., Inc., 1996.

Sebastian, Liane. *Electronic Design and Publishing: Business Practices*. New York: Allworth Press, 1995.

Seuss, Bernhard J. *Mastering Black-and-White Photography*. New York: Allworth Press, 1995.

Shaw, Susan D., and Rossol, Monona. *Overexposure: Health Hazards in Photography*. New York: Allworth Press, 1991.

Smith, Cynthia. *A Woman's Guide to Starting Her Own Business: How to Turn Talent into Profit*. New York: Carol Publishing Group, 1994.

Snyder, Jill. *Caring for Your Art*, rev. ed. New York: Allworth Press, 1995.

Society of Photographer and Artist Representatives. *Do-It-Yourself Kit*. New York: SPAR, 1989.

Stewart, Marcia. *Leases and Rental Agreements*. Berkeley, Calif.: Nolo Press, 1997.

Strong, William S. *The Copyright Book: A Practical Guide*. 4th ed. Cambridge, Mass.: The MIT Press, 1995.

Tabet, Joseph, and Jeffrey Slater. *Financial Essentials for Small Business Success*. Dover, N.H.: Upstart Publishing Co. Inc., 1994.

Taylor, Russel R. *Exceptional Entrepreneurial Women: Strategies for Success*. Westport, Conn.: Greenwood Publishing Group, 1988.

Trautmann, Carl O. *The Language of Small Business*. Dover, N.H.: Upstart Publishing Co., Inc., 1994.

U.S. Department of Commerce. "Basic Facts About Trademarks." Washington, D.C.: U.S. Government Printing Office, 1992. Free *pamphlet*.

Uva, Michael, and Sabrina Uva. *The Grip Book; or How to Become a Motion Picture Film & Video Technician*. Valencia, Calif.: Independent Cinema Technology and Videos, 1989.

Vitali, Julius. *The Fine Artist's Guide to Marketing and Self-Promotion*. New York: Allworth Press, 1996.

Weisgrau, Richard. *Formalizing Agreements*. Princeton Junction, N.J.: ASMP, 1996.

Weisgrau, Richard. *Photographer's Guide to Negotiating*. New York: ASMP, 1992.

Wilson, Lee. *The Copyright Guide*. New York: Allworth Press, 1996.

Wylie, Peter and Mardy Grothe. *Can This Partnership Be Saved?: Improving (or Salvaging) Your Key Business Relationships*. Dover, N.H.: Upstart Publishing Co., Inc., 1993.

Wylie, Peter and Mardy Grothe. *Problem Employees: How to Improve Their Performance*. Dover, N.H.: Upstart Publishing Co., Inc., 1991.

Zuckerman, Laurie B. *On Your Own: A Woman's Guide to Building a Business*. Dover, N.H.: Upstart Publishing, 1993.

Publishers and Book Sources

Allworth Press, 10 East 23rd Street, Suite 210, New York, N.Y. 10010; (800) 491-2808. *Phone orders accepted.*

Amphoto, 1515 Broadway, New York, N.Y. 10036; (212) 764-7300, (908) 363-4511. *Phone orders accepted.*

Eastman Kodak Co., Dept. 412L-209-AP, Rochester, N.Y. 14650; (800) 233-1650. *Call for catalog.*

Graphic Artist's Book Club, P.O. Box 12526, Cincinnati, Ohio 45212; (800) 937-0963. *Call for catalog.*

Nolo Press, 950 Parker Street, Berkeley, Calif. 94701; (800) 992-6656, (800) 955-4775.

Peachtree Publishers, 494 Armour Circle NE, Atlanta, Ga. 30324; (404) 875-2578. *Call for catalog.*

Upstart Publishing Co., 163 Central Avenue, Suite 4, Dover, N.H. 03820; (800) 235-8866. *Call for catalog.*

Watson-Guptill Publications, Inc., 1515 Broadway, New York, N.Y. 10036; (212) 536-5359.

Periodicals

Advertising Age, Crain Communications, Inc., 740 Rush Street, Chicago, Ill. 60611; (312) 649-5200

Adweek, 1515 Broadway, New York, N.Y. 10036; (212) 536-5336, (800) 722-6658

Afterimage, 31 Prince Street, Rochester, N. Y. 14607; (716) 442-8676

American Photo, Hachette Filipacchi Magazines, Inc., 1633 Broadway, New York, N.Y. 10019; (212) 767-6000

Archive, 915 Broadway, New York, N.Y. 10010; (212) 673-6600

Art and Design News, Boyd Publishing Co., Inc., P.O. Box 501100, Indianapolis, Ind. 46250; (317) 849-6110

Art Direction, 10 East 39th Street, 6th Floor, New York, N.Y. 10016; (212) 889-6500

Art Education Journal, National Art Education Association, 1916 Association Drive, Reston, Va. 22091; (703) 860-8000

Art Marketing Handbook, ArtNetwork, 18757 Wildflower Drive, Penn Valley, Calif. 95946; (916) 692-1355

ASMP Bulletin, American Society of Media Photographers, Inc., 14 Washington Road, Suite 502, Princeton Junction, N.J. 08550; (609) 799-8300

Camera Work, 70 12th Street, San Francisco, Calif. 94103; (415) 621-1001

The Commercial Image, PTN Publishing Corp., 445 Broad Hollow Rd., Suite 21, Mellville, N.Y. 11747; (516) 845-2700

Communication Arts, P.O. Box 10300, 410 Sherman Avenue, Palo Alto, Calif. 94303; (415) 326-6040; (800) 258-9111

Creativity, Crain Communications, 6500 Wilshire Blvd. #2300, Los Angeles, Calif. 90048; (213) 651-3710

DoubleTake, 1317 West Pettigrew Street, Durham, N.C. 27705; (919) 681-2596. *Documentary photography.*

Electronic Photography News, Photofinishing News Inc., 10915 Bonita Beach Road, Bonita Springs, Fla. 33923; (813) 992-4421

Exposure, Society for Photographic Education, Box 222116, Dallas, Tex. 75222; (817) 273-2845

Free-Lance Photographer's Handbook, New York Institute of Photography, Inc., 211 East 43rd Street, New York, N.Y. 10017; (212) 867-8260. *Marketing periodical.*

The Future Image Report, 1020 Parott Drive, Burlingame, Calif. 94010; (415) 579-0493

Graphic Design: USA, 1556 Third Avenue, New York, N.Y. 10128; (212) 534-5500

Graphis (USA), 141 Lexington Avenue, New York, N.Y. 10016; (212)532-9387

Guilfoyle Report, AG Editions, Inc., 41 Union Square West, Suite 523, New York, N.Y. 10003; (212) 929-0959. *For nature photographers.*

International Report on Stock Photography, Westlight, 2223 South Carmelina Avenue, Los Angeles, Calif. 90064; (310) 820-7077

News Photographer, National Press Photographer's Association, 3200 Croasdaile Drive, Suite 306, Durham, N.C. 27705; (919) 383-7246

Outdoor Photographer, Werner Publishing Corp., 12121 Wilshire Blvd., Suite 1220, Los Angles, Calif. 90025; (310) 820-1500

Petersen's Photographic, Petersen Publishing Co., 6420 Wilshire Blvd., Los Angeles Calif. 90048; (213) 782-2000

Photo District News, A/S/M Communications, Inc., 1515 Broadway, New York, N.Y. 10036; (212) 536-5222; (800) 669-1002

Photo Electronic Imaging, PPA Publications and Events, Inc., 57 Forsyth Street NW #1600, Atlanta, Ga. 30303; (404) 522-8600

Photo Bulletin, PhotoLetter, PhotoMarket, PhotoStockNotes, PhotoSource Intl., Pine Lake Farm, 1910 35th Road, Osceola, Wis. 54020; (715) 248-3800

Photographer's Forum, Serbin Communications Inc., 511 Olive Street, Santa Barbara, Calif. 93101; (805) 963-0439; (800) 876-5425

The Photo Review, Photo Review, 301 Hill Avenue, Langhorne, Pa. 19047; (215) 757-8921

Popular Photography, Hachette Filipacchi Magazines, Inc., 1633 Broadway, New York, N.Y. 10019; (212) 767-6000

PRC Newsletter, Photographic Resource Center, Boston University, 602 Commonwealth Avenue, Boston, Mass. 02215; (617) 353-0700

Print, RC Publications Inc., 3200 Tower Oaks Blvd., Rockville, Md. 20852; (301) 770-2900; (800) 222-2654

Professional Photographer, PPA Publications and Events, Inc., 57 Forsyth St. NW, Suite 1600, Atlanta, Ga. 30303; (404) 522-8600;

Publishers Weekly, 19110 Van Ness Avenue, Torrence, Calif. 90501; (800) 278-2991

PWP Newsletter, Professional Woman Photographers, c/o Photographics Unlimited 17 West 17th Street, New York, N.Y. 10011, (212) 807-0399

Rangefinder, Rangefinder Publishing Co., 1312 Lincoln Blvd. #1703, Santa Monica, Calif. 90401; (310) 451-8506

Select, Select America Ltd., 153 West 18th Street, New York, N.Y. 10011; (212) 929-9473

Shots, P38149, Dallas, Tex. 75238; e-mail: shots1234 @ aol.com; http://members.gnn. com/afterimage/shots.htm

Shutterbug, Patch Communications, 5211 South Washington Avenue, Titusville, Fla. 32780; (407) 268-5010

Single Image, Scott & Daughters Publishing, Inc., 940 North Highland Avenue, Los Angeles, Calif. 90038; (213) 856-0008

Southwest Photographic, 535 Cordova Road, Suite 175, Santa Fe, N.M. 87501; (505) 982-7905

SPAR Newsletter, Society of Photographer and Artist Representatives, 60 East 42nd Street, #1166, New York, N.Y. 10165; (212) 779-7464

Stock Photo Report, Brian Seed & Associates, 7432 North Lamon Avenue, Skokie, Ill. 60077; (847) 677-7887

Studio Magazine, 124 Galaxy Blvd., Toronto, Ont. M9W 4Y6, Canada; (416) 675-1999

Studio Photography, PTN Publishing Co., 445 Broad Hollow Road, Suite 21, Melville, N.Y. 11747; (516) 845-2700

Taking Stock, 110 Frederick Avenue, Rockville, Md. 20850; (301) 251-0720

The Natural Image, Lepp and Associates, P.O. Box 6240, Los Osos, Calif. 93412; (805) 528-7385

The Wedding Photographer, Wedding Photographers Intl., 1312 Lincoln Blvd., # 2003, Santa Monica, Calif. 90406; (213) 451-0090

The Wolfman Report, Hachette Filipacchi Magazines, Inc., 1633 Broadway, New York, N.Y. 10019; (212) 767-6000. *Report on the photo industry.*

Women Artist's News, P.O. Box 3304, Grand Central Station, New York, N.Y. 10163; (212) 666-6990

Computer Software

The Boss (Business management for MS-DOS), Boss Development Co., 310 Mockingbird Lane, South Pasadena, Calif. 91030; (818) 799-3400

Colleague (Business management for Macintosh), Colleague Business Software, 11606 DK Ranch Road, Austin, Tex. 78759; (512) 258-6023

fotoQuote (Stock photography pricing program for MS-DOS) Cradoc Corporation, P. O. Box 10899, Bainbridge Island, Wash. 98110; (800) 679-0202

Full Spectrum (Business management for Macintosh), Parhelion, P.O. Box 107, Cornish Flat, N.H.; (603) 675-2966

Grip (Business management for Windows), Grip Software, 420 North 5th Street, No. 707, Minneapolis, Minn. 55401; (612) 332-0052

Images IIIa (Business management for MS-DOS), Blue Moose Software, 230 Old Turnpike Road, Barrington, N.H. 03825; (603) 942-9917

InView (Business management for Macintosh), HindSight, P.O. Box 4242, Highlands Ranch, Colo. 80126; (303) 791-3770

PhotoByte (Business management for Macintosh or Windows) Vertex Software Inc., 31 Wolfback Ridge Road, Sausalito, Calif. 94965; (415) 331-3100

Silent Partner (Business management for Macintosh or Windows) The Medi Group, 180 Black Rock Road, Oaks, Pa. 19456; (215) 666-5911

StockView (Stock caption and tracking for Macintosh), HindSight, P.O. Box 4242, Highlands Ranch, Colo. 80126; (303) 791-3770

StrucSure (Business management for Macintosh or Windows), StrucSure Software, P.O. Box 11633, St. Louis, Mo. 63105; (314) 993-7577

The Viewfinder (Business management for MS-DOS), Retail Merchandise Systems, 8122 SW 83rd Street, Miami, Fla. 33143; (305) 274-6220

Video- and Audiotapes

"The Business of Images" (videotape). ASMP and The Newhouse School, Syracuse University with the support of Eastman Kodak Co. Available from ASMP (609) 799-8300.

"Get it in Writing!" American Society of Media Photographers. 90-minute audiotape, Richard Weisgrau, New York: ASMP, 1992.

"How to Find Clients and Get Paid" (four videotapes) by Maria Piscopo. Turner Communications, (800) 382-9417.

"Techniques of the Masters." Eastman Kodak.

"Working Solo" (two audiocassettes) by Terri Lonier. Audio Prod., ISBN 1-8832282-90-X.

Web Sites

Professional organizations

Advertising Photographers of America, APA: www.apanational.com

The American Institute of Graphic Arts, AIGA
 AIGA National: www.aiga.org
 AIGA Atlanta chapter: www.aiga-atl.org
 AIGA Colorado chapter: www.aigacolorado.org
 AIGA Los Angeles chapter: mach98.maddocks.com/aiga_la
 AIGA New York chapter: www.aiga.com/ny

The American Society of Media Photographers, ASMP
 ASMP National: http://www.asmp.org
 ASMP members only forum: http://www.asmp.org/asmp/private/memonly.nclk
 ASMP Chicago chapter: www.chimwasmp.org
 ASMP Houston chapter: www.mediaplace.com/asmp
 ASMP New England chapter: www.lsphoto.com/ASMP

ASMP Ohio/North Coast chapter: www.zdepth.com/asmp

ASMP Oregon chapter: www.teleport.com/~asmpor

ASMP Pittsburgh chapter: www.techlinx.com/pghasmp

Australian Institute of Professional Photographers, AIPP: colombus@ica.net.au

Canadian Association of Photographers & Illustrators in Communications, CAPIC; www.capic.org

Copyright Clearance Center, Inc.: www.copyright.com

National Press Photographers Association, NPPA: sunsite.unc.edu/nppa/

Picture Agency Council of America, PACA: paca@earthlink.net

Schools and Workshops

Art Center College of Design: www.artcenter.edu

Brooks Institute of Photography: www.brooks.edu

Rochester Institute of Technology, School of Photographic Arts and Sciences: www.rit.edu/~rckpph

Rhode Island School of Design: www.risd.com

Southern Illinois University, Applied Arts Department: www.siu.edu:80/departments/ctc/apartphp

The Maine Photographic Workshops: www.meworkshops.com

Santa Fe Winter Workshops: www.nets.com/sfworkshop.html

Time and Weather

Get the correct time from a really good clock: tycho.usno.navy.mil/cgi-bin/timer.pl

WeatherNet: the Internet's premier source of weather information. Providing access to thousands of forecasts, images, and the Net's largest collection of weather links: cirrus.sprl.umich.edu/wxnet

Topical sites of interest

Dast Library of Photography is a photo resource on a variety of topics: www.goodnet.com/~tibbits

Global Photographers Search is an Internet site that features searchable databases as a sourcebook for professional photography services: www.photographers.com

Photo District News provides a thorough photo industry watch: www.pdn-pix.com

The Photo News Network is a set of specialized forums and discussion groups where vital photography subjects and issues are discussed: www.photonews.net/forums

NETLOOK Photographic Magazine is an on-line magazine with photos, editorial comment, technical information, and interviews: www.netlookmag.com

Stock Solution's Top Photo Site of the Week. A list of links to top-quality photographs on the Web: www.tssphoto.com/foto_week.html

The STOCKPHOTO Web site allows stock photographers, stock photography libraries, stock photo buyers, students and anyone else interested in stock photography to participate in a moderated stock photo newsgroup and a discussion on topics of professional interest: www.S2F.com/stockphoto

World Wide Art Resources is the only complete registry of arts information on the Internet. Over 7,800 artists and over 100,000 other arts resources are listed: wwar.com

World Wide Web search aids
(a foot in the door for searches on anything to do with art)
Galaxy—Arts
www.einet.net/galaxy/Humanities/Arts.html

Yahoo—Arts
www.yahoo.com/Arts

Other
Business Tips Maria Piscopo: http://www.e-folio.com/piscopo
Eastman Kodak Information Center (800)-242-2424: www.Kodak.com/go/professional
Media Photographers' Copyright Agency, MP©A: www.mpca.com

Directories

American Showcase, Corporate Showcase, KliK! Showcase Photography, New Media Showcase, American Showcase, 915 Broadway, 14th Floor, New York, N.Y. 10010; (212) 245-0981

Art Director's Index to Photographers, Rotovision SA, Watson-Guptill Publications, Inc., 1695 Oak Street, Lakewood, N.J. 08701; (800) 451-1741

Art Galleries and Dealers, American Business Directories Inc., 5711 South 86th Circle, Omaha, Nebr. 68127; (402) 593-4600

California Image, Serbin Communications Inc., 511 Olive Street, Santa Barbara, Calif. 93101; (805) 963-0439; (800) 876-5425

Chicago Creative Directory, 333 North Michigan Ave., Chicago, Ill. 60601; (312) 236-7337

Chicago Creative Sourcebook, Rocky Mountain Creative Sourcebook, Southwest Creative Sourcebook, Texas Creative Sourcebook, Twin Cities Creative Sourcebook, Everest Publishing, 7002 East 1st Avenue, Suite 101, Scottsdale, Ariz. 85251; (602) 994-5024; (800) 240-2332

The Creative Black Book, The Creative Black Book Photography Listings, The Creative Black Book Portfolio Edition, Black Book Marketing Group, 10 Astor Place, 6th Floor, New York, N.Y. 10003; (212) 539-9800

Creative Directories, The Alternative Pick, 1133 Broadway, Suite 1404, New York, N.Y. 10010; (212) 675-4176

Creative Source, Corporate Source, Wilcord Publishing Ltd., 194 Merton Street, Suite 300, Toronto, Ont. M4S 3B5, Canada; (416) 487-7414

Creative Sourcebook: Photography and Illustration, Sumner Communications, Inc., 4085 Chain Bridge Rd., Fairfax, Va. 22030; (703) 385-5600

Digital Directory, 301 Cathedral Pkwy. #2-N, New York, N.Y. 10026; (212) 864-8872

Direct Stock, Direct Stock, Inc., 10 East 21st Street, New York, N.Y. 10010; (212) 976-6560

The European Creative Handbook, Reed Information Services Ltd., Windsor Court East Grinstead House, East Grinstead, West Sussex RH191XA, England; 44 03 4 2-32-6972

Eye, N.Y. Gold, New York Gold, Inc., 10 East 21th Street, 14th Floor, New York, N.Y. 10010; (212) 254-1000

Eyes: The Sourcebook for Black and White Art, Eyes Publishing, 6 Clark Court, Suite 101, Kendall Park, N.J. 08824; (908) 821-3937

The Design Firm Directory, Wefler & Associates, P.O. Box 1167, Evanston, Ill. 60204; (708) 475-1866

Gale Directory of Publications, Gale Research Inc., 835 Penobscot Bldg., Detroit, Mich. 48226; (313) 961-2242; (800) 877-4253

Gebbie Press All-In-One Directory, Gebbie Press, P.O. Box 1000, New Paltz, N.Y. 12564; (914) 255-7560. *Publications.*

Green Book, AG Editions, Inc., 41 Union Square West, Suite 523, New York, N.Y. 10003; (212) 929-0959. *Natural history stock.*

The Guide to Photography Workshops and Schools, Shaw Guides, Inc., 10 West 66th Street #30H, New York, N.Y. 10023; (212) 799-6464

Industry Directories, Artist's Market, Photographer's Market, Writer's Digest Books, F&W Publications, Inc., 1507 Dana Avenue, Cincinnati, Ohio 45207; (513) 531-2222; updated annually.

LA 411, 611 North Larchmont Blvd. #201, Los Angeles, Calif. 90004; (213) 460-6304

Madison Avenue Handbook, The Image Maker's Sourcebook, Peter Glenn Publishing, 42 West 38th Street #802, New York, N.Y. 10018; (212) 869-2020

O'Dwyer's Directory of Public Relations Firms, J. R. O'Dwyer Co., 271 Madison Avenue, New York, N.Y. 10016; (212) 679-2471

PACA Stock Agency Directory, P.O. Box 308, Northfield, Minn. 55057; (507) 645-6988

Photographers—Commercial; Photographers—Portrait, American Business Directories Inc., 5711 South 86th Circle, Omaha, Nebr. 68127; (402) 593-4600

Photographer's Market, Writer's Digest Books, 1507 Dana Avenue, Cincinnati, Ohio 45207; (513) 531-2222

Photography Market Place, R.R. Bowker, 1180 Avenue of the Americas, New York, N.Y. 10036

Professional Photo Source, A/S/M Communications, Inc., 1515 Broadway, New York, N.Y. 10036; (212) 536-5222; (800) 669-1002. *Resource directory, updated annually.*

SPAR Membership Guide, Society of Photographer and Artist Representatives, 60 East 42nd Street #1166, New York, N.Y. 10165; (212) 779-7464

Standard Directory of Advertisers; Standard Directory of Advertising Agencies (The Red Books), National Register Publishing, P.O. Box 31, New Providence, N.J. 07974; (908) 464-6800; (800) 521-8110

Standard Periodical Directory, Oxbridge Communications, Inc., 150 Fifth Avenue, New York, N.Y. 10011; (212) 741-0231; (800) 955-0231

Standard Rate and Data Service, 3004 Glenview Road, Wilmette, Ill. 60901; (708) 256-6067; (800) 323-4601

Stock Photo Deskbook, Photographic Arts Center, Ltd., 163 Amsterdam Avenue, Suite 201, New York, N.Y. 10023; (212) 838-8640

Stock Photo Fees in Europe, Presse Informations Agentur GmbH, Stefanienstrasse 25, 76530 Baden-Baden, Germany; 07221-25348; English edition.

Thomas Register of Manufactures, Thomas Publishing Co., 1 Penn Plaza, New York, N.Y. 10001; (212) 695-0500

Ulrich's International Periodicals Directory, Reed Reference Publishing, P.O. Box 31 New Providence, N.J. 07974; (908) 464-6800; (800) 521-8110

Who's Who in Professional Imaging, PPA Publications and Events, Inc., 57 Forsyth Street NW, Suite 1600, Atlanta, Ga. 30303; (404) 522-8600

The Workbook: The National Directory of Creative Talent; Regional Workbook Directories: East, Midwest, South, West; Stock Workbook 9, Scott & Daughters Publishing, Inc., 940 North Highland Avenue, Los Angeles, Calif. 90038; (213) 856-0008

Working Press of the Nation, Reed Elsevier New Providence, P.O. Box 31, New Providence, N.J. 07974; (908) 464-6800; (800) 521-8110

Organizations

Professional organizations are listed as marketing resources and for the identification of professional services.

Accountants

American Accounting Association, 5717 Bessie Drive, Sarasota, Fla. 34233; (813) 596-6200

American Institute of Certified Public Accounts, 1211 Avenue of the Americas, New York, N.Y.; (212) 596-6200

American Society of Woman Accountants, 1755 Lynnfield Road, Suite 222, Memphis, Tenn. 38119; (901) 680-0470

National Association of Black Accountants, 7249A Hanover Parkway, Greenbelt, Md. 20770; (301) 474-6222

Advertising Agencies

American Advertising Federation, 1101 Vermont Avenue NW, Suite 500, Washington, D.C. 20009; (202) 898-0089

American Association of Advertising Agencies, 666 Third Avenue, 13th Floor, New York, N.Y. 10017; (212) 682-2500

Communication Specialists

International Association of Business Communicators, 1 Hallidie Plaza, Suite 600, San Francisco, Calif. 94102; (415) 433-3400

Galleries

Art Dealers Association of America, 575 Madison Avenue, New York, N.Y. 10022; (212) 940-8590

Association of International Photography Art Dealers, 1609 Connecticut Avenue, Suite 200, Washington, D.C. 20009; (202) 986-0105

Council on Fine Art Photography, c/o Lowell Anson Kenyon, 5613 Johnson Avenue West, Bethesda, Md. 20817; (301) 897-0083

Graphic Designers and Art Directors

American Center for Design, 233 Ontario Street, Suite 500, Chicago, Ill. 60611; (312) 787-2018

American Institute of Graphic Arts (AIGA), 1059 Third Avenue, New York, N.Y. 10021; (212) 752-0813

Art Director's Club, 250 Park Avenue South, New York, N.Y. 10003; (212) 674-0500

Association of Professional Design Firms, 1 Story Street, Cambridge, Mass. 02138; (617) 864-7474

Design Management Institute, 107 South Street, Suite 502, Boston, Mass. 02111; (617) 338-6380

Graphic Artists Guild (GAG), 30 West 20th Street, New York, N.Y. 10011; (212) 463-7730

Society of Newspaper Design, P.O. Box 4075, Reston, Va. 22090; (703) 620-1083

Society of Publication Designers, 60 East 42nd Street, Suite 721, New York, N.Y. 10165; (212) 983-8585

Illustrators

Society of Illustrators, 128 East 63rd Street, New York, N.Y. 60018; (212) 838-2560

Insurance

Independent Insurance Agents of America, 127 South Peyton, Alexandria, Va. 22314; (703) 683-4422

American Society of Chartered Life Underwriters and Chartered Financial Consultants, 270 Bryn Mawr Avenue, Bryn Mawr, Pa. 19010; (215) 526-2500

National Association of Insurance Women International, 1847 East 15th Street, Tulsa, Okla. 74159; (918) 744-5195

National Association of Professional Insurance Agents, 400 N. Washington Street, Alexandria, VA 22314; (703) 836-9340

Labs

Association of Imaging Service Bureaus, 5601 Roeanne Way, Suite 608, Greensboro, N.C. 27409; (800) 844-2472

Association of Professional Color Laboratories (APCL), 3000 Picture Place, Jackson, Mich. 49201; (517) 788-8146

International Mini Lab Association, 2627 Grimsley Street, Greensboro, N.C. 27403; (910) 854-8088

Marketing

American Marketing Association, 250 S. Wacker Drive, Suite 200, Chicago, Ill. 60006; (312) 648-0536

Photo Retailers

Photo Marketing Association (PMA), 3000 Picture Place, Jackson, Mich. 49201; (517) 788-8100

Photographic Educators

Society for Photographic Education (SPE), P.O. Box 222116, Dallas, Tex. 75222; (817) 273-2845

Photographic Equipment Repair

National Association of Photographic Equipment Technicians, 3000 Picture Place, Jackson, Mich. 49201; (517) 788-8100

Picture Editors, Researchers, and Archivists

American Society of Picture Professionals (ASPP), c/o Woodfin Camp & Assoc., 2025 Pennsylvania Avenue NW #1011, Washington, D.C. 20006; (202) 223-8442

Professional Photographers Organizations

Advertising Photographers of America (APA), 7201 Melrose Avenue, Los Angeles, Calif. 90046; (800) 272-6264

Advertising Photographers of New York (APNY), 27 West 20th Street, New York, N.Y. 10011; (212) 807-0399

American Society of Media Photographers (ASMP), 14 Washington Road, Suite 502, Princeton Junction, N.J. 08550; (609) 799-8300

Professional Photographers of America (PPA), 57 Forsythe Street, Suite 1600, Atlanta, Ga. 30303; (404) 522-6800

Professional Woman Photographers, c/o Photographics Unlimited, 17 West 17th Street, New York, N.Y. 10011; (212) 807-0399

National Press Photographers Association (NPPA), 3200 Croasdaile Drive, Suite 306, Durham, NC 27705; (800) 289-6772

University Photographers Association of America, c/o Mark Philbrick, C-327 ASB Brigham Young University, Provo, Utah 84602; (801) 378-7322

Wedding Photographers International, 1312 Lincoln Blvd. #2003, Santa Monica, Calif. 90406; (310) 451-0090

Public Relations

Public Relations Society of America, 33 Irving Place, 3rd Floor, New York, N.Y. 10003 (212) 995-2230

Sales Representatives

Society of Photographer and Artist Representatives (SPAR), 60 East 42nd Street #1166, New York, N.Y. 10165; (212) 779-7464

Stock Agencies

Picture Agency Council of America (PACA), P.O. Box 308, Northfield, Minn. 55057-0308; (800) 457-7222

Women in Business, National Association of Women Business Owners, 1413 K Street NW, Suite 637, Washington, D.C. 20005; (301) 608-2590

ASMP and MP©A Information

The American Society of Media Photographers, Inc. (ASMP)

14 Washington Rd., Suite 502
Princeton Junction, N.J. 08550-1033
TEL: (609) 799-8300
FAX: (609) 799-2233
E-MAIL: Info@ASMP.org
WEB SITE: http://www.asmp.org

The American Society of Media Photographers (originally the Society of Magazine Photographers and later the American Society of Magazine Photographers) was founded in 1944 by a handful of the world's leading photojournalists to protect and promote the rights of photographers whose work was primarily for publication. ASMP was formed at a time when photographers were forced to shoot on speculation and when credit lines were unheard of. The organization was born out of need, and that need has driven it for more than half a century.

Today, ASMP is your link to professional business practices, up-to-date standards in the photographic industry, and is every photographer's voice in lobbying and advocacy efforts at state and federal levels. The nonprofit Society, with more than 5,000 members, is the largest organization of its kind in the United States and has won international recognition for its efforts on behalf of photographers. The Society has members in more than thirty countries, with the majority based in the U.S.

Besides its primary mission of protecting and promoting photographers' interests, ASMP is dedicated to promoting high professional standards and ethics and to cultivating friendship and mutual understanding among photographers. Its membership consists of photographers in every field with most working in the areas of advertising, editorial, commercial, and photojournalism. Through the efforts of its national office and its thirty-seven chapters nationwide, the ASMP is instrumental in educating its members and other photographers in good business practices. ASMP has a Code of Ethics to guide members in their dealings with clients and colleagues.

ASMP is very active in the areas of copyright, promoting better conditions for photographers, combating work-for-hire, and providing legal advocacy and lobbying. It promotes business education through seminars and publication of business books and forms. It has helped frame copyright legislation, and Society representatives have often given testimony before Senate and Congressional committees and in courts of law.

ASMP also provides a variety of member benefits including life insurance, comprehensive medical, equipment, and other insurance, discounts on numerous services (e.g., car rental, delivery services, stationery supplies, and others). The Society will also refer inquiries for photography to its members by region or specialty.

Above all, by being a member of ASMP you are establishing your credentials as a professional photographer who really cares about your profession. And you will be in the company of photographers such as Arnold Newman, Jay Maisel, Eric Meola, Walter Iooss, Yousuf Karsh, Richard Avedon, Eve Arnold, Jodi Cobb, and numerous other illustrious photographers.

The ASMP Advantage

Credibility: ASMP membership is recognized worldwide as a commitment to professionalism, quality, ethics, and as a sign of proven experience. This credibility makes a difference in the buyer's mind.

Communication: We start in the business by learning from others, and we can grow in the business the same way. Continuing dialogue among photographers is an indispensable element in an orderly industry. ASMP provides the setting through its local chapters for photographers to meet and share experiences, solutions, and ideas.

Alliance: Corporate America has discovered the strategic alliance: a means of tapping into the expertise, resources, knowledge, and assistance of others. ASMP is the strategic ally of professional photographers, organized to improve their interests by joining resources in a unique organization working uniquely for you.

Education: Being informed isn't enough. Knowing what, isn't knowing how. ASMP is committed to the education of its members, whether through its local chapters or national office. ASMP provides the educational opportunity to learn how to do what you have to do.

Information: The technology revolution requires photographer evolution, which is not possible without timely, accurate information. ASMP is the industry clearinghouse for the information you'll need to keep abreast in an ever-changing business.

Advocacy: ASMP helps its members when they are in need of sound advice, solid representation, and decisive action. In buyer's conference rooms, in federal and state legislatures, and in the courts, ASMP sets and reaches the agreements, drives the amendments, and sets the precedents that protect you. The Society has established a Legal Action Fund for special legal initiatives.

The ASMP Business Bible: a guide for professional media photographers. This publication is packed with the kind of information that the professional publication photographer needs to run a business. Designed to keep up with a constantly changing marketplace, the ASMP Business Bible will be periodically updated by a supplement service. As conditions mandate changes in business practices, the book will be updated, making it the most definitive and timely guide for professionals. ASMP members receive it free.

ASMP Bulletin: The Society's magazine presenting news and features, free to all members and affiliates.

ASMP Hotline: Late-breaking news and latest information on special pages in the Bulletin. It contains news, alerts, marketing information, as well as legal and business information.

ASMP Home Page on the World Wide Web: A database of members, searchable by region and specialty, membership information, news, publications, features, and links to other important industry sites are on the ASMP Web site. Find it at http://www.asmp.org

Membership Directory: Published annually, lists all members and affiliates with their addresses and phone numbers. General members may list up to five specialties. Provided free to all members and affiliates, and made available to thousands of photography buyers.

White Papers: Special publications dealing with specific concerns of photographers such as copyright, form agreements, magazine photography, stock photography, and other topics. Free to general and associate members; discounted for other members.

Chapter Affiliation: The ASMP chapter network now covers thirty-seven cities, states, or regions. These local chapters provide a wide range of seminars, workshops, and local news, as well as the opportunity to exchange views and information with your colleagues. Networking is a major benefit of ASMP membership.

ASMP Specialty Groups: Within professional photography there are business practices and concerns of particular interest to practitioners in certain fields. To address those needs, ASMP has created special-interest groups in areas such as architecture, photojournalism, sports, and stock.

Insurance: Life insurance, comprehensive medical, major medical, disability insurance, accidental death, and dismemberment plans are available. ASMP pioneered Prosurance, a liability and camera insurance policy for the professional photographer. A variety of other insurance, including workers' compensation, weather, cast/models, losses incurred through incorrect processing by labs, are available.

Good offices: Members receive consultation and advice on business problems and concerns from expert staff at ASMP's national office.

Other benefits: Include an ASMP Press Card, car rental discounts, travel discounts, x-ray protection labels, and access to discounted overnight delivery services and stationery supplies.

ASMP National and chapters are always seeking new benefits for members, and the list increases.

Membership Categories

All applicants must be persons of good moral character and reputation.

General Member: This is a photographer whose images are created primarily for publication, who has at least three consecutive years of substantial professional publication experience, and for whom the majority of earned income comes from the publication of their images.

Associate Member: Individuals otherwise eligible to be general members, except that they have had at least one year, but less than three years, of publication experience.

Regular Affiliate: Individuals who are not eligible for general or associate membership and who are actively engaged as professional photographers and who derive a portion of their income from such activity, or are educators, assistants, or employees of general or associate members.

Sustaining Affiliate: Individuals who are professionally associated with photography or photographers, but not eligible to be general, associate, or affiliate members.

Student Affiliate: Full-time students at college level or above, in the visual communications field. Proof of student status is required.

Partner/Spouse Member: Members whose situation warrants consideration for this category must meet all the requirements for membership, and the category is only available to individuals who have a "legal connection" with an existing general member.

Media Photographers' Copyright Agency, Inc. (MP©A)

14 Washington Rd., Suite 502
Princeton Junction, N.J. 08550-1033
TEL: (609) 799-9677
FAX: (609) 799-2233
WEB SITE: http://www.mpca.com

ASMP has also established the Media Photographers' Copyright Agency, MP©A to promote and protect its members' work in the digital environment. The ASMP board of directors voted to establish MP©A on the fundamental premise that ASMP members have the greatest depth and breadth of content of any group of photographers in the world.

Only ASMP members can join MP©A, and members can control what images are licensed and what prices they agree to. MP©A is not a stock agency, but an agent for the photographer. MP©A will make recommendations about prices, but the member-photographer can depart from those recommendations. Additionally, the photographer receives 70 percent of sales.

MP©A has formed a strategic alliance with Copyright Clearance Center, Inc., and Applied Graphics Technologies, the largest prepress facility in the U.S. MP©A members' images will be marketed under the alliance's new name of MIRA, the acronym for Media Image Resource Alliance.

In addition to being an agent for its members, MP©A has also received international recognition as a model for other countries who are developing photographer-controlled licensing agencies.

More information about MP©A can be obtained by writing, calling the above phone number, or exploring the agency's Web site.

About the Authors

Craig Aurness, the president of Los Angeles–based Westlight stock agency, is one of the most respected authorities in the stock photography industry.

David Barnes, an ASMP member and an experienced stock photographer based in Winthrop, Washington, markets his work internationally.

Bruce Blank is a Philadelphia, Pennsylvania, photographer who now heads ASMP's member operations and business education programs.

Professor **Thom Bunting** is a London, England, Internet authority and Web site consultant who consults internationally.

James Cook, a Denver, Colorado, ASMP member, is an editorial photographer and software producer.

Jon Feingersh, a former ASMP chapter president, from Rockville, Maryland, is one of the country's leading stock photographers.

Ira Mark Gostin, ASMP member from Reno, Nevada, is a co-chair of the ASMP corporate image committee.

Paul Henning, director, Third Coast Stock Source Inc., Milwaukee, Wisconsin, is a past president of the Picture Agency Council of America, PACA.

Scott Highton, an ASMP member and former director from San Carlos, California, is a photographer, writer, and authority on electronic technology.

Bill Hurter, a veteran photography industry writer/editor and consultant, is a principal of LandMine Productions, Los Angeles, California.

Don Luce, an ASMP director and former vice-president, is a commercial photographer and educator based in Cleveland, Ohio.

Jean Miller, a freelance editor in Cleveland Heights, Ohio, has an extensive background in education and editing.

Annette Laabs Paajanen is a Shorewood, Minnesota, writer/editor who specializes in corporate communications.

Victor S. Perlman, Esq., an attorney experienced in the photography industry and copyright law, is ASMP's general counsel.

Maria Piscopo, an artists' and photographers representative, consultant, and author, is based in Santa Ana, California.

Allen Rabinowitz, an Atlanta-based writer, has been writing for many years on photography and other visual communications topics.

Roger Ressmeyer, a leading magazine photographer and former ASMP director, is a senior editor at Corbis Corporation, Seattle, Washington.

Barbara B. Roberts, president of FPG International Corp., is an authority on the stock photography industry and has a strong corporate business background.

Stephen Seeger, a Dallas, Texas, photographer and ASMP director, is also a lecturer and educator.

Peter Skinner, a writer/photographer with an international background in newspaper, magazine, and corporate journalism, is ASMP communications director.

Richard Steedman, president and co-founder of The Stock Market agency, has been a leading authority on the stock photography industry for many years.

Amy Stone, a photographer, writer, and Internet consultant, is a principal of LandMine Productions, Los Angeles, California.

Vince Streano, a veteran stock photographer based in Anacortes, Washington, was an ASMP director for many years.

Susan Turnau, president, Sharpshooters, Inc., a leading Miami, Florida, stock photography agency, is president of the Picture Agency Council of America, PACA.

Mark Tucker, an ASMP member and former chapter president, is an editorial and fashion photographer in Nashville, Tennessee.

John Uppgren, an authority on communications, is chief information officer for the Gage Marketing Group, Minneapolis, Minnesota.

Emily Vickers is a consultant and partner in Mason Vickers Productions of Hopewell, New Jersey, offering full production services to photographers.

Richard Weisgrau, ASMP executive director and author of several publications, is a respected authority on the business of photography.

Index

Books from Allworth Press

Pricing Photography, Revised Edition by Michal Heron and David MacTavish (softcover, 11 × 8½, 144 pages, $24.95)

The Photographer's Guide to Marketing and Self-Promotion, Second Edition by Maria Piscopo (softcover, 6¾ × 10, 176 pages, $18.95)

How to Shoot Stock Photos That Sell, Revised Edition by Michal Heron (softcover, 8 × 10, 208 pages, $19.95)

Stock Photography Business Forms by Michal Heron (softcover, 8½ × 11, 128 pages, $18.95)

Business and Legal Forms for Photographers by Tad Crawford (softcover, 8½ × 11, 192 pages, $18.95)

Legal Guide for the Visual Artist, Third Edition by Tad Crawford (softcover, 8½ × 11, 256 pages, $19.95)

The Law (in Plain English) for Photographers by Leonard DuBoff (softcover, 6 × 9, 208 pages, $18.95)

The Copyright Guide by Lee Wilson (softcover, 6 × 9, 192 pages, $18.95)

Mastering Black-and-White Photography by Bernhard J Suess (softcover, 6¾ × 10, 240 pages, $18.95)

The Digital Imaging Dictionary by Joe Farace (softcover, 6 × 9, 256 pages, $19.95)

The Photographer's Internet Handbook by Joe Farace (softcover, 6 × 9, 224 pages, $18.95)

Overexposure: Health Hazards in Photography, Second Edition by Susan D. Shaw and Monona Rossol (softcover, 6¾ × 10, 320 pages, $18.95)

Please write to request our free catalog. If you wish to order a book, send your check or money order to Allworth Press, 10 East 23rd Street, Suite 210, New York, NY 10010. Include $5 for shipping and handling for the first book ordered and $1 for each additional book. Ten dollars plus $1 for each additional book if ordering from Canada. New York State residents must add sales tax.

If you wish to see our catalog on the World Wide Web, you can find us at Millennium Production's Art and Technology Web site:
http://www.arts-online.com/allworth/home.html
or at **http://www.interport.net/~allworth**